The Strategic Use of Information Technology

The
Executive
Bookshelf

Sloan Management Review

The Strategic Use

of Information

Technology

Edited by

Stuart E. Madnick

New York   Oxford

OXFORD UNIVERSITY PRESS

1987

Oxford University Press

Oxford   New York   Toronto
Delhi   Bombay   Calcutta   Madras   Karachi
Petaling Jaya   Singapore   Hong Kong   Tokyo
Nairobi   Dar es Salaam   Cape Town
Melbourne   Auckland

and associated companies in Beirut   Berlin   Ibadan   Nicosia

Copyright © 1987 by Sloan Management Review

Published by Oxford University Press, Inc.,
200 Madison Avenue, New York, New York 10016

Oxford is a registered trademark of Oxford University Press.

Library of Congress Cataloging-in-Publication Data
The Strategic use of information technology.
(The Executive bookshelf)
A selection of articles from the Sloan management review.
Bibliography: p.   Includes index.
1. Management—Data processing. 2. Management information systems.
3. Strategic planning—Data processing.
I. Madnick, Stuart E. II. Sloan management review. III. Series.
HD30.2.S79 1987   658'.05   87-1606
ISBN 0-19-505048-7

9 8 7 6 5 4 3 2 1

Printed in the United States of America on acid-free paper

Foreword

The Executive Bookshelf reflects the mission of the *Sloan Management Review,* which is to bridge the gap between the practicing manager and the management scholar. Based on real-world business concerns, *SMR* articles provide the practicing manager with state-of-the-art information on management theory and practice. These articles are of particular benefit to the executive who wants to stay abreast of some of the best research and analysis coming from top business schools.

This series draws together *SMR* articles that make significant contributions to the management fields they cover. Each book is edited by one of the Sloan School of Management's most respected professors in the field, and begins with the editor's introduction, which guides and broadens the reader's understanding of the subject at hand.

The great value of these collections lies in how the articles complement one another. The authors do not always agree, but each has something important to say. Consequently, when read in its entirety, each book will challenge the reader to think more carefully about specific management issues. The editors' selection of, and introduction to, the articles will help readers interpret the various perspectives that are presented.

The usefulness of this series is enhanced by the *Sloan Management Review*'s rigorous editorial standards. Articles must not only have a practical focus, but they must also be accessible to the reader. Before an article is accepted for publication, it must be reviewed and accepted by an independent referee. The combination of applicability, academic seriousness, and solid writing assures that the series is readable and authoritative. The language is nontechnical, with minimum discussion of research and methodology, and the authors are influential leaders in the field of management.

The qualities that make these books useful to managers also make them invaluable as assigned readings in academic executive development programs and in private sector management training. In addition, they are helpful to students needing practical information to complement the theoretical materials in standard textbooks.

On a broader scale, this series is an extension of the Alfred P. Sloan School of Management. As one of the leading business schools in the country, the Sloan School complements its educational programs with research intended to produce new and better solutions to management problems. The *Sloan Management Review* in general, and this series in particular, reflects this combined research and training orientation.

The *Review* has a tradition of facilitating communication between executives and academics, and this series is an exciting addition to that tradition. We hope that you share our enthusiasm and that these books help you to become increasingly challenged, informed, and successful.

Cambridge, Mass.   Abraham J. Siegel
March 1987   Dean, Alfred P. Sloan School of Management
                           Massachusetts Institute of Technology

Preface

The Strategic Use of Information Technology brings together for the first time some of the best and most influential articles that have appeared in the *Sloan Management Review*. The book is intended to provide practicing managers with a systematic approach to pursuing ideas and applications in the burgeoning field of information systems for managers. Designed for easy reading and reference, the book should be equally valuable to specialists and nonspecialists alike.

The business and popular press is awash with success stories of companies that have seized competitive advantage through strategic use of information technology: Merrill Lynch, Federal Express, Toys R Us, USA TODAY, etc. *Time* magazine even named the computer "Man of the Year."

This book attempts to go beyond superficial stories and to develop a proactive approach to planning for the strategic use of information technology. The chapters have been carefully selected, assembled, and organized to provide an effective three-part action plan.

The first part, entitled "Integrating Information Technology into Corporate Strategy," presents frameworks for identifying strategic opportunities for an organization and explains how to mobilize the organization to seize these opportunities.

As a result of this more comprehensive and strategic use of information technology, the role of the traditional information systems (IS) organization is undergoing dramatic changes. In the second part of this book, "Planning for the New Era of Information Technology," appropriate roles and responsibilities for the IS organization are identified and discussed. A primary focus is on the role of chief information officer (CIO), the newly coined title for the top information systems executive, and on how the CIO can be effective in relating to peer executives and, at the same time, effectively guide the IS organization.

The book concludes by looking beyond the obvious operational concerns and challenges us to recognize and act upon our "Responsibilities to the Organization and Society," the third part of this volume.

The Strategic Use of Information Technology would not have been possible without the creativity of the authors of the articles included and without the persistence and valuable efforts of the staff of the *Sloan Management Review* in establishing such a quality journal and shepherding the book through the publication process. Rosemary Brutico is especially to be acknowledged. The editor is honored to be part of such an endeavor.

Cambridge, Mass.   S.E.M.
November 1986

Contents

Contributors

Philip Adler, Jr., is Professor of Management in the College of Management at the Georgia Institute of Technology and Professor of Rehabilitation Medicine in the School of Medicine at Emory University. He has acted as a consultant for federal and state government agencies and as a management development lecturer for top organizations.

John F. Akers is Chairman and CEO of IBM Corporation. He is a director on the boards of the Home News Publishing Company and the Council for Financial Aid to Education and is a member of the Board of Trustees of the California Institute of Technology, Institute for Advanced Study, the Advisory Board of the Yale School of Organization and Management, and the Board of Governors of United Way of America.

Robert I. Benjamin is Manager, Corporate Strategies and Programs, at Xerox Corporation and a Visiting Scientist at the Center for Information Systems Research at the Sloan School of Management, MIT. He is the author of *Control of Information System Development.*

Andrew C. Boynton is a Ph.D. candidate at The University of North Carolina at Chapel Hill where he concentrates in management information systems. His professional interests include technology diffusion within organizations and the strategic implications of information technologies.

John C. Camillus is Associate Dean and Professor of Business Administration at the Graduate School of Business of the University of Pittsburgh. His research, teaching, and writing interests are in the areas of strategic planning and management control. He is the author of *Budgeting for Profit.*

Adam D. Crescenzi is Vice President of Index Systems Inc. He is responsible for all business operations of Index's Management Systems Group and is a member of the firm's Policy Committee.

Albert L. Lederer is Assistant Professor of Business Administration at the Graduate School of Business of the University of Pittsburgh. His major professional and research interests are in the areas of planning, developing, and managing information systems and using information systems to manage the human resources function. He is a contributing editor to *Personnel.*

Henry C. Lucas, Jr., is Professor of Information Systems at the Graduate School of Business Administration, New York University. His research interests include implementation and the managerial and organizational problems in the use of information systems. He is the author of

The Design, Implementation and Management of Information Systems and *Information Systems Concepts for Management.*

Stuart E. Madnick is Associate Professor of Management Science at the Sloan School of Management, MIT. He is a member of the Center for Information Systems Research and an affiliate member of the Laboratory for Computer Science, MIT. He is the author of numerous books and articles in the field of information systems, including the widely adopted textbook, *Operating Systems.*

Darrell E. Owen is Information Systems Program Coordinator at Bonneville Power Administration (BPA), a Federal Power Marketing Agency located in Portland, Oregon. His professional interests include the application of management principles to information systems technology, the management of personal computers in the corporate setting, and office automation as the predominant form of automation in the 1980s.

Charles K. Parsons is Associate Professor in the College of Management at the Georgia Institute of Technology. His professional interests include office automation and the use of microcomputers in organizations. He is engaged in organizational research that examines how employees adopt new technologies and their reactions to information technology. Dr. Parsons is the coauthor of *Item Response Theory: Application to Psychological Measurement.*

John F. Rockart is Director of the Center for Information Systems Research and Senior Lecturer of Management Science at the Sloan School of Management, MIT. His current interests lie in the areas of the critical success factor concept, top managerial information use, linking business strategy with information systems strategy, and the management of end-user computing. He has written numerous articles and is coauthor with Michael S. Scott Morton of *Computers and the Learning Process.*

Michael S. Scott Morton is Professor of Management and Faculty Chairman of the Senior Executives Program at the Sloan School of Management, MIT. His active professional contacts with major U.S. and foreign corporations, as well as his teaching activities and areas of personal research, involve strategic planning, computer-based decision support systems, and management control systems. He is coauthor with Peter G. W. Keen of *Decision Support Systems: An Organizational View.*

Cornelius H. Sullivan, Jr., is President and founder of the Information Technology Planning Corporation in Chicago, where he assists companies in the development and implementation of more competitive information systems and strategies.

Jon A. Turner is Associate Professor and Director of the Ph.D. program of the Information Systems Area, Schools of Business, New York University. His research interests include job design, systems evaluation, implications of information system policies, and the human factors of computer interfaces.

John Wyman is Vice President, Marketing, at AT&T. Mr. Wyman is a member of the Society for Information Management and serves on the editorial review board of the *Journal of Marketing.* He is coauthor of *Successful Telemarketing.*

Robert W. Zmud is Professor in the School of Business Administration at The University of North Carolina at Chapel Hill. His professional interests include information systems management, management of technology, and technology diffusion.

Scott B. Zolke is Assistant Athletic Director and a legal councilor for the Georgia Tech Athletic Association. He is a member of the Association of Trial Lawyers of America, the American Bar Association, the Illinois State Bar Association, the State Bar of Georgia, and the Justinian Society of Lawyers. He is also a member of the trial bar in the U.S. District Court for the Northern District of Illinois, the U.S. Court of Appeals for the Seventh, Ninth, and Eleventh Circuits, and the U.S. District Court for the Northern District of Georgia.

The Strategic Use of Information Technology

Introduction: Perspectives on the Effective Use, Planning, and Impact of Information Technology

Stuart E. Madnick

Integrating Information Technology into Corporate Strategy

Information technology (IT) has moved demonstrably into the limelight as a major force to be reckoned with in corporate America. Examples of promises of "competitive advantage" to those that exploit "strategic computing" abound in all the major business publications. One of the earliest, and now classic, examples is American Hospital Supply (see Chapter 1).

American Hospital Supply (AHS), a leading manufacturer and distributor of a very broad line of products for doctors, laboratories, and hospitals, has since 1976 evolved an order-entry distribution system that directly links the majority of its customers to AHS computers. Over 4,000 customer terminals at various locations are linked today to the American Hospital Supply system. As well as providing the customer with direct access to the AHS order-distribution process, the system allows customers to perform functions, such as inventory control, for themselves, thereby generating incremental revenues for AHS. The American Hospital Supply system has been successful because it simplifies ordering processes for customers, reduces costs for both AHS and the customer, and allows AHS to develop and manage pricing incentives to the customer across all product lines. As a result, customer loyalty is high, and AHS market share has been increasing.

A corporation must consider three factors if it seeks success through information technology (see Figure I.1). First and second, an understanding of strategic applications and information technology is critical. But a third, and often overlooked, critical dimension is the importance of planning organizational changes

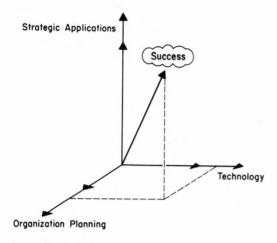

Figure I.1 Factors Critical to Success

that are necessary if strategic applications using information technology are to succeed. Such planning activity is the focus of this introduction.

Framework for Integrating IT into Corporate Strategy

Top management needs a framework to understand how to integrate information technology into its corporate structure and an action plan to seize the opportunities made possible.

A starting point for such a framework is found in Michael Porter's work on competitive strategy.[1] He suggests that, for any company, significant strategic actions consist of diminishing supplier or customer power, holding off new entrants into its industry, lowering the possibility of substitution for its products, or gaining a competitive edge within the existing industry.

All four elements of Porter's strategy appear in the American Hospital Supply case. This generic framework can be extended in various ways to focus on information technology more directly.

The strategic opportunities matrix in Figure I.2 provides a simple but powerful way of thinking about the strategic use of IT.

The opportunities arena may occur in internal operations within the corporation, such as Xerox's improved service-dispatch system, or in external relationships with customers and/or suppliers, as in the American Hospital Supply order-entry system. Furthermore, the organizational change brought about or facilitated by IT may be fairly low, as in the case of Xerox and American Hospital Supply, or it may be significant, as in Digital's restructuring of its computer configuration-design process or in Merrill Lynch's expanded role into many banking services through its cash management account (CMA).

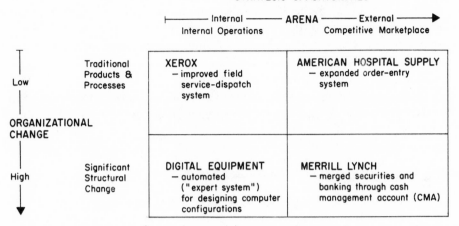

STRATEGIC OPPORTUNITIES

├────── Internal ────── **ARENA** ────── External ──────▶
Internal Operations   Competitive Marketplace

Low	Traditional Products & Processes	**XEROX** — improved field service-dispatch system	**AMERICAN HOSPITAL SUPPLY** — expanded order-entry system
High	Significant Structural Change	**DIGITAL EQUIPMENT** — automated ("expert system") for designing computer configurations	**MERRILL LYNCH** — merged securities and banking through cash management account (CMA)

ORGANIZATIONAL CHANGE (vertical axis)

Figure I.2   Strategic Opportunities Matrix. (Adapted from Figure 1.1.)

Positioning IT in the Organization

Technological myopia can stifle an organization's ability to seize new opportunities. In Chapter 2, John Wyman notes the importance of top-management positioning. He cites a survey of the organizational level and role of the top IT position that reflects the corporation's attitude toward information technology (see Figure I.3).

At the lowest tier in this matrix, data processing (DP), office automation (OA), and telecommunications (TP) are perceived as three separate islands, each with its own manager and budget. The firm sees these three distinct functions as expenses in need of control.

	Full Sample	+ $500 M Sales	Top IS Position	Planning Role	Attitude
High	8%	17%	CIO	Strategic	Priority
	27%	30%	VP, MIS	Tactical	Necessary Investment
	27%	17%	Dir, MIS	Operational	Necessary Expense
Low	38%	36%	Mgr, DP (or TP, OA)	Budgeting	Expense to Control

Figure I.3   Strategic Positioning Matrix. (Adapted from Figures 2.1 and 2.2.)

In contrast, at the highest level, the management of what is now integrated technology moves to the senior-officer level—a chief information officer (CIO), a counterpart of the chief financial officer. Here, the planning task is to develop the firm's strategic use of information technology. When information is viewed in this context, it becomes very valuable, something to be treated as a priority investment equal in importance to labor or capital. Wyman reported that the larger organizations, those with over $500 million in sales, were twice as likely as smaller organizations to have a CIO position already established.

Matching IT to the Organization's Corporate Strategy

It is not sufficient merely to identify strategic opportunities and to establish a supportive organizational structure. It is important that the information technology strategy selected match the organization's strategic posture as well. Three dimensions of such a strategy are identified by John C. Camillus and Albert L. Lederer in Chapter 3.

1. Transaction processing systems (TPS) vs. decision support systems (DSS): A TPS is a system set up to process large numbers of transactions efficiently and accurately (e.g., an order-entry or reservation system). A DSS is intended to aid managerial decision making. Although the TPS–DSS choice actually represents a continuum, the TPS is inherently oriented toward programmed decisions; DSS, on the other hand, is more appropriate for semistructured problems and nonprogrammed decisions.
2. Mainframe vs. independent microcomputers: A large-scale mainframe computer can provide a high-performance centralized database capability, such as may be needed for an airline reservation system. Independent microcomputers, on the other hand, may be appropriate in a consulting organization where each specialist has very different data and analysis needs.
3. Strict vs. flexible: The policies for hardware acquisition, data control, staffing, etc., may be either strict or flexible. Where efficient execution of a clearly defined strategy is important, a comprehensive and strict set of policies is probably warranted. A flexible approach to these policies would promote creativity, independence, and adaptive behavior.

These three dimensions are independent, and an organization could select a separate position on each; however, matching these information technology strategies with corporate strategies leads to certain likely relationships, as suggested in Figure I.4. In this figure, the key elements of strategy alternatives proposed by Glueck (a),[2] Porter (b),[3] and Miles and Snow (c)[4] are depicted.

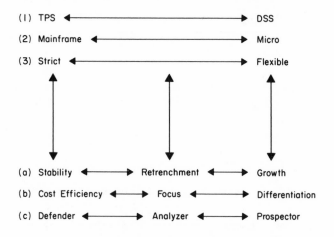

INFORMATION TECHNOLOGY STRATEGY ALTERNATIVES

(1) TPS ←——————————→ DSS

(2) Mainframe ←——————————→ Micro

(3) Strict ←——————————→ Flexible

(a) Stability ←——→ Retrenchment ←——→ Growth

(b) Cost Efficiency ←——→ Focus ←——→ Differentiation

(c) Defender ←——→ Analyzer ←——→ Prospector

CORPORATE STRATEGY ALTERNATIVES

Figure I.4 Matching IT Strategy and Corporate Strategy. (Adapted from Figure 3.3.)

A stability (a), cost-efficiency (b), or defender (c) stance mandates an orientation that can enhance profits without an increase in volume of activity—suggesting a TPS mainframe information technology with strict policies. On the other hand, a growth (a), differentiation (b), or prospector (c) corporate strategy might be best accomplished by a flexible orientation utilizing micros with DSS capabilities.

Each situation, of course, must be examined separately, but this framework helps to structure the evaluation process. The important point is that an explicit matching be done between corporate strategy and IT strategy.

Control of IT

The previous section noted the importance of matching corporate and IT strategies. There are various ways of accomplishing this goal, ranging from informal to fully integrated corporate/IT strategy planning. In Chapter 4, Henry C. Lucas and Jon A. Turner suggest the alternatives listed in Table I.1.

In the independent situation, information systems are not linked to any corporate strategy other than performing their tasks with operational efficiency; this corresponds to most traditional payroll, inventory, and order-entry systems. In the policy-support situation, IT is used to help develop corporate strategy, for instance, by producing sales forecasts and testing assumptions during the planning process.

Table I.1 Integration of Information Technology and Corporate Strategies

	Level of Integration	Primary Objective	Secondary Objective
I.	Independent	Operational efficiency	Manage information
II.	Policy support	Aid decision making	Understand problem dynamics
III.	Fully integrated	Open new products, markets, and directions	Change decision process, consider alternatives

Adapted from Table 4.1.

Explicit control of IT and full integration into corporate strategy formulation are necessary prerequisites for the successful exploitation of IT strategic opportunities. In extreme cases, IT strategy is the corporate strategy, as illustrated by the following case (see Chapter 4).

Information Resources, Inc., developed a corporate strategy that is intertwined with information technology. The firm purchased grocery-store point-of-sale scanning equipment and gave it free to fifteen supermarkets in two towns, which were selected on the basis of their demographic makeup. There were 2,000 households in each of the two test markets using the scanning equipment: Their purchases were recorded on an Information Resources computer in Chicago. Since each product was marked by the universal product code, researchers could pinpoint a family's purchases by price, brand, and size and then correlate the purchase information with any promotions, such as coupons, free samples, price adjustments, advertising, and store displays.

This technology means that Information Resources can conduct economical scientific tests of marketing strategies to determine the most effective approach to its customers. For example, through cooperation with a cable TV network, the firm can target different TV spots to selected households and analyze the resulting purchases. The imaginative use of this technology, in fact, allowed the firm to gain a competitive lead over much larger, better established market-research firms.

Assuming that one is appropriately motivated to want to seize such strategic advantages, how does one structure the corporation's information systems organization and develop a process for planning for this new era of information technology? These issues are addressed in the next section.

Planning for the New Era of Information Technology

Role of the Chief Information Officer

The role of the top information systems (IS) executive is fundamentally changing from the "technical" orientation of the 1960s and 1970s to a "managerial" orientation for the 1980s and 1990s. But how does the IS executive develop this managerial orientation, focus energy and efforts, and develop effective relationships with peer executives?

A powerful tool for identifying ways of meeting these needs is the critical success factors (CSFs) methodology developed by John F. Rockart (see Chapter 5).[5] CSFs help identify those few key areas of activity in which favorable results are absolutely necessary for a particular manager to reach his or her goal. In a survey of nine major companies that generally were regarded as outstanding in their use of information technology, the CSFs of the top IS executives were elicited and summarized in the following four key categories: service, communication, IS human resources, and repositioning the IS function.

A general profile of successful IS executives emerged from this study. These executives see their role as general business managers, not as information systems technicians. They also see the information systems function as significant to the success of the company, and they are constantly communicating this perspective to others. Each IS executive interviewed had a crisp, clear view of his or her own critical success factors. In short, all had well-defined perspectives on IS technology and a clear vision of where their corporations should be going with that technology.

Finally, almost all of the executives interviewed spoke of their organizations from a "political" perspective as well as from a "rational" one. Emphasis was often placed on the need to get key "power" individuals to understand and act in ways beneficial to the organization. The use of the CSF methodology is effective in both accomplishing this goal and starting the planning for the exploitation of information technology within the firm.

An Assessment of Critical Success Factors for Planning

Originally, the CSF procedure, which involved interviews between an analyst and a CEO, was intended to identify critical areas of concern for that executive and to provide initial descriptions of information measures that reflected those concerns. Subsequently, Bullen and Rockart broadened the definition of CSFs and proposed that they be used as a management of information systems (MIS) planning tool.[6] When CSFs are used in this way, managers from multiple levels of an organization's hierarchy must be interviewed and the resulting CSFs are synthesized into a collective set for the entire organization.

A number of organizations have employed CSFs successfully in these ways. In Chapter 6, Andrew C. Boynton and Robert W. Zmud report on a study they conducted to determine the strengths and weaknesses of the CSF methodology as applied to MIS planning and requirements analysis. They suggest that the CSF method has two key strengths that make it successful. First, it generates user acceptance at the senior-management level. Senior managers intuitively understand the thrust of the method, and consequently they strongly endorse its application as a means of identifying important areas that need attention. Second, the CSF method facilitates a structured, top-down analysis or planning process. It initially focuses a participant's attention on a core set of essential issues and then proceeds to refine the issues in a manner that allows an evolving design to be examined continuously for validity and completeness.

In strategic planning, CSFs form a bridge between corporate strategic interests and strategic planning efforts of the information function. Since an organization's CSFs are those factors that must function well for the organization to succeed, a link is provided between an organization's tactical and strategic planning objectives.

In their study of CSF effectiveness, Boynton and Zmud did find that the more removed managers and other personnel were from the senior-management level, the more difficult it became to develop meaningful corporatewide CSFs. They categorized their findings about critical success factors into strengths and weaknesses (see Table I.2).

By understanding these strengths and weaknesses, the CSF method can be effectively applied to help a corporation perform strategic information technology planning.

Top-Management Participation

As the previous discussions indicated, active top-management participation, direction, and support are crucial to the strategic use of information technol-

Table I.2   Strengths and Weaknesses of the CSF Method

Strengths
- Provide effective support to planning processes
- Develop insights into information services that can impact a firm's competitive position
- Are received enthusiastically by senior management who identify with the thrust of the CSF concept
- Serve as the top level of a structured analysis and promote structured analysis process

Weaknesses
- The more removed managers are from senior positions within the organization, the more difficult it is for them to identify meaningful organizational CSFs
- Managers not involved with strategic and tactical planning can experience difficulty in dealing with the conceptual nature of CSFs
- It is difficult for certain managers to ascertain their information needs using only CSFs

From Table 6.2.

ogy. There are many ways to accomplish this, and John F. Rockart and Adam D. Crescenzi propose a three-phase process (see Chapter 7):

I.   Critical success factors
II. Decision scenarios
III. Prototyping

The use of critical success factor analysis in phase I not only provides the linkage between business strategy and information technology, but it also establishes the active top-management participation needed to carry through with phases II and III.

The decision scenarios explored in phase II have two major goals: To develop systems priorities and to gain managerial confidence that the systems priorities will support the corporation's key objectives.

Phase III involves creating prototypes and implementing actual systems. A prototype provides enormous benefits by reducing monetary and business risk and by allowing a manager to inspect, work with, and actively participate in the development of the system.

Portfolio of Systems Planning Methodologies

A variety of systems planning methodologies has been proposed over the years. Each can serve an important role depending on the circumstances. Two important factors are infusion and diffusion. Infusion refers to the degree of penetration of information technology into the organization, usually with a focus on decreasing costs and/or increasing revenues. Diffusion refers to how widely the information technology is decentralized and disseminated.

Using these two dimensions, Cornelius H. Sullivan, Jr., in Chapter 8, identifies four planning environments and the most promising methodology for each (see Figure I.5).

The stages of growth (SOG) method, first proposed almost twenty years ago, suggests that the changes introduced by IT must be assimilated by organizations through a predictable sequence of stages, starting with initiation and expansion and followed by consolidation and maturity. This situation is rapidly being changed by increasing infusion and diffusion, but it remains viable and appropriate in "traditional" environments with low infusion and diffusion.

The business systems plan (BSP), developed by IBM, focuses on conceptualizing and designing the overall corporate data resource. This approach works well in a "backbone" environment where computing is strategic to the company, yet it is still centralized in the manner of its deployment and operated in a manner analogous to a factory.

The critical success factor (CSF) approach, because of its ability to be cus-

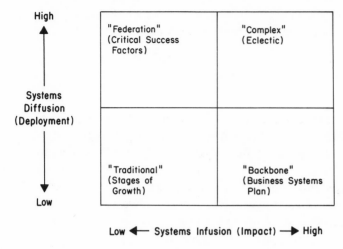

Figure I.5 Technology Planning Environments. (Adapted from Figure 8.2.)

tomized to individual executives and departments, is ideal in the environment in which technology is to be distributed among communicating "federations."

No single method appears to dominate in the "complex" environment of high diffusion and high infusion. Thus, many complex corporations draw upon these three methods to develop their own uniquely eclectic approaches, often incorporating additional factors such as data-resource management, network-resource management, and new organizational designs.

Pressures on the Information Systems Organization

In most information systems organizations, two important forces are at work that must be realized and addressed. The traditional information systems organization, depicted in Figure I.6a, could be divided into three levels of management hierarchy: the head of IS, the middle-level IS management, and the IS operations management. This organizational structure is evolving through (1) the elevation of the CIO and (2) the introduction of information centers (ICs), as depicted in Figure I.6b.

In other words, as information technology has taken on a more important strategic role, the head of information systems—increasingly being called the chief information officer—has been elevated in the organization's hierarchy. As early as the fall of 1984, the CIO function was identified in 30 percent of the Fortune 100 companies surveyed.[7] This elevation, however, not only raises expectations, but also produces disappointment, especially if the lower levels of an IS organization hierarchy continue to operate as if no change had occurred.

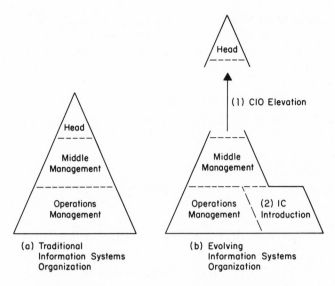

Figure I.6   Pressures on the Information Systems Organization

Another major change has grown out of the information center concept. Conceived by IBM Canada in 1976, this concept envisages an organization that supports technology for end users. In a 1983 study by the Diebold Group of New York (see Chapter 9), over 66 percent of the companies surveyed had introduced information centers. Today, these information centers provide end users with increased self-sufficiency and productivity aids, thereby reducing the amount of traditional IS resources needed.

The information center's predominant focus has been on the use of technology, usually without explicitly addressing the management of technology. Thus, the operational level of the IS hierarchy has broader responsibilities for supporting new technologies—yet often without corresponding management adjustments.

The combination of CIO elevation and information center introduction is leading to disruptions within many IS organizations. Recognition of these forces is necessary, as are adjustments to the organization to support the CIO's new role and to manage the technology. An example of such a structure has been proposed by Darrell E. Owen in Chapter 9.

Besides the internal concerns, such as the IS organization's structure, a corporation must also be cognizant of the environment in which it exists and of its responsibilities to the employees of the organization and to society. Specific examples of these issues are highlighted in the next section.

Responsibilities to the Organization and Society

The pervasive and critical role of information technology necessitates certain responsibilities to customers, the organization, the industry, and society at large. As John F. Akers, Chairman and CEO of IBM, states in Chapter 10, "If we don't conduct ourselves responsibly, governments and other institutions will erect barriers that could restrain our growth and limit the usefulness of our industry."

One particularly important area to consider is managerial security—that is, the policies and procedures adopted by management to determine authorization and to ensure the security of their data and computer installation against unauthorized access or modification.

A framework to categorize management policies and procedures has been developed in Chapter 11. This article identifies four primary areas: organizational considerations, organizational impact, economics, and objectives and accountability. Accountability warrants special attention since its assignment is often not explicitly performed or monitored.

In Chapter 12, Philip Adler, Jr., Charles K. Parsons, and Scott B. Zolke address these issues in the context of personnel administration. Their research identifies specific management implications and concludes with the development of a four-step proposal:

1. Develop a formal practices plan.
2. Encourage active employee involvement.
3. Accumulate only relevant and recent data.
4. Carefully control and monitor release to the outside.

Although externally developed social, legal, and technical factors may influence or constrain options, primary decisions continue to be based on internal management decisions. As our reliance upon information technology continues to heighten and propel us toward an ever more comprehensive "information society," these issues will become increasingly critical.

Conclusions

Corporations stand at the threshold of a new age. Confronted with worldwide turbulence and competition, information technology is the new weapon that is capable of dramatically changing the balance of power. An effective battle plan and the ability to mobilize resources are essential. This introduction has presented the steps needed to integrate information technology into corporate strategy, plan organizational changes, and be alert to the impact of information technology upon society at large.

PART I

Integrating Information
Technology into Corporate
Strategy

1

Information Technology:
A Strategic Opportunity

Robert I. Benjamin

John F. Rockart

Michael S. Scott Morton

John Wyman

In this article, the authors claim that information technology (IT) has generated strategic opportunities that all U.S. industries should take advantage of if they want to maintain their competitive edge. But before these opportunities can be seized, the authors argue that the gap between the opportunities created by IT and the effective utilization of this technology must be closed. In analyzing the current business climate, they provide senior management with a framework for exploring IT strategic opportunities. Case studies of leading-edge companies that have successfully implemented IT into their corporate strategies are presented. *SMR.*

Today, senior executives are barraged by the business press with the message that personal computers, computer-aided design, telemarketing, and a myriad of other applications of electronic technology will give them and their companies new muscle tone and greater profits. But behind this ever-increasing assault is the reality of an ever-expanding gap between the opportunities created by information technology (IT) and the effective utilization of this technology. The gap is caused by two factors:

- An unprecedented increase in functionality and cost performance of information technology, which in effect is creating strategic opportunities for many companies.

From *Sloan Management Review,* Spring 1984, Vol. 25, No. 3. Reprinted with permission.

- Most senior managers have little or no experience or background in managing information and telecommunications technologies. Thus, they do not have an experiential base to relate this new form of strategic opportunity to their business.

It was only a few years ago that Alan Kantrow wrote, "The past decade reveals managers' growing awareness of the need to incorporate technological issues within strategic decision making. They have increasingly discovered that technology and strategy are inseparable."[1] But the reality is that, while most managers have increasingly focused on the *basic* technologies underlying their respective industries as ingredients of strategy, far too many have missed the significance of the new *computer* and *communications* technologies that affect all industries today.

Within the past year, we discussed this situation with top executives and technology managers in two dozen companies. In some cases, we performed in-depth studies of significant exploitation of IT.

In order to provide senior management with some rough guidelines for applying information technology to their strategic needs, we will discuss five key issues:

- The driving forces underlying information technology that are creating business strategy;
- A senior management entrepreneurial attitude;
- Ways in which leading-edge companies are utilizing information technology to improve their strategic position;
- A simple, but useful, framework, called a strategic opportunities matrix, for exploring IT strategic opportunities; and
- A managerial approach, which is a summary arising from our studies, that appears appropriate for effective application of information technology.

Driving Forces

There are two steady forces driving information technology:

1. New Information Technology Economics

This economics is summed up by an unrelenting year-after-year 30 to 40 percent improvement in cost performance of circuitry and mass storage, with steady smaller cost-performance improvements in telecommunications. Below are several examples that illustrate the dynamics of this cost-performance progress:

- *Processors*. Today's $5,000 personal computer is almost equivalent in capability to the million dollar computer of the 1960s.

- *Telecommunications*. Long-distance fiber-optics circuits will be installed during the rest of the decade at one-tenth the cost of the conventional circuits they will replace. This will provide a radical change in telecommunications cost performance.

- *Software*. Despite the publicity given to hardware, software is the area of most dramatic change. Languages and applications that facilitate new uses and users of information technology are coming to market at an ever-increasing rate. For example, not much more than a decade ago, it cost hundreds of hours and tens of thousands of dollars to program financial proforma capability. Today, a "spread sheet" program like VISICALC costs a few hundred dollars. Literally, hundreds of thousands of copies have been sold to end users in the marketplace. And ever more powerful and more easily usable software is being produced at an increasing rate.

2. Challenging Business Environment

All businesses face the unrelenting pressures of a business environment characterized by an intense global competition, which was recently described by Levitt.[2] Moreover, this increasingly competitive world has developed against a backdrop of difficult economic conditions, including long-term high inflation, high interest rates, and low real growth.

The interaction of these two variables—information technology economics and a challenging business environment—has generated what might be called the economic imperative of information technology. Organizations that do not take advantage of the growing opportunities provided by IT are likely to slip behind in the competitive business world.

One example clearly illustrates this point. The revitalization of the manufacturing industry in the United States leans strongly on information technology. For companies to compete effectively internationally, several technologies must be utilized. These include computer-assisted design and manufacturing, automated factories and robotics, and new approaches to inventory flow, such as the Japanese "Kanban," which requires close interconnection between production facilities and key suppliers.

Senior Management Entrepreneurial Attitude

Kantrow argues persuasively that in order to exploit strategic opportunities arising from technology, a senior management entrepreneurial attitude is required to:[3]

- View new technology as a central part of business thinking;
- Examine how the key decisions of senior managers can be affected by the new technology;
- Examine cross-functional organizational utilization of the technology; and
- Consider the planning and production processes required to exploit the technology.

Today, an increasing number of companies are adopting this attitude with regard to the basic technologies that are relevant to their industries. However, we did not see significant evidence of this kind of thinking with respect to information technology in our discussions with companies, many of which are in the multibillion dollar class. Out of these discussions came the following observations:

- Only a handful of companies demonstrated that managerial attention was focused on the potential impact of information technology on corporate strategy. These companies had clearly delineated formal processes to ensure information technology input to the development of strategy. In the remainder, IT input, where it existed, was informal at best.
- In almost all cases, this input was a relatively new phenomenon, occurring for the first time in the past twelve to eighteen months.
- Even where IT input was available at the corporate level, managers to whom we talked believed that it was *not* being effectively included in the planning process at lower levels.

This last point is particularly relevant, since, as we will note later, our research indicates that strategically oriented information technology applications can be generated at all organizational levels. In fact, most of the effective applications we have seen have been developed spontaneously at lower levels within the organization. Although, in a few cases, these applications arise from a corporate executive's strategic business vision, this is not the primary source of the strategic application of the technology that we have seen.

Utilization of IT by Leading Companies

Despite a general lack of managerial attention given to the significance of IT, a number of companies have seized the opportunity to use information technology to gain a competitive advantage. Five significant examples are:

- American Hospital Supply (AHS), a leading manufacturer and distributor of a very broad line of products for doctors, laboratories, and hospitals, has since 1976 evolved in an order-entry distribution system that directly links the majority of its customers to AHS computers. Over 4,000 customer terminals at various locations are linked today to the American Hospital Supply system. As well as providing the customer with direct access to the AHS order-distribution process, the system allows customers to perform functions, such as inventory control, for themselves, thereby generating incremental revenues for AHS. The American Hospital Supply system has been successful because it simplifies ordering processes for customers, reduces costs for both AHS and the customer, and allows AHS to develop and manage pricing incentives to the customer across all product lines. As a result, customer loyalty is high, and AHS market share has been increasing.

  AHS's initial move to electronic ordering was begun by the manager of a regional distribution center working to fill the needs of a single customer. A far-sighted senior management has continually supported the system "with management attention and development funds."

- Digital Equipment Corporation (DEC) has utilized the recently developed software technology for "expert systems" to improve significantly a system configuration problem. Because of the tremendous variety of possible configurations of its equipment and the difficulty of ensuring that each system was appropriately configured, DEC was faced with a problem of reworking manufactured configurations at field installation time. In addition to the expense involved, the necessary rework caused lost revenue as a result of deferral of invoicing and customer complaints. However, in conjunction with Carnegie-Mellon University, DEC engineers captured the "expert rules" used by the most knowledgeable design and field service engineers in a computer program. This system ensures that expertly designed configurations are developed for every system for manufacture and subsequent field installation. It has proved extremely successful and is now being accessed, on a trial basis, by sales personnel in their order-generating process. Thus, customers in the field can be assured that their orders are appropriate and fully specified at the time they are entered.

- *USA TODAY* was largely the conception and creation of Allan H. Neuharth, president of Gannett Newspapers, who devoted much of a year's time to studying the information generation and transmission technologies needed to create the first "national" newspaper and to transmit it by satellite to seventeen geographically dispersed printing plants. The paper was introduced in September 1982, and by October 1983 1.1 million copies a day in nineteen metropolitan areas were being sold. Satellites and other information technology allow a thirty-six-page edition to be created, transmitted in eight hours, and printed with full color quality.

- In 1977, Merrill Lynch & Co. established the cash management account (CMA) and shattered the traditional boundaries between the banking and securities industries. The CMA is a combination of charge card, checking account, and brokerage service all rolled into one product. Implementation required a complex information technology interface of communications and data processing between the Merrill Lynch brokerage offices and Bank One, which acts as the check and credit-card processing center for the CMA accounts. By February 1983, more than 915,000 accounts were in place. Accounts were being added at a rate of 5,000 a week. Other financial institutions such as Shearson-American Express have introduced competitive offerings and are fighting vigorously to gain a share of this newly created market made possible by IT.

  The cash management account's origin was a 1975 study by Stanford Research Institute for the then chairman Donald Regan. The planning organization at Merrill Lynch developed the initial vision into today's highly successful CMA system.

- In the years 1979–1982, Xerox implemented a fieldwork support system to provide better and more cost-effective service to its very large worldwide customer base of office equipment. The system is operational on over fifty distributed minicomputers in the U.S., Canada, and Europe to facilitate the way thousands of Xerox customer-service representatives support their customers. The system provides the work-support representatives with computerized access to information about customers, previous call histories, and workloads of technical representatives in the area. Upon the completion of a call, the work-support representative schedules the customer-service representative to the next customer site. The customer-service representative is also provided with information about the problem he or she will encounter and parts most likely needed. Additionally, a substantial number of problems are diagnosed over the telephone, thus reducing the total number of calls made.

  The fieldwork support system is strategically important to Xerox because it improves customer satisfaction through faster, high-quality response time and improves productivity of the large tech rep force by increasing the number of calls each can make.

From the above examples, it is clear that some companies are implementing systems of strategic importance. Some senior managements are acutely aware of the strategic potential of information technology and are leading the change, while other senior managements have merely created a climate that supports IT innovation.

A Strategic Opportunities Framework

Senior executives need to be able to determine where strategic opportunities for use of information technology exist. This section will present our approach, called the strategic opportunities matrix, which we feel is a simple, but insightful, framework that senior managers can use. Before describing the matrix, however, a number of other methods appearing in the literature should be noted.

Michael Porter's framework for developing strategy in a competitive environment is a starting point for some useful frameworks.[4] Porter suggests that, for any company, significant strategic actions consist of either diminishing supplier or customer power, holding off new entrants into its industry, lowering the possibility of substitution for their products, or gaining a competitive edge within the existing industry. Other authors using this framework in discussing IT and strategy provide checklists of ways in which to make any of the strategic moves through the use of IT.[5] Suggestions for companies following each of Porter's three "generic strategies" (low cost, differentiation, and niche) are also made.

Alternatively, a thorough search of the "value-added" chain for the most useful application of IT is suggested by some authors.[6] Here, the manager carefully analyzes all steps in the business process from R&D and purchasing through final sales to ascertain the critical points at which IT can be best applied. Other approaches abound.[7]

We believe, however, that, in light of today's technology, each senior manager should focus on two significant questions:

- Can I use the technology to make a significant change in the way we are now doing business so my company can gain a competitive advantage?
- Should we, as a company, concentrate on using IT to improve our approach to the marketplace? Or, should we center our efforts on internal improvements in the way we currently carry out the activities of the firm?

The first question is important because there exist today significant opportunities in some industries to utilize IT in order to deliver revolutionary new products—in effect, changing the industry—or to redefine vastly current approaches to manufacturing, purchasing, etc. This huge competitive "leap" should be a foremost concern of senior management; if it is not undertaken by one's own company, it is open to exploitation by others. Alternatively, if no such opportunity appears feasible, attention should turn to improving the current business through IT.

Moreover, there are two ways in which any business can be made substantially better: (1) improving the organization's impact in the marketplace; and (2) improving *key internal operations,* thereby lowering costs or improving services. Our second question is meant to place emphasis on both ways. Most attention today focuses on using technology to improve the organization's impact in the marketplace. Most of the companies that we have seen, however, have significant opportunities to improve key internal operations. Today's technology provides a myriad of ways to improve these operations (e.g., CAD/CAM for faster, better integrated manufacturing processes, electronic or voice mail for improved communications, etc.).

Taken together, the two questions suggest a four-cell strategic opportunities matrix, which is shown in Figure 1.1. We believe it presents a simple, but powerful, way of thinking about strategic use of IT. Each of the five companies presented below occupies a cell of this matrix.

Significant Structural Change: Competitive Marketplace

Porter states that "the power of technology as a competitive variable lies in its ability to alter competition through changing industry structure."[8] Gannett's creation of *USA TODAY* is a significant structural change in the production and distribution of newspapers leading to the creation of the Focus Metromedia Newspapers. If it is a long-term success, it will cause a significant restructuring of the publication industry.

Significant Structural Change: Competitive Marketplace

The Merrill Lynch cash management account has directly changed the types of financial services offered to the consumer, resulting in significant structural change in the financial services industry.

Significant Structural Change: Internal Operations

The Digital Equipment Corporation "expert system" is an example of applying new advanced software technology to an internal set of manufacturing processes. The result is a computer-based configuration of computers, not a relatively frail manpower-intensive process.

	Competitive Marketplace	Internal Operations
Significant Structural Change	Gannett—*USA TODAY* Merrill Lynch General Electric	Digital Equipment
Traditional Products & Processes	American Hospital Supply Bank of America Toyota	Xerox United Airlines

Figure 1.1   Strategic Opportunities Framework

Traditional Products and Processes: Competitive Marketplace

The American Hospital Supply order-entry system is a strategic application of information technology that takes traditional internal products and processes (American's own order-entry and distribution system) and links them directly to customers, thus creating a potentially defensible barrier to competition.

Traditional Products and Processes: Internal Operations

Xerox has taken a traditional process—the dispatching of field service personnel—and, through an effective communication-computer system, has significantly increased both technical representative productivity *and* customer satisfaction.

In most companies, there are strategic opportunities in all quadrants of the matrix (see Figure 1.1). Several other examples are given to make the application of the opportunities matrix more concrete:

- United Airlines (UAL) began using teleconferencing services over ten years ago for emergency situations and daily executive briefings, both of which are critical to the success of the airline's operation. Very favorable, ongoing experience with teleconferencing has led UAL to stretch its application into matters as delicate as labor negotiations. Success has been reported in at least one key teleconferencing negotiation that resulted in significant time savings. In the context of the opportunities matrix, this is a refinement of a current internal process through use of information technology.
- A recently hired junior employee of a Bank of America line division became interested in developing cash management analysis tools on a personal computer. Once a rough prototype was working, it was demonstrated to the division's senior management, and funds were allocated to develop a full-fledged prototype of a working system. The prototype system was tested by four major customers of the Bank of America. The results of the

experiment disclosed a sizable opportunity to enhance the bank's relationship with corporate treasurers. Several very useful functions could be provided on the personal computer. These include facilities for analysis of corporate balances; a direct linkage into the Bank of America funds transfer system; and, via Bank of America, linkage to the other major money center banks. In this instance, the strategic opportunity is focused on the competitive marketplace and is a significant refinement of a traditional process of providing information to customers.

- Toyota U.S. has established an extensive system to support its widespread dealers' network. The system provides Toyota with timely order- and inventory-control data as well as providing the dealers with an on-site system to run their own businesses. The system is composed of the Toyota data center, which is linked by Toyota's telecommunications network to dealers who have minicomputers of different capacities and functionality geared to their own business needs. Toyota benefits through more accurate sales and inventory data. Moreover, the dealers are able to manage their own businesses better and are linked more tightly to Toyota in their business relationship. The Toyota system is externally focused and combines a traditional process (order-inventory) with a new powerful addition—a system to support the dealer in managing his or her own business.

- In 1980, General Electric (GE) found that consumers did not feel that GE was adequately responsive to their inquiries. Consumers wanted more product information before their purchase and additional information after the purchase. The GE Answer Center, utilizing an "800" line for toll-free calling, was opened as part of an overall strategy in the consumer-products sector to better meet customer needs. The system now covers all GE products and handles over 1.5 million calls per year. Computers are used to retrieve 500,000 pieces of information about GE's 8,500 products. Some 94 percent of the customers who use the system express satisfaction with the results. In this case, GE has restructured the way they deal with their end-point customer, the consumer.

Summary: A Managerial Approach

Many opportunities for strategic use of information technology exist today, and more are constantly emerging with the increasing flow of lower cost technologies that provide significant new capabilities. As competitive pressures grow, these opportunities are being seized. What steps, then, should senior management take to move the strategic application of information technology forward within the organization? We suggest three straightforward actions:

1. Ask the two basic questions noted earlier, with the first question taking precedence. There are significant opportunities for competitive advantage through IT.
2. Focus attention on information technology at the top of the corporation. In most of the cases where significant structural change has been effected, it has been the result of a senior person's vision (e.g., *USA TODAY*, Merrill Lynch). The business understanding for this vision and the ability to implement it are rarely found in the lower parts of the organization.
3. Generate awareness of the potential advantages of IT, and incentives to take advantage of it, throughout the organization. Our research indicates that *most* of the strategic improvements in current processes have bubbled up through the organization. This is consistent with von Hippel's research on innovation, in which he concludes that the majority of technological innovation emerges not from the supplier's research and development but from creative uses of existing technology by an organization's customers.[9] It is necessary, therefore, to maintain alertness to possible new uses of the technology at all levels of the organization—especially among those personnel who have customer contact. As Joseph L. Dionne, CEO of McGraw-Hill, Inc., notes, "Customers are the key to creating the new generations of electronic products and services. . . . Every time the customer asks for a new application of the technology, McGraw-Hill responds by creating a new product that can then be marketed elsewhere."[10]

In short, senior management should work to *create an environment* in which information technology is considered an important strategic weapon. The appointment of a senior "technology officer" reporting at a high level in the corporation is one possible way to effect this. The exact actions taken, however, will be different from organization to organization and with each business's strategy, structure, and culture.

Perhaps one of the most comprehensive approaches toward underscoring the importance of IT for all levels of the organization has been taken by Emhart, a manufacturer of shoe-machinery hardware. After considerable research into strategic options, the CEO and president concluded that the company would have to invest heavily and creatively in all types of technology—the emphasis being on information technology. To signal this corporate emphasis to the organization, two new roles were created—a director of technology and a director of information technology. More significantly, a new subcommittee of the board of directors was formed—a subcommittee of technology to receive reports from the two directors at its periodic meetings.

These moves have served to indicate clearly and successfully to the organization the motive of the technological thrust underlying Emhart's ambitious new goals.

Not all companies will choose this same organizational approach. Yet, those organizations that continue to conduct business as usual in the midst of a major information technology revolution will, we believe, be overlooking a very major opportunity.

2

Technological Myopia: The Need to Think Strategically about Technology

John Wyman

Technological myopia—a form of business short-sightedness—is an affliction to be avoided. In its internal or external form, an industry or company fails to comprehend technological progress. Here, the author states that an inappropriate attitude toward technology is often the cause. He outlines a four-phase process—assessment, involvement, selection, and integration—that can be used to overcome technological myopia, a process that incorporates a change in perspective. The author draws on examples from several firms to illustrate his points regarding information technology and its level of priority within a firm. He maintains that the key to the successful implementation of technology lies in choosing a strategic approach. *SMR.*

Some years ago, Theodore Levitt took managers to task for too narrowly perceiving their businesses. In his classic example, he cited the railroads as seeing themselves as being in the railroad business instead of in the broadly defined transportation business—a strategic oversight that led them to miss opportunities in the growing trucking and airline industries. Levitt termed this kind of business short-sightedness "marketing myopia."[1] One might argue, however, that the railroads were not myopic so much in a marketing sense as in a technological sense: They failed to see how advances in highway construction and airplanes would affect the demand for rail transportation. European and Asian railroads, in contrast, managed to compete with these new developments by adopting new railroad technology.

Technological myopia is an affliction with two varieties. The first is the external form: an industry, as in the railroad example, that doesn't broaden its vision to see how technological progress in its own or related industries will affect it. The second is *internal* myopia, which occurs when a company or

From *Sloan Management Review*, Summer 1985, Vol. 26, No. 4. Reprinted with permission.

industry has advanced technology available but doesn't see how to apply it in a strategic way. The Stakhanovite movement in Stalinist Russia is a classic example of internal technological myopia. Stalin ordered workers to increase production norms and deployed the latest technologies to make it happen. The technology performed admirably—but not strategically—the result being that the workers glutted the economy with goods for which there was no significant demand.

Internal myopia is either a failure to utilize technology's full power or to put it to the wrong use. External myopia amounts to not understanding—or even being aware of—an emerging technology. Both are hazardous to a company's health, and both can be corrected—if one is willing to undergo the cure. Luckily, there is no shortage of purported cures requiring the attention of the CEO. Parsons, for example, urges the CEO to develop an explicit technology strategy.[2] McFarlan suggests that the CEO insist upon an accounting of the competitive impact of technology expenditures.[3] And Rockart and Crescenzi focus on identifying the critical success factors needed to support the business.[4]

I applaud all of these ideas and suggest they can be even further enhanced by the addition of an assessment process. It is important, I think, for a firm to examine its attitudes toward technology. An inappropriate attitude is often the cause of technological myopia in its external or internal form. A change in attitude is a change in perspective. It improves decision making and, more importantly, strategy. My approach, then, incorporates a four-phase process that one can employ to overcome technological myopia.

Phase I: Assessment

The Strategic Value Matrix

One way to assess strategic perspective is through what I call the Strategic Value Matrix. You can effectively measure the degree of technological myopia by the position of a firm on this matrix (see Figure 2.1).

On the lowest tier, data processing, office automation, and telecommunications are perceived as three separate islands, each with its own manager and budget. (And putting together a budget is about the extent of the planning that takes place for each function.) The firm sees these three distinct functions as centers of expense needing control. At the next tier, the three functions are organizationally placed under one director who prepares an operational plan, but senior management still views information systems as an area of expense, albeit a necessary expense.

The next step elevates information systems to the vice-presidential level. Planning becomes more systematic and integrated. The plan also addresses

High

	Organization	Planning	Value
	Chief Technology Officer	Strategic Business Plan	Priority Investment
Strategic Value	Vice President, Information Systems	Tactical Support for Strategic Plan	Necessary Investment
	Director, Management Information Systems	Operational Plan	Necessary Expense
	Manager	Budget	Expense to Control

Low

Figure 2.1   Strategic Value Matrix

how it will support corporate objectives and, in fact, a document is usually produced with a title something like "Information Systems Strategic Plan." The document then normally outlines the information systems strategy for four or five years. But that plan usually doesn't address the strategic goals of the firm; at best, it offers tactical support. However, at this point there is an interesting—and critical—shift in the value the firm places on information systems; it changes from necessary expense to necessary investment.

At the highest level on this matrix, the management of what is now integrated technology moves to the senior officer level. We've got a new position—chief technology officer—a counterpart of the chief financial officer. Here, the planning task is to develop the firm's strategic use of information technology, and when information is viewed in this context it becomes very valuable, something to be treated as a priority investment equal in importance to labor or capital.

As a point of reference, let me cite some figures that show where information managers place their companies on this matrix. In a recent McGraw-Hill study of MIS managers, only 8 percent put their company in the top slot in terms of seeing information technology as a priority investment. The next two groups both drew 27 percent. And fully a third viewed information technology as an expense to be controlled. In a sample of companies with annual sales of $500 million or more, 17 percent saw information technology as a priority investment, 30 percent as a necessary investment, 17 percent as a necessary expense, and 36 percent as an expense to be controlled. While the larger companies have a more strategic view, the bulk of the responses are clustered at the bottom of the matrix, which suggests that there are still plenty of opportunities to exploit. This chart can serve as a good vehicle for facilitating discussion with senior executives (see Figure 2.2).

High

Value	Full Sample	+$500M Sales
Priority Investment	8%	17%
Necessary Investment	27%	30%
Necessary Expense	27%	17%
Expense to Control	38%	36%

Strategic Value

Low

Figure 2.2   Results of the McGraw-Hill Study

Now let me turn to a few examples of companies I believe have reached the top tier on the strategic value matrix.

- Back in 1980, Ed Schefer, vice-president of information management for General Foods, started working with his senior management to involve information technology in the strategic planning process. One of his tactics was to turn everyone in his information services department into consultants and send them throughout the company to teach as many people as possible to utilize end-user computing. With information technology so diffused, it became an integral part of almost everyone's work and planning. And soon it became an integral part of planning the business strategy.
- Donald Siebert, chairman of J. C. Penney, has said that the leaders in retailing in the 1980s and 1990s will not necessarily be the best merchandisers, but rather the ones who capitalize on the advantages that technology provides. In keeping with Siebert's remarks, Penney's is now a leader in point-of-sale systems that provide optimal inventory, provide cash controls, and make it possible to have instant credit authorization. This last feature has opened up a whole new line of business for Penney's. They now market credit-card authorization and verification to other companies and list Shell and Gulf Oil among their major customers.
- Citicorp is another example. The giant bank holding company has set up a high-level technology committee to explore strategic applications, and they also publish a newsletter on technology to keep officers abreast of new applications. And to give you an idea of the bank's future commitment to technology, John Reed, the new chairman, was the architect of much of the firm's technological innovations over the last ten years.

Phase II: Involvement

Strategic Question Set

After assessing where you are on the strategic value matrix, you might ask yourself how you can improve your strategic use of information. The obvious way to begin is by looking at the marketplace. Ask yourself, what strategic approach will give you an advantage over your competitors? Michael Porter of the Harvard Business School has some helpful suggestions on this point. Porter identifies three generic strategies for outperforming other firms in an industry: being the low-cost producer; differentiating the product; or focusing on serving a particular segment of the market.[5]

There are, of course, several permutations of these strategies. For example, one can become the low-cost producer in a specialized market niche, or differentiate the product and at the same time be the low-cost producer. What really counts is the strategic focus of the approach. Once a strategic route has been decided upon, you can creatively examine how information technology can help implement the plan by asking a series of strategic questions:

- In becoming a low-cost producer, how can technology help optimize inventory or improve productivity?
- In using differentiation, how will technology help improve customer service, physical distribution, or quality control?
- In focusing on just a small segment of the market, how can technology help develop business opportunities and serve the market better than competitors?

Those questions are just a start, but their importance lies in the fact that they all focus on opening up new opportunities.

Phase III: Selection

Strategic Focus Matrix

The key to the successful implementation of technology lies in choosing a strategy that makes sense for your business. Research recently conducted at AT&T found that the biggest payoff from information technology will come from automation of those items that affect the customer throughout the entire selling cycle. One could categorize these items as having a customer focus on the one hand and an operations focus on the other. Customer-focus examples might be product information or new product development, while an operations example might be materials management. One can then relate the particular focus with the competitive strategies already discussed: differentiation, low-cost production, and niche marketing.

Differentiation/Customer Focus: Merrill Lynch

Let's start with the combination of customer focus using a product differentiation strategy (see Figure 2.3). The Merrill Lynch cash management account, or CMA, is my favorite example. In 1977, Merrill Lynch introduced CMA as a new product totally based on modern information technology. The CMA is a combination of charge card, checking account, money-market fund, and brokerage service all combined into one product. Merrill Lynch set out to permanently change the shape of the financial marketplace by taking several existing but separate services and tying them together through information technology to create a new service that shattered the traditional boundaries between the banking and securities industries. For those firms afflicted with technological myopia, CMA was an eye-opening experience, and competitors were left playing catch-up.

Today, the Merrill Lynch CMA has more than a million customers, and while there are now a host of similar services in the marketplace, none of them has more than a fraction of CMA's market share. A strategic use of information technology produced a lasting competitive advantage for the first firm into the marketplace.

Differentiation/Operations Focus: Singer

Singer recently embraced a strategic focus that differentiated the firm in the operations arena. The strategic focus resulted from Singer's goal of providing better customer information and order processing for its national accounts. In an effort to reduce costs and at the same time give customers more control over their orders, Singer put computer terminals in customer locations. Their customers can now directly order merchandise, check the status of orders,

	Differentiation	Low Cost	Niche
Customer	Merrill Lynch	General Tire	American Airlines
Operations	Singer	Pitney-Bowes	American Hospital Supply

Figure 2.3   Strategic Focus Matrix

check prices and availability, and arrange for shipment of the merchandise. In addition, Singer is now contemplating a special incentive for customers who use this system.

Low-Cost Producer/Customer Focus: General Tire

General Tire arranged to have a telemarketing center take over the service support functions that previously had been performed by the field sales force. Telemarketing specialists handle questions like "Have you got it?" "How much is it?" "Did it ship?" and "There's something wrong with my bill." This lowered General Tire's unit costs by freeing the field sales force to devote more of their time to selling. General Tire then decided to let the telemarketing center take over the selling and account management role for some of the company's marginally profitable accounts—accounts that couldn't be profitably serviced by the sales team. In the first month of operation, General Tire's telemarketing people sold more to these accounts than the field sales force had sold to them over the entire previous year.

Low-Cost Producer/Operations Focus: Pitney-Bowes

Pitney-Bowes has found a strategic application of information technology in the way it dispatches its service people. Currently, they dispatch over 3,500 customer engineers from each of their ninety-nine branch locations throughout the U.S. Drawing upon a central data base in Danbury, Connecticut, and twenty dispatch centers that feed into it, Pitney-Bowes has found a very efficient way to send out its customer engineers. The customer calls in on an 800 number and identifies his problem, and someone at Pitney-Bowes puts it into a diagnostic system to see if it can be solved over the phone—thereby saving the cost of dispatching a customer engineer. If not, he checks the data base to find not only the service engineer who is in nearest proximity to the customer but also the engineer who can handle it at the least possible cost. Before the new system was put in place, every customer engineer had to be trained to service every kind of machinery in his area; now the company can assign someone who has a skill that matches the problem, so that the high end of their product line does not suffer because of problems at the low end. The customer benefits from this arrangement not only by having a specialist work on his problem, but by having a 30 percent improvement in response time.

Niche Marketing/Customer Focus: American Airlines

A few years ago, American Airlines decided to go after the high air-mileage passenger market with a product called AAirpass: five years of air transportation providing 25,000 miles a year for a flat $20,000 cash up front. Because of its high dollar value, American used a telemarketing center to qualify leads for the product. Later, however, the product manager learned that the telemarketing center staff was actually selling AAirpass over the phone. Drawing upon the telecommunications technology available in the center, the manager redrafted his marketing plan using telemarketing as the primary channel of distribution.

Niche Marketing/Operations Focus: American Hospital Supply

American Hospital Supply, as its name suggests, has selected the health-care industry as its niche in the wholesale business. To gain an important edge over its rivals, American Hospital Supply pioneered an order-entry distribution system that links most of the firm's customers to its computers. In addition to ordering merchandise, the system also allows customers to control their inventories, increasing the likelihood of their coming to rely upon American Hospital Supply as a key supplier. The fact that the company's initial move to electronic ordering was spearheaded by a regional manager seeking to meet the needs of a single customer suggests that starting small may be a key to success.

Rockart makes the point quite tellingly in his discussion of creating prototypes and implementing actual systems.[6] He writes, "A prototype allows a manager to inspect, work with, and shape the product as it is being developed to a point where he or she feels comfortable with it in all its dimensions."

Phase IV: Integration

Even after selecting and implementing a strategy, however, technological myopia may persist. What is needed is some means of instilling a strategic approach to technology. Successful solutions are the product of an enlightenment process that links technological applications to business strategy. But arriving at those solutions—or even thinking that they are achievable through technology—is quite often a long road littered with obstacles.

The biggest obstacle is corporate culture. In a company at the lowest tier of the strategic value matrix, nothing short of a cultural revolution is going to move it to the top, and to bring about that revolution, strong leadership is needed. CEOs must believe—and make others believe—that their firms' fortunes hinge upon the successful application of technology. And if CEOs are mired in the outdated culture, nothing short of a major competitive threat will cure them of their myopia.

Conclusion

To bring about the integration phase, begin by giving this article to the senior management team. Once the team's interest is piqued, suggest attendance at seminars on information technology and perhaps even arrange to show them some firms that are using technology to achieve major corporate goals. Once senior management become believers, you can take things a step further, going so far as to arrange meetings between your executives and those of companies currently using technology in a strategic way. You might also suggest that the board of directors convene for a quarterly briefing on information technology, or establish a technology committee, not unlike the audit and other committees that report to the board. The technology committee would be in charge of reporting strategic applications of technology within the company, or in other companies within the same industry. In time, and with persistence, your company's top management will come to see information technology in the same light as labor and capital—as a resource that can differentiate products, streamline operations, and earn a high return on equity.

3

Corporate Strategy and the Design of Computerized Information Systems

John C. Camillus

Albert L. Lederer

Computerized information systems (CIS) have been a source of much controversy in recent years. Some argue that the wealth of information available allows senior managers to keep close tabs on both their operations and their subordinates, while others maintain that advances in the design of CIS—such as wide availability of computer terminals—allow decision making to be contained within the lower levels of management. Yet another school of thought holds that the impact of such systems on top management is relatively unimportant. The authors present all three points of view as valid. In this article they discuss the importance of selecting a CIS whose design is in keeping with the strategic management processes of the organization. The alternative designs fit various strategy frameworks, and they feel that a "match" between the CIS and the strategic management objectives of the organization enhances productivity to an incomparable degree. *SMR.*

The implications for strategic management of computerized information systems have been the focus of much speculation in both practitioner and research journals. It has been argued, for instance, that the explosive improvements in computer hardware technology and related software design have made it possible for senior managers to exercise close supervision and control of subordinates whose performances they would not otherwise have been able to track in a timely and detailed fashion.[1] For instance, senior managers can now directly access the data bases of managers reporting to them and can develop their own measures of performance in addition to those that are formally reported. The reliability of the information they obtain is also presumably enhanced as a consequence.

From *Sloan Management Review*, Spring 1985, Vol. 26, No. 3. Reprinted with permission.

On the other hand, convincing arguments have been presented that advances in the design of decision support systems (DSS) and the availability of computer terminals and personal computers to a broad spectrum of managers decentralize decision making to an unprecedented, and unexpected, degree. For example, plant managers can exercise control over labor utilization and production scheduling with minimal involvement from corporate or division management.

A third perspective that has recently been offered is that despite all the excitement and the apparently stunning breakthroughs, the impact of computerized information systems on top management has been and will continue to be negligible.[2]

These three highly disparate points of view have been advanced in a most convincing fashion with apparently unassailable logic and are supported by empirical, albeit somewhat anecdotal, evidence. It is not the intention of this article to champion or denigrate any one of these points of view. In fact, we consider all three perspectives to be valid. The first two points of view, that both centralization and decentralization are supported by CIS, suggest that alternatives that vary a great deal are offered by CIS. The third point of view, that the impact of CIS on the nature of top management responsibility has been and will continue to be insignificant, is not inconsistent with the contention that the way in which this responsibility is discharged can be influenced by the design of the CIS.

We interpret the empirical evidence as indicating that very different alternative designs and purposes of CIS exist. Here we discuss how to select and orient the design of the CIS in order to obtain the desired impact upon the strategic management processes of the organization.

The Impact of CIS on Strategic Management

CIS design that is chosen to be consonant with the strategy, structure, and style components of an organization's administrative system will contribute to more effective management.[3] The rationale underlying this proposition is that the CIS, as an element of the organization's planning and control system, should meet with the consistency imperative of effective administrative system design. The experiences of companies that have been proactive and pioneering in CIS design tend to support this proposition. There have been instances of both gratifying success[4] and dismal failure,[5] thus strongly corroborating the importance of appropriate design.

CIS capabilities today offer management more choices in terms of alternatives than those previously available to organizations. That CIS capabilities offer new options and strategic advantages has been amply demonstrated. For instance, the war between Walden Books and B. Dalton has been fought mostly on the CIS battlefield.[6]

Based on these propositions, it follows that identifying the range of CIS options and selecting the most suitable is of critical importance. We identify here what we view as key dimensions of choice with regard to the design of the CIS that managers should consider. Furthermore, we offer guidelines with regard to how to best tailor and exploit CIS capabilities from the perspective of alternative management viewpoints. These key dimensions and guidelines are discussed below.

Key Dimensions of CIS Design

The designers of the organization's administrative system have begun to recognize the fundamental differences between computer systems that have been set up to process a large number of transactions (record-keeping) efficiently and accurately and systems that are intended to aid managerial decision making.[7] While it is not entirely impractical to implement both transaction processing systems (TPS) and decision support systems effectively, it must be recognized that the hardware, software, expert personnel and, most importantly, management style needed to perform each of these two tasks efficiently are vastly different.[8]

Tradeoffs will almost inevitably have to be made and it is better for them to be conscious rather than arrived at by default. A key design choice, therefore, is where on the TPS–DSS spectrum the organization should position itself in terms of hardware, software, and personnel choices. The TPS is inherently oriented toward programmed decisions,[9] whereas the DSS is more appropriate to semistructured problems and nonprogrammable decisions.[10]

It is important to note that the practical extremes of the TPS–DSS continuum do not entirely exclude either capability. There is a minimum or threshold TPS capability that all CIS should possess. A similar argument might be made for DSS capability. One might go a step further and maintain that, in fact, if TPS are inadequate or not at critical mass, then DSS are not possible because of the lack of essential data in electronic form. However, the relative importance given to either orientation is what is at issue, in the universal context of scarce resources.

A second key decision related to the TPS–DSS posture is the choice of hardware configurations. At one end of the spectrum one can visualize mutually independent microcomputers and, at the other end, a single mainframe, possibly with remote terminals. Between these extremes lies a wide variety of options, such as networked minicomputers connected to a central, host mainframe.

The independent microcomputer extreme may be appropriate, for example, for an organization engaged in engineering consulting, with dedicated micros in the various departments such as civil, electrical, and chemical engineering, whose strategy is based on the distinctive competence of the professionals in these departments. Each engineering department, it could be argued, needs to have immediate access to its own data without necessarily having to share it with the other departments. At the other extreme is an airline emphasizing efficiency and customer service with a large mainframe hooked up to numerous remote terminals. Reservations must be current and accurate, while being shared by all agents throughout the country. In between these two extremes would lie the manufacturer of a large variety of automotive parts in different locations throughout the country whose viability depends on the ability to maintain quality, control costs, and manage inventories in each of its nationwide manufacturing locations. Slight inaccuracies, however, may be tolerable in order to achieve larger savings. In this last case, a headquarters mainframe and distributed minicomputers may best serve the organization's strategy.

The third key dimension is not so readily obvious as the previous two. A subtle, but significant, influence on CIS design is the nature of the related policies adopted by the organization. These policies could address, among other issues, the following:

- The criteria for acquisition of hardware and software. For example, should all new microcomputers be required to be compatible with a particular mainframe?
- The locus of authority for data entry and retrieval. For example, who may retrieve confidential computerized marketing information?
- The appropriate use of consultants.[11] For example, may functional departments hire their own computer consultants?

A flexible approach to these CIS-related policies would foster different managerial responses and attitudes than would a rigorous and strict set of policies.[12] In organizations where strategies demand creativity, independence, and adaptive behavior among managers, as in innovative consulting organizations, a flexible approach to policy formulation is probably appropriate. On the other hand, where the efficient execution of clearly defined responsibilities is at the heart of an organization's strategy, a bias toward a comprehensive and strict articulation of policies is probably warranted.

The preceding three dimensions are perhaps the most important determinants of the appropriate design of the CIS. Several other dimensions can be identified, some of which will be discussed later; however, it does appear as though choices made with regard to the TPS–DSS posture, the micro-mini-mainframe configuration, and the flexible-strict policy stance are crucial.

Once these choices are made, the pattern of decisions with regard to the other characteristics of CIS appears to be largely determined.

Granting, for the moment, that this assertion regarding the dominance of these three dimensions is essentially correct, it follows that the choices with regard to CIS are defined by a three-dimensional space. This conceptualization of the feasible (and vital) space for decision making regarding the design of the CIS is diagrammed in Figure 3.1.

The significance of these three dimensions of choice in CIS design is readily apparent in Figure 3.1. Organizations appropriately positioning themselves at one extreme (0, 0, 0) would of necessity be vastly different in strategic characteristics than organizations that justifiably select the other extreme (1, 1, 1). On the one hand, one can visualize a large, centralized, efficiency-oriented, stable organization with a top-down approach to decision making. On the other hand, one can conjecture a smaller, decentralized, effectiveness-oriented, growing organization with a bottom-up decision-making style.

Organizations positioned at the (0, 0, 0) corner of the matrix would appear to be "transactional" in character. The (1, 1, 1) corner of the matrix, in contrast, would appear to be the appropriate location of organizations that can be characterized as "decisional." To facilitate further discussion, we shall, therefore, refer to the (0, 0, 0) corner as "transactional" and the (1, 1, 1) as "decisional."

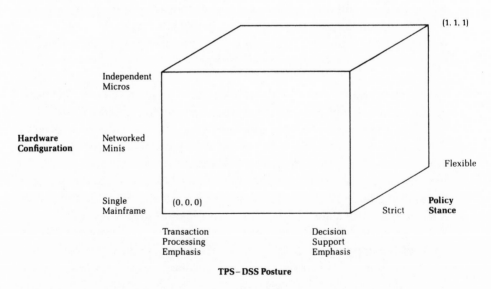

Figure 3.1   Key Dimensions of Strategic Choice in CIS Design

Additional Dimensions of CIS Design

A variety of other decisions relating to CIS design appear to be closely linked to the organization's administrative system. These decisions, however, are substantially driven by the choices made with regard to the TPS–DSS posture, hardware configuration, and policy stance. Consequently they are perhaps best made following a determination of the organization's preferred positioning along the three key dimensions. The endeavor in the context of the additional dimensions identified below is to ensure that consistent decisions are made. An erroneous decision or an undesirable situation resulting from the failure to make a decision with regard to these dimensions could lessen the positive impact of correct, mutually consistent decisions along the three key dimensions.

These additional dimensions essentially reflect aspects of the structure of the MIS function in the organization:

- The emphasis on personnel who are "dedicated" functional specialists with close ties to particular user departments.[13] Examples of these specialists would be the accounting-systems analysts and personnel database administrators. Alternatively, the emphasis would be on personnel whose capabilities are in the areas of information technology in general, and who are primarily associated with the corporate headquarters rather than departments or functional areas. The dedicated, functional specialists would fit in with a more decentralized, flexible, decision-support-oriented approach. The other extreme would be more in keeping with the choice of centralized information technologists.
- The existence of CIS–MIS departments in the subunits of the organization, possibly in addition to a centralized department in the corporate office. The obvious extreme alternative here is to have only a single centralized CIS–MIS department.
- The reporting relationship of the head of the CIS–MIS department to corporate management. The department could report to a "line" general manager (CEO–COO/Executive VP) in the situation where decision support is given a great deal of importance. Alternatively, where transaction processing dominates, the CIS–MIS department head could report to a corporate-level staff executive such as the controller or financial vice-president. This possibility was often adopted in the early days of CIS–MIS development.

The proposed relationship between these three structure-oriented dimensions of CIS design and the original three key dimensions of choice is illustrated in Figure 3.2. As the preceding discussion of the structural aspects of the CIS

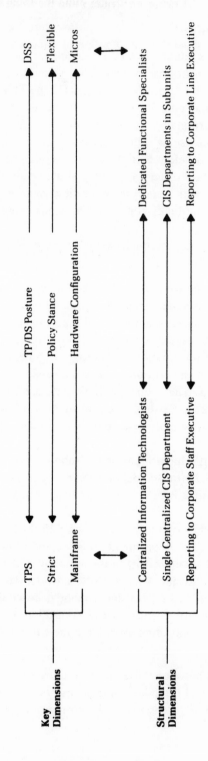

Figure 3.2 Key Design Dimensions and the CIS Departmental Structure

function suggests, the choices that are made vis-à-vis the key dimensions identified earlier can greatly facilitate the making of effective and consistent decisions in other aspects of CIS design.

Generic Strategies and CIS Design

The significance and conceptual validity of the three key dimensions can perhaps be assessed by evaluating the relationship between these dimensions and the concepts of generic strategy that have earned widespread credence in recent years. Three of these accepted definitions of generic strategy have been developed by Glueck (1976), Miles and Snow (1978), and Porter (1980).[14]

Glueck identifies growth, stability, and retrenchment as basic alternatives among which organizations should choose. A growth strategy makes a flexible decision-support orientation imperative in order to provide the information base and climate that can sustain organizational growth. Stability, on the other hand, mandates an efficiency orientation that can enhance profits without an increase in volume of activity.

The relationship of retrenchment strategies to the key dimensions is possibly less clear-cut. Retrenchment that focuses on determining which business segments or product lines should be eliminated from the corporate portfolios would require a continuing emphasis on decision support. Transaction processing in relation to the components of the business that are dropped can be eliminated, thus reducing the absolute magnitude of the TPS component of the CIS. On the other hand, retrenchment that relies on merely reducing the volume of activity across the board places few demands on the DSS component of the CIS. The TPS component should probably receive more attention in this mode of retrenchment, as volume reductions will have to be accompanied by increases in efficiency if the organization is to enhance or regain profitability.

Porter's three generic strategies also appear to map quite well onto the three dimensions of CIS design. Cost-efficiency strategies demand a transactional $(0, 0, 0)$ (Figure 3.1) posture, whereas the need to identify and maintain differentiation strategies can be readily linked to the decisional $(1, 1, 1)$ end of the spectrum. A strategy of focus, however, does not a priori suggest a bias in favor of one or the other extreme along the dimensions of CIS design. If focus means doing a few things well, a transactional emphasis may be appropriate. If focus means identifying niches on an ongoing basis, because the organization wishes to grow, the bias could be more toward the decisional extreme.

Finally, the Miles and Snow typology displays a logically supportable relationship with the key dimensions. An organization that is a defender would clearly be best served by a transactional emphasis in CIS design. A prospec-

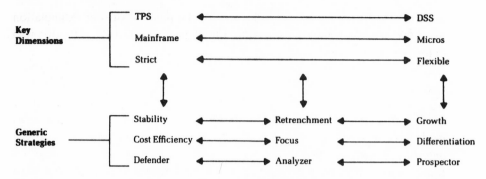

Figure 3.3   Generic Strategies and the Key Dimensions of CIS Design

tor, on the other hand, almost by definition, requires a decisional orientation. An analyzer requires a more balanced posture that can vary depending on top management's decision-making style.

The relationship between these generic strategies and the key dimensions is illustrated in Figure 3.3.

Applying the Framework

The practical significance of this framework can be assessed by reviewing its applicability to two different corporate contexts. For example, a company in the business of overnight pick-up and delivery of small packages illustrates the "stability, cost-efficiency, and defender" (Figure 3.3) end of the spectrum of generic strategies. At the "growth, differentiation, and prospector" end of the spectrum would be an acquisition-oriented conglomerate.

In the overnight, small-package business, reliability and cost efficiency are the key requirements for survival and success. Both reliability and cost efficiency in this business are obtained by selecting the most appropriate equipment (aircraft, communications, trucks, etc.), by taking advantage of economies of scale, and by careful routing of the daily itinerary of individual aircraft. These imperatives should, therefore, drive the choice of integrated communications and computer equipment and practices. For instance, one of the most successful companies in this business recognized the implications of these basic requirements for organizational success when computerizing the daily, real-time routing of its pick-up vans.

At first glance, the obvious avenue to computerizing the company's van routing appeared to be a decentralized, flexible, DSS-oriented approach with microcomputers located at each office or airport with voice communication to individual van drivers, as is done by taxicab companies. A closer examination of the situation suggested, however, that a strict, centralized, TPS-oriented approach using mainframe computers and satellite-based communications, with identical, dumb terminals in vans would be preferable for a variety of reasons.

First and foremost, the key to reliability and cost efficiency in terms of daily operations was seen to lie in the routing decisions for aircraft. These decisions could best be made centrally with a real-time awareness of package volume at each airport location. This volume results from thousands of individual transactions, aggregated at hundreds of airports. Second, voice communication with individual drivers of vans was severely impeded by the fact that, unlike taxi drivers, these drivers had to be out of their vans for substantial periods of time in order to pick up and hand-deliver packages. The use of satellite-based communications, between a central computer facility and terminals in vans, was seen as desirable. The terminals would receive updated routings even when the driver was out of the van. Centralized receipt of pick-up requests would also enable more efficient routing of vans to locations served by more than one local office, thus ruling out the use of microcomputers in the individual offices. Third, the algorithms for optimal routing of aircraft and even of vans were complex and required mainframe capacities and speeds for timely operations. Fourth, and finally, these algorithms were constantly being improved and it was simpler to test and introduce innovations in one central location, as opposed to dozens or hundreds of decentralized computing facilities.

The relevance and value of the framework that we propose is corroborated by this example. Application of the framework suggests apparently counterintuitive solutions to a key problem in a particular strategic context. These solutions upon further examination, however, appear to be the correct approach to adopt in this context.

In the second example, at the other end of the spectrum, the decision as to appropriate acquisition targets for a conglomerate appears to require a flexible, DSS-oriented approach, using microcomputers. The acquisition analysis carried out at the corporate level would initially require the use of microcomputers as terminals to access external data bases and pull out information for subsequent analysis using the internally developed search routines. This exercise would result in the development of a preliminary list of acquisition candidates. This list would then be subject to further intensive, spreadsheet-oriented analyses.

In this growth-oriented context, where the mode is one of prospecting for new opportunities, CIS decisions suggested by the framework developed in this article again appear to be valid. Both examples reinforce the validity and utility of the framework, particularly in the first example, where the counterintuitive solution suggested by the framework was shown upon analysis to be justified.

Conclusion

The basic thrust of our article, that there should be a match between the design of the CIS and the strategic management choices of the organization, has been explored from a pragmatic perspective. The key dimensions of the design of the CIS that have been identified define possible alternatives that display vastly different characteristics. These very different characteristics are related to particular strategies. Managers with strategic responsibilities and CIS designers thus have the beginnings of a framework for a fruitful dialogue. This article, it is hoped, offers preliminary guidelines as to the nature and direction of the decisions that are likely to promote a mutually supportive relationship between the design of the CIS and the strategic management of the organization.

4

A Corporate Strategy for the Control of Information Processing

Henry C. Lucas, Jr.

Jon A. Turner

Although the use of information processing has become widespread, many organizations have developed systems that are basically independent of the firm's strategy. However, the authors in this article argue that the greatest benefits come when information technology is merged with strategy formulation. The article includes examples of how this has been done and presents a framework for top management direction and control of information processing. *SMR.*

How can information technology contribute to the development of corporate strategy? How should top management control information processing in their organizations? It seems that many managers have difficulty answering these questions. The president of a medium-sized manufacturing company remarked: "I receive about the same information today as was provided thirty years ago before our computers. Only now I spend millions to get it." The chairman of a $3 billion conglomerate has commented repeatedly: "I get nothing from our computers."

We have observed that many top executives feel that existing information processing activities are not well managed. However, the focus of many of these managers is on the problems created by computers and on growing budget requests, rather than on ways in which the firm's strategic objectives can make use of this technology. If managers believe they are unable to control the quality of information services provided within the firm, they are unlikely to rely on these services in meeting critical goals. Thus, the purpose of this article is twofold: to demonstrate how some firms have incorporated information

From *Sloan Management Review*, Spring 1982, Vol. 23, No. 3. Reprinted with permission.

processing technology into corporate strategy and to present a framework for top management direction and control of information processing.

Information Processing Technology and Corporate Strategy

It is probably safe to say that the average general manager knows more about all the other functional areas of his company than he does about information processing. The CEO who came up through the sales organization is also likely to understand accounting, finance, and production, because all of these specialties are involved in bringing a product to the marketplace. But does the CEO have an equivalent knowledge of information processing? The answer in most cases is "no." To be successful in the next decade, however, executives must learn to deal equally well with information processing technology. The executive does not have to become a computer expert, but he or she does have to apply accepted managerial techniques to information processing. In addition, top management must devote time to information processing activities if they are to be successful.

A key task of top management is to formulate corporate strategy. Executives should ask such questions as: "What does the corporation do well?" "How do we apply our resources to achieve corporate goals?" "What are competitors doing?" In this respect, a corporation has two choices: It may continue to support its present corporate strategy, maintaining momentum where it is doing well; or, it may change its strategy dramatically by choosing a new direction for development. For example, a single-product, single-market firm might try a diversification strategy to reduce both the cyclical fluctuations in product demand and the impact of major change in consumer buying patterns. Or a large energy company might decide to enter a new market by purchasing a number of high-technology firms and integrating them into a new subsidiary in order to cope with the uncertainties in its primary petroleum market.

Impact on Corporate Strategy

How does information processing technology have an impact on corporate strategy? Three types of relationships between information processing technology and corporate strategy are shown in Table 4.1. In the first case, we find independent information systems that help the firm implement strategy by creating greater operational efficiencies. These systems are not directly linked to the strategy formulation process or integrated with a strategic plan. The need for such a system is usually perceived by an operational unit, and its primary objective is to improve efficiency. Most existing information systems

Table 4.1 Information Technology and Corporate Strategy

Level of Integration with Strategy Formulation	Primary Objective	Secondary Effect
Independent	Operational efficiency	Managerial information
Policy support	Aid repetitive decision making	Better understanding of problem dynamics
Fully integrated	Open new products, markets, directions	Change decision-making process; alternatives considered; evaluation criteria

fall into this category: They process routine transactions, produce output that goes to customers, and provide exception reports.

A more direct contribution to strategy comes from policy support systems, which are designed to aid the planning process. In this second case, the system helps in formulating the plan, but is not a part of it; that is, the system is not part of an end product or service produced by the firm. A good example of one of these policy-support systems can be found in Hamilton and Moses.[1] The forecasting data needed by a large conglomerate are contained in a common data base accessible through a computer. A set of analytic tools, including a large mathematical programming routine and econometric and risk-analysis models, is used iteratively to generate different courses of action over a multiyear planning horizon and to test assumptions during the planning process. In this case, the computer is used as an administrative device to interface the various components of the planning system and to actually execute the models.

The most exciting possibilities exist when the technology itself becomes a part of the strategy, for it expands the range of strategic alternatives considered by the firm. As Kantrow notes: "Technology should be viewed as a central part of business thinking at all levels and not as a kind of a line phenomenon to be held at arm's length by all but R and D engineers."[2] In this third case, technology bears an integral relation to a company's strategic thinking by helping to define the range of possibilities. At the same time, it provides a good portion of the means by which the strategy, once chosen, is to be implemented. Several examples may help to illustrate this type of integration between technology and strategy.

Technology and Strategy Integration

Data Resources, Inc. (DRI), now a subsidiary of McGraw-Hill, was founded by Professor Otto Eckstein of Harvard. The firm began by offering forecasts developed from Eckstein's econometric model of the U.S. economy. While such models were theoretically possible before the advent of electronic computers, computational requirements made them impracticable to solve. The development of information technology made it possible to create the kind of model that forms the nucleus of DRI's business. Furthermore, DRI offers a variety of services in which the customer accesses a DRI computer: These services are made possible only because of the options provided by new technology. When DRI's product became fully integrated with information processing technologies, the firm experienced substantial growth.

In another example, a major brokerage firm, whose goal is to become one of the leading financial institutions in the U.S., is offering a service in which a customer's cash in a brokerage account is automatically invested in the brokerage firm's liquid assets fund when the cash is not invested in securities. Thus as positions are liquidated or dividends paid, the cash immediately begins earning the highest interest available to the customer. Through an arrangement with a commercial bank, the customer can write checks ($500 minimum) against the balance. Although the brokerage firm no longer receives interest from the investment of customers' idle cash, the firm expanded its market share and increased revenues through its new business.

On a smaller scale, information processing technology makes it possible for a new market-research firm to offer a service that could not be obtained from its competitors.[3] Information Resources, Inc., developed a corporate strategy that is intertwined with information technology. The firm purchased grocery-store point-of-sale scanning equipment and gave it free to fifteen supermarkets in two towns which were selected on the basis of their demographic makeup. There were 2,000 households in each of the two test markets using the scanning equipment: Their purchases were recorded on an Information Resources computer in Chicago. Since each product was marked by the universal product code, researchers could pinpoint a family's purchases by price, brand, and size and then correlate the purchase information with any promotions, such as coupons, free samples, price adjustments, advertising, and store displays.

This technology means that Information Resources can conduct economical scientific tests of marketing strategies to determine the most effective approach to its customers. For example, through cooperation with a cable TV network, the firm can target different TV spots to selected households and analyze the resulting purchases. The imaginative use of this technology, in fact, allowed the firm to gain a competitive lead over much larger, better established market-research firms.

These examples illustrate how the integration of information processing technology with strategy formulation expanded the opportunities for each firm. At

DRI the technology allowed the firm first to create an econometric model and then to use time-sharing services to market its product directly to the customer. This technology created the opportunity for a new form of business and later helped to increase revenues through new services. In the brokerage firm, the technology made it possible to offer a new service that probably expanded the market share of the firm and increased the size of its liquid-assets fund. Information processing also helped the market-research firm gain a competitive edge and set a new standard for service in the industry.

Capitalizing on Information Technology

How does the firm take advantage of information technology and achieve a high level of integration between technology and strategy? To accomplish this, top management must follow three steps:

1. Look for ways to incorporate technology into a product or service. Does information processing provide an opportunity for a new approach to business? Does the technology make it possible to differentiate your product and services from the competition? Technology can help open new markets or increase existing market shares. Note this suggestion means that information processing expenditures will have to be viewed as an investment as well as an expense!

2. To integrate technology with planning, the firm needs information about likely future technological developments. To conduct a technology assessment, the organization must invest resources in R&D. The company can collect information from a number of sources to estimate technological trends. The firm can invest selectively in university programs to keep up on research, and it can sponsor or subscribe to studies conducted by consulting firms.

3. Exert control over information processing in the firm. As we have mentioned, one of the greatest impediments to using information technology for strategic purposes has been an inability on the part of top management to control successfully the information-systems function. In the next section of the article, we present a framework to help manage information processing in the organization.

Accomplishing the first two tasks above is difficult, particularly for someone who is currently an employee of the organization. For these two tasks, we recommend the creation of a new position; namely, the technological strategist, who must report to a high-level manager in the firm in order to have real influence.

The technological strategist needs to have as a primary talent an understanding of information processing technology and of its likely development during the next two decades. This individual also must become knowledgeable about the mission of the organization and its products and services. The technological strategist must be given resources and the freedom to make unusual and possibly outrageous suggestions. (Management then evaluates the ideas and chooses suggestions that make a contribution to overall corporate strategy.) The technological strategist can be evaluated on the quality of ideas generated and on whether the suggestions are implemented. The final evaluation, however, will be whether technology makes a contribution to achieving the overall strategy of the corporation.

Managing Information Processing

Why is the need to control information processing such a major roadblock to achieving the full integration of information technology and corporate strategy? If senior management lacks confidence in information processing, then it will not want to risk the future of the firm on a strategy that depends on information systems.

Consider the following example. A major electronics firm considered itself the industry leader. But its strongest competitor made a bold move by placing computer terminals connected to its computer in the offices of electronics-parts distributors. Now the distributors can order electronically from the competitor, obtaining parts in a shorter time with less paperwork required. The industry leader, on the other hand, suffered for many years from a lack of effective information processing management: It did not have the confidence, capacity, or skills to match what the competition had done. To counter this aggressive use of information processing, the industry leader, however, began a price war that contributed to its first annual loss in many years.

Obviously there were many factors influencing the firm, and difficulties with information systems were not the sole cause of its problems. Still, this example demonstrates that senior management must be able to control information processing if it is to be relied on as a part of corporate strategy. It is our contention that effective control of information processing is a necessary prerequisite to the integration of technology with strategy. If information processing is viewed as a failure, managers will refuse to rely on it for a major role in the formation and execution of corporate strategy.

Through our research, we have come to an important conclusion. Generally, the management of information processing is relegated to an immediate subordinate or even to middle-level managers. However, our experience has convinced us that senior managers are, or at least should be, interested in the guidelines for obtaining control over information processing. The delegation of responsibility for this activity has not been successful in many firms. Thus, the framework that follows is intended to help the senior manager understand the key considerations in the management of information processing, so that he or she can guide other managers and the information services staff.

Identifying Lack of Control

Any of the following problems might indicate that information processing is not under control:

1. Managers and other users are uncomfortable with the method and priorities by which new applications are chosen;
2. Cost displacement or return on investment—rather than opportunity fulfillment—is the only criterion for selecting new computer applications, leading to the rejection of all but "independent" systems;
3. One or more new computer applications are experiencing significant cost and/or schedule overruns;
4. There are many complaints about the quality of information processing service;
5. Most senior managers are not supported by systems that relate to their most important responsibilities;
6. There is no formal top-management policy for information systems.

If an organization has more than one of these symptoms, it may be depriving itself of the opportunity to gain a major competitive advantage through the creative use of technology.

Special Considerations for Computing Technology

Information processing technology differs from other types of technology partially because it is less visible. Certainly one can see terminals and computer equipment, but the process of systems analysis and design and the nature of computer programs remain obscure to most individuals outside of the profession. One can observe a numerically controlled machine tool at work, but there is much less to see when a computer is functioning at high speeds.

In addition to being abstract, computing technology has a different impact from many other types of technology: The secondary effects of computing are often more important than its primary ones. As an example, consider a transaction processing system designed to automate an accounts receivable function. The primary objective of such a system might be to reduce errors in posting receivables and to maintain correct account balances. The secondary effect of this system, combined with a payments system, is that the firm now knows its exact cash position at the end of each day. By reducing uncertainty in the firm's cash position, the treasurer may have a significant new source of funds for short-term investment.

A Framework for Management Activities

Figure 4.1 presents a framework for viewing management decision areas involved in controlling information processing. Many of the points in this framework have been discussed in isolation in the literature, but Figure 4.1 links these management activities together and shows the interrelationships among them. It is our contention that positive management action is needed in all areas in the figure. Management can and should control information processing; if not, decisions will occur by default.

Table 4.2 summarizes the actions for management in each of the areas discussed below. Where possible, we offer recommendations for management policy. Where the recommendations depend on circumstances unique to the firm, Table 4.2 lists some of the factors that should be taken into account in the development of a policy.

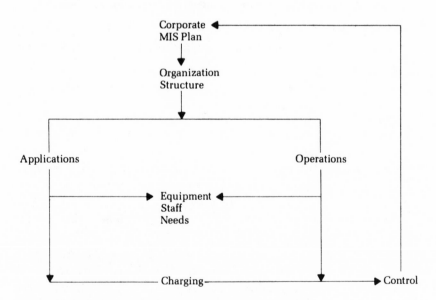

Figure 4.1   A Framework for Managing Information Processing

Table 4.2 Management Action for the Development of a Policy

	Issue	Recommendation
I. Corporate MIS Plan	Mechanism	Operational plan: 1 year; longer-term plan: 3–5 years; technology assessment; link to organizational plan; separate IS planning officer
	Involvement	User and management input
	Contents and format	Applications needs; operations needs; implications for staff and equipment
	Priorities	Senior-level committee to choose applications areas
	Reporting	Annual report of MIS tied to plan
	Issue	**Alternative**
II. Organization Structure	Type	Centralized, distributed, decentralized for operations and analysis design
	Evaluation	Criteria: service levels; cost responsiveness; flexibility; history of organization
	Control	Balance local autonomy with corporate needs
	Issue	**Recommendation**
III. New Applications	Generate new ideas	From plan; also, procedures for requests
	Package	Evaluate: functional fit to needs
	Selection	Multicriteria scoring models[a]
	Development	Extensive user input; management involvement setting goals; reviewing system
	Change	Preparing organization to manage and cope with change
	Conflict	Ways to use conflict constructively
	Issue	**Recommendation**
IV. Operations	Measurement	Develop user-oriented measures
	Evaluation	Administer regular evaluations including variety of measures
	Issue	**Recommendation**
V. Equipment/Staff Needs	Evaluation and choice criteria	Develop evaluation methodology
	Compatibility among vendors	Establish vendor compatibility policy
	Technological assessment	Factor likely technology changes into decisions
	Issue	**Alternative**
VI. Charging	To charge	Yes or no; advantages and disadvantages[b]
	Charging mechanism	Full or partial charge out: accounting techniques
	Issue	**Recommendation**
VII. Control	Overall evaluation	Compare results to plan
	Frequent feedback	Monitor progress on systems development projects; conduct user surveys as discussed under "Operations"

[a]H. C. Lucas, Jr., and J. Moore, "A Multiple-Criterion Scoring Approach to Information Project Selection," *INFOR,* February 1976, pp. 1–12.
[b]J. Dearden and R. Nolan, "How to Control the Computer Resource," *Harvard Business Review,* November–December 1973, pp. 68–75.

A Corporate MIS Plan

- See that a three- to five-year plan is developed;
- Participate in the planning process.

A plan for information processing should be coordinated with corporate strategy. The plan should serve as a road map to show the direction of the systems-development effort and implications for operations. It also furnishes the basis for later evaluation of the performance of the information processing function.

A corporate information systems plan should show how information systems technology will be used to meet corporate goals. The plan should contain a statement of corporate goals and the specific information systems tasks that must be accomplished to meet these goals. A typical plan describes the breakdown in activities and resources required for the development of new applications and the operation of existing systems.

Many organizations we have observed agree that such a plan is needed, but they have not developed one. A frequent reason is that the three- to five-year information systems planning horizon is not compatible with the planning horizon of the organization. In other instances, the corporations do not have a plan at all.

We feel that it is both possible and highly desirable to develop an information processing plan even without a formal corporate plan, as the technology is too pervasive and fast moving for planning to occur by default or solely through decisions made by personnel in the information services department. Leaving the plan to the computer staff tends to produce a document that reflects information services priorities rather than those of the corporation. We recommend that a special group be created, consisting of members from corporate staff, user management, information services management, and executive staff, to generate the plan. A broad-based composition tends to better reflect corporate-wide priorities.

Selection of Applications Areas

A key task for the organization is to identify areas for new applications of technology. What are the applications areas with the highest return? What applications will best further the strategic goals of the corporation? What new opportunities does the technology provide?

Application systems have useful life spans of five to ten years. As a result of rapid technological advances, computer hardware tends to have a shorter life than application systems. Decisions made today regarding these systems restrict future options. For example, a decision to implement a particular application system acts to constrain future hardware choices to those that are compatible with the present equipment. Therefore it is important to select carefully applications areas, since these decisions may shape the firm's information processing during the next decade.

Finally, the plan should outline and set priorities for applications areas, for example, marketing or production control, based on the expected corporate contribution. To establish these priorities, a high-level planning group should make the tradeoffs among functional areas. Using a management group ensures that the decision on priorities is a management decision, rather than one that is controlled by a single operating unit, or a choice left to the information services staff. A major purpose of this component of the plan is to shift attention from equipment to applications, which are the real payoff to the firm.

Organization Structure

- Evaluate various patterns for providing computing services so as to choose the most effective alternative;
- Develop a policy that balances coordination costs and local autonomy.

Existing information technology offers considerable flexibility in developing patterns for the structure of the information services function. The firm must identify possible processing patterns, evaluate them, and choose an alternative for implementation.

Processing alternatives can be divided into three broad groups that represent points on a continuum. At one extreme is complete centralization: All systems analysis and design are performed by a central group and all equipment is operated centrally. All corporate data are also centrally located and controlled. At the other extreme is complete decentralization: All equipment resides at local sites, and these sites have their own staff for analysis and design work. Data are also decentrally located and controlled. Distributed processing occurs when central and local sites are tied together in some type of communications network that permits resource sharing.

Management must trade off the benefits perceived by users in having and controlling their own computer system resources against the need for overall coordination and standardization in the organization. Allowing the proliferation of small computers can lead to high costs if the organization decides to connect diverse equipment through a network. Also, the firm must ask if there are opportunities to develop common systems that can be used in multiple locations to prevent the duplication of development efforts.

New Applications

- Develop a mechanism for selecting alternatives that obtains input from those who must interact with the system;
- Be sure that a realistic number of alternatives are considered, including the "status quo" or the "no systems" alternatives.

Rarely today are totally infeasible applications suggested by users. Instead, some type of feasible system can always be undertaken to improve information processing. The question is what is both feasible and desirable. A corporate group should choose applications areas as part of developing a plan for information processing. Now the task is to decide what type of system, if any, will be developed. Management must consider the existing portfolio of applications and provide *guidance* on the magnitude of the investment possible and the *balance* of the portfolio. For example, the firm will want to have some low risk/low payoff projects under way to offset projects with a high risk of failure.

Advances in package design have resulted in packages becoming usable alternatives to the internal development of a custom system. In general, packages require somewhat less time and effort to implement and maintain than do custom systems, but they can lead to higher operational costs and possible omission of desirable features. Management should ensure that alternatives to custom development are always considered.

Selection and Implementation of New Applications

We advocate a decision procedure in which the information services department involves users in the selection of alternatives for a new application. First, the users should agree with the information services department on the number of alternatives for a single application. An example of alternatives is the use of an applications package, an online system, a batch system, or the maintenance of the status quo.[4] The selection group then agrees on a series of criteria to be used to evaluate each of these alternatives. Finally, an alternative is selected from the several possible choices considered for this application.

All computer applications involve changes ranging from simple procedural change to major organizational alterations. It is important for change to be implemented carefully so that a system will be successful. Management should set the objective for a system and, where possible, make any desired organizational changes independently of system implementation.

It is likely that the participants in the development process will not all have the same objectives, so that conflicts are certain to arise. Liaison agents, joint user-system designer-project teams, and frequent review meetings help resolve conflict in a constructive manner.

Systems analysis and design is an area that requires a great deal of management attention. Managers must demonstrate that they support the development of a new system, and they must see that there is adequate user input in the design process. Often courses are used to prepare the systems staff and users for the development of a new system. These courses are followed by frequent group review meetings during the design process. Top management participates in these meetings and makes clear that it supports the changes that are expected to come from the system.

Operations

- Establish criteria for measuring the performance and service levels of computer operations;
- Measure and evaluate the operations function regularly.

The concerns in the operation of existing systems are credibility and service levels. It is very difficult to gain enthusiasm or cooperation in the development of new systems if existing service levels are unsatisfactory. Management must be sure the information services department is providing effective service as perceived by its customers. Often when the measures used to evaluate service are created and evaluated in the information services department itself, they tend to have little meaning for users. However, management sees a report that describes, for example, the percentage of output reports processed on time and the availability of the computer, and it assumes that adequate measurement is taking place.

To improve performance evaluation, the firm can conduct user surveys of service levels to supplement measures of on-time performance or computer up-time supplied by the computer-operations group. These surveys can be treated statistically to extract key factors (combinations of items on the survey), which serve as a measure of performance. Over time the survey is repeated, the factors computed, and the progress of the operations function evaluated. Such a technique provides a measurement and evaluation, which include criteria important to users as well as indicators from the operations group.

Equipment/Staff Needs

- Review equipment recommendations;
- Authorize adequate staffing levels.

The need of the organization to operate existing systems and the resources required to develop new applications determine staff and equipment requirements. One of the by-products of the planning process is the identification of needed resources: Requirements are compared with available resources to determine what incremental equipment and staff are needed. Top management must make the decision of what action to take when there is a discrepancy between the resources needed to accomplish the plan and the resources available.

Management must examine the alternatives available for processing, including the use of outside services, a facilities management contractor, internal computers, etc. Also the firm must forecast changes in the technology to balance costs versus the risk of obsolescence.

There are a large number of options for equipment, and management must help develop criteria for comparing alternatives. One important issue today is the extent to which compatibility among different vendors is stressed. If many incompatible systems are acquired, the organization will be unable to take advantage of common software.

For the staff, the obvious way to expand resources is to hire more individuals. However, there is a limit to the number of people who can be absorbed productively into the organization. Another alternative is to use more packaged programs to improve staff productivity. Outside contractors can be employed to develop systems or to supply staff.

All trends for the future point to the conclusion that hardware costs will continue to decline and that there will be an insufficient number of computer professionals to develop systems. These observations suggest that the organization will have to give more responsibility for systems to users. The firm should acquire user-oriented languages, such as report generators, and encourage users to retrieve their own data and design reports. One recommendation is to invest in a data base management system and query language to extend the computer to the end user.

Charging

- Determine the objectives of a charging policy;
- Design and implement the policy.

There are a number of advantages and disadvantages to charging for information processing services. Management should realize that a charging policy will influence user behavior, and they should choose the policy accordingly. A full charge-out scheme using a pricing mechanism is advocated to allocate computer resources. For this approach to work, the user group has to be fairly knowledgeable and has to have an interest in the budget. The user must know how his or her behavior can influence charges for services.

Overhead charging is advocated for organizations that are trying to encourage use of the computer. Here, it is assumed that users are more naive and reluctant to make use of the computer resource. But by making the computer a free good, its use is encouraged. Partial charging schemes feature overhead charging for systems analysis and design or for corporate-wide systems and use charge-back schemes for operating expenses. Operating costs are easier to determine and fluctuate less than charges for developing new applications. Thus this dual approach creates more certainty for users and means that the corporation absorbs some of the budgetary risk for new systems development.[5]

Control

- Evaluate the contribution of information systems to corporate goals and strategy;
- Evaluate information services performance with respect to the plan;
- Take the needed corrective action to achieve the plan, e.g., add resources or modify schedule.

Management control is concerned with the broad question of whether information technology is making a contribution to corporate strategy. This contribution can be in the form of independent systems, policy-support systems for planning, or through a close linkage between technology and strategy formulation. One way to gain control over information processing is to participate in the decisions mentioned above and to be knowledgeable about information processing activities in the organization.

Specific Control Mechanisms

For design activities, the firm can conduct a postimplementation audit and compare achievements with original goals, budgets, and specifications. On an operational level, one control mechanism is to compare actual results with the information processing plan. On a more frequent basis, user reactions to service levels can be measured and reported, and progress on individual systems development projects can be monitored. Management should establish performance criteria, and the information services department should report on them.

One major management problem is what action to take when it appears that some part or all of the information processing function is out of control. A common solution, though not necessarily the best, is to replace the manager of the information services department. Instead, top management should take a careful look at how it is contributing to controlling information processing. The framework in Figure 4.1 is one starting point for such an examination. Has management helped develop a plan for information processing? Is management involved in the selection of applications and the determination of priorities? Do top managers set the objectives for new systems and participate in their design?

In some instances, changes in personnel may be appropriate when the operation is out of control. However, in others, the best action is to provide additional resources. Possibly, processing schedules are not being met because of a lack of manpower or computer power. The design of new systems is an R&D activity, as there can be high uncertainty. If a high risk or complex system is experiencing delays, and yet it appears to be managed well, then the appropriate action might be to add resources or extend the schedule.

In summary, the first step in exerting control is knowing what to measure and conducting the evaluation. The second step is determining what action is most likely to improve the situation if part of the operation is out of control.

Conclusion

This article has described relationships between information processing and corporate strategy. We argue that most organizations have developed systems that are basically independent of the firm's strategy, for they help achieve some objective through greater efficiency or through better management. Policy support systems contribute to the planning process directly. However, the greatest benefits come when information technology is merged with strategy formulation: Technology serves to expand the range and number of strategic opportunities considered by the firm. In the future, information technology will be an increasingly important component of corporate strategy.

The second part of the article presented a framework for top management control of information processing activities in the organization. If information technology is to make a contribution to strategy formulation and to the operation of the firm, management must become more adept at coping with information processing activities in the organization. The framework for control stresses the importance of the planning process, the development of organizational structures for information processing, the identification and development of new applications, the operation of existing systems, the identification of equipment and staff needs, and the charging for services and monitoring information processing performance. The purpose of the framework is to assist top management in determining the key issues for concern and action in managing the information processing resource.

By including considerations of information technology in the development of corporate strategy and by managing information processing activities effectively in the organization, this technology will make its maximum contribution to the organization. Managers will no longer have to ask, "What am I getting from information technology?" Instead they will be able to point out the nature and extent of the contribution that technology makes to the organization.

PART II

Planning for the New Era of Information Technology

5

The Changing Role of the Information Systems Executive: A Critical Success Factors Perspective

John F. Rockart

As the information systems (IS) field has evolved over the past decade, the concerns of the IS executive have shifted from technical issues to broader management questions. This article attempts to identify those factors critical to the success of the modern IS executive. Based on extensive interviews conducted in nine firms, the author has developed a composite of today's "model" IS executive and has uncovered some of the fundamental issues that this executive will face in the 1980s. *SMR.*

There is little doubt today that the job of the information systems (IS) executive is changing. The role of the computer in major organizations and the tasks of its chief executives have shifted significantly. Throughout the profession there is a fundamental feeling that the "technically oriented" information systems executive of the 1960s and 1970s is rapidly being replaced by a "managerially oriented" executive of the 1980s. Precisely what this means, however, is still unclear. This article presents the results of one research study aimed at increasing our understanding of the evolution of the IS executive role.[1]

Even to a casual observer of the information systems field, it is clear that the way an IS executive must conceptualize his job is changing. The information systems field itself is also undergoing significant changes. Through the 1970s there was a rapid evolution from "centralized data processing" to "distributed data processing." Under the centralized mode, all machines and systems personnel were located in one, or very few, geographic locations under a single line IS authority. Managerial reporting relationships were straightforward and uncomplicated. Now, however, under "distributed data

From *Sloan Management Review*, Fall 1982, Vol. 24, No. 1. Reprinted with permission.

processing," the geographic sites of machines and personnel are widespread. Geographically dispersed data processing managers report both to local line supervisors and to the information systems executive (who must thus cope with the time-consuming added burdens of matrix management).

In addition, recently, a profusion of new technology supporting a diverse array of new computer-based activities has burst upon the scene. This new, more effective and increasingly efficient technology, combined with changing external conditions (e.g., inflation, younger executives' increased understanding of computer technology, increased competitive pressures), has initiated an age in which end-user–oriented systems—such as on-line data inquiry and analysis, office automation, electronic mail, and teleconferencing—are rapidly becoming widespread in major organizations. The growth rate in each of these end-user tools at all levels in the corporation is very high, ranging from 30 to 100 percent per year in a set of companies recently studied.[2] As we move through the 1980s, it is predicted that terminals ultimately will be present on all desks (on those of clerks, managers, and senior executives).

In short, in just a few years, the domain of the IS executive has grown dramatically. Only a decade ago, the typical IS executive was concerned solely with a limited accounting-centered application set, a few centrally located people, and one or two large computers over which he had close and almost absolute control. In contrast, today's computer environment involves a diverse set of applications supporting fundamental operational activities in almost all parts of the organization. Computer hardware is widespread and is supported by geographically diverse IS personnel whose clientele is rapidly expanding to include almost every person in the organization.

The Current Study

In a recent research study we focused on the evolution of the IS managerial role in this changing environment. Extensive interviews were conducted in nine major companies whose top IS executives hold an excellent reputation in their fields. In all cases these executives focused their efforts and those of their departments primarily on meeting the major needs of the business and only secondarily on advancing the technical excellence of the IS department. The companies studied were selected at random from a list of twenty firms that were suggested as being outstanding either by academic colleagues or by industry contacts.

A primary emphasis in the study was placed on understanding these executives' "critical success factors" (CSFs)—those few key areas of activity in which favorable results are absolutely necessary for a particular manager to reach his or her goals.[3] By zeroing in on those areas perceived by these executives as most significant for the well-being of their organizations, we hoped to identify the fundamental issues to be faced by IS executives in the 1980s. From this critical success factors base, it was felt that a role model for the IS executive would emerge.

Research Method

Since any definition of the objectives, critical success factors, and operating methods of a "model" IS executive must be subjective, we elected a research method that was case-based and inductive. Interviews were conducted with the head of information systems, three to five of his or her subordinates, his superior, and two or three key users in each company. We asked all these individuals to discuss the objectives, immediate goals, critical success factors, organization structure, planning processes, and control systems of the IS organization. Evaluative comments as well as descriptive comments were sought from each individual. On the average, one and one-half to two days were spent at each company—the average interview with the head of IS consuming half a day and other interviews lasting approximately two hours each.

Within each company studied there was substantial agreement with the IS critical success factors described by the IS head. Because of this agreement, the article will focus on the critical success factors cited by the IS executives.

The companies selected were large, but generally not industry giants. We restricted our sample to firms in which the head of information systems still has primary line responsibility for the function. Omitted from the sample, therefore, were companies of the stature of Exxon and General Motors and some smaller companies where the chief information systems executive plays only a staff, coordinating role for almost independent divisional information systems groups. Although this class of information systems executive also deserves study, we targeted the more numerous IS executive who has in the early 1980s *both* line and staff responsibility. Our sample was dispersed over several different industries. It included two of the top twenty banks, a major insurance company, one of the five largest airlines, one of the five largest railroads, and four manufacturing firms—three of which are in the *Fortune* top 200.

Results

Although many interesting facts and ideas emerged from our interviews, three major findings are perhaps most relevant:

1. The critical success factors, as stated by each executive, differ from company to company, but they can be summarized as a set of four distinct factors that we term an "IS executive CSF set."
2. Each IS executive has established a distinctive and broad set of managerial tools, techniques, and processes aimed at facilitating good performance in "critical" areas.
3. Although individual executives differ in several ways, there are striking similarities in the managerial viewpoint of these nine executives. They exhibit many common managerial behaviors, as evidenced in the interviews and as described by others. This "profile" is worth considering as a role model for the IS executive of the early 1980s.

These three major findings are discussed in subsequent sections of this article. First, however, in order to provide the reader with a better feel for the results, we will detail the particular circumstances and resulting CSFs for three firms from our sample.

CSFs of IS Executives

The critical success factors for each of the nine IS executives are summarized in Table 5.1. Each of these CSFs is a shorthand statement of those limited number of areas where "things must go right" for the IS function to be successful and for the IS executive's goals to be attained. In order to understand these briefly stated CSFs better, we will first examine the executives in Companies A-C. Although differences in their companies lead to differences in their CSFs, many similarities can be noted.

Company A: Railroad

The head of information systems in this large railroad is a multiple-decade veteran of the organization who reports directly to (and enjoys a close personal relationship with) the president. Since the company is in a rather mature and not highly profitable business, resources for the IS function are limited and must be used efficiently. Three of the five critical success factors for this IS executive reflect this concern (see Table 5.1).

The first CSF reflects this executive's need to have the tools, techniques, and processes in place to manage most effectively the limited cadre of information systems people available to him. As is reflected in CSFs #2 and #5, it is equally important to ensure that his people are "working on the right projects." With limited resources, his priorities must be selected with care.

Table 5.1 Information Systems Executive's CSFs in Nine Companies

Company	Critical Success Factors
Company A: **Railroad**	1. Effective management of human resources 2. IS priorities aligned with business 3. Delivery of service 4. Users—especially the CEO—having favorable perceptions of IS 5. Continued direct reporting link to the CEO
Company B: **Major Bank**	1. Reliable, high-quality IS service 2. Communication of service quality and reliability to top line 3. High-quality IS human resources 4. Ensuring IS services evolve with needs capabilities 5. One IS executive in top-management inner circle
Company C: **High Technology** **Manufacturing**	1. Successful implementation of two new key systems 2. Top-management communication 3. Top-management education 4. Meeting service standards 5. Human resources
Company D: **Airline**	1. Increased visibility for IS within company 2. Good and better operating performance 3. More involvement in corporate planning process 4. IS morale 5. Downplay responding to users: Increasingly taking leadership in helping users define information needs 6. Restructuring IS in line with new technology
Company E: **Insurance**	1. Maintaining top-management user contract 2. Other top-management to review IS planning for approval and visibility 3. Providing planning role model for company 4. IS planning—IS leadership 5. Increasing user "direction" of IS projects 6. Maintaining managerial perspective
Company F: **Manufacturing**	1. Retaining trained, high-quality personnel 2. Ability to interact with top management 3. Improving "software hardware" 4. Enhancing job satisfaction for IS personnel 5. Improving management control
Company G: **Bank**	1. High-quality personnel 2. User and top-management satisfaction and involvement 3. Efficient use of human resources 4. Service levels (actual and perceived) 5. IS value perceived by organization 6. New IS role communication to top management
Company H: **Manufacturing**	1. Attract, train, and retain high-quality people 2. Plan effectively 3. Top-management communication 4. Utilization of best productivity tools 5. Internal and external recognition of MIS 6. Support from top management 7. Decentralization of MIS function
Company I: **Manufacturing**	1. Involvement in mainstream application 2. Involved, active, knowledgeable users 3. Systems competence of people 4. Effective, efficient systems 5. High performance on perceived service levels

It is, therefore, important that he have close ties with the operating officers of the railroad: His direct link with the chief executive officer is most important in this regard. Toward the end of the interview, the IS executive said he foresees some near-term movement toward increased end-user computing, but he feels that this movement will be slower in his company than it will be in other firms. Therefore, this executive continues to place heavy emphasis on ensuring the most effective and efficient use of centralized IS personnel.

Like most other heads of information systems in our sample, he believes that "delivery of service" (CSF #3) is a critical success factor for IS. The ability to deliver dependable, on-time, low-cost service is the bedrock upon which IS stands. Moreover, he says that good service, by itself, is not enough. It is necessary for users to *perceive* that the service is good in order to foster sound user relationships (CSF #4). These relationships in turn further the user-IS communication needed to ensure that IS priorities are aligned with the business. Thus we circle back to CSF #2.

Company B: Major Bank

At the time of our interview, the executive in charge of information systems in Company B had only recently been recruited from outside the organization. Prior to his arrival, the reputation of the information systems function with regard to day-to-day service and on-time, within-budget development of new systems was less than satisfactory. Therefore, his top two critical success factors address this situation (see Table 5.1). First he feels that the development of high-quality, reliable service (CSF #1) is essential to his organization. In addition, he feels strongly that the now emerging results of his department's efforts to improve service must be fully understood by senior management in all user areas (CSF #2).

CSFs #3 and #4 in Company B originate from the IS executive's belief that his function is in the process of a major change. This will be a rapid evolution from having IS "doing everything itself" to a role that will be increasingly oriented toward supporting end-user efforts to develop many of their own reports and systems through the use of steadily improving end-user programming languages. As a result, he notes: "I have to change the people mix I have in information systems. We need more consulting-oriented people who really like to work with line management. It will be critical for me during this decade to continually upgrade the quality of people in IS while retaining the best that we already have [CSF #3]." Because of this situation, he believes that the tools and techniques with which the IS function works and the services it offers are going to evolve throughout the 1980s. He feels he must ensure that the services his organization offers keep pace with both the needs of the users and the technical capabilities provided by the vendors (CSF #4).

Finally, the IS executive of Company B feels that he must participate in the key top-management discussions of the business and of the directions it is to take (CSF #5). Such corporate involvement is necessary for him to ensure that his organization is working on the appropriate priorities and providing the services that are required by the business as it grows and changes.

Company C: High-Technology Manufacturing Company

The CSFs for the executive in charge of information systems in Company C are of particular interest, for he reports at the lowest level of any of the executives in our study (see Table 5.1). While all the other executives report either directly to the president or to a person reporting to the president, the information systems executive in Company C is "buried," with three managerial levels between him and the top executive officer. It is clear to him that he is viewed and evaluated as a functional manager and not as a participating corporate executive. As a result, his most significant critical success factor is the implementation of two major new systems: "Although this is changing as a result of my efforts, there is no doubt in my mind that I am judged primarily on our ability to complete and install major new systems [CSF #1] as well as to provide ongoing service [CSF #4]."

The other critical success factors for this IS executive, however, are aimed at changing the role of IS in his firm: "We need to move more rapidly toward better end-user computing services, toward using IS resources to provide *information*, not just *paperwork processing*, and to expand the ability of our line managers to better use information systems. The only way we'll get this done is if top management understands what I believe is the evolving role for IS." Thus, his other critical success factors include top-management communication (CSF #2), top-management education (CSF #3), and human resources (CSF #5). The last of these is aimed at hiring individuals who can and do communicate with management regarding the need for new and better systems. However, he also expends a significant percentage of his own time in the "very critical process of helping top management to understand that we are in a very different era of information systems use, that the new technology presents a multitude of opportunities for our company, and that we must organize effectively and devote the necessary resources to take advantage of these opportunities."

A CSF Set for IS Executives

Previous work on critical success factors has demonstrated that although CSFs differ among companies because of factors such as size and competitive strategy, each industry has a generic set of CSFs.[4] More recent studies show that occupational roles also have generic sets of CSFs.[5] A manufacturing manager, for example, will have a set of CSFs that includes inventory levels, product costs, and efficient plant scheduling.

The case studies summarized in this research similarly suggest a generic set of role-related CSFs for executives. Of course, since individual differences exist from company to company, this generalized set can serve only as a "model" against which each company—and its IS executive—can test its particular set of CSFs. Abstracting from the CSF material generated in interviews at the nine companies, it appears that there are four CSFs for this type of IS executive: service, communication, IS human resources, and repositioning the IS function.

I. Service CSF

The first, and most obvious, CSF is service, which appears in the lists of almost all of our company respondents. This CSF refers not only to the effective and efficient performance of necessary operations (e.g., terminal response time or the on-time, within-budget development of information systems) but also to the *perception* of that service by user and corporate management. Most of the executives in our sample have developed measurement devices to enable them to understand both the current status of their service and users' perceptions of that service.

II. Communication CSF

Every executive in our sample identified one or more critical success factors associated with a strong need to understand the world of key users and top line executives, as well as to have these individuals understand the IS environment. It is important to note that this "communication CSF" concerns a *two-way* communication. One communication direction is from the IS executive to the line. This involves the responsibility of IS to educate top management and key users about the potential impact of information technology on their industry and their company.

The other side of the information flow concerns the communication of user needs and priorities to the IS function. As will be noted later, a sample of executives used a significant number of processes (including planning, involvement in top management councils, and interpersonal communication) to facilitate this communication.

In short, in naming this particular CSF, these IS executives are underlining the death of the technically oriented, stay-in-the-office information systems chief. In his place, they are affirming the birth of a new corporate executive who is oriented toward active communication and leadership in the use of information technology to meet the full spectrum of business needs.

III. IS Human Resources

The third generic CSF is human resources in the information systems function. Almost all of the executives interviewed stressed that the information systems function is changing. As IS moves away from accounting applications (which require IS personnel who are relatively unskilled interpreters of existing written rules and traceable processes as well as diligent coders of programs) to applications that assist executives to develop and use information data bases of their own, the characteristics of effective IS people will change.

During the 1980s, there will be a need for an increased supply of technically literate, but managerially competent, information systems people to help line management understand their own needs and build their own systems. The supply of such people is limited. The attraction of these people to, and their subsequent retention within, information systems is viewed as a critical success factor by all. At the same time, the IS executives agree that it is also critical to retain and provide incentives for the best of the "COBOL-shop" personnel to develop further and maintain the existing massive paperwork processing systems. From any perspective, information systems is a people-intensive process. For any IS executive the quality of his people is a key ingredient in success or failure.

IV. Repositioning the IS Function

The fourth generic CSF—repositioning the information systems function—involves four basic components: technical, organizational, psychological, and what is referred to here as "IS managerial." All contribute to change the IS role from a limited "automated back office" to a more ubiquitous function involved in all aspects of the business.

The *technical* component of repositioning provides users with a new set of tools, techniques, and processes that allow them to access and to use information as espoused in the literature on decision support and executive information support.[6] This part of the repositioning process moves end-user computing activity from the fringes of "data processing" to a more central role in the IS function.

The *organizational* restructuring of the IS function requires integrating all telecommunications, information processing, and information gathering and disseminating functions into a single functional unit. Each of these capabilities becomes part of an indivisible information function. This organizational change can facilitate the increased involvement of information systems in the mainstream product line of the firm. For example, IS technology is heavily involved in new product offerings in the banking and insurance industries. Most of the manufacturing firms in our sample have also extended their communication systems network to their customers and vendors. This extension of IS capabilities not only facilitates the selection and sale of the company's products, but also provides increased service to its customers.

In addition to these technical and organizational changes, a *psychological* repositioning of the IS function must occur. Within many firms this department is viewed merely as "data processing," an automated accounting and paperwork function. Yet, in order for the IS function to reposition itself, it must communicate to users that it handles not just data but also information. This information should be viewed as a key product of the firm that is valuable to internal planners, customers, and suppliers.

Finally, many of the executives in our sample believe that in order to implement these first three changes they will have to restructure the IS *managerial* role. This involves repositioning themselves in the organization from essentially a line department that supervises the hardware and systems-development people to a functional, staff-oriented department (with line computing responsibilities distributed to various departments and divisions of the organization). This restructuring is necessary, they believe, to allow IS management to focus on planning and on executing all of the above repositioning processes.

Variations from the Model CSF Set

Although this generic set of CSFs is readily apparent in the nine companies studied, the specific CSFs do differ from one IS executive to another. Even some of the four model CSFs are absent from individual lists. This variation suggests that any particular head of IS should not expect to have exactly the same four CSFs that were described in the generic set of IS CSFs. Concomitantly, the definition of his or her current role may differ somewhat from the general model postulated here. What is the cause of this variation in actual CSFs? They are undoubtedly the result of a number of contingencies that need further research and analysis. In this study, however, they seem to differ for four major reasons.

The first, and perhaps most important, reason for differences in IS CSFs is the stage of development of the IS organization studied. Almost all of the nine companies in our sample were either in late stage three or in early stage four in Gibson and Nolan's typology. (Gibson and Nolan describe four stages of the growth of a data-processing department organization as it proceeds from inception to a mature function.)[7] Subsequently, we have interviewed many other executives in the early portion of stage three—the control stage. Not unexpectedly, their CSFs fall into a pattern that stresses "remaining within budgetary constraints" and various aspects of service delivery. The repositioning CSF found among our respondents is rarely, if ever, viewed as "critical" by these early stage three organizations.

Second, the recent organization history of the IS function heavily influences each executive's perception of his or her own critical success factors. Companies in which service has been a problem often have service-oriented CSFs predominating, often to the exclusion of other factors. Those in which IS personnel have been a particular problem will tend to stress the human factor.

Third, the human, organization, and financial makeup of a company will also affect IS CSFs. For example, IS CSFs are different in organizations where top management is well aware of the technology and its implications as opposed to those companies where it is not.

Finally, the perspective or "world view" that the IS executive has on the field and on his or her role in the company is a very significant generator of CSFs. The CSF lists compiled above reflect the views of nine proactive, business-oriented IS executives. In subsequent interviews we have found a few IS individuals who believe that theirs is essentially an internally oriented, responsive function. These executives tend to be more technically oriented and often play a reactive, rather passive role in their corporations. Their CSFs, as can be imagined, are quite different. Thus CSFs are obviously a reflection of an executive's personality and perspective on his or her role.

For all four of these reasons, the CSFs *stated* by the IS executive will differ from company to company. It is up to such an executive and his or her top management to ensure the correct pace of evolution of the IS role.

Techniques to Ensure Performance

The mere statement that things are critical is not enough. One searches for evidence that this view of the job is adopted through managerial actions. In the companies studied, a well-defined set of tools, techniques, and processes is in place to ensure that significant managerial attention is given to critical areas. This section details the most widespread of these managerial methods.

For the *service* CSF, the most important approaches in these companies involve not only techniques for the actual delivery of service but also several techniques that focus on measuring user perception of service delivery. These measurement devices vary. They include: a daily "sign-off" inquiry presented to each on-line terminal user; monthly, quarterly, or annual surveys of user opinion through internally generated questionnaires; and, in one case, a structured set of interviews administered by an outside consulting organization. These techniques are important since they not only allow the measurement of user perceptions but also permit the IS executive to communicate the resulting, hopefully favorable, perception back to the users and to corporate management. In this way, the image of IS, and therefore IS credibility and its ability to affect corporate actions, can be maintained or improved.

The *communication* CSF is supported by a wide-ranging set of techniques and processes that contributes to effective communication between our sample of executives and their constituencies. Prominent among these processes is strategic planning. Each interviewee, with one exception, has an ongoing strategic planning process as a means of communicating with his or her users about the nature of the IS environment and about what they should jointly be doing to adapt to and exploit it. The only executive who does not have a well-defined process is the one in the railroad company. And even there, an information systems strategy is developed—although primarily through the intense relationship between the IS executive and the CEO.

A second essential aspect enhancing effective communications is that almost all of these executives report at or near the peak of their organizational pyramid. As noted earlier, the one executive in our sample who did not was working intensely to remedy this.

All but two of these executives have developed steering committees for communication purposes. Generally, these committees are seen as a vehicle both to understand user priorities and to educate users and others in the firm about what is happening in the IS organization. These executives have also placed emphasis on considerable informal contact and communication within the organization. To further this, several have established an IS top-management team that consists of a chief executive officer, who is responsible for contact outside the IS organization, and a chief operating officer, who is responsible exclusively for the management of internal IS operations. This arrangement, which several other executives are thinking of establishing as well, frees up the senior executive to interact with other senior executives on general issues of corporate management.

In addition, these executives have begun to facilitate more effective communication with users by increasingly aligning their systems development groups directly with user or customer units. In doing so, they are, at the very least, moving away from a centralized, pooled organization of system developers to a system development organization structure that is aligned with specific functional or divisional responsibilities. In an increasing number of these organizations, the systems development staff reports, or will soon report, directly to the user division or departmental management. All of this is being done to ensure vitally needed system development personnel/user communication.

The *human resources* CSF is supported by several processes. All but one of the executives have established a career-development process to provide support and incentives for the IS staff. Many have a program for interchanging their IS people with the rest of the organization. Line personnel are brought in to improve functional knowledge within IS. Similarly, IS staff are moved out to other parts of the organization in order to enhance staff development and promotional opportunities. In addition, there is an emphasis in these IS organizations on increasing the number of people who have a generalist, managerial focus. Most organizations have a program for hiring MBAs. Some actively promote an image of IS as a reservoir of talented people for the organizations. This enhances the organization's ability to recruit competent, highly motivated graduates. As one IS executive respondent put it: "The more knowledge I can get out there of our technical capabilities, and how to use them, the better off I am."

To ensure the *repositioning* CSF for the new era of information management, these executives have implemented a wide range of approaches and techniques. They uniformly are placing an increasing emphasis on developing methods to manage data as a corporate resource. Although none of them is entirely sure of the ultimate implications of this concept, they all emphasize its increasingly evident importance and the need to explore its possibilities. In addition, they are active in creating new methods to further the development of decision support systems for managers. Most of these companies have either established or are in the process of developing separate end-user support organizations as a responsive approach to users whose requirements are oriented toward their own manipulation of available computerized data bases.

Finally, as noted briefly above, in most of these companies, there is a trend toward recasting the organization structure to reposition corporate IS primarily as a staff organization. This is another reason why systems development people and hardware are being transferred to divisions and functional departments. Given this elimination of day-to-day line responsibility, corporate IS can focus its attention on developing the necessary tools, techniques, standards, and methods to facilitate the corporatewide dissemination of computer technology. It can also work to plan and facilitate the necessary convergence of word processing, telecommunications, and related information technologies.

A "Profile" of the Excellent IS Manager

Just as IS CSFs reflect an executive's view of his or her role, so do they also mirror the executive. In analyzing each of the nine interviews, several common attributes of these executives became apparent. In effect, a common profile (or model) of these "excellent managers" emerged—a profile that no one executive fits exactly, but one that describes each of them in most respects.

With one exception, these IS executives see themselves (and are seen) as corporate officers: All report either to the president or to a general manager (such as an executive vice-president) who reports directly to the CEO. All see their roles as general business managers, not as information systems technicians. With only one or two exceptions, they view themselves as candidates for top-line management jobs in their organizations. (In fact, since our study, two have been promoted to top general management positions in a major division of their corporations.)

Additionally, all our respondents see the information systems function as very significant to the success of the company: They are constantly communicating this perspective to others. They are all high-profile people in the thick of corporate discussions. They view their job as one of "getting the message across" to those who do not have an understanding of the technology, and their image as company "leaders" throughout their organizations facilitates this.

Like most effective line executives, they appear to enjoy the "battle" to accomplish their goals. Almost all of the executives interviewed often spoke of their organizations from a "political" perspective as well as a "rational" perspective. Emphasis was often placed on the need to get key "power" individuals to understand and act in ways beneficial to the organization.

Finally, each IS executive interviewed had a crisp, clear view of his own critical success factors. There was little, if any, hesitation in identifying a concise list of areas that were critical to success. Moreover, the action plans that were being implemented to improve performance in each of these areas were foremost in the minds of these executives.

In short, the executives interviewed have a well-defined perspective on IS technology and a clear vision of where their corporations should be going with that technology. They have a strong sense of their roles in the corporation and of the steps they must take to implement both their desired IS strategies and their own personal strategies.

Conclusion: The New IS Executive Role

In attempting to define the new IS executive role, we focused on three aspects of our sample of IS executives: their CSFs, the key techniques and processes they use to manage critical areas, and their common individual attributes. Taken together, these aspects provide a profile of an aggressive, proactive, communication-oriented executive who focuses heavily on helping his or her organization adapt to a changing technical environment.

Today, executives see their role as one that assures that rapidly evolving technical opportunities are understood, planned for, and implemented in his organization. This, in many cases, calls both for significant changes in the way the organization does business and for a significant evolution in his own job.

No longer can the IS executive in medium-sized to large-sized organizations directly "control" all the computer-based activities of the firm. Increasingly, he or she must give away day-to-day line responsibility to local IS executives, and assume the more stafflike role of counterparts in such industrial giants as IBM and Exxon. Only through this shift will IS executives have the time to focus on the more staff-oriented tasks of IS strategy, planning, standard setting, and management of research into technological directions and is to applying the new technology to the organization. Increasingly, he or she is a disseminator and "salesperson" of ideas and techniques rather than a direct implementor.

Three of the four model critical success factors (communication, IS human resources, and repositioning) directly reflect this evolving staff-oriented role definition. In most cases our executive sample has decided that the service CSF must be brought into line with this new role. Operating responsibility for local IS units is increasingly being transferred to local line managements. The top IS executive today is a "thinker, planner, and coordinator" rather than a direct "implementor and doer."

6

An Assessment of Critical Success Factors

Andrew C. Boynton

Robert W. Zmud

The critical success factors (CSF) method has attracted considerable attention as a means of supporting both the management of information systems (MIS) planning and requirements analysis. Using insights gained from two case studies, the authors assess the strengths and weaknesses of this methodology. They find that the CSF method is particularly effective in supporting planning processes, in communicating the role of information technologies to senior management, and in promoting structured analysis processes; and that it is not so effective when used with lower-level managers or as the sole means of eliciting information requirements. The article concludes with suggested guidelines for the effective application of the CSF method. *SMR.*

The critical success factors method can be applied as a means of supporting both the management of information systems (MIS) planning and require-ments analysis. Although experiences in applying the CSF method have gener-ally been quite favorable, there is some debate about the strengths, weak-nesses, and appropriate use of CSFs as an information systems methodology.

This article provides insight into the strengths and weaknesses of the CSF method. First, we will discuss the CSF methodology, define CSFs, and review the broad range of uses of the CSF method. Second, we will describe models of both the MIS planning and requirements analysis processes, and then examine the way in which each might be supported by the CSF method. Third, we discuss two case studies relating experiences in applying the CSF methodology in order to assess the identified strengths and weaknesses of the CSF method. Finally, we will suggest guidelines and strategies for how and when to use CSFs.

From *Sloan Management Review,* Summer 1984, Vol. 25, No. 4. Reprinted with permission.

The CSF Concept

Critical success factors are those few things that must go well to ensure success for a manager or an organization, and, therefore, they represent those managerial or enterprise areas that must be given *special* and *continual* attention to bring about high performance. CSFs include issues vital to an organization's current operating activities and to its future success.

The CSF methodology is a procedure that attempts to make explicit those few key areas that dictate managerial or organizational success. CSFs emerge from structured dialogues between a skilled CSF analyst and the key personnel of a firm. A series of dialogues between the analyst and a manager should result in an explicit statement disclosing that individual's personal CSFs. CSFs should be elicited from managers who represent a cross section of the organization's major functional areas. This will provide a collection of consistently referenced CSFs that can be extracted and refined into a set of organizational CSFs.

Development and Application of the CSF Method

The use of the CSF concept as an information systems methodology was first introduced by John Rockart as a mechanism for defining a chief executive officer's information needs.[1] Rockart's concepts were developed from ideas stated much earlier by Daniel.[2] Rockart outlined a procedure by which interviews between an analyst and a CEO result, first, in a set of CSFs and, then, in performance measures that represent these CSFs. Rockart did not specifically advocate using the CSF method to develop a detailed set of requirements specifications, but rather to identify critical areas of concern and to provide initial descriptions of information measures that reflect these critical areas. Rockart stressed two points: CSFs provide a focal point for directing a computer-based information system (CBIS) development effort, and the CSF method should result in an information system useful to a CEO as it pinpoints key areas that require a manager's attention.

Bullen and Rockart later broadened the definition of CSFs and proposed that they be used as an MIS planning tool.[3] When using the CSF method as a planning tool, managers from multiple levels of an organization's hierarchy must be interviewed. The resulting CSFs are synthesized into a collective set for the entire organization. Rockart and Bullen suggest that information resources and activities should then be targeted at enabling the organization to realize these collective CSFs.

Two studies in the literature report that the CSF method has been successfully used to identify the key concerns of senior MIS managers.[4] Munro compared these two studies for consistency, and the resulting positive assessment suggests that the CSF method is, in fact, a reliable technique.[5]

Application of the CSF Method beyond the MIS Arena

Munro and Wheeler suggest that CSFs can be used to direct an organization's efforts in developing strategic plans.[6] In addition to applying CSFs to fabricate a set of strategies, they can also be used to identify critical issues associated with implementing a plan. Anderson observes that CSFs can be used by managers and organizations to help achieve high performance.[7] Through the explicit identification of organizational CSFs, managers can help ensure that resources under their authority are directed toward important areas. Ferguson and Dickinson suggest a slightly different role for CSFs: Boards of directors can use them to establish guidelines for monitoring a corporation's activities.[8]

Qualities of the CSF Method

The CSF method has been cited for weaknesses in three principal areas. First, it has been asserted that the CSF method is difficult to use and is, therefore, not appropriate for organizations whose analysts do not possess the capability to successfully apply the method. While it is true that the CSF method must be directed by a skilled analyst, the same statement could be made about all nonautomated information system methodologies.

Second, the validity of the CSF method has been questioned because of the threat of analyst and manager bias introduced through the interview process. However, Munro's study showed that two independent CSF analyses yielded comparable results, thus indicating that these potential biases can be overcome.[9] It is unlikely that these independent studies would have been consistent if there had not been considerable validity to their findings. Moreover, in both cases very skilled CSF analysts directed the study.

Third, Davis raises several concerns regarding the applicability of the CSF method as an appropriate requirements analysis methodology.[10] Given that humans have a limited capacity to deal effectively with complexity, the CSF method may very well yield an information model that is simple and thought provoking but not accurately representative of the actual environment. As humans often exhibit difficulty in dealing with causality, any association between CSFs and organizational success as interpreted by a manager may not represent a true causal relationship. The analysis procedure that leads to CSF identification may be biased by the manager's or analyst's beliefs and values or by the available data. Although there has also been concern that the CSF methodology is heavily influenced by recent events, this concern has largely been negated, since it is felt that short-term memory does not apply to the CSF formulation process.[11] It is not clear to what extent limitations such as these imperil the use of the CSF method. Research results and case experiences of applying CSFs should eventually provide a better understanding of such issues.

Our experience and the experience of others suggest that two key strengths of the CSF method contribute to much of its success. First, the CSF method generates user acceptance at the senior managerial level. Senior managers seem to intuitively understand the thrust of the CSF method, and consequently, they strongly endorse its application as a means of identifying important areas that need attention. Second, the CSF method facilitates a structured, top-down analysis or planning process. It initially focuses a participant's attention on a core set of essential issues, and then proceeds to refine the issues in a manner that allows an evolving "design" to be continuously examined for validity and completeness. Our case studies provide support for these two assertions regarding the CSF method.

The Application of CSFs to MIS Planning and Requirements Analysis

It is evident that CSFs can be used for both MIS planning and requirements analysis. Precisely what does the CSF methodology bring to these two activities? In order to answer this question, we will examine the possible roles of CSFs in MIS planning and requirements analysis.

CSFs Applied to MIS Planning

We will use the MIS planning model proposed by King and Zmud.[12] An information function planning context addresses the traditional technical activities undertaken to deploy information system products within an organization. An information resource planning context, on the other hand, addresses the management of information technologies from an organization-wide perspective. Both the information resource and information function planning contexts should be evident in a comprehensive MIS planning effort.

Three levels of planning arise within both the information resource and information function contexts: operational planning, strategic planning, and policy planning. Operational planning involves those activities required to implement specific computer-based information systems; strategic planning attempts to link an organization's strategic interests with information technologies; and policy planning is aimed at establishing an organizational culture that is able to make appropriate use of information products and services.

An assessment of how CSFs could support MIS planning leads to some preliminary ideas about the manner in which the CSF methodology should be applied. Table 6.1 summarizes the relation between the information resource and information function contexts. Our discussion will first focus on the information resource context and then on the information function context.

CSFs in Information Resource Planning

At an operational level, CSFs help ensure that critical organization information processing needs are explicitly addressed. The development of organizational CSFs and their use as a guideline for bounding and directing implementation efforts also provide a means to improve the overall integration of information systems efforts. In strategic planning, CSFs form a bridge between corporate strategic interests and the strategic planning efforts of the information function. Since an organization's CSFs are those factors that must go well for the organization to succeed, a link is provided between a corporation's tactical and strategic planning objectives. CSFs, then, provide a means of explicitly relating information resources to an organization's strategic plan-

Table 6.1   Activities of the Two Planning Contexts

Information Resource Planning Context	
Policy	Cultivate core group of organizational proponents Define information technology role throughout organization
Strategic	Ensure that CBIS portfolio is consistent with corporate strategy Define global information technology role
Operational	Address critical organization information processing needs

Information Function Planning Context	
Policy	Develop strategies to manage change Ensure that information manager wears corporate hat
Strategic	Merge information-related technologies Engage in resource planning for future needs Establish sound user-support staff trained in business, technologies, and organizational issues Develop programs to diffuse particular information technologies
Operational	Build solid CBIS base for future DSS Develop career paths within information function Establish documentation standards Develop requirements analysis process for proposed systems

ning efforts. Further, CSFs enhance communication between the organization's general management and those individuals responsible for deploying information resources by providing a common schema that both groups can easily comprehend. The popular call for information systems managers to don a "corporate hat" can be partially answered when such managers participate in a CSF analysis and gain knowledge of an organization's internal and external environment. As a policy planning tool, CSFs can help develop a core group of information technology proponents throughout the organization, particularly when it is recognized that information technologies provide strategic opportunities. The CSF method also seems very adept at establishing a mutual understanding between managers and analysts, thus enhancing the information technology group's image and improving their usefulness to the corporation.

Similar gains are obtained by applying the CSF method as a strategic and policy planning tool. In both instances, the information function is thrust into the mainstream of the organization's activities. Through CSF interviews focused on organizationwide strategic issues, information managers can align their strategic plans with those of other influential managers, and develop closer ties between the information function and those individuals who set organizational directions.

CSFs in Information Function Planning

There appears to be less application of CSFs to the information function planning context. One obvious operational level use of CSFs is as a requirements analysis methodology. CSFs provide a sound methodology for understanding the information needs of managers, and they can be an important tool in an analyst's repertoire. Strategic and policy roles for CSFs within the information function planning context revolve around their use as tools to identify those issues that merit close management attention within the information function itself. Such analyses should enable information function managers to develop a better understanding of their environments, and this should be reflected in improved tactical as well as strategic planning efforts. Since information function planning must be sensitive to both changing technical and organizational environments, the CSF method brings to the surface key issues that must be addressed in managing change within information function policy.

In summary, CSFs can be applied effectively throughout the information resource planning context but only sporadically within the information function planning context.

Planning in both the information function and information resource contexts is a process heavily dependent on conceptual thought. Similarly, CSFs

represent a high-level conceptualization of issues that are extremely important to a manager's or an organization's success. "High level" refers here to
the robust nature of CSFs in that they are impacted by numerous organizational or managerial actions. Given that the CSF method has tended to be
enthusiastically received by senior managers, it appears to provide an ideal
means of bringing structure and consistency to the MIS planning process
through a clear vision of vital factors.

CSFs Applied to Requirements Analysis

We will use the requirements analysis model suggested by Zmud.[13] Simon's
early ideas are prominent in this view.[14] As Figure 6.1 illustrates, the requirements analysis process follows a top-down, structured approach. The conceptual design phase represents an effort to arrive at an information system
design that evolves from an overall understanding of an organization's or a
manager's environment and important opportunities and problems. This conceptual phase is then followed by a detailed design process that links this
overall vision with organizational realities to arrive at a specification of relevant, feasible information requirements.

To be successfully performed, the conceptual design phase requires an ab-
straction of the major external and internal forces that influence organizational
behaviors. This normative organizational model provides a centerpiece for the

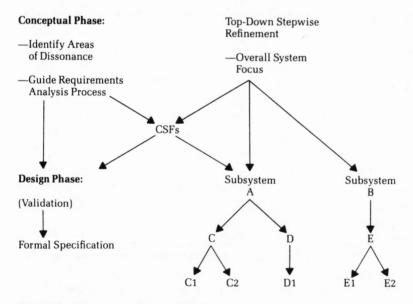

Figure 6.1   The Requirements Analysis Process

requirements analysis process. As CSFs can be thought of as representations of those important external or internal conditions that permeate the organization's environment, they provide such a normative model. A CSF requirements analysis effort seems to parallel Simon's challenge that managers selectively scan their environments.[15] The CSF method seems ideal as a tool for establishing sound conceptual components from which to base a requirements analysis specification. In this sense, the conceptual design phase is the highest entity of a structured, top-down requirements analysis approach.

Rockart initially advocated the use of CSFs both for conceptually identifying a manager's key concerns and for developing specific measures that capture a manager's information needs. In other words, Rockart suggested that CSFs are applicable to both the conceptual and the detailed design phases of the requirements analysis process. It is not immediately apparent how an extremely conceptual technique such as the CSF methodology can be successfully applied in defining specific information needs for *most managers,* outside of providing an initial high-level specification to be refined by other tools and techniques.

It is important to observe that the initial set of managers using CSFs for requirements analysis were corporate CEOs. There may be a relationship between a CEO's ability to conceptually identify specific information needs and his or her preoccupation with planning, a high-level managerial activity that requires broad strokes of conceptual thinking. It is also likely that a CEO's information needs are themselves a high-level representation of an organization's information processing activities.

In summary, CSFs appear valuable as a means of building a conceptual model of the key facets of an organization or of a manager's role in an organization. Such a model can then be used to drive the requirements analysis process. However, because certain managers may experience some difficulty in dealing with conceptual thought processes, the CSF methodology may not be universally appropriate. Because rather concrete thought processes are required to arrive at a detailed specification of information requirements, the CSF method might not, by itself, be an effective requirements analysis tool.

Case Study of a Financial Services Firm

The CSF method was used at a small, rapidly growing financial services organization to plan the firm's future information technology infrastructure, to define specific information needs (of a monitoring nature) for management, and to provide management with information about nonrelated system areas (e.g., organization design and strategic planning). Figure 6.2 shows a map of

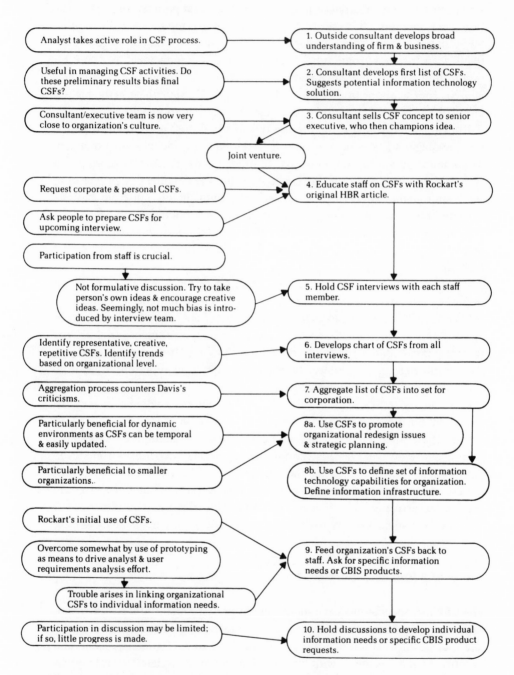

Figure 6.2 Map of CSF Procedure at Financial Services Firm

the CSF activities that were employed. Steps 1 through 10 depict actual events, and the ancillary balloons contain interpretive remarks regarding this CSF process. Some important features of this case were:

- The consultant developed a thorough understanding of the industry and the organization prior to using the CSF method.
- One of the firm's senior-level managers developed a great interest in CSFs and championed the project.
- CSF interviews were conducted at every level of the organization, and involved clerical, staff, line, and senior managerial personnel.

After factoring out the nuances of the case situation, four assertions can be made. First, the CSF method provided an excellent vehicle to identify the firm's future information infrastructure. The following list of CSFs was derived for the firm:

- Prevent losses through risk management,
- Increase diversification of the customer base,
- Increase professional staff productivity, and
- Enhance the corporate image with the firm's markets and the public.

This set of CSFs helped develop insights into a number of information services that could significantly impact the corporation's competitive position. Because of the momentum established by the CSF exercise, the firm has begun to expand its information resources to include new staff, hardware, and software. Perhaps most importantly, because of the CSF-based analysis, senior management now perceives information technologies to be resources that are vital to the corporation's future.

Second, the CSF exercise provided senior management with important information for strategic planning efforts. The explicit identification of CSFs sharpened management's understanding of those factors central to the firm's success. Corporate reorganization efforts were accelerated by the CSF exercise, and they are likely to be more successful because of it.

Third, it proved difficult to formulate specific management information needs using the CSF method. Managers, especially those who were not at senior levels in the organization, had considerable difficulty with the transition from manipulating conceptual CSFs to defining concrete information needs.

Fourth, the farther managers and other personnel were from the senior managerial level, the more difficult it became to develop meaningful corporatewide CSFs. Interestingly, the senior executive who was championing the CSF project developed a list of personal CSFs that closely paralleled the final aggregation for the firm as a whole. On the other hand, those managers and personnel involved with specific operating areas tended to identify CSFs that were limited in scope (but which they viewed as being corporatewide in nature).

It is important to note, however, that the comments and CSFs gleaned at all levels throughout the organization contributed to the organizational understanding achieved by the analyst. It is doubtful that the resulting high-quality set of organizational CSFs would have been derived if these multiple CSF perspectives had not been obtained.

The difficulty experienced by lower level personnel in identifying meaningful CSFs might simply reflect the nature of this particular organization, where a heavy reliance on role specialization undoubtedly results in rather parochial views of the firm's activities. However, the inability of these individuals to arrive at specific information needs cannot be attributed to this intensive specialization. One would expect just the opposite as these narrow organizational roles should result in a much clearer understanding of individual information needs. It is interesting that the only individuals who were able to actually define concrete information measures were the senior managers.

Case Study of a State University

In this case, CSFs were used in a large state university's career placement function for the purpose of exploring CBIS alternatives. CSF interviews were held with managers and staff to discover the major issues confronting the organization and to arrive at specific information needs.

This case reinforced an important finding made in the more robust study of the financial services firm. The CSF concept was enthusiastically received by the director of the career-placement function, who also responded with an excellent list of issues prior to the first CSF interview.

A second observation consistent with the first case study was that lower level managers and administrative personnel had difficulty working with the CSF concept. In most instances, lower level personnel tended to react to day-to-day events within their individual responsibilities, rather than to adopt a more proactive, conceptual orientation to their and the organization's working environment. This suggests that managers who do not approach their responsibilities from a planning mode may find the CSF method frustrating.

Although the manager and analyst found CSFs extremely useful for locating enterprise areas ripe for information system solutions, specific information requirements were not arrived at through the CSF methodology. This change in procedures by the CSF analyst was a direct consequence of the prior case experience. Instead, available information resources (e.g., microcomputer-based application generators) were used to develop prototype infor-mation system designs that included reports and input screens. An iterative process was put in place in which the analyst/manager team worked together to refine the manager's information needs. Nonetheless, a link between this requirements analysis process and the CSF method does exist. For example, one major CSF was consistently identified during the interview process. Since this CSF appeared to be particularly important, the prototype information system stressed this facet of the organization very strongly.

Discussion of the Case Study Findings

From the two case studies, we can summarize the strengths and weaknesses of the CSF method (see Table 6.2).

Insights into the CSF Method

Much of the attractiveness of the CSF method may be due to the enthusiasm it generates from senior managers. CSFs enable MIS analysts to establish a positive relation and a meaningful dialogue with users. The earlier assessment of MIS planning indicated that CSFs should improve user communications and build managerial support for information technologies. The case studies strongly support this assertion.

The normative analysis of CSFs also indicated that the CSF methodology was a useful tool for information resource planning. In both case studies, CSFs were particularly successful in defining organizational information infrastructures.

The experience with the first case study indicates that CSFs can be used to

Table 6.2 The Strengths and Weaknesses of CSFs

Strengths
- Provide effective support to planning processes
- Develop insights into information services that can impact a firm's competitive position
- Are received enthusiastically by senior management who identify with the thrust of CSF concept
- Serve as the top level of structured analysis and promote the structured analysis process

Weaknesses
- The more removed managers are from senior positions within the organization, the more difficult it is for them to identify meaningful organizational CSFs
- Managers not involved with strategic and tactical planning can experience difficulty in dealing with the conceptual nature of CSFs
- It is difficult for certain managers to ascertain their information needs using only CSFs

arrive at specific information needs for high-level managers. However, the experiences of both case studies indicated that lower level managers may have considerable difficulty in defining specific information measures related to CSFs. This may be attributed to their lack of experience in conceptual thinking.

The earlier assessment of the requirements analysis process suggested that CSFs would best serve as a normative information needs model, which could then be used in a top-down requirements analysis effort. The case experiences also support this assertion, though not as strongly.

CSFs and planning both involve conceptual thought processes that require managers to put aside day-to-day activities and focus on broader organizational concerns. Since planning is a major activity of senior-level managers, these individuals are likely to be more comfortable with conceptual thought processes than lower level managers. The CSF method enables senior managers to adopt a more structured approach to their planning efforts.

Guidelines for Using the CSF Method

This analysis suggests several guidelines on when, where, and how to use CSFs. CSFs are flexible and do not require a rigorous format in their use of interpretation. This offers an advantage as CSFs can be tailored to different applications, as is seen in the growing number of uses proposed for CSFs in MIS and other organizational domains. A disadvantage is that the flexibility of CSFs may lead to an overly casual approach to their application. If this occurs, the CSFs will communicate invalid signals to both analysts and users. The guidelines that follow are intended to direct an effective application of the CSF method.

1. CSFs are an excellent tool for information resource planning. The CSF method seems particularly useful for organizations considering a more aggressive information technology posture, as identified CSFs locate key business thrusts. CSFs are also very useful in prioritizing potential information system projects by identifying those information services that address critical organizational concerns.

2. When attempting to translate CSFs into specific information needs for a manager, the use of prototyping is recommended as a means of product development. Except for a small cadre of top managers, it seems very difficult for managers to bridge the chasm between the conceptual nature of CSFs and specific management information requirements. Reports and screens developed using application generators can serve to bridge this chasm and facilitate the identification of specific information needs. By using application generators for rapid prototyping with CSFs as a guiding

element in the design effort, an analyst and manager can quickly run through several iterations of potential solutions and home in on a set of information specifications that address crucial managerial concerns.

3. The individual managing the CSF effort should have a thorough understanding of the organization or should, at least, be literate in the organization's principal area of business. This requirement is particularly important, since the dialogue between the manager and the analyst largely determines the quality of the CSF effort. The analyst must manage this dialogue if it is to be successful.

4. Because it is desirable to access managers throughout the organization in some CSF projects, it is useful to identify and cultivate a senior-level manager to champion the project. The CSF method represents an intrusion on the normal activities of most managers. For those individuals uncomfortable with high-level conceptual thinking, this intrusion may even be threatening. Although the CSF concept usually generates a positive response once it is under way, there will be less resistance if training materials are provided on the CSF method.

5. Do not make an overt attempt to identify CSFs with information technologies when conducting interviews. The blockages and biases that come up when discussing information systems are significant deterrents to an enlightened CSF interview. The analyst must exploit this opportunity to discuss organizational issues and should not retreat to comfortable and familiar, yet largely unproductive, technical ground in CSF interviews. Managers who are unable to deal with conceptual thought seem to have a strong tendency to begin talking in terms of concrete information outputs. If useful CSFs are to be generated, such a tendency must be countered, particularly in the initial interview.

6. Planning efforts can be enhanced by conducting CSF interviews on multiple levels of the organizational hierarchy. However, the analyst should not expect individuals throughout an organization to readily relate to the CSF concept. Senior management should exhibit a better grasp of the issues that are critical to an organization and should be better able to develop CSFs as conceptual entities. However, CSFs gleaned from lower level management or staff can be productively used to validate the results of high-level CSF interviews.

Conclusion

The weaknesses attached to CSFs can be largely overcome through a careful application of the CSF method. Although the CSF method is difficult to use and requires an analyst comfortable in dealing with business concepts, the CSF method is probably easier to use than most other techniques once an analyst becomes skilled in the CSF methodology. If an analyst understands its strengths and weaknesses, the CSF method can be applied across a wide range of settings to facilitate the rapid accumulation of meaningful information.

The CSF method has numerous strengths. Senior-level managers are receptive to the CSF concept of identifying important organizational issues. CSFs provide a common language for managers and analysts that threatens neither party and provides insights useful to both. Furthermore, a structured approach to the analyst-manager dialogue is made possible. CSFs represent a high-order entity at which an intensive analysis of important issues can be focused. Finally, the CSF method does not require a large commitment of organizational resources. CSFs can be developed by a skilled analyst after several one- to two-hour interviews. These CSFs can then be continually revised to reflect the important issues that confront a manager in a dynamic environment.

If the method is applied correctly, reliability should not be a problem with CSFs. The analyst must understand that some managers are more comfortable with high-level conceptual organizational issues than other managers and must weigh the responses accordingly.

At least in terms of MIS planning, most, if not all, of the criticisms identified by Davis can be overcome if an analyst aggregates CSFs obtained from interviews conducted across a diagonal slice of an organization.[16] With requirements analysis, a similar strategy (such as interviewing a manager's subordinates and peers) may also provide a means for validating a set of information needs.

In summary, there are two major findings regarding the use of the CSF method as an appropriate MIS methodology. First, CSFs can induce a structured design process for eliciting both MIS plans and managerial information needs. This structured approach lends a sense of consistency and completeness to these MIS efforts by emphasizing and then refining important organizational or managerial issues. Second, CSFs are generally more useful in MIS planning than in requirements analysis. This is probably because MIS planning takes place on a much more conceptual plane than requirements analysis. A successful CSF-led requirements analysis effort is likely to be supported by other more concrete techniques, or it is likely to involve a manager who has a proactive, rather than reactive, organizational perspective.

7

Engaging Top Management in Information Technology

John F. Rockart

Adam D. Crescenzi

In this article, the authors present a three-phase process that they believe successfully engages top management in information technology (IT). Through a case study of a steel service industry, they outline the various steps involved in capturing senior executives' attention and in expanding their awareness of the many potential benefits of IT. While the authors realize that successful implementation of this process depends on many outside factors (i.e., timing, management's eagerness to get involved, competitive pressures), they feel that once a company commits itself to the process, the rewards will be self-evident: management will improve their delivery of products and services and increase their effectiveness and productivity in managing the business. *SMR.*

During the past three decades, innumerable systems have been computerized to improve efficiency in accounting and operational activities. More recently, decision support systems (DSSs) have come into their own and are flourishing in many companies. Now, with the advent of the personal computer, computer-based assistance for *all* functions of the business is becoming widespread in a number of corporations.

In the midst of this computer-based explosion, however, one significant ingredient has been noticeably missing. For the most part, top management has stood—uninvolved—at the sidelines. Senior executives have been merely spectators in the development and use of information systems. With a few notable exceptions, they have given little thought to improving corporate effectiveness through their own involvement in systems planning and prioritization.

From *Sloan Management Review,* Summer 1984, Vol. 25, No. 4. Reprinted with permission.

Until very recently, this posture made some sense: information systems were considered primarily paperwork-processing systems, which were thought to have very little impact on organizational success or failure.

Today, however, managers are confronting forces that are indicating that widespread change is imminent. These forces include recognition of the limits to growth in the "smokestack industries"; competition for strategic niches; and new organization structures, which will often lead managers to unfamiliar territories. Thus, executives are eager to obtain the right information that will help them *manage change*.

How Information Technology Can Help Management

The movement of information systems hardware and software capabilities from merely facilitating the automation of clerical tasks to providing direct on-line support for decision making and other managerial processes has opened up new ways for top executives to view their information needs. Today, information technology (IT) gives managers an opportunity (1) to improve delivery of their products and services, and (2) to potentially increase their effectiveness and productivity in *managing* the businesses.

Finally, and, perhaps, most important, the new information/communication technology is having a significant impact on business strategy itself. For example, such companies as Merrill Lynch, American Hospital Supply, and McKesson have demonstrated that significant competitive advantages can be gained through judicial use of new technology.[1]

Clearly, it is time for top management to get off the sidelines. Recognizing that information is a strategic resource implies a clear need to link information systems to business strategy, and, especially, to ensure that business strategy is developed in the context of the new IT environment. In short, senior executives are increasingly feeling the need to become informed, energized, and engaged in information systems.

Our tenet in this article is that active engagement of top management with information systems is highly desirable in organizations of every size. Through a case study of Southwestern Ohio Steel (SOS), we present a three-phase process that we believe is instrumental in engaging top executives. The process is based on three major concepts:

- Critical Success Factors: to engage management's attention and ensure that the systems meet the most critical *business* needs;

- Decision Scenarios: to demonstrate to management that the systems to be developed will aid materially in the decision-making process; and
- Prototyping: to allow management to quickly reap system results that are to be a part of the development process, and to minimize initial costs.

Tying these three concepts together in a single development process accomplishes two major ends. First, it engages top management in the information systems planning process in a manner that is managerially meaningful. Second, it keeps management's attention and involvement throughout a rapid development process, since the systems priorities are targeted to support their decision-making processes.

Southwestern Ohio Steel: A Case Study

Southwestern Ohio Steel is one of the top three steel service centers in the U.S., with sales of approximately $100 million. Located in Hamilton, Ohio, with a processing plant in Middletown, Ohio, it employs more than 400 people. SOS is in the business of purchasing steel of differing quality, including primes and seconds as well as overruns, from major steel companies and selling it directly to hundreds of customers throughout the Midwest and contiguous states. The majority of the steel is processed (e.g., slitted, sheared) to some extent at the SOS plant before it is shipped to customers. By paying close attention to merchandising and manufacturing processes, SOS has developed an image of quality and service to both its customers and suppliers. A key contributor to SOS's image is its ability to provide customized products quickly as a result of extreme flexibility in its production schedule.

A Changing Environment

In early 1982, SOS utilized its existing computer installation to perform only routine accounting functions. However, several factors convinced management that a major review of its information systems capability was needed. These factors included:

- The company's planning process indicated that, despite possible stagnant growth in the steel industry, SOS could be expected to continue to grow significantly. Steel service centers were becoming an increasingly accepted and utilized service by American industry. Service centers' share of the steel end-market had grown from 17 percent in 1960 to 23 percent in the early 80s and was expected to be in the high 20s by 1990. Two competitive advantages facilitated SOS's decision. First, the steel centers' ability to hold and preprocess steel vastly decreased the inventories needed to be maintained by their customers. Second, as more firms turned to the essentials of Japanese management, a growing trend toward "just-in-time" delivery-oriented steel manufacturers was gaining a competitive edge over the less delivery-oriented ones.

These very positive factors, however, were in turn making the steel service-center business increasingly complex. Thus, the complexity of inventory and manufacturing management at SOS had grown significantly. With customers maintaining lower inventory levels, a vastly increased number of "hot orders" (or next-day delivery) was complicating plant operations. In addition, an increasing number of SOS customers were using manufacturing requirements planning (MRP) systems and were, therefore, calling for smaller lots and more frequent deliveries.

- At SOS, the information systems capability was strained. While existing systems, which were installed by the company's accounting firm, were doing a superb job of providing the accounting personnel with data, all key managerially oriented information remained manual.
- Finally, SOS's management team was changing. The first-generation management of the family-owned organization was giving way to a newer, younger managerial team, two of whom were sons of the original top management. Still, there was a need for departing key executives to pass on knowledge and to build into the systems some of the expertise and perspectives they had gained over the years.

Management's first impulse was to turn to a consulting firm it had used in the past. However, the solution this firm proposed came as a shock to the senior executives of the steel firm. It was a series of on-line computerized information systems based on "tried-and-true" conventional systems design and implementation processes. The cost was estimated at $2.4 million over the course of four years. Furthermore, major results and benefits would not be apparent until after the fourth year.

Management, therefore, rejected this approach. All members of the management team felt quite uncomfortable with the price tag, timeframe, and overall risk associated with the project. Most important, the exact tie between the systems proposed and the real needs of the business was unclear.

At this point, Tom Heldman, the chief financial officer, embarked on a search: "I wasn't quite sure what I wanted. But I knew there had to be a more creative approach toward assisting top management to understand its systems needs and to bring up systems more quickly, with reduced risk and cost." Heldman found what he wanted in the process described below.

A Three-Phase Process for Managerial Involvement

Figure 7.1 outlines the three major phases of the process used at Southwestern Ohio Steel. Each phase has two or three subparts and a particular "key technique" associated with it. The three techniques are what assure managerial involvement from the earliest planning stages through a very interactive implementation process. The three phases are:

- Linking information systems to the management needs of the business. Using critical success factors, management develops a clear definition of the business and comes to an agreement on the most critical business functions. In addition, management takes a first cut at stating its information systems needs in these critical areas.
- Developing systems priorities and gaining confidence in the recommended systems. Using the key technique, decision scenarios, management develops an understanding of how these systems, which were defined in phase one, would deliver the necessary information to support key decisions.
- Building low risk, managerially useful systems. Utilizing the key technique, prototyping, initial, partial systems are built and brought up very quickly at low cost. In working with early, limited—but operational—versions of these systems, management is able to grasp more fully their usefulness and to authorize, with significantly greater comfort, continued system development. As a by-product, initial financial benefits from these systems are received very quickly.

Phase One: Linking Information Systems to the Business

This phase emphasizes understanding the business, focuses on the few factors that drive the business, and actively engages management in the process. Only at the very end of this phase is the initial link made to information requirements for the key areas of the business. As Figure 7.1 shows, the first phase is divided into three steps: (1) an introductory workshop, (2) critical success factors (CSFs) interviews, and (3) an all-important "focusing workshop" in which the results of the interviews and their implications are evaluated and discussed very thoroughly.

Step 1: Introductory Workshop

Five key members of the SOS management team participated in this workshop. They were William Huber, chairman of the board; Joseph Wolf, presi-

Phase One: Linking Information Systems to the Management Needs of the Business. Key Technique: Critical Success Factors Process

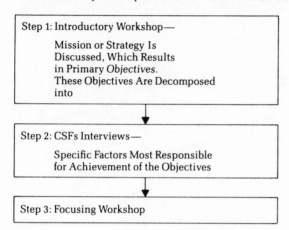

Step 1: Introductory Workshop—

Mission or Strategy Is
Discussed, Which Results
in Primary *Objectives.*
These Objectives Are Decomposed
into

Step 2: CSFs Interviews—

Specific Factors Most Responsible
for Achievement of the Objectives

Step 3: Focusing Workshop

Phase Two: Developing Systems Priorities and Gaining Confidence in Recommended Systems. Key Technique: Decision Scenarios

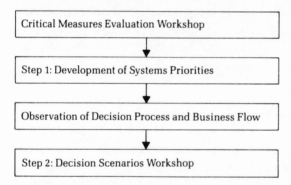

Critical Measures Evaluation Workshop

Step 1: Development of Systems Priorities

Observation of Decision Process and Business Flow

Step 2: Decision Scenarios Workshop

Phase Three: Rapid Development of Low Risk, Managerially Useful Systems. Key Technique: Prototype Development, Implementation, Use, & Refinement

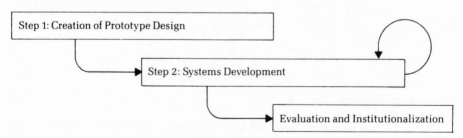

Step 1: Creation of Prototype Design

Step 2: Systems Development

Evaluation and Institutionalization

Figure 7.1   A Three-Phase Process for Managerial Involvement

dent; Tom Heldman, vice-president of finance; Jacque Huber, vice-president of sales; and Paul Pappenheimer, vice-president of materials.

In the first workshop session, the consultants—having already completed their introductory "homework" about the company—presented the three-phase-process approach to determine what the company's information needs would be. The CSF method and the prototype concept were also described here. The major step was to discuss and agree upon company objectives.

William Huber found this approach very much to his liking, even though he was initially skeptical. Before the workshop, he told Heldman: "Don't let anybody ask me what information I need. People don't know what they need." Nonetheless, the approach of developing information systems based on the *understandable* information imperatives of critical business functions, not on vaguely guessed-at information "needs," caught his attention. Consequently, he became an active and influential participant throughout the workshop, passing on to the younger management team much knowledge that he had acquired in the several decades of his managing the business.

Four benefits emerged from the workshop:

1. A *managerial* perspective for systems development, that is, one of linking information systems needs and priorities to the most important business activities of the executives, was established;
2. An initial step was made toward the establishment of business priorities through the definition—essentially, a redefinition—of corporate goals;
3. Active involvement of the key member of the executive team, the chairman of the board, was obtained; and
4. The techniques that were to be utilized during the process were explained to the SOS executives.

Step 2: CSFs Interviews

The critical success factors method is a technique designed to help managers and system designers identify the management information necessary to support the key business areas.[2] For an individual manager, CSFs are the few key areas in which successful performance will lead to the achievement of the manager's objectives. In effect, critical success factors are the means to the objectives—which are the desired ends. On a corporate level, CSFs are the key areas on which the company must focus in order to achieve its objectives.

The CSF interview process is designed to have each manager explicitly state those factors that are critical, both for himself and for the corporation. By voicing these CSFs, managers are able to sharpen their understanding of the business's priority areas. The ways in which the CSFs might be measured are also discussed, which leads to considering what information is necessary.

At SOS the five key executives and ten other key managers were interviewed. In addition to further communicating the desire to link all systems development strongly to the needs of the business, the interviewing process also helped to clarify the understanding of the business, the role of each individual, and the culture of the organization.

Step 3: Focusing Workshop

Preparation for the focusing workshop on management's part consists of reading interview summaries, which are then distributed after they have been reviewed by the individual participants. At the workshop, the consultants present a "strawman" of corporate mission, objectives, and CSFs—all constructed from the analysis of the introductory workshop and interviews. The strawman provides a basis for extended, often intense, discussion and the key to uncover varying perceptions and disagreements among the management team. This is the most significant and difficult step in the first phase, for different individual perspectives, managerial loyalties, and desires emerge. Thus, leadership by corporate management is essential in untangling the myriad of differences and focusing on the core elements of the business. The end result is agreement on the company's missions and goals.

During the focusing workshop at SOS, corporate objectives developed in the introductory workshop were reaffirmed. Most of these objectives were related to financial and marketing aspects of the business. From a set of forty initially suggested critical success factors, which were obtained through the interviews, four CSFs emerged:

- Maintaining excellent supplier relationships,
- Maintaining or improving customer relationships,
- Merchandising available inventory to its most value-added use, and
- Using available capital and human resources efficiently and effectively.

As Tom Heldman notes: "This is the key meeting. The interviews are merely a preliminary, a 'softening-up' process in which managers get an initial opportunity to think deeply about the corporation, as well as to develop relationships with the consultants."

In the course of the focusing workshop, what had previously been implicit was made explicit—sometimes with surprising and insightful results. In Jacque Huber's words: "We all knew what was critical for our company, but the discussion—sharing and agreeing—was really important. What came out of it was a minor revelation. Seeing it on the blackboard in black and white is much more significant than carrying around a set of ideas which are merely intuitively felt."

Another SOS executive portrays the managerial insights gained from focusing on the organization's CSFs in a somewhat different way: "During the meeting, our concept of our organizational structure went from an organizational chart that looked like [Figure 7.2] to one that looked like [Figure 7.3]. This was important. It affected our system's design enormously. More importantly, it has affected the way we manage the business."

Although the interpersonal skills and business knowledge of the consulting team running the focusing workshop are very significant, the workshop technique itself readily captures the attention and involvement of the management team and eases the seminar leadership job. Again, Heldman sums it up: "Focusing on 'what makes the company a success' intrigued almost all of top management. It appealed to a group of good managers, allowing them to engage in a discussion of what they knew best and what seemed important to them."

Phase Two: Developing Systems Priorities

In the second phase, another workshop is held to define the set of measures that would be used to evaluate the CSFs (see Table 7.1). The measures are hard and soft data which managers use to monitor the performance and behavior of each CSF. In the SOS workshop, for example, current measures and data used for decision making were examined through observations of business activities.

Finally, initial steps are taken to assess from management's viewpoint the implications of the set of objectives, CSFs, and measures for information systems priorities. As Figure 7.1 illustrates, phase two has two major steps:

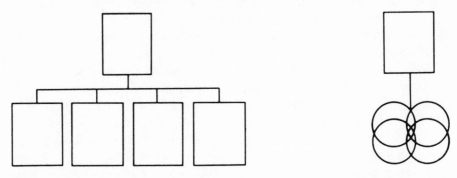

Figure 7.2   **Figure 7.3**

Table 7.1 Measures of One CSF

CSF	Measures	Data Type	Current Measure
Customer	Volume	H	M
Relations	Inquiries	H	M
	Order/bid ratio	H	M
	Complaints and/or rejections of materials	H	M
	Customer turnover or lost accounts	H	M
	Decline in volume with customer	H	M
	Program account actual volume vs. customer and SOS forecasts	H	A
	New accounts	H	M
	Conversions to program accounts	H	U
	On-time delivery:	H	A
	—to first promised date		
	—to final need date		
	Trends in credit rejections	H	U
	Tone of voice (*esp. during late delivery calls*)	S	A
	Finance and credit "handling" feedback	S	A

Key:
H=Hard
S=Soft
M=Measured
A=Data Available
U=Data Unavailable

(1) the development of systems priorities and (2) the gaining of managerial confidence, through the use of decision scenarios, that the systems priorities will support key decisions.

Step 1: Development of Systems Priorities

At the same time that the results of the interviews and sessions were being reviewed, the project team began studying the business in more depth. At the end of this period, three distinct systems priorities that would support the fundamental managerial processes were identified: the buying and inventory process, the marketing of steel, and the production scheduling process.

An analysis of these three proposed systems showed that each would significantly affect the CSFs of the firm. Inventory management would affect all of the CSFs, especially supplier relationships and efficient use of resources. The marketing system would have a direct impact on customer relationships and merchandising. Finally, production scheduling would be significant with regard to the critical areas of efficient and effective use of resources, merchandising, and customer relationships.

In general, the transition from a business focus on objectives and CSFs to one on systems definition is not a straightforward, simple process: It is more an art form than a science. In other words, such a transition relies heavily on the technical expertise, systems knowledge, and all-around expertise of the design team. But at SOS, as in other cases in which we have been involved, the significant systems needs were strongly indicated from the preceding *managerial* discussion of goals, CSFs, and measures.

Step 2: Decision Scenarios Workshop

While observing the key managers in their daily activities, the project team noted recurring decisions along with the questions managers asked of themselves and others in order to make these decisions. From these "decision situations," a set of "decision scenarios" was developed. Each decision scenario was concerned with a particular managerial event and the questions that might have been instrumental in the formulation of a decision. All relevant questions, both those which could be answered by computer-based data and those which could not, were included in the scenario.

In another session, the three proposed prototype systems were outlined to the managerial team. This particular session, however, centered on the "decision scenarios." A sample decision scenario is presented in Tables 7.2 and 7.3. By working through a series of scenarios, the managers were able to gain a much greater familiarity with and insight into the workings of the proposed systems. They were able to see what questions would be answered by the new systems, what questions would not be answered, and how the data would be presented through "paper models" of proposed screen formats.

During this session, the technical environment necessary to support the systems, the necessary data in the system, and the source and frequency of data collection were also discussed. After the SOS management confirmed that the systems were appropriate, the project team began working on the design details of the system.

Phase Three: Creating Prototypes and Implementing Actual Systems

As Figure 7.1 shows, the final phase of the process contains two major steps: (1) the creation of an initial, detailed prototype design and (2) actual systems development.

Step 1: Creation of a Prototype Design

Even after the systems are agreed upon, the exact method of prototyping must be decided and the right type of prototype must be selected. So far,

Table 7.2 A Sample Decision Scenario

Purchasing Scenario: The inventory manager receives a call from a supplier offering an extremely attractive purchase opportunity: a 15-ton slab that can be rolled to any width from 57¼ to 59¾ in either cold rolled or galvanized prime coil. The price is 19 cents per pound.

Questions Asked:
What does the economy look like overall?
How have orders been keeping up?
—Are contract customers meeting expectations/using their reserves?
—What was last week's order volume in prime roll?*

What are prime cold rolled inventory levels?*
—Are we particularly low in any gage?
—Have we been too high in this area?
—What can I expect to use in the next two months?

What is the supplier's situation?
—Is this a "once-in-a-lifetime" situation?
—How badly do they need us here?
—Is this price likely to be offered again?

What have I paid for this item in the past?*

Who will get it if we refuse it?

*Denotes questions that can be answered by the proposed system.

Table 7.3 Paper Model of Output: Inventory Levels

To Review Cold Rolled Steel Inventory Levels

Product Description: CR
Grade: SOS
Gages[1]:   ALL

Gage[2]	On Hand	On Order	Total	Available to Promise[3]	Percent Available to Promise	Last Month Sales	Weeks of Sales[4]
.022	232	51	283	35	12	50	25
.026	636	0	636	101	16	135	20
.032	1,450	474	2,014	234	12	328	27
.044	6,213	1,352	7,565	945	13	1,324	25
.055	5,769	1,256	7,025	939	14	1,229	25
.068	192	87	279	0	0	41	30
.097	143	0	143	0	0	31	20
.112	67	0	67	0	0	14	21
Total	14,792	3,220	18,012	2,250	12.5	3,152	—

[1]A specific gage (i.e., .031), range of gages (i.e., .031, .044), all gages=ALL.
[2]Gages without inventory do not appear.
[3]Neither reserved for program account nor assigned.
[4]On hand plus on order less open orders (last month's sales/days in month: Column 7).

it appears that there are three significantly different kinds of prototypes: an information data base, a pilot system, and a "classical" prototype. Interestingly enough, all three prototypes were called for at SOS.

- An information data base for marketing support. By its very nature, an information data base, which is a collection of data made accessible to users, is a prototype. No matter how carefully designed the initial system is, it is impossible to have a manager define the exact information he or she will use to make decisions. Most decision-making processes are tenuously understood at best, and knowledge of the data needed for them prior to automation is incomplete. Moreover, as managers use a data base, they gain further insight into the data they really need and the methods of access that they desire in order to use that data.

    At SOS, sales support was provided by an information data base originally designated to include information on customers, potential customers, open orders, and accounts receivable. The majority of the CSF measures stated in Table 7.1 were included in one form or another. This prototype was, in current parlance, a decision support system.

- A pilot system for inventory management. Pilot systems and pilot plants have been built as part of research and development processes for decades. These systems are a miniature replication of the final production plan. Tests are made to make sure that the pilot will perform the needed function. If all goes well, the process is then expanded in scale to the full production system. The "pilot" class of prototype works similarly: A piece of an entire system with all its functions is developed. The pilot that was developed at SOS was an inventory management system: One separable segment of the inventory, approximately 15 percent, was initially put on the computer.

- A classical prototype: production scheduling. A prototype system—which, according to a dictionary definition, "exhibits the essential features of a later type"—is built with an initial fundamental, yet incomplete, set of functions. The prototype system is then exercised to illustrate what it can do. Its functionality is expected to increase later on.[3]

    At SOS, a production scheduling prototype was designed to allow managers to queue work at machines, generate schedules based on job priorities, and minimize set-up time. In DSS mode, the computer performs some functions automatically and interacts with schedulers to perform other functions. Increased functionality is continually being built into the prototype.

A major feature of each of the prototype systems developed at SOS is its ability to provide some data for all levels of management. (Most systems that are routinely developed today emphasize only a single-level management

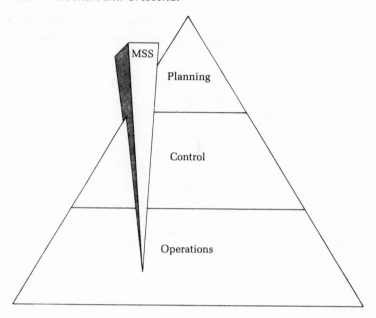

Figure 7.4   Management Support System (MSS)

function—for example, operational control, management control, or strategic planning).[4] At SOS, however, a top-down managerial approach ensures that the systems not only contain the relevant data for operational purposes, but also provide the raw material necessary for managers to make decisions regarding management control applications and strategic planning. Figure 7.4 shows that emphasis is placed on the last two functions, indicated by the heavy wedge of the slice at the top of the figure.

At SOS, not all of the key executives were committed until after the prototyping concept was fully evident. Although most of them, during the CSF phase, were intrigued, and even excited with the idea of actually linking systems to business needs, Paul Pappenheimer, for one, was not. He remained skeptical: "I had heard a great number of computer horror stories," he recalled. He was fearful that control of the inventory would be lost in the conversion process and that the computer could not support his somewhat unique inventory needs. (Each item of inventory is different at SOS in that it varies in quality, size, and many other attributes. Each steel coil needs a full description.) It was not until decision scenarios were utilized and an early prototype design was well under way that Pappenheimer fully understood the prototype approach and felt comfortable with it. He finally perceived the prototype concept as a means of lowering the company's (and his) risks to an acceptable level. Recalling his experience, Pappenheimer says: "I would have slept better at night if they [the consultants] would have fully communicated the prototype concept from the beginning. Once the idea finally struck me, it really turned me on. I went from negative to highly enthusiastic."

Finally, it was Heldman who articulated the unique advantage of the prototype concept: "We're not just talking about monetary risk here, although this is certainly a factor. Managers at all levels are also concerned about the risk in the development of a nonviable system to which the company is committed because of the expenditure. For some, it is only when they realize that they can get their hands on the prototype at an early stage and assess its utility before going forward that they can relax."

In short, a prototype:

- Reduces monetary risk,
- Reduces business risk, and
- Allows a manager to inspect, work with, and shape the product as it is being developed to a point where he or she feels comfortable with it in all dimensions.

Step 2: Systems Development

Actual development of all of the prototypes was done on an IBM System 38, using RPGIII. The system now has twenty-eight terminals with additional terminals on order. The final detailed design and programming were performed by the SOS staff with the aid of an outside programmer who was proficient in RPGIII. The initial prototype development period was short for all systems. For example, the initial inventory prototype was up in two months. After three months of operation, a significant redesign added new functions. This redesign process was repeated again after an additional six months, fully illustrating the concept of "evolutionary design."[5]

The systems are now used by operational personnel and managers at all levels. Some standard reports are issued, but most of the interaction is through menu-based interactive processing. More significant, today a number of SOS personnel at all levels are learning the available query language for the System 38 that will allow them to interrogate the files on their own. In fact, one of the first persons to attend the query school and to use the facility actively was Jacque Huber: "If I could tell a staff person what I wanted in the past, I can write my query today. I get my answers faster."

Summary

Figure 7.1 summarizes the three-phase process as perceived by the SOS management. The figure, however, does not show the considerable "backroom" effort that was made by both the consultants and the systems developers. It should be stressed that it is imperative that the consultants gain some background knowledge about the company before the first phase. There is also a need for them to understand the details of some of the operational activities before the prototypes are sketched out. These behind-the-scenes steps are necessary if one wishes to implement this three-phase process. (The actual creation of data bases and the development of control procedures to assure the appropriate updating of data must be carried out by operational personnel during the prototype system development stages.)

The Benefits of the Three-Phase Process

Much has been accomplished at SOS through the use of this process. On one level, all three systems are up and functioning, thereby providing the usual advantages of computerizing marketing data, inventory control, and production scheduling. The advantages gained include:

- Immediate access to order status. "Now," says saleswoman Brenda Grant, "you can check exactly where your order is in the production system while keeping the customer on hold. You don't have to check with the plant and then make those long-distance calls back." Both internal and external telephone tag is avoided. Another salesman comments: "With the new system, what used to take an hour now takes only a minute or two."
- A significant increase in the number of sales calls that can be made per salesperson. Time that used to be "wasted" in answering customer queries and in searching for raw material inventory status has been eliminated. In addition, customer and prospect data, which are available in the marketing information data base, enables salespeople to prepare for "cold calls" more efficiently.
- Improved understanding of customers. By using the available query system, Jacque Huber and the sales personnel are able to analyze customer buying patterns to improve production efficiency.
- Improved management of slow-moving inventory. Both visibility into the entire inventory status and analytic capability make this kind of management possible. Pappenheimer cites the particular ability to get to past usage data which "previously were only in my head."

- More accurate inventory control. John Antes, manager of inventory and material assignment, says: "The computer is faster and more accurate. There are controls and validations. There were some errors before with the manual system."
- Improved production scheduling. Greg Parsley, manager of the first shift in the plant, notes: "The system allows us to foresee problems and to react to them sooner. Before, we never knew where we would be in the future until we were there."
- Reduction in plant personnel. With the introduction of the system, plant management has reduced its staff while still maintaining the workload. A combination of factors made this possible: improved scheduling, reduced need to interact with sales personnel, reduced time in searching for or correcting lost or inaccurate paper work, and improved visibility into aspects of the plant.

On a more significant level, the three-phase process has strongly affected the management team in a very positive way. The questions one asks in evaluating a system are:

- Did it work? Was something beneficial accomplished?
- What is management's attitude?
- Is management moving ahead?

The answer to the first question is given in the section above. As to the second question, there is a clear sense of both success and comfort in the top-management team at SOS today. As Wolf, the president, notes: "Our good feelings today come from an approach to information systems that is based on managing the business." Jacque Huber says that the SOS management team, which initially was highly nervous that it would "mess with something that works" and "lose control," was able to "come together," through this process, on a systems plan. In addition, he says: "We have achieved in nine months at far lower cost what we expected would take six years under the previously proposed plan." Managerial attitude also appears to have been affected by four other results of the process:

- A sharper focus in the minds of all top managers on the few important things to which they must direct their attention.
- An increased understanding of the interdependence of the various parts of the business and the ability, through the computer system, to take advantage of this knowledge.
- The transfer of a sizable segment of this knowledge from the retiring chairman to the younger management team. This was made possible through the multiple workshops in which various aspects of the business, particularly

the most critical ones, were discussed. For Heldman, who was the newest member of the management team, "the insights gained into the company" were extremely useful. He further notes: "I believe that for any information systems officer who may have been slightly on the 'outside,' this process would provide tremendous insights into the company and the ways in which top management thinks."

- The direct terminal-based access that management now has allows them to gather data on various aspects of the status of the company. Huber and Pappenheimer rely on this daily.

It is also clear that the process will have a continuing effect on the company. For example:

- The three existing prototype systems are continually being expanded on in scope and functions;
- CEO Wolf has just commissioned a prototype system to develop a "cost model" for SOS—a system that he will be able to access directly;
- Additional personnel is being sent to "query" school; and
- CSF use is being extended. Jacque Huber states: "A good manager and his team can use CSFs in all phases of business activity. What is needed is a broad educational program to introduce and promote the concepts of CSFs. I plan to introduce CSFs to my sales managers soon."

Can the Process Work in Other Companies?

Is the process replicable in other companies? SOS is a medium-sized company in a single industry with a capable management team. (It goes without saying that good management *is* necessary, for no consulting team can help inadequate management develop a clear focus.) However, this process does not work only in medium-sized single industries. Index Systems Inc., for example, has used the CSF and prototyping phases many times with management teams in half-billion-dollar companies and divisions of multibillion-dollar organizations. Decision scenarios, the newest input into the process, also appear to be working well in other organizations.

It should be stated that we believe this process will *not* work at all times in all companies. Timing is key. Management must be ready to be involved. Competitive pressures, a felt need to rethink computer priorities, or sheer awareness of the increasing strategic importance of information systems are all among a long list of factors on which the outcome of the process is dependent. Given that these conditions are increasingly evident in many organizations, successful implementation of the process occurs because of the following:

- An easy and quick link to top management is made. As Jacque Huber notes: "The businessman can relate to CSFs. They make sense. They are a natural extension of objectives and the planning process."
- Management focuses on those areas of the business it deems important. Thus management feels comfortable about building information systems to support these areas. Huber again states: "The businessman needs to be reminded to focus on the means after the ends have been determined. The CSF process is the best focusing device I have ever been exposed to."
- Real management involvement is engaged. Heldman notes: "Most top executives really provide only token 'support' for information systems. In this process, management spent considerable time talking about its own business. They were involved. And a great amount of energy of the executive group went into the process. Token 'support' is not enough. One winds up with systems that do not affect the guts of the business."
- The consultants (whether internal or external) gain significant insight into the business and therefore are more effective. In addition to providing managerial focus, this process enables the system designers to better understand management and its needs. Several days of managerial interaction centered on the business itself provide a wealth of company-specific knowledge. As Pappenheimer notes: "The previous consultants who submitted the $2.4-million bid never grasped the business. They were working from an information technology and systems capability viewpoint, rather than from a business perspective. Index grew to know us."
- Finally, managers recognize that this process involves lower risk. There is a strong managerial bias against committing vast sums of money in areas one does not fully understand. The CSFs provided the knowledge confirming why the systems should be developed. Decision scenarios convinced management that the particular systems would provide the information they needed to ask major questions at all levels of management. And the prototypes made it possible for management to see what the systems' capability would be on a small scale before they committed all the funds to the project. In summary, Heldman states: "The organizational impact and change as a result of the systems have been profound. In a year when our marketplace is collapsing, we have been able to stay ahead, respond, and serve our customers better. This is a success story."

8

Systems Planning in the Information Age

Cornelius H. Sullivan, Jr.

Senior executives in American business are attaching increasing importance to information technology, and their line managers are taking greater responsibility for it. As these trends continue, interest naturally grows in systems management disciplines, particularly strategic planning. This article analyzes past and current systems planning practices, and introduces the idea of information technology architecture planning. Results of empirical research are presented to show which kinds of planning work best in different environments. Finally, a frame of reference is developed to suggest how to make planning relevant and effective in the emerging information age. *SMR.*

"Are we moving forward or not?" asked the bewildered vice-president in charge of strategic planning for information systems at a large financial services institution. "Clearly, we are spending a lot of money on systems. More employees and customers than ever rely on our technology. My boss reports three levels higher in the management hierarchy than he did ten years ago. So do I.

"On the other hand," he went on to admit, "my manager now has only one-fifth the number of people working for him that he had four years ago. Today he controls about 30 percent of the systems budget, down from 80 percent as recently as 1978. My guess is that we don't know where half the computers in our company are anymore. Many of my phone calls are not returned.

"How do we function in this environment?" he mused. "What is our role? How should we plan? Need we bother to try?"

Reservations about the efficacy of strategic planning for information systems have become widespread, and they are frequently justified. Many companies, like this firm, have actually used a series of different approaches. Yet, these changes of approach have been indicative neither of aimless wandering nor of futility. On the contrary, each methodology has made its legitimate

From *Sloan Management Review*, Winter 1985, Vol. 26, No. 2. Reprinted with permission.

contribution to our growing understanding of the challenge of effective planning. In the long run, however, all have turned out to be partial viewpoints with only temporary appeal. Something *new* is necessary: In the information age, many firms are turning from conventional approaches to an architectural perspective.

Information Systems Planning in Transition

Viewing information technology from an architectural perspective is a radical departure from the past. Almost twenty years ago, when formal information systems planning was first initiated at many firms, the leading approach was a method called the stages of growth (SOG).

The Stages of Growth Approach

Typically, when SOG came into vogue, a massive computer room was being built, substantial numbers of programmers and analysts were being hired, and the first large-scale systems development projects were being undertaken. The task at hand was to build an unfamiliar and expensive enterprise within an enterprise. The planning response was to borrow from the social sciences a notion that organizations must assimilate this kind of change through a predictable sequence of steps at a modest pace. The theory held that the sequence, with stages of initiation and expansion followed by consolidation and maturity, would be similar at all firms.[1]

The idea of stages of growth has been used to explain almost everything—from sex and childhood to grief and revolution. In the salad days of data processing, there were observable patterns of expenditure and organizational learning. The stages of growth hypothesis institutionalized the process of benefiting from the experience of others, primarily by promoting management controls during the crucial transition from a period of great expansion to one of consolidation. SOG planning had the virtue of looking at the data-processing resource in a holistic fashion. It also killed the old notion that the best data-processing manager was simply the best programmer; the computer room was becoming professionalized.

SOG Dated by Technological Change.
However valuable it may once have been, the stages of growth approach has been seriously dated by technological change. Specifically, two broad transformations have occurred since the initial explosion of business data processing in the early- to mid-1960s. First came data resource technology, in the form of inexpensive mass-storage devices and com-

mercial database management packages. Second, on-line systems spurred a massive new wave of ideas for applying technology to business purposes. The exploitation of on-line technology depended more on the ability of a company to retrofit stored data than on strict adherence to prescribed organizational development processes. Including the separation of a corporation's abstract data structures from its applications programs, on the one hand, and from its physical storage media, on the other, this retrofitting caused a change in perspective, with the emphasis in information systems shifting from applications and processing management to data and information resource management. With this fundamental shift came a different set of planning requirements.

Business Systems Planning

The planning response to this new environment is well represented by IBM's business systems planning (BSP) package. BSP focuses less on developing organizational structures and disciplines necessary to manage the computer room than on conceptualizing and designing the overall corporate data resource. Rather than identifying isolated applications projects, BSP takes a coordinated intersystem view. Unlike the theory-driven stages of growth approach, BSP is business oriented: BSP recommendations derive from the construction of an empirical model of a particular business enterprise and its information resource. While shifting the perspective from applications to information, BSP also changes the planning goal from one of following universally prescribed actions to one of developing highly customized goals.[2]

The Limitations of BSP.   Despite these advances, BSP has limitations. While SOG realistically stresses the need to know where a company stands today before trying to plan where it can go tomorrow, BSP is idealistic: it assumes—quite incorrectly in most cases—the opportunity to rationalize data structures as if there were no legacy from the past. With sales to fulfil and books to close, it is a rare firm that can afford to build a corporate database in one dramatic effort; the process must be gradual.

The other major limitation of BSP is that it was designed for centralized environments. This is not surprising, considering that it was developed and promoted by IBM during a period when the firm's principal products were mainframe computers. Nothing in the original methodology helps an organization if its computing resource has become organizationally or physically decentralized—that is, if a centralized mainframe database management program will not work.

The Impact of Decentralization

Decentralization is precisely what began to take place in the late 1970s. The technological vanguard of this outward thrust included minicomputers with dedicated applications packages to mechanize specialized business functions. Growing experience and comfort with information technology among line managers, coupled with a clearer sense of the impact of technology on their business operations, caused them to assert more direct control over systems activities. Emerging technologies such as office automation, robotics, and CAD/CAM also contributed to the process. Personal and home computing have accelerated the trend. (Just wait for smart phones.)

As minis and micros saturate a company, and as systems responsibilities appear in the job functions of more and more employees, organizational learning continues to take place, but varies too much from one part of the organization to the next to use SOG as a proactive basis for planning. Nor is BSP, with its assumption of a central repository of data, particularly relevant.

Both approaches have been enhanced to reflect underlying changes in technology and the way it is commercially deployed and managed. More stages and a new learning curve have been added to the original SOG worldview. BSP has also changed substantially, and data resource planning has been generally superseded by the broader notion of information resource management (IRM). IRM retains the information focus of BSP, but brings back into the planning process the management issues of organizational change and commitment. By combining the data orientation with the management perspective, IRM integrates many of the best aspects of stages of growth and BSP planning.[3]

Nevertheless, with information technology not only growing in size and importance but also becoming increasingly decentralized, neither of these planning perspectives has proven entirely satisfactory, even with updating. Today, one characteristic question that managers increasingly ask of information systems professionals is "Where is what I want?" In a world of multiple systems and multiple databases, decision support has become a complex task of fetching, revising, condensing, assembling, interpreting, and presenting information from many sources to numerous destinations.

Critical Success Factors

A new planning response to this environment has been critical success factors (CSFs) planning. This approach assists management in the increasingly important job of identifying the individual requirements for information systems. It generally boils down to a list of crucial information and analyses that are not currently at hand, but that subsequent systems development efforts could make available. In this sense, critical success factors planning is one of the first planning efforts to be communications oriented. Rather than focusing on processing or data, as have its predecessors, CSF begins to take a networking perspective.[4]

Although extremely useful, CSF planning is not a complete planning methodology. It assumes a good deal of awareness about information systems on the part of the user, and is more helpful in designing support systems for isolated senior executives than in resolving companywide issues of integrated information systems. While it fills a niche, the limitations of this approach for interdepartmental systems projects make it no more of a methodological panacea than its predecessors. As the bank vice-president mentioned above put it, "We need some overarching perspective, some way of looking at the whole problem. So far we have been dealing with isolated pieces, and tending to deal with them serially, one at a time."

Planning in Today's Systems Environments

The quest for an effective methodology motivated us to conduct a thorough review of information systems planning efforts at thirty-seven major U.S. companies. In each case the systems environment was profiled in terms of a variety of organizational and technological factors. Then a sample of managers, users, and technicians in each company rated the overall effectiveness of their planning process. Analysis of the profiles and ratings revealed that only two of the measured factors are closely correlated to high ratings for the particular planning methodology used in a company.[5]

Infusion

One of the correlated factors is *infusion*. This is the degree to which information technology has penetrated a company in terms of importance, impact, or significance. Traditionally, information technology has been of only tactical significance in most companies—for payroll, accounting functions, and isolated sales or production reports. Increasing numbers of firms, however, are using computers in ways that dramatically change their competitive postures. Sometimes this is by lowering costs significantly; more frequently it is by increasing revenue, as information systems become the basis for new or enhanced products and services. A company with a low degree of information technology infusion finds that computers are not yet strategic to its business. A firm with a high degree of infusion finds the technology crucial.

Diffusion

The other factor is *diffusion*. Diffusion means decentralization, or the degree to which technology has been disseminated or scattered throughout the company. Diffusion may take place in organizational terms, as companies use information technology in support of more and more functions and business units. Diffusion may occur in physical terms, as companies install minicomputers, word processors, process control devices, and micros. Diffusion may also take place in terms of responsibility, as line managers take more control of systems design, development, and operations.

A company with a low degree of diffusion is one with centralized mainframe computers and a strong data-processing function consolidating all systems design, development, and operations within one management hierarchy. A company with a high degree of diffusion is one in which a considerable number of minicomputers and microprocessors have appeared in different places, systems management functions are not necessarily controlled by the same management team, and business unit and functional managers have taken considerable responsibility for the development and operation of their own information systems.

Correlations with Planning Methods

The degrees of infusion and diffusion of technology have no significant correlation with the kinds of planning processes used by twenty-two of the companies analyzed, which view their current planning methodology as no more than moderately effective. However, the connection between type of planning and the extent of infusion and diffusion is quite clear at the fifteen firms studied that rate themselves as having highly effective planning. If the degrees of infusion and diffusion are used as the coordinates on a two-dimensional matrix, and companies with high effectiveness ratings are plotted in the matrix, as in Figure 8.1, the results are striking.

Four Systems Environments

Figure 8.1 shows that each of the three major approaches to information systems planning seems to work in one particular quadrant of the matrix. Names are given to these quadrants in Figure 8.2. The stages of growth method applies in what we call a *traditional environment,* in which both infusion and diffusion are low. This is the conventional data-processing shop, consisting of a computer center and the associated support organization. It operates as a corporate utility and endeavors to achieve economies of scale. The strategic planning objective is to manage this basic processing resource

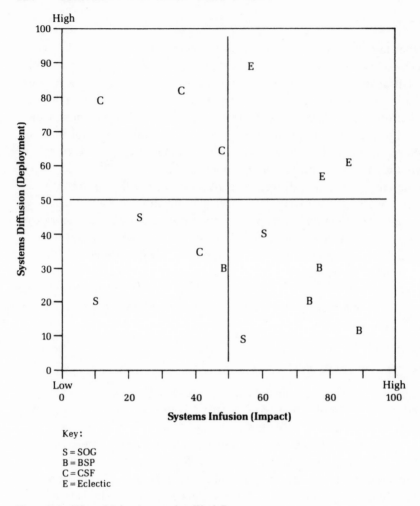

Figure 8.1   Where Major Approaches Work Best

efficiently. Capacity planning and systems development methodologies are major planning elements.

Business systems planning and information resources management work in the backbone environment, in which computing has become more strategic to the company, but it is still centralized in the manner of its deployment. Here, the computing effort begins to take on qualities of a factory. A key issue, as in any factory, is achieving engineering flexibility for retooling. The disciplines of data and information resource management are called upon for this flexibility, resulting in a focus on activities such as implementing and supporting a

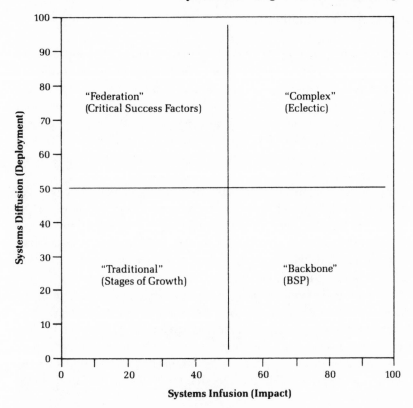

Figure 8.2 Technology Planning Environments

database management system, retrofitting existing systems to it, introducing a data dictionary, and educating senior managers about the importance of viewing information as a corporate asset.

CSF planning apparently is best suited to the environment in which technology is more distributed than it is crucial—high diffusion but low infusion. This is a *federation,* a collection of loosely coupled entities. As in the Hapsburg Empire, some degree of cooperation is necessary. If it doesn't exist, it generally must be invented to enable the organization to accomplish basic systems tasks. Here the central issue is deciding what information to share and allowing reasonable access to remote data and programs. Some kind of shared communications utility or networking umbrella frequently emerges in this environment to coordinate otherwise separate and independent processing and data resources.

Planning Issues in the Information Age

What about the fourth quadrant? The problem of our planning vice-president, and that of his counterparts at an increasing number of companies, is not that they have failed to use and master appropriate planning disciplines as their firms have assimilated progress in information technology. They seem, albeit intuitively, to have stayed on track while moving through the matrix over time from one quadrant to another. But now they are in a complex environment, in which both infusion and diffusion are high. Essentially, they have entered the information age.

Companies in the complex environment are discovering that there is as yet no planning methodology well suited to their needs. Certainly none of the popular packages works especially well. Instead, in this quadrant, firms have been developing eclectic approaches tailored to meet specific needs. Ironically, these are some of the same companies that, as a matter of policy, are increasingly turning outside whenever possible for software packages and turnkey systems for new applications. They are deciding to focus in-house development attention not on software programming, but on strategic planning. As information technology becomes embedded in the firm, the process of ensuring that it is effective is no longer entrusted to mechanistic planning procedures from a bygone era. Rather, the consensus is that a company must find or develop an approach with features that match its unique information-age requirements.

Transforming the Applications Development Portfolio

In the course of developing a unique approach to information planning, companies find that a series of fourth-quadrant planning issues appear. One is the transformation of the applications development portfolio. Previously focused on mechanizing existing business activities and functions, the new development thrust becomes product oriented. Many firms find that information technology can be the basis of new products or can better differentiate existing ones. This is fairly obvious in the financial services and information industries, such as banking and publishing. But it is frequently no less the case in manufacturing, distribution, and other sectors of the economy. It often seems as if the more conventional, mundane, and commoditylike the products of a firm, the easier it is to find—and the greater the advantage there is in finding—ways to add value to products by using information systems. In fields as diverse as hospital-equipment supply, industrial abrasives, agricultural implements, and building materials, cases abound where an ingenious systems executive has joined forces with line managers and the marketing department to get information technology out of the back office and new products out the front door.

Retooling Management Disciplines

A second fourth-quadrant issue is the retooling of management disciplines. In the presence of a problem, a standard American response is to commence counting things. The common data-processing reaction to office automation, for example, was to take elaborate inventories of word-processing equipment. One bank made use of an elegant relational database management system for the purpose. But why? Arithmetic is no substitute for insight and foresight. By nurturing emerging technologies, the effective information systems executive will become less of a controller than a change agent. But by delegating routine systems development and operation to line units, he or she will assume more responsibility for education and experimentation.

Supporting New Organizational Designs

In the information age, technology must be used to support new forms of organizational design. Matrix management enjoyed a certain vogue two decades ago, but fell abruptly into disrepute. This was largely because it did not work, at least not in large corporations. While becoming diversified and multinational, a company clearly needs to find a way to manage across functions, business units, products, markets, and geographical regions. Although advances in the practice of accounting seemed to make this feasible as early as the 1960s, the array of management schemes required incredible volumes of information exchange in nonhierarchical patterns in order to succeed. Communications technologies at the time were limited largely to the nineteenth-century telephone system, the eighteenth-century mail system, and the cultural tradition of face-to-face meetings, which probably dates from the Pleistocene era. More recently, a rich variety of teleconferencing and store/forward technologies promise to close the gap in communications tools through which matrix management once fell.

Networking Resource Management

Closely related to the task of supporting new forms of organizational design is networking resource management. Coordination of information exchange throughout a company frequently begins in the federation quadrant, but becomes an overriding concern in the complex environment. Planning processes for traditional and backbone environments are processing based and data based, respectively; networks are viewed as peripheral elements, and communication is almost an afterthought, a cost to be minimized. In the information age, applications processors and databases multiply and become widely dispersed. In an effort to link them back together for legitimate business purposes, such as consolidated statements and cross-selling of products, the information exchange network of an enterprise becomes a key system component. Processing and data, which had been viewed as central, begin to look peripheral. Communication, which had been peripheral, begins to appear central. Accordingly, companies turn to information exchange: The network becomes a viable point of coordination in an otherwise highly distributed systems investment. When this happens, information flow finally stands alongside information processing and information storage and retrieval as a major element of the overall investment in information technology.

Developing Information Systems Architecture

One final information age issue is architecture. Companies in traditional, backbone, or federation environments tend to focus narrowly on either information processing, data, or communications, respectively, developing technical expertise, management experience, and a planning perspective in each area serially—as our planning vice-president put it, "One step at a time." However, after assembling these three basic building blocks, a company (typically in the fourth quadrant) will eventually discover the close interrelationship of all three planning perspectives. General systems theory, after all, tells us that information processing, storage, and communication are the three basic parts of a computer. They must eventually be well coordinated for a firm to realize the benefits of the information age, just as the components of an individual computer must be well tuned and managed to operate efficiently and effectively. When that happens, a fourth-quadrant business may be realistically and profitably viewed as one large system, with hundreds, or even thousands, of processing, storage, and communications elements, all interacting with the correct degree of freedom and coordination in order to be as responsive as possible to the diverging marketplace requirements of different business units, as well as to the countervailing need for standardized information exchange by the corporation as a whole.

A firm developing an information systems architecture considers the requirements and relationships among different business processes, data, and information flows. At the same time, the firm evaluates the capabilities of technologies that are currently used to support the business. Alternative technologies are also considered as supplements or replacements. In cases where considerable opportunity for improvement in functional quality exists, a business case is developed. The combination of a chance to realize a dramatic functional improvement and the expectation of a reasonable return on investment motivates new development.

The analysis of systems architecture opportunities may propel a firm toward more distributed computing, or it may produce changes in the way data resources are deployed. Frequently, the network will emerge as a crucial central element. Not only do specific new applications of technology appear, but the architectural view often produces corporate standards and utilities. A standard is a set of rules, protocols, or gateways to be shared by different business entities in order for them to interact. A utility is a shared system, such as a communications network, which would not be feasible or desirable for only one information flow, but which yields economies of scale and integration benefits for a set of flows. Taken together, the specific applications, logical standards, and physical utilities for processing, storage, and information flow constitute the information technology architecture of an enterprise. With this overall architectural strategy, a firm is prepared to determine the nature and extent of systems integration that most closely matches its unique business requirements.[6]

Avoiding Irrelevant Planning

All strategic planning efforts—whether they produce systems plans or business plans—are vulnerable to the charge of irrelevance. Planning is invariably time-consuming; it may serve a marginally useful budgeting function, it rarely results in a truly strategic change in direction, and it never produces a new product idea. So why bother? Only by focusing on strategic issues of information-based services, organizational transformations, appropriate management disciplines, and the development of an overall information technology architecture can those in the complex environment of the information age have confidence that planning is worthwhile.

A Contingent Approach to Planning

The research and resulting framework described above enable us to see how and why some companies have adjusted their approaches to planning for information technology, but the implications extend considerably beyond taxonomy and historiography. The matrix can be used for prescriptive purposes as well as descriptive ones. Since each of the quadrants is associated with a high probability of success using a particular approach to planning, knowing where our organization stands in the model enables us to manage our methodology to fit our circumstances.

In practice, however, it turns out that the overall corporate position in the matrix is, by itself, an inadequate starting point to optimize the planning effort. Several important dynamic conditions can exist and must be taken into consideration. One condition is movement through time: A company cannot expect to stay in one quadrant forever, and managing the movement from one quadrant to another is itself an objective. Also, a discrepancy can exist between a company's position in the matrix and that of its competition or industry. There may also be a difference between the perception and the reality of a system, in which case the planning activity takes on an educational burden. And, perhaps most important, there can be substantial variation within a company, particularly a large, diversified, or geographically dispersed one.

Because of these discrepancies, a uniform, monolithic application of one planning approach from year to year and throughout a company is frequently undesirable. Although it might be argued that most enterprises are moving relentlessly into the information age—the fourth quadrant—the speed and even the desirability of this movement are uneven among business units and across time. Accordingly, it can be helpful and necessary to vary the nature and extent of planning within a company and from one year to the next. Differential planning of this kind can give the best of both worlds: It can maximize responsiveness to business and technological change throughout the corporation without sacrificing the need to see the big picture. A contingent approach can resolve an irony of the information age: It can overcome the gnawing fact that specialized management of technology is disappearing (through diffusion) just as its strategic importance is peaking (through infusion).

In view of the highly publicized difficulties associated with strategic planning, it is understandable that not everyone advocates it. In fact, the challenge of the information age has motivated a substantial retreat away from planning into unpremeditated action. As this happens, two critical fallacies become apparent. One is the notion that foresight is no longer possible. Making a virtue of necessity in the absence of a decent methodology, this position advocates free-form experimentation. This is the viewpoint that says we must "experience the technology." It is reminiscent of a certain theory of child rearing, according to which a baby can do no wrong. The more messy, the more creative, the better. The inevitable result is clutter.

The other extreme is backsliding into determinism. Here an analogue of the opposite view of child rearing appears, emphasizing the need to observe schedules, routines, predictability, stages. But what could be less helpful (or less true) today than the notion that all firms will pass lockstep through some uniform sequence? Just the reverse is happening: As technology becomes increasingly embedded in a company, that firm's experience with the technology becomes more idiosyncratic. Competitive companies in the information age are the ones breaking out of the mold. They demonstrate that there are no predictable stages of growth.

Between these two extremes lies another approach. This middle way holds that progress is both possible and desirable, but stresses that effective systems must be closely interwoven with business purposes. Development should focus on product differentiation and support for new forms of organizational design. Management disciplines ought to concentrate on facilitating change. Finally, application planning and information management must be supplemented by a new emphasis on networking resource management and on information systems architecture.

9

Information Systems Organizations: Keeping Pace with the Pressures

Darrell E. Owen

Information systems organizations have come under tremendous pressure in recent years, both from top management and from rapid advances in technology. In this article, the author stresses the changing role of the data-processing manager—now the information systems manager and soon to be the information manager—as well as the structural elevation of the IS organization. He assesses the various adjustments that organizations have made in order to deal with the changes and makes recommendations for future adjustments. *SMR.*

Over the last decade, information systems (IS) organizations in virtually every corporation in the country have had to face two universal pressures. First, from the top, corporate management is simply expecting more. ("Demanding" may be more appropriate.) Second, there is the pressure caused by technology. More of it, and all of it changing! While these aren't necessarily new pressures, they are greater than ever before. And there is little likelihood that these pressures will abate in the near future.

There was a time when IS organizations actually sought management's attention to help establish their credibility within the corporation. But now management's incessant demands have more than compensated for their earlier apathy. Technology at one time was thought to be the salvation because it provided enabling tools. The blitz of new technology is often more than the IS organization can deal with effectively.

The purpose of this article is twofold: to assess typical IS organizational adjustments instituted to accommodate these two, sometimes conflicting, pressures and to recommend the further structural adjustments needed to add depth and continuity to what are viewed as initial "quick fix" solutions.

From *Sloan Management Review*, Spring 1986, Vol. 27, No. 3. Reprinted with permission.

A quick word on perspective. It must be remembered that, while this article examines the organizational structure, structure is but one dimension. The critical dimension is the actual performance of the functions within this structure. And structure is similar to the role played by computer hardware: It's the frame upon which the computing is performed. In this analogy, activities are the corresponding software—the intelligence that makes the structure perform according to its design. As such, the analysis contained herein should be viewed as but a single piece in the overall puzzle of managing information systems technologies.

Background

The seeds of increased demand for information processing can be traced to the basic restructuring of the Western economy. As the economy has moved away from producing goods to producing services, the relative importance of information has increased. Acknowledgment of this fundamental shift from an industrial to an information society was the key trend in John Naisbitt's 1982 bestseller, *Megatrends*.[1] In many respects, it provided the basis for the entire book. Citing a government-sponsored study by Dr. Marc Porat conducted in 1967, Naisbitt states that 46 percent of the GNP (53 percent earned income) was "information economy" based. That was two decades ago! And the information industries are the fastest growing industries in the country. In citing a study by David Birch, Naisbitt continues to point out that 90 percent of the jobs created since 1970 are information, knowledge, or service related: only 5 percent are related to manufacturing. Relative to economic history, we are in the infancy of this new era.

With this heightened emphasis on information, management's response could not be far behind, and in most corporations, it wasn't. Top management has come to recognize that information—hence information systems—is a vital element in doing business. As such, there have been increasing demands for significant contributions from the IS organization.

As an initial display of this new focus, top management has responded almost across the board by elevating the IS organization within the corporate structure. During the past decade, IS managers have been on a steady ascent from the computer room in the basement corner to the executive suite. It is not uncommon to find IS managers playing key roles within the corporate superstructure. As a simple illustration, until approximately three years ago, Datamation's Annual DP Salary Survey reflected the top IS-related position as "Corporate Director of DP/MIS." Their most recent surveys include "Vice-President" as the top position. Corporate Director of DP or MIS is shown as the number two position.[2] The job description guides for the 1984 survey further reflect that the elevation is not in name only:

- Vice-President: The senior executive for all corporate information systems. Responsible for long-range planning, budgeting, and operations.
- Director of DP: In charge of all DP at the divisional or departmental level. Responsibilities parallel those of corporate officers, but may be at least partially guided by decisions made at corporate level.

The guide for the 1980 survey showed the Corporate Director of DP or MIS as the "top executive for all computer processing."

This elevation is due to the recognized importance of information and supporting technologies. In many industries, information processing has become a strategic element in posturing the company for gaining a competitive advantage in the marketplace. In others, it's a matter of basic survival.[3]

Concurrent with management's increased focus and expectations have come advances in the enabling technologies. If there were a single phrase to describe the state of the IS organization in dealing with this new technology, "semi-ordered technologically induced chaos" would be a telling choice. The balance between the "semi-ordered" and the "chaos" varies from company to company depending on the extent to which this new technology is put to use. But most IS organizations are suffering from this common ailment. For example, it's hard to imagine any IS organization during the last two years that has not had to make adjustments for personal computers. A survey conducted by Datamation reflects spending in the Fortune 1000 companies for PCs to be 3.8 percent of the total DP budget.[4] Considering the numbers of PCs that can be bought for these dollars, and the fact that it was zero just a few years ago, the impact of this one change alone is staggering. Software sales for PCs are estimated at $1.9 billion for 1984. At an average of $200 per package, that's 950,000 new software packages sold in one year. Projections are for this $1.9 billion to be $10.9 billion by 1989![5]

Office automation and changes in communications technology are two other raw nerve "technologically induced" changes—each with its fair share of chaos. By comparison, PCs are simple and stable relative to what is currently taking place in telecommunications technology.

The prior generation data-processing manager was just that: a manager of data-processing technology. Note the singularity! Today the head of the new IS organization is a manager of multiple IS-related technologies (plural). No longer is the mainframe computing environment the sum total. There are minis, office systems, micros, local-area networks, PBXs, etc., etc., and etc. And the pace of change within these new technologies is even more staggering!

Many IS organizations have accommodated this increased pressure of technology by establishing an Information Center. Originating from IBM (Canada) in 1976, the information center concept includes the establishment of a new organizational entity devoted to new technologies employed to satisfy the new "end-user." It's the "user-friendly" group within the IS organization. While no two are implemented exactly the same, when IBM spoke, IS organizations listened, and they are acting according to the script in increasing numbers. A survey conducted by the Diebold Group, Inc. (New York), in 1983 revealed that two-thirds of the thirty-two major companies surveyed had planned on implementing two or more information centers by 1985. Many major companies, such as Atlantic Richfield Oil, Union Carbide, Lockheed, and Chase Manhattan Bank, have had them in place for several years.[6]

Assessment

With the pressures identified and the common responses isolated, the question of the sufficiency of these changes can now be addressed. Are these structural changes sufficient to accommodate these pressures? If not, why? Also, if not, what further changes should be made?

Organization Elevation

By itself, relocating any function intact will result in little if any change. Elevating the IS organization may result in an added focus that may eventually lead to changes, but little can be expected by this change alone. There is one exception—likely to be followed by a second. First, it will yet further raise management's expectations. And second, it will eventually result in disappointment in meeting these expectations!

The pyramid diagram can be used to illustrate the situation resulting from elevating information systems. Figure 9.1 represents a typical IS organization.[7] The IS manager is at the top, midlevel managers are in the center, and the operations level is at the base.

Elevating the IS organization has the impact of separating the IS manager from the remainder of the IS organization. This "elevation gap" is reflected pictorially in Figure 9.2. The result is that the IS manager is now at a higher level—with the remainder of the IS organization relatively unchanged and remaining at the prior level. The midlevel managers and the operations level are basically the same as before the change. While referred to in different terminology, this gap was discussed from various perspectives by both John Diebold[8] and Joseph Mallory[9] as early as 1982. Both addressed the situation

Figure 9.1 Typical IS Organization

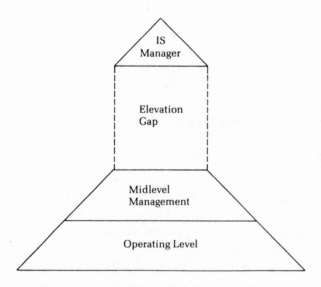

Figure 9.2 Elevated IS Organization

of higher level IS-related positions being established while the organization was still floundering in its newly appointed roles/responsibilities.

The IS manager is now concerned with the corporate issues, associated strategies, directions, policies, and so forth. That was, in part, the purpose of the repositioning.[10] Unfortunately, and through no fault of the IS manager, little time is left to manage the IS organization. It is unlikely (if not impossible) that the IS manager can pull the organization up to this higher level. After all, they still have to write code, install cables and terminals, operate the computer, etc.

While having an IS manager who is more manager than technical specialist

is a major step forward, the direct improvement of the IS organization resulting from this move upward will be very slow at best. If we look at the long-
term trend, we observe that the data-processing manager of yesteryear is
becoming today's information systems manager. Whereas he used to be the
manager of technology, now he is responsible for managing information systems; he is responsible for both the technology *and its use*. In many corporations, pressure from the top is moving the IS manager higher still—to the
executive level. And the pressure has still not abated![11]

Seeds are already being scattered, and in some places taking root, for the IS
manager or IS executive to become an information manager. Chief information officer, while still rare, is the logical next step. Today information resource management (IRM) is a more commonly heard buzzword. In the
federal sector it's an edict established by the "Paperwork Reduction Act of
1980" (public law 96–511). According to this law, all federal entities will
manage information as a resource—or at least diligently attempt to! Under
this scenario, the manager's responsibilities include not only managing technology and its use (the mainstay of the IS manager), but also managing the
actual information.

The weakness in simple structural elevation of the IS organization should
be readily identifiable. If the DP-to-IS organization elevation has caused a
disconnect between the IS manager and the IS organization, any future elevation (IS-to-ISM) will only increase this gap.

Information Center

The second common structural adjustment within the IS organization is the
introduction of the information center (IC) concept. While there are an infi-
nite number of variations in its implementation, the driving motivation behind
the information center is new technology. In effect, the information center is
IBM's answer to the infusion of new technology. Specifically, the information
center is aimed at supporting new technologies targeted for the end-user.

Various IBM publications state the IC mission with some variation, but the
following is a typical mission statement:[12]

The information center mission is to provide the Headquarters user community with
computer productivity aids, allowing authorized users access to computer data while
remaining responsive to their requirements for education and assistance in application
developmental problem resolution. The intent is to increase the self-sufficiency of the
user in the access of data, reducing his/her requirement for programming resources
from the Information Systems Department.

The productivity aids provided by the information center consist of user-oriented languages for information retrieval, personal computing, education, planning, and text processing and retrieval. These languages function in a "demand processing" environment, or one in which the user carries out his/her own programming, job submissions and reporting, either interactively or through the walk-in center.

There is little argument that there has been a significant increase in the technologies that now must be accommodated by the IS organization. And a large share of these are in support of the newly emergent "end-user." Thus far, the information center points in the right direction. However, it falls short of the target by simply failing to go far enough. It's not so much a total long-term solution as an initial reaction in the right direction.

The major weakness of the information center is twofold. First, it carries with it the necessity of leaving what is, as is, and responds by adding a new group to deal with the new technology. The root problem with this approach should be obvious: Leaving what is, as is, is not taking full advantage of the new technology. Nor will it optimally support the IS manager in his increasingly elevated role. There is a need for the entire MIS organization to think and perform differently. The corporation needs to infuse the new technology as a whole. For example, decision support system (DSS) software is often an information center product bought for and used as a financial modeling tool by users in the financial area. It offers much more. It has significant contributions to make in mainstream applications development activities well beyond financial modeling for such things as report writing, prototyping, etc. The same applies to fourth-generation languages.

The net effect of adding new technology is that it broadens the IS's organizational responsibilities. This leads to the second major weakness: It does not provide for corresponding adjustments in management. Again using the organizational pyramid to illustrate, the infusion of new technologies moves the IS organization from the original state as reflected in Figure 9.1, to that reflected in Figure 9.3. Via the information center, new technology is most frequently put into use with no one assigned management responsibilities. It is not uncommon for an organization to have hundreds of personal computers with no single manager responsible. Software products are installed, training conducted, help provided, but no one is responsible for ensuring the products are compatible and consistent with the overall IS direction.

However, even Figure 9.3 is partially misleading because it portrays the added technologies as being under the management of the IS organization. Frequently this is not the case. For example, voice communications is seldom included within the responsibilities of the IS manager, yet the PBX is a newer technology with significant information-systems-related capabilities.

The information center response has as its predominant, if not sole, focus the use of the technology, without properly addressing the management of the

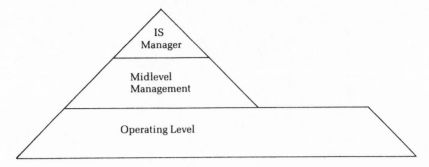

Figure 9.3 Technologically Expanded IS Organization

technology. The operating level now has broader responsibilities for supporting new technologies used throughout the organization—yet without corresponding management adjustments.

This alone is a critical if not fatal error associated with the establishment of the information center concept, especially when one considers that the IS manager is no longer in a position to be the manager of these technologies. Even if he or she were, remember that we are talking about new technologies: technologies that have likely emerged or changed significantly since the IS manager was at this technology level.

When combined with the separation caused by the IS organizational elevation, a clearer representation of the IS organization in many of today's corporations emerges, as shown in Figure 9.4. In summary, the IS organization is simply being pulled apart—spread too thin to be totally responsive to demands.

Both the organizational elevation to support management's interest and the addition of an information center to support new technologies are well-intentioned adjustments. But in and of themselves, they are insufficient to accommodate the continual pressures being applied to the IS organization. As reflected in Figure 9.4, while the adjustments are of value, they are also the cause of yet additional problems.

Structural Readjustments

If we analyze the responsibilities of the data-processing managers of yesteryear, we quickly discover that they primarily managed technology: usually a single technology, a central processing-oriented technology. Unlike today's environment, the manager wasn't too concerned with top management (un-

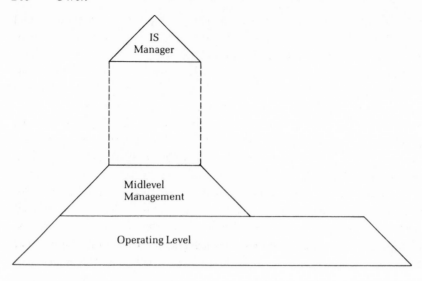

Figure 9.4 Resultant IS Organization

less the payroll didn't run), nor did he have to worry about a vast array of rapidly changing technologies. Things were relatively stable. (Relatively!)

Today, the IS manager finds himself in a totally new world. The IS manager must concern himself daily with meeting top management's requirements. Yet at the same time, he must also be responsible for managing an evergrowing, rapidly changing set of technologies—technologies that didn't even exist as little as two to three years ago. And many of these technologies are the very ones that will enable the manager to be responsive to the demands from the top. As illustrated in Figure 9.4, the IS manager is faced with adding breadth to his organization's responsibilities and, at the same time, bridging the gap between himself and the rest of the MIS organization.

In the flurry of this transition, the one critical ingredient that has unwittingly been lost is that of a technological manager. We have lost sight of the fact that while technology is changing, management remains management. Someone must be in charge, responsible and accountable. Technology doesn't change this aspect of management. And this technological management role, once played by the DP manager, is not being played by the IS manager. He is too far removed, and the technology base is too broad. And it is no longer a single role to be played by any one individual. It's multiple, because there are now multiple technologies, all of which can be individually larger than the single technology of days past!

Unfortunately, with the IS manager not filling this role, frequently neither is anyone else. When management accommodations are made, they are often in the form of a new committee or a new staff position assigned special responsibilities. Yet another frequently occurring accommodation is that of the traditional host-oriented organization absorbing the change in one fashion or another. It is this latter alternative that, because of tradition or momentum, most frequently fulfills the responsibility of the IS manager. It's the default position—the one taken when no one acknowledges the need.

If we analyze the IS organizational structure, we will find that, for the most part, it has remained virtually unchanged during this time of changing responsibility. Most IS organizations consist of an operations department and an applications development department. In addition to these two main components there are a variety of add-ons, possibly even the new information center, but applications and operations are still the core ingredients of the typical IS organization. Central processing, distributed processing, micros, office systems, communications, etc., are likely to be crammed within the same basic structure that was designed twenty years ago to accommodate the management of a central processing-oriented technology.

Just as the responsibilities of the DP manager have changed to those of the IS manager, structural accommodations must also be made to change the DP organization to an IS organization. This transition requires that things be done differently and, in many cases, the restructuring of the organization to better accommodate new roles and responsibilities.

The organizational chart in Figure 9.5 presents an alignment of the IS organization to remedy the problems addressed earlier. This structure is presented in a "generic" form without biases for existing in-house structures, traditions, areas of unique focus, etc. As such, it should be viewed as a prototype to which alterations may be required. For example, Central Systems, Distributed Systems, Office Systems, and Communications are the reflected technology breakdown. Another logical split for some organizations would be Business, Technical, Office Automation, and Communications, and there are other alternatives. The important thing is to recognize the adjustments that are needed to accommodate the management of a growing inventory of technology, and to adjust this need to the environment into which the IS organization must fit.

IS Manager

This restructuring acknowledges the IS manager's shift in responsibility from that of technological manager to that of strategic manager. This is accomplished in part by establishing the intermediate-level technology managers. This allows for the continuation (if it already exists) of the strong executive management liaison role. The net result is that the IS manager is now able to

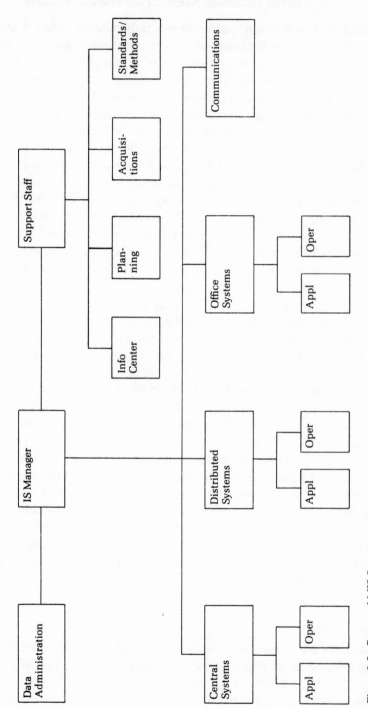

Figure 9.5 Proposed MIS Structure

become an IS executive—a role into which he is being thrust. The establishment of a data administration function is a preliminary move aimed at paving the way toward the IS manager becoming the (or supporting the future) corporate information officer (CIO). The four technology managers, with the support staff, keep the reporting clear, yet, at the same time, provide the checks and balances associated with managing IS technologies.

Technological Managers

The loss of the technological manager role is significant and may very well be a critical factor in the future success of the IS organization in its expanding role. As proposed, these managers all have similar responsibilities except that each has a separate area—Central Systems, Distributed Systems, Office Systems, and Communications. These managers have a "cradle-to-grave" type of responsibility, similar to the role previously played by the DP manager. The establishment of these managers will resolve the problems brought about by bringing in new technology and supporting its use, but without any manager(s) directly responsible. Two critical aspects of the overall management of the information systems technology will be accomplished: First, the new managers will fill the gap between the new IS manager and operations of the technology. Second, managers are established who are accountable for each of the new technologies.

Substructures within each of these four managers can vary, but should include support for applications development and operations. Database management (if it exists) is best located within the central systems application substructure. In this way, it becomes integrated with the actual applications development being carried out by the IS personnel, not just the end-users. Data administration has the overview, information-management-oriented responsibilities.

The establishment of the Office Systems manager addresses the area where most businesses are currently bleeding—office automation and personal computers. This organization will have its hands full for a few years. Luckily, this need is beginning to be recognized, and adjustments similar to those proposed here are already under way in many companies. A 1985 survey conducted by Software Access International, Inc., indicated that companies are rapidly moving in this direction. Thirty percent of the Fortune 500 companies had already established "micro managers" by the end of 1984. Only 15 percent had such a position at the end of the prior year. The reason? Anticipated growth in PCs. The Diebold Group, Inc. (New York), predicts that by 1990, 30 percent of a business's data processing expenditures will be in microcomputers.[13]

The communications manager would again be new in most IS organizations. Specifically, this organization would add focus to the increasingly critical aspect of managing a key "enabling technology" required to support the other primary information systems technologies. The exact split between the communications manager's role and operationally based communications (within each of the other technology managers) is a configuration-by-configuration call. Also, its actual growth into the area of voice communications must be tailored site-by-site. Preferably, this organization should have all communications-related responsibilities (voice, data, image, etc.). The key is that by being placed within the IS organization, close coordination is ensured. This will become more critical as the information-related technologies merge.[14]

Data Administration

For most corporations, this will be a newly recognized responsibility. Primarily, the establishment at this level is an investment in the future. Management's pressure on the IS organization ultimately focuses on having information available when and in the form required. While the IS organization is designed to accommodate this pressure, the predominant tool at its disposal is technology—the enabling resource. This position requires a technologist who will provide support to the IS manager in his evolution toward becoming the information manager of the corporation. In part, it's an in-house R&D effort set aside to prepare for the next move—a move already upon many IS managers. In the meantime, there is more than enough to accomplish in establishing and administering data-administration policies and procedures.

Support Staff

This collection of staff functions includes the information center, central planning, acquisition, and standards/methods. With separated technologies, and technologies that are moving rapidly, it is increasingly important that these functions be coordinated/managed from the top. The planning function here should be one of facilitating, not actual planning. Planning is management's responsibility and, under this proposed structure, it rests with each of the technology managers. The central acquisition is a clearinghouse and expediting function to support end-users and the technology managers. With the broad range of technologies available today, acquisitions must be screened for compatibility and quantity discounts.

The information center would primarily serve an "if you don't know who else to call, call us," function. Also, coordination of end-user consulting and training would be a major responsibility of this unit. By reporting to the IS manager, the information center provides balance between the technological managers and the using community. Including it with other staff functions introduces an element of the "real world" into activities that otherwise tend to become very sterile and separate from the rest of the IS organization they are established to serve. Responsibilities now in the typical information center may need to be redistributed to the appropriate technology manager.

Conclusion

The common remedies of organizational elevation and establishment of information centers are both needed and excellent starting points. They are viewed here as initial reactions in response to real needs: the increased importance of information to the corporation and the need to accommodate the newer technologies.

However, these actions are but partial measures to resolve problems associated with these pressures. Further action is needed to imbed the new focus and changing technologies into day-to-day operations. The proposed structure of the IS organization should be viewed as a major step in further adjusting the IS organization structure to this changing role and environment. The new structure fills the gap between the IS manager and the IS organization and, at the same time, acknowledges the broader scope brought about by the newer technologies.

Restructuring is seldom a panacea, nor should the structuring presented in this paper be viewed as such. It is not. Rather, it is designed to allow the IS organization to get back to the basics: providing a framework for managing technology. It allows this to take place concurrently with providing an opportunity for the IS manager to be involved with corporate-level direction-setting activities. From here the real work begins. The new and changing technologies must be employed effectively to satisfy the specific needs of each using organization and the corporation as a whole.

As a postscript, many corporations are now moving into a relatively new phase of information-systems-related management, commonly referred to as information resource management (IRM). Frequently, the IS manager is the target for this new responsibility and in future years we can expect to see IS managers become corporate information officers—if they are prepared.

This movement has already begun in many of the larger corporations. In a recent survey of sixty Fortune 100 companies (Fall 1984), the CIO function was identified in 30 percent of the firms surveyed. While titles varied, all reported directly to the CEO or chairman.[15] In these situations, the role of the IS manager is again significantly expanded to include management of information, not simply the systems upon which this information resides. This paper has focused on the management of the enabling information systems— the technologies and their application. In doing so, it has laid the groundwork for the next phase.

PART III

Responsibilities to the Organization and Society

10

A Responsible Future: An Address to the Computer Industry

John F. Akers

The future of the information processing industry seems virtually unlimited except to the extent that, by default, the industry itself might encourage society to restrict its functions. In this article, the author addresses problems that could threaten the growth of the industry and outlines a threefold responsibility: to customers, to the industry itself, and to society as a whole. He maintains that the industry must concern itself not just with leading-edge technology, but with leading-edge ethics as well, and predicts that the information processing industry will continue to merit the public's trust as it grows to its full potential. *SMR*.

At IBM, we usually avoid making predictions, but here's one: The future of the information-processing industry is unlimited—unless we encourage society to impose shackles upon us. Technology will continue to move ahead, creating new applications and exciting opportunities, so the industry should sustain its dynamic pace as far into the future as it is possible to see. But looming not too far ahead there are problems that threaten our growth, obstacles not so much technological as human. If these problems are not adequately addressed, they could sap our energy and block the path of our continued progress. This article identifies some of these human problems and presents guidelines for dealing with them.

A brief survey of technology, current and future, is a good place to begin. Progress in our industry has been so fast that it seems to be a never-ending series of breakthroughs, continuing at a very rapid rate. Someday soon I believe we'll see workstations at the desks of almost every professional and administrative employee of industry, government, and academia, and in their briefcases and their homes, too. In college dormitories, computers will be part

From *Sloan Management Review*, Fall 1984, Vol. 26, No. 1. Reprinted with permission.

of the furniture. An ever-improving price/performance relationship will continue to spur the advance. For about the price of today's personal computer, I can already foresee a 32-bit workstation operating at 10 MIPS, with up to 16 megabytes of main storage and 400 megabytes of disk storage.

The centralized system, or "glasshouse," will continue to grow, with multiple systems per center and multiple centers per enterprise. Networks will tie the various levels of computing together. Larger systems will have 100-MIPS uniprocessors, a hierarchy of storage speeds and sizes, and transaction rates of 10,000 per second. Then there will be integration of data, text, image, and voice. We'll see PBXs with data-processing functions built in, and the converse, data systems with voice capability.

There will be electronic mail between enterprises, file sharing among nonsimilar workstations, software that integrates systems across the network, and data portability. Artificial intelligence tools and techniques will be widely available to help generate new applications, improving the productivity of programmers and users. And all these systems will be connected by networks: centralized systems, distributed systems, department systems, and workstations. The key to all this growth will be software, with systems that are much more comfortable to use. In summary, technology will continue to create tremendous opportunities for the industry and its customers.

In the past thirty years, the computer industry has grown to about $250 billion; by the early 1990s, its sales will exceed $1 trillion. The reason for this explosive growth is simple supply and demand. Mankind creates the demand with its ever-growing list of problems. They are everywhere: in health care and education, in brokerage houses and food distribution, in institutions public and private. Fortunately, the information industry can help supply solutions to many of these problems. Our ability to deliver these solutions is growing at 15 to 20 percent annually in revenue terms and more than twice as fast in terms of computing capacity.

This is a global industry: There never was another so truly universal in scope and application. Automobiles and oil may have greater revenues today, but ultimately their growth will be limited by the nature of their products. The information industry, however, will keep on growing virtually forever because the world will never run out of problems to solve and never have too much information.

Nevertheless, there are potential limitations to this growth. These limitations are not technological, but societal, and they could be serious if the industry fails to meet its responsibilities to society. High among our short- and long-term objectives should be developing an industry that's not only dynamic and innovative, but responsible as well. If we don't assume these responsibilities willingly, others will force us to do so in ways that we'll find restrictive and stifling, and the results of that could slow our progress.

The biomedical industry faces an analogous situation. Advances in science and technology have brought new opportunities, but also new dilemmas. The ability to splice genes, to control conception, and to prolong life have led to new questions: What is life? When does it begin? When does it end? And what are the responsibilities of the medical profession in answering these questions? In our industry, the issues are rarely life and death, but the implications are far-reaching. They compel us to take a new look at such old problems as quality, privacy, data security, fraud, and fair play.

Our industry has a great deal of which to be proud. To a degree almost unmatched in business history, our products are safe, reliable, and highly productive. On ethical issues like privacy, we have performed a service for society by enhancing public understanding and promulgating safeguards. And we deliver an exceptional product for a bargain price. As people in the industry are fond of pointing out, if transportation technology had progressed as rapidly in price/performance, people would now be able to go around the world in a matter of minutes for a fraction of today's airfares. There are, however, exceptions to this record of achievement, and we have an obligation to address them. Our responsibilities fall into three categories: a responsibility to our customers and the users of our products; a responsibility to ourselves, as an industry; and a responsibility to society at large, which goes beyond our own interests and those of our users.

Responsibilities to the Customer

What do we owe our customers? Clearly, our customers have a right to expect highly reliable products and systems. The recent quality history of this industry demonstrates what can be done. The concept of "zero defects," once an impossible dream, is becoming a reality, but, as our IBM ads say, "If your failure rate is one in a million, what do you say to that one customer?" It's not just a matter of avoiding the regulations and recalls that have burdened other industries. Rather, quality is sound and responsible business.

Prevention, doing it right the first time, is the key in both hardware and software. At IBM, we plan to reduce by more than 50 percent over the next few years the costs associated with rework and repair. For the industry as a whole, such improvements could bring billions of dollars in savings and, even more important, continued public trust, which is beyond price. As our products multiply, we must intensify our efforts to ensure that every product is defect-free and truly reliable. And as service evolves toward remote diagnosis, we must ensure that the people responsible are not also perceived as remote when the human touch is needed.

Finally, we have a responsibility to provide users with systems that are safe, comfortable, and easy to use. We have already seen what happens when we fail to convince people that all necessary safety precautions have been taken. A current example is the controversy surrounding video display terminals and the fear of radiation. Around the world, these fears have led to strikes, prolonged labor negotiations, and the loss of public confidence, despite the fact that some medical and scientific studies have challenged the validity of such concerns. Clearly we have a responsibility not just to provide systems that are safe and pleasant to use, but to communicate honestly and keep users fully informed on those issues as well.

Responsibility to the Industry

Our second responsibility—to ourselves as an industry—concerns the way we conduct ourselves. An industry that wants to earn the public's respect will not tolerate such dishonesty as, for instance, the appropriation of the fruits of another company's work. It is by no means only IBM that has suffered such misappropriation: Company after company has been victimized. Software copyrights have been widely violated by other companies and by individuals. Chips that cost millions of dollars to develop have been copied for a tiny fraction of their original cost. Whole systems have been pirated and sold to the public.

One result of these practices has been legislation, actual and proposed, to inhibit such conduct. And though much of this legislation is eminently necessary, we should beware of weaving a complex web of rules and regulations. To avoid unduly burdensome regulations, we must explain our positions and needs to the government, press, and public. We have not always done this well. Too often, the image we project to the media is that of warriors on a battlefield of cutthroat competition, and, to some extent, we have brought this reputation upon ourselves through our aggressive conduct. On the other hand, such one-dimensional perceptions also stem from a misunderstanding of the nature of the competitive process in this industry. The fact is, there is hardly an enterprise in our industry that is not dependent on the products of its competitors. The press and public need to understand that in this industry, yesterday's competitor is today's customer and tomorrow's partner in some joint venture.

This is an ultracompetitive industry, but the premise that for every winner there must be a loser is sheer nonsense. As long as this industry is growing at

15 to 20 percent annually, there will be many more winners than losers. We have a responsibility to communicate that fact to the press, and the press, in turn, has a responsibility to communicate it to the public.

Responsibilities to Society

Finally, what are the industry's responsibilities to the society at large? One of our key obligations is to education. There is a natural and growing interdependence between our industry and academia. On the one hand, scientific discoveries in universities can lead to major new developments in the industry; on the other, universities need industry's help if their scientific curricula are to keep pace with the rapid developments in the industry itself. Back in the 1960s, thousands of computer scientists were working in industry, but they had been educated as mathematicians, physicists, and engineers, and they learned computer science on the job—in effect, by apprenticeship. Not until 1964 was the first advanced degree in computer science awarded.

In the late 1960s and early 1970s, the industry became highly dependent on microelectronics, but no degrees were granted in large-scale integrated electronics until the late 1970s. The same holds true today about our dependence on magnetic technology, CAD/CAM, and other advanced areas. Industry is taking the lead in basic training, while the schools catch up. As we push the limits of technology, we find ourselves using materials in ways never before attempted. Our materials engineers require knowledge at the molecular level; thus, the dependence of industrial technology on leading-edge science deepens. At the same time, modern science owes an increasing debt to the latest in technology. Therefore it is enlightened self-interest for our industry to share our experience with faculty and students and to support their efforts in computing.

As for privacy, we have, as an industry, done a commendable job of defining and advancing privacy in the computer age. We have publicized the rights of the individual and helped put into place principles and policies to safeguard those rights. Still more needs to be done. Congress is concerned that the use of computers to gather and store personal information may be outpacing legal and ethical safeguards. Critics claim that dossiers assembled by political groups, corporations, and law-enforcement agencies could be used for purposes far different from those for which the information was legitimately collected. Unless our industry takes a constructive part in this debate, we will have only ourselves to blame when the laws that emerge are ineffective and unduly burdensome.

Another aspect of responsibility to society is our attitude toward computer crime, both crimes directed against computers and those in which the computer is an instrument for committing the crime. The American Bar Association estimates the losses from theft of tangible and intangible assets (including software), destruction of data, embezzlement of funds, and fraud at as much as $45 billion annually. There are proposals in Congress for bills to make computer fraud and the counterfeiting of credit cards federal offenses. A Bar Association survey shows widespread support for such legislation.[1] But interestingly, when the pollsters asked people how to prevent computer crime, most said the better way was not legislation but self-protection by business and education of users and the public about the vulnerabilities of their computer systems. This constitutes a direct challenge to our industry. Electronic locks and keys to safeguard data security already exist, but we have much to do to educate people in their full use and implementation.

Finally, we must realize that in the international arena the computer, which is fundamentally useful and wealth creating, is viewed with fear by some societies. They worry that they may be left behind in the general progress of humanity. Their fears are a jumble of the real and the imagined. We must do what we can to assist legitimate national goals and to see that the benefits of the computer are made available to all peoples of the world. This can be achieved only in a spirit of cooperation and partnership.

Summary: Ethical Responsibilities

The bottom line is economic. For the reasons I've mentioned, people won't use our products fully unless we merit their trust. And if we don't conduct ourselves responsibly, governments and other institutions will erect barriers that could restrain our growth and limit the usefulness of our industry. Society must know that ours is not an industry that turns a blind eye to computer crime, fraud, or unethical behavior of any kind, and it's incumbent upon all of us to see that the evidence bears this out. In our industry, therefore, we must concern ourselves not just with leading-edge technology, but with leading-edge ethics as well.

Recently, two business school professors surveyed business executives about what they thought should be emphasized in the education of the entrepreneurs of the future. Somewhat to their surprise, 72 percent said ethics. Ethics could and should be taught as part of the curriculum, they said. One of the respondents summed it up with this comment, "If the free enterprise system is to survive, business schools had better start paying attention to teaching ethics. The entrepreneurs of the future should know that business is built on trust, which in turn depends on honesty and sincerity."[2]

In conclusion, these are my three predictions: The technology of our industry will continue to make dynamic strides; there will be great elasticity of demand; and the information-processing industry will see that it can and must merit the public's trust so it can grow to its full potential. These are responsibilities that are not someone else's job, but direct challenges to our companies and to each one of us—challenges deserving a high priority.

11

Management Policies and Procedures Needed for Effective Computer Security

Stuart E. Madnick

Although many security issues are controlled by legislative ruling and social standards, or are constrained by technological limitations, many other important matters of operational computer security are directly or indirectly under managerial control. The author argues that the necessary control policies and procedures will become increasingly critical as our reliance upon computer-based information systems continues to increase. This article presents a comprehensive framework for understanding the various aspects of computer security. Through this framework, those areas controllable by management are identified, and possible actions are proposed. *SMR.*

In general, much of the literature and research on computer security-related matters has focused either on privacy and its associated social and legislative implications[1] or on technical mechanisms to enforce a specific security objective.[2] In comparison, the managerial and organizational issues, lacking the emotional tone of the privacy issues and the precision of the technical implementations, have received limited attention. This situation is especially unfortunate since, even after generally accepted privacy legislation is enacted and the major technological security mechanisms refined, the managerial security issues, by their very nature, will persist.

Managerial security (sometimes called operational or administrative security) is concerned with the policies and procedures adopted by management to ensure the security of their data and computer installation. Although certain of these policies and procedures may be externally defined, such as those relating to privacy laws or government regulations (e.g., IRS rules), most are internally defined.

A typical definition of data security found in the literature might be: "Pro-

From *Sloan Management Review*, Fall 1978, Vol. 20, No. 1. Reprinted with permission.

tection of data against accidental or intentional disclosure to unauthorized persons, or unauthorized modifications or destruction."[3] Key to such a definition is the notion of authorization. Major managerial control issues include the questions:

1. Who should be authorized?
2. How is this determined?
3. How is the authorization process operated?

In recent years various authors have attempted to address some of these policy and procedural issues.[4] With few exceptions these studies either have been imbedded in elaborate privacy or technical security reports or have been intended to serve as introductions to particular aspects of the problem. As a result, the literature on managerial security is diffuse and unorganized. This article introduces a comprehensive framework for organizing and studying the diverse aspects of managerial security. This framework places issues of management policies and procedures into four categories:

I.   Operational considerations
II. Organizational impact
III. Economics
IV. Objectives and accountability

Using this framework, the key issues regarding management policies and procedures for effective computer security are categorized and analyzed. Specific emphasis is placed on proposals regarding surveillance and authorization.

I. Operational Considerations

Many managerial decisions must be made regarding the procedures to be used in the operation of an organization's computer facility. Although most of these decisions are intended primarily to increase the degree of data security, they must also be viewed in light of the organization's overall objectives.

Operating Environment

Physical and operational procedures can be used to limit significantly the number of people that have any access to the computer facility. The three major categories of access are:

1. Closed. Only a very small number of operators have direct access to the computer facility. All computation to be performed is submitted to one of the operators, who then oversees the actual run.
2. Open. In principle, any member of the organization may have access to the computer facility. The user must physically appear at the computer facility to perform computations and can be screened at that time.
3. Unlimited. Access to the computer facility is via communication lines, usually the public telephone network. The user need not ever physically appear at the computer facility nor have any personal contact with the operators of the facility.

There are, of course, variations on the operating environments listed above. Each environment has implications for the organization's data security as well as the utility of the computer facility. By severely limiting access, such as in a closed environment, controls similar to those used for a bank vault can be enforced. In fact, most high-security military installations use this approach, and the "computer room" is often actually a vault. Although a closed environment can provide high physical security, it may not be consistent with the organization's needs. Many of the important modern applications of computers are dependent upon the concept of on-line access—leading essentially to an unlimited-access environment.

The open- and unlimited-access environments introduce different types of risks. In an open environment it is possible to screen out external intruders, but the computer facility is still exposed to the actions of internal users who have legitimate physical access to it. An unlimited-access environment cannot easily constrain access by external intruders, but direct physical contact with the computer can be prevented, and the actions that can be performed via communication lines can be restricted in various ways.

Types of Authorization Control

As noted previously, operational security is, to a large extent, concerned with the authorization process. The most critical aspects of this process relate to:

1. Who wishes to access or alter information?
2. Which information will be accessed or altered?
3. What operation is to be performed on the information?

These aspects should be analyzed in terms of the controls appropriate to and/ or necessary for the individual firm's security goals. (A complete security system would likely include controls on when, from where, and why information is accessed or altered.)

Identification and Verification.   The verification process usually involves something that the user: (1) knows (e.g., a password), (2) carries (e.g., a badge), or (3) is (e.g., a physical characteristic, such as a fingerprint). In many organizations, surrogates, perhaps administrative assistants, may be permitted access to obtain reports for the president. Considerable attention should be paid to the technical mechanism for assigning such roles, such as giving the surrogate the "president's badge," and the procedural mechanisms for ensuring the correct and legitimate behavior of an individual acting for someone with more security authorization. In many systems there is no way to distinguish among the several individuals that are allowed to take on a specific role (e.g., acting for the president). But without a differentiation procedure, it is difficult to audit effectively such a system or to trace responsibility.

Classification of Information.   The classification procedure can be complicated by many factors, such as granularity and security level. Granularity denotes the level of detail of information to be classified: an entire document, a record, or a specific data item. A single document may contain a variety of information that may warrant separate classifications. Furthermore, in certain types of computerized data bases, the concepts of documents or even records may not explicitly exist. In such a situation it becomes necessary to authorize on the basis of specific data items or data types.

The use of security levels is largely motivated by the military concept of security classifications, such as confidential, secret, and top secret. Most nonmilitary organizations also use this concept to some extent (e.g., company confidential, company registered confidential, etc.). Various combinations of information-classification schemes can be employed in organizations. Combining "horizontal" partitioning (i.e., functional) with a "vertical" partitioning (i.e., security level) is a common choice.

Operations upon Information.   Once the "who" and the "which" have been established, it must be determined what actions are to be allowed. As a simple example, one can distinguish between the operations "read" and "write." In the first case, an individual may be authorized to obtain certain information, such as a customer's bank balance, but have no authority to change it. In the other case, authorization to change the information may be given.

Variations on these two basic operations should be considered. For example, the actions of "creating" or "destroying" records are often treated differently from "reading" and "writing." An inventory-control clerk may be authorized to update the inventory balances, but only the engineering department personnel may be authorized to create new part records. Other versions of "reading" can be used. For example, some systems allow access to statistical information (e.g., average salary) without providing access to the individual salary information. Also, especially for proprietary software, there is the notion of "execute-only" access, where someone may be authorized to use the program but not to modify or read it. (Reading the program would allow it to be copied and thereby stolen.)

Operational Ease

Security mechanisms can cause additional hardship or inconvenience for users. If such mechanisms are not easy to operate, they will not be used effectively. For example, an inventory-control clerk's primary responsibility is to maintain up-to-date information on the company's inventory. If the security mechanism requires extra time to update the inventory status, it will be at odds with the primary job function of the clerk, who may then take shortcuts that compromise the security mechanism.

When one is devising an authorization and security mechanism, it is important to consider the operational environment and pick an approach that is likely to be easy and convenient to use. This decision may involve compromises between degree of security and ease of use.

Reliability and Recovery

As the capabilities and cost effectiveness of information systems have increased, the systems have become closely integrated into the operation of many organizations. This has, in turn, increased the concern for reliability and recovery.

In some cases, reliability and recovery procedures are concordant with security procedures. For example, reliability mechanisms often include additional tests for potential errors in either the hardware or software. Some of these tests may be used to test for potential security violations. On the other hand, other reliability mechanisms produce redundancy and duplication. For example, one way to safeguard the company's key files and provide for effective recovery is to make one or more copies.[5] Thus, if the original is destroyed, a copy can be used. Unfortunately, these copies may increase the exposure to security violations. In fact, since under normal operation the duplicates are not used, stolen or replaced copies may never be missed. In order to address this specific problem, many companies are adopting new procedures whereby both the original and copy are used in normal operation, such as on alternate days. In this way it is more likely that missing information will be detected. In addition, the reliability of the copies can be confirmed. In one organization a spot check of their "backup copies" revealed that 25 percent were not usable due either to errors during the copying operation or to deterioration during storage.

Transition

At times of transition, the system is extremely vulnerable to security violations, especially if the transition is from a manual to a computerized system.

This vulnerability is caused by various factors: (1) Most users are not used to the new system and are likely to be careless; (2) the system itself may not include all the "ultimately desired" security facilities, and the facilities provided may not be fully tested; and (3) the operational and technical problems that usually accompany a transition may act as significant diversions for concurrent security violations. Security considerations must be carefully factored into the transition plan to minimize these vulnerabilities.

II. Organizational Impact

Computer system security often requires or causes organizational changes. Some of these changes are desirable and are concordant with the security objectives. Other impacts may be detrimental to the security objectives and, possibly, to the organization as a whole. Several of these key issues are discussed in this section.

Awareness and Education

The degree of awareness of data security as an issue and the possibility of security threats vary widely. Although awareness is increasing, it is likely that the situation has not changed significantly from that reported in one study where it was concluded that only a small proportion of computer users use security features.[6] As one senior manager of a time-sharing firm stated, "Some customers are concerned about security, some are not; but they are all naive." Furthermore, it was found that although most systems provided various special security mechanisms, only a handful were actually used and those only by the most sophisticated users. The majority of the users assumed that the computer system was secure and that they were adequately protected.

Surely the need for user education is an important aspect of improved and effective security procedures and enforcement. Part of this increased education and awareness will come about as a result of external factors, such as (1) press and media coverage, (2) increases in direct personal contact with computer systems as these systems become more pervasive in organizations, and

(3) advances in security, in both technique and cost effectiveness, that would provide a more natural and easier use of modern systems. Organizations may also find it valuable to accelerate the awareness process by developing or sponsoring specific security education activities.

Attitude

When extensive computer security is introduced into an organization, some personnel may react negatively because of a difficulty in getting their work accomplished and/or a feeling of loss of power. The first problem was briefly discussed earlier.

In a secure system people no longer can have unlimited, unrestricted access to the entire system. Management must explicitly determine each individual's access rights. To the extent that possession of information is a form of power, individuals may resist and resent any decrease in information access rights, even if the information is not necessary for the normal operation of the individual's job. Furthermore, restrictions on or the elimination of "hands on" computer access by most applications and systems programmers is often a serious blow to the programmers' egos.

Personnel and Responsibility

To a large extent the security-related aspects of personnel selection and assignment are very similar in both the computer and noncomputer environments; thus, much of the existing literature on such subjects (e.g., embezzlement) is applicable.[7]

Computerized systems have introduced several new problems:

1. A computerized system often allows for much more streamlined and efficient operation by eliminating many of the traditional steps. The loss of an intermediate step may also negate an existing internal check.
2. The operation of computerized systems introduces many new roles and procedures for which the concepts of division of responsibility are not well established from experiences with prior manual systems. Since computer programs, to a large extent, act as surrogates for what were traditionally manual steps, one individual may inherit the conflicting responsibilities of writing both operational and auditing programs.
3. Finally, the separation of responsibilities between computer programmers and operators can easily lead to conflicting company objectives. For instance, whereas in some cases it would be advantageous to hire only operators with no programming ability, the company's advancement op-

portunities may contrarily encourage operators to aspire to positions as programmers. The correct balancing of these potentially conflicting objectives must be carefully studied. Various additional procedures and checks and balances can be developed to lessen the potential exposure due to security violations by computer operators.

III. Economics

Key issues that must be resolved in order to determine security economics include: (1) a determination of the value of information; (2) an assessment of likely threats to the information; and (3) a determination of the costs of available security mechanisms and their effectiveness. Aspects of these issues are discussed below.

Value of Information

It should seem obvious that the determination of the value of information is a crucial step in any security decision as well as in normal information management. Unfortunately, the evaluation process remains very subjective. The process not only requires placing a value on information, but also consideration of the fact that the same information may be perceived to have different values by different groups of individuals. At least three separate interest groups are involved:

1. Keeper—the organization that has and uses the information;
2. Source—the organization or individual that provided the information, or to whom the information pertains;
3. Intruder—an individual or organization that may wish to obtain the information.

The value of information depends, further, on its type. The following are general categories of information type:

1. Critical operating information, such as this week's sales orders and production schedule, may have a very high value to the keeper, but considerably less value to its sources (i.e., the customers) or potential intruders.
2. Personal information (e.g., an individual's census data or medical information in the employee personnel file) may have a much higher value to the source (i.e., the individual) than to either the keeper or intruder.
3. Proprietary information, including marketing-forecast data gathered by a company, may be much more valuable to an intruder, such as a competing

company, than to either the sources (i.e., sample customers) or the keeper, who may have already finished analyzing the data.

The categories listed above are aggregations. The value of a specific type of information may be perceived differently by different keepers (or different individuals or groups within the "keeper" organization), sources, and intruders.

Threats

In evaluating threats, one wants to know the economic impact (usually interpreted as a loss or expense to the keeper or source) should a particular operation be performed on certain information. Threat operations can be divided into major categories, such as:

1. Interrupt—disrupt the normal processing of the information. Note that an interruption may be an important concern even though the information itself may not be affected in any way.
2. Steal or disclose—read or copy information for use by either the intruder or a third party (e.g., publishing the medical records of a competitor).
3. Alter—change information, such as the intruder's bank balance. This is probably the most obvious threat to most people.
4. Destroy—permanently destroy the information, by erasing a magnetic tape, for example.

There are, of course, alternative categorizations of threats as well as additional factors that may be considered, such as whether the action was intentional (e.g., an intruder breaking in) or unintentional (e.g., someone inadvertently losing the data). Although the intentional threats are often of most concern, the unintentional may be more frequent and, possibly, have greater economic impact.

Risk

The threat assessment is intended to determine the value of a certain action upon information. In order to develop a rational security plan, it is necessary to assess the probability of each threat occurring. A common objective of most risk-assessment strategies proposed is to arrive at a quantitative statement of risk, such as a decision-analysis calculation of the expected value of the loss for each threat.[8] However, numerous problems are encountered in attempting to perform such a risk assessment. First, determining the precise monetary value of a threat may be very difficult. Second, there is usually a reluctance to assign a monetary value to threats that have social impact, such as disclosure of confidential medical information. Third, as noted earlier, different individuals and organizations may assign different values to a given threat.

There is also considerable difficulty in determining the probability of a threat occurring. Computer threats are too diverse and too recent for much statistical information to have been gathered. A threat assessment is, therefore, the most subjective aspect of the economics of computer security, and thus each assessment must be calculated in its particular context.

Countermeasures and Costs

For each risk usually one or more countermeasures are possible.[9] Countermeasures are intended to decrease the risk either by decreasing the probability of the threat occurring, or by decreasing the impact of the threat should it occur. For example, the probability of losing information can be decreased by adding new procedures to monitor the use and location of the information. The impact of lost information can be decreased either by having copies of the information available or by setting up procedures in advance that enable rapid and inexpensive reconstruction of the information.

The two major considerations for each countermeasure are its effectiveness and its cost. This information can provide the basis for a rational economic-security plan.[10] In particular, a countermeasure is economically reasonable if its effectiveness, in terms of decreased risk, exceeds its cost. The organization can establish maximum risk levels and then select one or more economically justified countermeasures, as necessary, to reduce the total risk below the maximum risk levels. Of course, many of the same problems that prevent precise threat and risk assessment exist in determining countermeasure effectiveness and cost. On the other hand, several efforts have been made to enumerate countermeasures and, at least qualitatively, rate their effectiveness and cost.[11]

One final issue often studied in the context of threats by intruders is the cost of the threat. In theory an economically rational intruder will not expend more to initiate a threat than the expected gain from that threat (e.g., one would not reasonably spend $5,000 to break into a vault that one believed only contained $10). Thus, one of the significant objectives of a security countermeasure is to increase the costs to an intruder, so as to raise the price above the value the intruder anticipates. The intruder's costs include resources necessary, such as technology, expertise, time, and opportunity. In addition, penalty costs, such as the possibility of detection and the resulting economic, personal, and social losses, represent a potential expense to the intruder. Therefore, countermeasures based on ex post facto detection rather than prevention of threats may be equally effective in reducing the risk of an intruder threat. This point will be discussed in more detail later.

IV. Security Objectives and Accountability

As part of a meaningful security plan it is necessary to consider the objectives to be accomplished and the specific organizational responsibilities necessary to carry out the plan. For example, security violations by authorized insiders far outnumber those likely to occur by external intruders. Thus, a plan focusing only on the outside intruder may not provide much increase in security. Unintentional mistakes by insiders may also be a comparatively important problem in many organizations.

Validation and Consistency

Techniques and procedures to validate the reasonableness and consistency of data are important in reducing the frequency of unintentional errors and in providing a means of detecting or preventing various forms of intentional security violations by either insiders or external intruders. Simple format and range checks are common to most, but not all, information systems. A typical format check would verify that the zip code of an address is five digits long. A range check would verify that an employee does not report working more than sixty hours a week.

More complex consistency checks can be very valuable, though they are less frequently used. For example, range checks on salaries may be conditioned on organizational position. For the president of the company, a wage payment of $2,000 per week may not be unlikely, whereas it would be for a clerk. In the same manner, shipments being sent to an address different from the customer's normal address may be suspicious. Such consistency checks are much more complex and time-consuming, both to construct and to execute, than simple range checks, since the procedures require comparing several different sources of information to determine consistency within individual records. Although the specific mechanisms for actually performing validation and consistency checks are largely technical issues, a determination of the extent of validation and the specific rules and procedures to be followed requires careful managerial consideration.

Surveillance

As noted earlier, computerized systems have often provided ways to stream-line operations and greatly reduce the number of steps and amount of paper-work involved in various activities. These systems can also greatly increase the difficulty in detecting security violations. A simple example, based on an actual "computer crime," may help to illustrate this point.

A certain company uses an on-line order-entry system to allow salesmen in the branch offices to place an order directly to the warehouse by telephone. A salesman, former employee, or outsider who has learned how to remotely access and use the system may place a large order early in the month, then rent a truck and pick up the merchandise at the warehouse. (Since the order was in the system, the warehouse personnel would be expecting the pickup.) Before the order is transferred to the billing system at the end of the month, the thief can cancel the order and thus remove all traces of it from the computer system. Over time the company may notice that its inventory rec-ords differ from the physical inventory. In a large warehouse with annual inventory turnover of $100,000,000 or more, a $500,000 discrepancy may be attributable to breakage or normal losses. If the discrepancy is large enough to be viewed as a problem, the most obvious assumption would be that the warehouse workers are stealing the equipment or that an intruder is breaking into the warehouse. The remedy would then likely be to install closed-circuit televisions and increase the number of security guards. The thief at a remote terminal would not be a likely suspect. (Don Parker, Stanford Research Insti-tute, has studied and documented several hundred actual computer crime cases.)[12]

Using the computer's capabilities, special surveillance procedures can be incorporated into the system to circumvent this type of crime.[13] There are at least two major forms: (1) audit log and (2) monitoring.

Audit Log.   Basic to the concept of an audit log or audit trail is a permanent record of every significant action executed by the system. Thus, as in the days of quill pen journals and ledgers, one log record is made of every order placed and another of every order canceled (rather than merely discarding or erasing the order record). In principle, log records are accumulated and never changed. Such an audit log can be used for several important purposes:[14]

1. Security-violation detection. An audit log can be used to help determine and diagnose certain security violations because there is a permanent rec-ord of the order entry, order pickup, and order cancellation).
2. Traditional auditing. An audit log, at least in part, is essential to tracing

transactions through the system as required in normal financial-auditing procedures.

3. Minor and massive recovery. In an on-line system, an audit log of some type is essential to allow effective recovery from malfunctions caused by software or hardware during normal operations. The periodic (typically nightly or weekly) backup tapes do not contain records of the transactions for the current day. But with an audit log, it is possible to reconstruct information that may have been destroyed or invalidated due to the malfunction. In cases of minor malfunctions, a recovery can be automated and accomplished in a few minutes or even seconds.

4. Correction of errors. In many systems, especially on-line systems, an error may be detected by the user immediately, such as accidentally typing the wrong account number or incorrectly deleting a specific account. The audit log can be helpful in reconstructing data that may have been incorrectly altered.

5. Deterrence. The mere existence of an audit log may be a deterrent to many security violations, especially by insiders. Even if one knows how to circumvent a given system's security procedures and normal checks and balances, the fact that one's actions may be detected from the audit log can be a deterrent.

The concept of an ex post facto security mechanism as a deterrent is often neglected in the design of many security procedures. The important point to note is that the computer system is only one part of the security process. Just as in the case of a "successful" bank robbery, ex post facto pursuit and prosecution are important.

A careful managerial study is necessary to determine what information should be captured in the audit log and how it should be organized for most effective use. Furthermore, a definite plan of active examination is necessary if security violations are to be detected in a timely manner. In many installations, audit logs are generated and stored, but never used. The audit logs should be used in both a systematic and nonsystematic manner. In the former case, standard reports should be devised that can be used to detect unusual situations, such as an unusually large number of invalid or incorrect log-in attempts, exceptionally large orders from certain customers, etc. An intruder who has sufficient knowledge of the standard report procedures, may find a way to violate system security that does not appear on any of the standard security-check reports. (The standard cliché in movie burglaries is for one of the robbers to say, "The guard makes his rounds every thirty minutes; that gives us twenty-five minutes to break into the safe.") But nonsystematic behavior can be accomplished by introducing an element of randomness into the examination, either by having the checking programs randomly select transactions for examination or by providing on-line access to the audit log, thus enabling security officers or management personnel to browse arbitrarily through the information.

Monitoring.   Monitoring is a more active form of surveillance. While the system is in operation, various forms of information and statistics can be gathered and displayed on special monitoring terminals. This type of facility can be used for a variety of security and nonsecurity related purposes:

1. Security-violation detection. Information system monitoring facilities can be used in a manner similar to closed-circuit television and intruder-detector systems. They may be used in a summary mode to note any unusual situations, such as an incorrect log-in attempt, numerous data input errors, or an exceptionally large order or withdrawal, or in a viewing mode to monitor in detail the actions of one or more specific terminal users.
2. Education. Such monitoring facilities can be extremely instructive to both new and current managers. By actually seeing the system in operation, at both the summary and detail levels, one can gain considerable insight into the operation of the organization. Many incorrect preconceived notions can be corrected and new patterns of operation observed.
3. System performance and utilization. By being able to monitor the system, its designers can explore possible areas of improvement. In one case it was observed that the lengthy "Englishlike" interface to the information system, though very popular with the infrequent management users, required excessive typing for the full-time system users and was the cause of most data-entry errors. This problem had not been brought to the attention of the designers during the previous six months of system operation, because the data-entry activity was organizationally and physically quite removed from the system designers.

There are two additional points that must be made about surveillance facilities. First, the audit-log and monitoring capabilities introduce additional possibilities for security violations (e.g., stealing the audit log may be easier than stealing the data base itself). Thus, the security of these facilities must be carefully studied. In some installations extensive precautions may be made to secure the computer facility and the operational data, while the backup and audit tapes are stored unguarded in the basement. Second, use of the audit and monitor facilities must itself be audit logged. Otherwise, a dishonest security officer or someone who finds out how to gain access to these facilities may be able to use them to violate security and operate undetected.

Needless to say, the various surveillance mechanisms and procedures described above have definite implications for the privacy of the system's users. The monitoring facility, for example, could essentially allow a manager to "look over the shoulder" of any terminal user indefinitely without the employee being aware of this monitoring activity. In this regard such facilities are similar to concealed closed-circuit televisions. Thus, careful consideration should be given to their mode and purpose for use, as well as the extent of knowledge about the existence of these systems that the company should allow.

Authorization

The authorization process is an extremely important issue with numerous facets. Two specific issues will be discussed in this section: (1) authorization control and (2) rigidity of authorization.

Authorization Control.   The access-control rules to be enforced by the system can be viewed, essentially, as merely another type of information in the system, but this information and the ability to change it have sweeping implications. A possible analogy is the safe that contains the combinations to all the other safes.

Changing the access-control rules (i.e., changes to authorizations) can be accomplished in various organizational ways. These methods can be divided into three major categories: centralized, hierarchical decentralized, and individual.

1. Centralized. A single individual or organizational unit, such as the security officer or data-base administrator, handles all authorizations.
2. Hierarchical decentralized. The central authorization organization may delegate some or all of its authority to subordinate organizations. For example, accounting files may be placed under the control of the head of accounting. Authority may then be further delegated (e.g., authorization control for certain accounting files may be assigned to different managers within the accounting organization). In most implementations the higher authorities in the authorization hierarchy retain the ability to revoke or override authorization decisions made by their subordinates.
3. Individual. In this situation no static authorization hierarchy exists. An individual may be allowed to create information (authorization to "create" may be controlled by either of the earlier two approaches), and the system would then recognize that individual as the "owner" of the information. The owner may authorize others to access the information, pass ownership to someone else, or establish co-ownership arrangements.

Each of these authorization approaches has advantages and disadvantages, which has led some organizations to develop combinations or variations of these basic strategies to meet their organizations' needs.

The centralized approach, not surprisingly, is largely motivated by the military concept of "security officers." With the increasing concern over the corporate "information resource" and the establishment of a data-base administration function in many organizations, this approach has been adopted by some companies and may be viable in small or highly structured organizations. However, in most large volatile or decentralized organizations, rapidly evolving functions and information, especially for test cases and development activities, as well as personnel turnover and reassignment, can result in an extremely large number of security authorizations being required every day. For example, in a study of a medium-sized but highly volatile organization (a university), it was found that authorization changes occurred at least once every three minutes.[15] Therefore, the centralized approach may not be desirable in organizations with a high volume of security authorization changes or where the organizational structure is too complex or decentralized to allow effective and intelligent centralized control over authorization changes.

The hierarchical decentralized approach has been widely recommended in the literature and is basic to the security implementation on certain systems, such as the Honeywell Multics system.[16] This approach allows the security authorization control to be delegated to the groups that can most effectively administer and monitor these controls. From an organizational point of view this may be very important. For example, if a division or function operates as a separate profit center with control over its own expenditures and plans, that division probably should have security-authorization control over its internal data.

A major problem with most implementations of this approach lies in the authority of higher levels in the authorization hierarchy to revoke or override all authorization decisions. This ability is usually viewed as necessary for organizational (i.e., "the boss is the boss") and operational (i.e., to correct mistakes in authorization assignments) reasons. However, no "private" information can exist in this system. By analogy to the normal office environment, this would be equivalent to banning locked drawers in employees' desks. This issue of "corporate privacy" (as opposed to the more commonly accepted concept of "personal privacy") has been a major factor in the reluctance of many groups within corporations to computerize their records. One salesman noted that he would rather destroy his personal notes on client companies, and the peculiarities of their purchasing agents, than risk having these notes computerized and thus allow the chance that this information could be seen by anyone else. Indeed, few individuals do not view as private at least some information, records, or notes pertinent to their organizations that they keep in the privacy of their offices. This problem is likely to increase significantly among white-collar workers and management as advances in office automation greatly increase the scope and diversity of information stored in computerized information systems.

The individual-authorization control is used in many simple systems. A convenient implementation is to allow the creator of a file to designate "owner" and "user" passwords for the file. The owner password allows one to change either of the passwords; the user password allows one to access the file. Various authorization objectives can be accomplished using such a system. Private information can be kept private simply by not divulging either of the passwords. (Note: it is assumed that no standard way is provided for anyone, whether president or systems programmer, to find the passwords for any file.) Access or ownership rights can be awarded by giving the passwords. One drawback to the password strategy is that it is impossible to identify all the people who know the password or to revoke access selectively. However, alternative strategies can be devised to accomplish the same results without using passwords in the manner noted above.

One problem with the individual-authorization approach, though, regardless of the implementation, is the potential for situations where it becomes necessary to override the security mechanism (e.g., the individual dies, becomes ill, leaves the company). In general, any security mechanism can be overcome, though some mechanisms, such as cryptographic encoding, are very difficult to break, even by the system's designers. If the mechanism is easy to break, the "privacy" assumed above will not exist; if it is very difficult to break, the organization may suffer if adverse circumstances occur.

Rigidity of Authorization.   Computer systems, lacking discretionary judgment, require that precise statements of access-control rules be enforced. Careful thought must be given to the establishment of these rules and the specific authorizations assigned.

The rigidity of the authorizations has posed various problems in the past. While testing the experimental Resource Security System (RSS), IBM's Federal Systems Center noted that "a major concern in FSC was that the use of a secure system would hamper our ability to react quickly to priority situations. . . . What this means, for purposes of system design, is that effective security overrides must be available to the installation."[17]

Most existing security systems either do not provide any security-override mechanism, or the override is in the form of a "panic" button that can be invoked by the security officer or computer operator to suspend all security enforcement. This approach is very crude, awkward to use, and may expose the system to security violations while security enforcement is suspended.

As an example, consider the situation of a doctor who desperately needs information about a patient admitted in an emergency. If the patient's regular doctor is currently unavailable to give the attending physician access to the patient's files, it should be possible to use a formal procedure whereby the attending physician can request access to the patient's file. The system will record this fact and the action will be subject to later review by the patient's regular doctor. Certainly, less rigid access-control rules are called for in such situations. For example, three levels of access control may be defined. The normal "access is allowed" or "access is prohibited" can be augmented by "access *may* be allowed." Thus, in environments where high ethical standards are the norm and/or ethical behavior is encouraged by practical constraints (e.g., ex post facto prosecution), certain users may be assigned "access may be allowed" permission to another user's private information. In these cases, any attempted access will trigger a special action to inform the user that the requested access is to private information. The user would then be required to acknowledge that this access is deliberate and to provide a brief explanation of the reason. The final decision as to the appropriateness of the access is deferred to human review at a later time.

This type of flexibility is rare in current security systems. Further development of these concepts and capabilities is essential in order to avoid the extremes of impairing effective use of the system or reverting to ad hoc emergency procedures all the time.

Security Responsibility

As should be clear from the preceding discussions, effective security requires the cooperation and planning of many people in an organization. Although certain aspects, such as awareness, require the active participation of almost everyone in the organization, most of the planning and decision-making issues are best resolved by a small number of people. Who should be responsible for security planning?

The problem of responsibility is complicated by the fact that at least three types of issues can be identified, each implying a potentially different type of organizational responsibility. These three issue types are:

1. Policy. Policy issues regarding the use and types of security procedures require the active participation, formulation, and acceptance by top-management personnel.
2. Operational. Mapping the policy decisions into practice requires a detailed

knowledge of the organization's information-processing activities and the available security-enforcement technologies. This type of activity would require the skills normally found in the data-base administration, systems programming, and computer operations functions.

3. Economic. It has been noted that many security issues are essentially economic decisions, involving uncertainty or incomplete information and risks. The decision to use a certain security procedure that costs X dollars and provides a specific but unquantified degree of protection against certain types of potential security violations is very similar to the decision to expend funds on a project to develop a new product. In this context the role of "risk managers" (i.e., individuals experienced in making such subjective decisions) has been suggested in the literature.[18]

The concept of risk managers has been used in a very broad context to accommodate the perception that important elements of risk exist at the policy and operational levels as well as for economic decisions. Therefore, some security experts have recommended to top management that ongoing risk-analysis teams be formed that include: (1) EDP operations management, (2) department managers, (3) applications programmers, (4) systems programmers, (5) internal auditors, and (6) physical security personnel.[19]

The specific security roles and responsibilities may vary from organization to organization, but careful planning and defining of responsibilities are essential to effective and operationally viable information system security.

Summary

This article has identified and categorized the key management policy and procedure issues relevant to the attainment of effective computer security. Although social, legal, and technical factors may be relevant in certain cases, the primary factors in each issue identified center on management decisions. Management must carefully weigh the operational, organizational, economic, and accountability implications of each of these decisions.

As our reliance upon computer-based information systems continues to increase and to propel us toward an even more comprehensive "information society," these issues will become increasingly critical.

12

Employee Privacy: Legal and Research Developments and Implications for Personnel Administration

Philip Adler, Jr.

Charles K. Parsons

Scott B. Zolke

The contemporary emphasis on privacy has created a myriad of complex personnel problems and associated approaches to handle them. These privacy-oriented problems generally involve social, ethical, legal, managerial, and even political considerations. Personnel administrators are constantly confronted with the privacy issue. This article attempts to synthesize privacy information relevant to personnel administration, and to provide personnel administrators with managerial guidance for handling employee privacy problems in the work environment. It places particular emphasis on differentiating between ethical and legal aspects of privacy in our society, and, accordingly, on clarifying existing confusion over the impact of so-called privacy laws on personnel administration. *SMR*.

Picture the following scenario. A supervisor's relationship with a subordinate has deteriorated to an antagonistic stage. The supervisor learns that the employee has been diagnosed by a physician as being paranoid. Seeking to strengthen his position and credibility in the matter, the supervisor circulates an interoffice memorandum indicating the physician's assessment of the employee's mental state. The employee challenges this action in court as libelous and an unnecessary invasion of privacy.

Can the previous situation occur? In fact, it has occurred and a state supreme court ruled in the employee's favor by stating that the employee's

From *Sloan Management Review*, Winter 1985, Vol. 26, No. 2. Reprinted with permission.

privacy had been violated by the interoffice memorandum.[1] This recent case, though another appeal is still possible, indicates the difficulty in maintaining the delicate balance between employer managerial interest and employee personal privacy. It also establishes another benchmark in the growing relationship between law and employee privacy that is now an integral area of concern within the field of personnel administration.

The issue of employee privacy has experienced a dramatic increase in attention from human-resource administrators during the past few years. After a relatively slow start, perhaps triggered by an Orwellian philosophy revolving around fear of "Big Brother," concern for personal privacy has rapidly moved from the realm of science fiction to the reality of governmental law and corporate ethics, becoming, in the process, a central issue of employee relations.

A right to privacy is routinely associated with citizenship in the United States. However, there is a growing debate concerning the extent to which the government should become involved as an explicit protector of this right. This debate is carried on in books, articles, technical reports, and other documents. Stone, Gardner, Gueutal, and McClure have reported that over 2,100 written documents have been recently published on the privacy issue.[2] In addition, both state and federal governments have become involved to some extent, continuing to gather information and to consider advocacy positions in the privacy area.

The fact that personal information is required in order to conduct business effectively in an increasingly complex society must be considered a principal contributor to the privacy issue. The question of what personal data is required to effectively conduct business affairs can be considered from a triangular perspective:

1. What personal data is actually required?
2. How will such data be obtained?
3. Under what circumstances will this data be released?

Use of personal data usually falls into two categories. The first category involves the use of personal information about the employees as an input to managerial decisions regarding hiring, work assignment, compensation and benefits, promotions, terminations, etc. The second category concerns the release of employee personal data to external individuals and organizations for such purposes as job references, credit checks, etc.

There appear to be two major sources of ambiguity when formulating and interpreting management policy in the area of employee rights to privacy. The first is, "What are the specific statutes and legal framework under which employees have a formal right to privacy?" The second is, "What information handling practices and managerial actions are likely to be perceived as privacy violations by employees?" We will address these two topics and discuss their implications for management policy making.

Legal Background of the General Privacy Issue

"There can be no public without full publicity in respect to all consequences which concern it. Whatever obstructs and restricts publicity, limits and distorts public opinion and checks and distorts thinking on social affairs."[3] Nevertheless, many societal functions would be ineffective were they not exercised in confidence.

The First Amendment serves to ensure the free flow of information and ultimately protects the idea of an informed public. This concept finds its origin as far back as the Magna Carta. However, the First Amendment freedoms are not absolute, and are tempered by three important restrictions: (1) the privilege to withhold records in safeguarding the national security; (2) compliance with statutory law; and (3) the prevention of unwarranted invasions of privacy.

Though commonly assumed to be a right of citizenship, the U.S. Constitution does not make specific mention of the right to privacy. However, as Duffy notes, Amendments 1, 2, 3, 4, 5, 9, and 14 have been interpreted as collectively providing some privacy protection. In addition, several states (Alaska, Arizona, California, and Washington) have enacted some degree of constitutional protection.[4] Rather than review these protections state by state, we suggest that interested readers further consult their particular state codes.

Although there is no general explicit constitutional right to privacy, many state and federal courts have recognized certain protected "zones" of privacy. The most widely recognized "zones" have centered on sex and marriage.

This growing concern for privacy has been the subject of many disputes, especially given the limited applicability of the Privacy Act of 1974. In resolving the tensions between the opposing needs of disclosure and confidentiality, the courts have been without any uniform rules.

The Privacy Act requires that: (1) federal agencies inform individuals (including federal employees) that there are personal data record-keeping systems containing information about them; (2) agencies permit individuals to copy, correct, and amend the recorded personal information; and (3) the type of data agencies may collect about an individual be limited. With certain exceptions, the agency must obtain written consent from the individual before making disclosures of personal information to outsiders.

The 1974 Privacy Act created the Privacy Protection Study Commission, which was to recommend to Congress principles and practices that should be required of private businesses. These recommendations, reported in 1977, include that the 1974 Privacy Act *not* be extended to the private sector, that employees be given some new privacy protection, and that private sector organizations adopt some privacy-policy protection on a voluntary basis.

As of 1981, nine states (Arkansas, California, Connecticut, Indiana, Massachusetts, Minnesota, Ohio, Utah, and Virginia) had passed privacy acts similar to the federal Privacy Act of 1974. Two other states (New York and Colorado) have passed less comprehensive laws. These laws, like their federal counterpart, apply to government agencies only. Eight states (California, Connecticut, Maine, Michigan, North Carolina, Oregon, Pennsylvania, and Wisconsin) now have legislation giving employees the right to inspect their own personnel file. Michigan's statute is the most detailed and provides safeguards as summarized by Duffy:

[E]mployees may, upon written request, examine and copy personnel records at a reasonable time and place. (The term *personnel records* appears to be broadly defined although the Act specifically excludes certain reference letters, comparative evaluations, medical reports, and investigative or grievance files maintained separately.) Employees may request that information in their personnel files may be amended or corrected. If the request is denied, they may file dissenting statements that are to be kept in a file with the disputed information. If the employer maintains investigative files, employees must be notified of their existence at the end of the investigation or after two years. Investigative files must be destroyed if no action is taken.

Duffy goes on to note that other states have not been as comprehensive, but specific information items have drawn attention. Polygraphs and other so-called truth-verification devices have at least some limitations on them in twenty-one states, with Massachusetts, New York, and Rhode Island absolutely prohibiting their use in the employment context. Other statutes limit the use of arrest records and restrict access to medical records and financial data by outside parties.[5]

In addition to the federal and state statutes, many courts now recognize an independent tort for invasion of privacy. The legal concept is founded upon that body of unwritten principles originally based on the usages and customs of the community, recognized and enforced by the courts. However, invasion of privacy is a separate and distinct entity from defamation.

Invasion of privacy occurs where information not reasonably related to a legitimate interest is disclosed. Defamation applies to those instances where false or misleading information is disclosed. In the context of employee-employer relationships, most courts will recognize the furtherance of the employer's business or the public good as constituting a legitimate interest.

Cases do exist where the disclosure of defamatory information, if reasonably believed to be true and necessitated by a need to protect a business interest, will not be actionable. On the other hand, disclosure of true, embarrassing, private facts to people who do not possess a legitimate interest in the subject matter, will constitute an invasion of privacy.[6]

One federal court has already recognized that an employer can be liable for negligence in the maintenance of a personnel file.[7] Along the same line of reasoning, Representatives Barry Goldwater, Jr., and Edward Koch introduced legislation in 1975 that would have set privacy guidelines applicable in the private sector. The "Comprehensive Right to Privacy Act" (H.R. 1984) was never voted upon; however, the findings of the seven-member Privacy Protection Study Commission are worthy of mention. The Commission recommended that legislation:

1. Require businesses to publish notice of their file and information systems;
2. Require businesses to collect, directly from the individual, only personal information necessary to accomplish proper business purposes;
3. Restrict the transfer of information between businesses;
4. Require businesses to ensure that personnel files are kept accurate and timely;
5. Allow individuals to inspect files;
6. Require businesses to provide written notice to any person concerning whom it has information;
7. Provide strong penalties for violations; and
8. Establish a board to oversee compliance.

It is suggested that regardless of which of these recommendations (if any) are codified by law, some type of uniform code is needed to clarify for the courts and personnel administrators those actions that are permissible. Consistent with the Commission's findings, most states' privacy statutes provide the employee with three procedural safeguards:

1. The right to be informed of the existence of the personnel file;
2. The right to inspect the personnel file; and
3. The right to correct inaccuracies in the personnel file.

Position of the Courts

In the decisions regarding privacy, most courts have concerned themselves with the preservation of two competing interests: the interest in avoiding disclosure of personal matters and the interest in providing for the free flow of information in making important business decisions. William Prosser, an authority on tort law in American jurisdictions, wrote that privacy could be categorized into four areas, two of which directly apply to the employment relationship: intrusion into private affairs and public disclosure of embarrassing private facts.[8]

Accordingly, when controversies arise regarding personnel files, employers will first have to be able to establish that they only retain information reasonably related to their business and that they have taken reasonable steps to preserve the privacy of their employees. For example, an employer's obligation to protect the privacy interests of its employees often conflicts with the needs of a labor union that seeks to review personnel files in order to protect its members from discriminatory hiring and firing practices. These conflicting interests require a careful balancing of the respective harms should such information be disclosed or withheld.

The privacy question has further been clouded by administrative investigations. When an employer receives a request to produce the personnel records of its employees, the employee has no standing from which to attack the request. It becomes incumbent upon the employer either to comply with the request, thereby breaching the employee's privacy, or to assert the employee's privacy rights and run the risk of being held in contempt for refusal to comply. These are the types of problems that, in the absence of uniform legislation, today's personnel administrators are faced with.

Landmark Court Decisions. Several noteworthy decisions indicate the direction that the United States Supreme Court is taking with respect to the privacy question. The most significant privacy case of the 1970s was *Whalen* v. *Roe*.[9] There, a state health agency required employers to disclose employee medical records in order to document the outbreak of contagious diseases. Roe contested this practice and argued that such disclosure was an unwarranted invasion of privacy. The United States Supreme Court rejected Roe's argument and held that the public interest in health was more important than the individual interest in keeping medical records private. Further, there was no showing of any immediate, physical, tangible injury, and hence the disclosure was upheld.

Privacy is often measured in terms of the expectations of the individual versus the public's interest in gaining access to the information. A recent decision by the United States Court of Appeals for the Sixth Circuit permitted a disclosure similar to that in *Whalen* v. *Roe,* but required the National Institute for Occupational Safety and Health to provide adequate security measures to protect the privacy of those employees whose medical records were reviewed.[10]

It would appear that when a federal agency governed by strict procedures for the safekeeping of records seeks access to confidential employee records, the courts will permit disclosure as long as there exists a reasonable relation to a job-related health hazard, and adequate safeguards are employed. However, one federal court has held that the interests in protecting employee health are superior to the privacy interests of the individual. As justification for such a position, the federal court held that the fact that the employees were willing to divulge sensitive information to their employer constituted a dilution of their privacy interests.[11]

Many times, before an agency can obtain employee records, the employee is asked to consent to disclosure. This is especially true in cases dealing with psychological testing data. The United States Supreme Court has ruled that where there exists substantial evidence of actual adverse effects to the employee from disclosure, a governmental agency cannot compel the employer to release sensitive information.[12] Hence, although the employee may have diluted his privacy interest by permitting the employer to accumulate sensitive information, any showing of actual harm will prevent forced disclosure.

As seen from these cases, the risk to the affected employee is a key component in determining whether information can be disclosed. Most government agencies have policies and procedures that minimize the risk that confidential information will be disclosed to noninterested parties. Should the disclosure pose such an adverse effect on the employee that to do so would offend reasonable sensibilities, most courts will refuse to compel an employer to comply with a request. On the other hand, as long as the agency has adequate safeguards, and the need for the information is related to health and safety, disclosure will be mandated.

Most courts have held that there is no infringement of privacy when ordinary sensibilities are not offended. So long as there is not a flagrant breach of decency and propriety, the courts will recognize that no individual can expect complete noninterference from the society in which he or she lives. Accordingly, information regarding salary, business connections, age, experience, education, and criminal convictions will not constitute an unwarranted intrusion into an individual's right to privacy.

Major Privacy Ambiguities

There continues to be confusion in the minds of many individuals, including personnel administrators, as to the legal status of employee privacy. The dividing line between legal and ethical controls affecting the privacy of employees is not so vague, however, as is frequently believed. In fact, there are actually few direct legal constraints protecting employee privacy. At present, there are no broad federal regulations protecting the privacy of private-sector employees. As noted earlier, the privacy of federal employees is protected by the Privacy Act of 1974. This federal law has been held by the courts to cover, in certain instances, state, county, and municipal employees.

Employees in the private sector, however, must still depend primarily upon the traditional legal implications of slander and libel, as well as ethical considerations, for the protection of personal data accumulated by their employers. However, due to the uncertainty of some personnel administrators about the existence and coverage of "privacy laws," private-sector employee privacy is often artificially protected by "government regulations" that, in reality, have no direct legal impact upon privacy matters. Some personnel administrators appear unaware that their "legal" concern for protecting employee privacy is actually based on governmental nondiscrimination laws, rather than on laws directly concerned with the employee-privacy issue.

Accordingly, private-sector employees may gain a certain subtle degree of privacy protection from their employers simply because of confusion about nondiscrimination laws with which managers desire to comply. Personnel administrators who believe they are complying with privacy laws that are actually nonexistent are basing their actions on familiarity with provisions of governmental nondiscrimination statutes.

In fact, a recent federal court decision has stated that an employer's invasion of employee privacy may constitute a civil-rights violation.[13] However, this issue arose because of the existence of pertinent civil rights legislation, rather than as a result of privacy laws per se. Thus, even if compliance occurs for the wrong legal reasons, personnel administrators "properly" protecting employee privacy will find themselves legally correct.

For another example, consider a recent case before the District Court of Appeals in Ohio. There, a jury verdict of $10,000 was sustained in an invasion-of-privacy case brought by an employee against his privately held corporate employer. The controversy centered on the employee's answer to a question regarding whether he had ever been convicted of a criminal offense. He answered in the negative and failed to note that he had previously been convicted of armed robbery in a juvenile-delinquency proceeding. Several months after he was hired, the personnel director learned of the juvenile proceedings from the local police. His employment was terminated as a result of the alleged false statement.

At the grievance hearing, wherein the nature of the juvenile conviction was disclosed, the personnel director, a union representative, and other employees were present. The employee's lawsuit sought damages for the invasion of his privacy, alleging that his employer should not have disclosed anything more than the existence of a juvenile-delinquency conviction.

In affirming the verdict, the appellate court noted that the right of privacy is concerned with a person's peace of mind that his private affairs will not be made public. Although an employer does have a qualified privilege to make limited communication to parties who possess a legitimate interest in the information, the publication of the nature of the juvenile offense, that is, the armed robbery, went beyond that privilege. This decision is especially significant inasmuch as the appellate court held that there exists no requirement that a plaintiff prove malice to sustain an invasion-of-privacy action.[14]

Currently, because of various court interpretations of the privacy issue, there is considerable question as to what is proper employee-privacy protection under civil-rights and nondiscrimination laws. The federal courts are clearly increasing their attention to the employee privacy issue, even if under the guise of civil-rights laws, and consequently, personnel administrators should be aware of a rapidly increasing number of pending cases and plaintiffs' awards in this regard. Accordingly, what may be "traditionally" accepted as proper protection of employee privacy is subject to sudden legal change.

Although the courts seem to recognize that employers must have a reasonable opportunity, relevant to possessing employee personal data, to conduct their business affairs, personnel administrators should not take this to mean they have a broad license regarding the collection and protection of such data. Even if employee personal data are kept secret upon acquisition by employer, the mere obtaining of some of that information may be a civil-rights violation. Thus, employers should be most cautious of asking the "wrong" questions (per court decisions) of employees, regardless of their opinion that such information is necessary to the conduct of "normal" business activity.

Summary of Legal Background

There are multiple indicators that protection of employee privacy will receive even more emphasis in the near future. First, as noted above, the right to privacy is commonly assumed to be a basic right of U.S. citizens. However, there are several trends in our society indicating that the protection of these rights is becoming more problematic. Many people have heard of the Privacy Act of 1974, but it is a common misconception that the Act applies to a wide range of employment situations. In fact, the Act only covers employees of federal agencies. It prohibits certain information-dissemination practices without employee approval, and it requires that employees be permitted to review their information files upon request. However, these protections have not yet been extended to the private sector.

Second, several states have passed some form of law to protect privacy rights, but these vary in comprehensiveness. Although most of the state laws are relatively new, it is probable that both interpretation and enforcement of the laws will be inconsistent across these states.

Third, there are commercial and governmental interests in information about people, and employers provide a potentially rich souce of this information. For instance, the concept of credit rating is based on the idea that credit bureaus should gather individual financial data, including present salary and salary history.

Fourth, there is also a growing capacity within organizations to gather, save, and rapidly transmit employee information through computers and telecommunications devices. The improvement in technological capacity has been accompanied by the creation of centralized databases within organizations that can gather many pieces of information about an employee that in the past had been scattered throughout the organization. All of these above conditions are viewed by some as threats to the basic right of privacy, leading to the continuing debate on workplace privacy.

On a national level, the debate will be fueled by incidents of employee privacy violation that gain national attention. For a given organization, the amount of conflict surrounding issues of employee privacy will be determined by the accumulation of privacy violations. Therefore, it becomes very important to understand what factors and information-handling practices affect employee perceptions of privacy violations. We will now review the recent research on perceptions of privacy violation.

Research on Perceptions of Privacy Violation

Research on employee perceptions of privacy is only beginning to accumulate. However, the studies that do exist suggest that there are a number of factors that affect perceptions of privacy violation. The first point of interest is whether or not employees know how their employers handle employee personal information. In a survey of 2,047 employees from five companies, Woodman, Ganster, Adams, McCuddy, Tolchinsky, and Fromkin found that across sixty information items (e.g., demographics such as age and sex, financial situation, medical information), employee beliefs about whether or not the company retained information were accurate an average of 68 percent of the time.[15] Management in each of the five companies had reported actual practices.

Employees tended to overestimate the maintenance of affiliation information (union, religious, political) and underestimate the maintenance of medical information. These inaccuracies are understandable because 85 percent of the employees reported that they had never inspected their personnel file. When asked whether or not they had experienced an upsetting incident in their company's handling of their personal information, 7 percent said yes to a disclosure within the firm and 3 percent said yes to some disclosure outside the firm. As a general reaction to the company's information handling practices, 44 percent were satisfied, 22 percent were dissatisfied, and 34 percent reported uncertain.

One of the most disturbing findings from this study is the general lack of knowledge about what is maintained and what is not. A lack of knowledge sets a fertile ground for rumors based on isolated incidents of privacy violations.

The same survey reported which information-handling practices employees felt were most disturbing.[16] Each respondent in the survey responded to one of sixteen hypothetical job situations that reflected different practices. The four factors studied were: (1) type of information (personality or performance); (2) permission for disclosure (yes or no); (3) consequences of disclosure (positive or negative outcome for employee); and (4) location of disclosure (released to sources within the organization [internal] or sources outside the organization [external]).

All factors were found to be statistically significant, with greater perceived privacy invasion occurring: (1) for release of personality rather than performance information, (2) for permission not obtained prior to release, (3) for a negative rather than a positive consequence, and (4) for information released to an external rather than an internal party. Probably more interesting was the finding that permission was the most important factor. In fact, when prior permission is obtained, there is no difference between releasing information to internal or external parties. Also of interest was the finding that the outcome of the information release (positive or negative) was a relatively minor factor compared to whether or not permission was obtained prior to disclosure. Clearly, an individual's perceived control over personal information (permission obtained before release) is more important than the eventual outcome as far as perceptions of privacy are concerned.

This latter conclusion was also supported in a study by Fusilier and Hoyer who used a hypothetical personnel selection situation. Respondents felt a greater degree of privacy invasion when personal information from their current employer was released without their consent than when permission was obtained.[17] In addition, if the respondent received a job offer, perceived privacy violation was lower than if he or she did not get the offer. In this study, the location of the disclosure (within a university or outside a university) and type of information (personality or performance) did not make a difference.

Though the current article has focused on the employer-employee relationship, there are many other institutions that gather, retain, and disseminate personal information (e.g., insurance companies, the Internal Revenue Service, lending and other credit-granting institutions, and law-enforcement agencies). The question about public perceptions of the relative likelihood of privacy violations in different institutions was the topic of a study. In interviews with 193 subjects, Stone et al. asked about individuals' values, beliefs, attitudes, experiences, and future intentions concerning information-handling practices in one of six different types of institutions, one of which was an employer. The researchers found that individuals felt more confident about their ability to control personal information maintained by their employer than their ability to control that maintained by any other type of institution. However, this difference in confidence did not produce significant differences in willingness to support legislation that would control information-handling practices in these different institutions. The researchers also noted that the average scores for the legislation-support scale were relatively high across all institutions.[18]

Managerial Implications and Conclusions

From our review of both the legal and psychological literature on workplace privacy, it is clear that the handling of employee information in organizations has important implications for personnel administrators. Present case law leaves many questions unanswered, and the private sector is not covered by legislation in most states. Therefore, the enactment of uniform guidelines incorporating the recommendations of the Privacy Commission would be helpful to personnel administrators.

Regardless of further governmental standards, personnel administrators essentially have two broad internal roles to perform regarding the protection of employee privacy. The first role relates to privacy considerations involved in carrying out their standard staff unit activities such as hiring, training, compensating, and grievance administration. The second role relates to providing staff technical guidance in the privacy arena for managers throughout their organization. Clearly, the performance of the first role establishes the basic pattern for handling employee privacy within that organization, since managers will likely follow the tone of the "examples" on this issue set by their personnel administrators.

Personnel administrators also have an external role to perform for their organizations relevant to protecting privacy of employees. This role involves the furnishing of employee personal information to third parties regarding job references, credit checks, legal investigations, insurance risks, etc. Ironically, this external role, with its lesser direct bearing on internal organizational operations, may create the most difficult and potentially dangerous employee-privacy challenges for management. We offer some of the more obvious implications and suggest that concerned readers follow up with more detailed suggestions provided by Duffy or Noel.[19]

1. Develop a formal information-practices plan. To avoid sensitizing people, do not use the phrase *privacy plan*. The plan should be written and circulated to all employees. Supervisors and managers must be made especially aware of their responsibilities concerning their own behavior and that of their subordinates.
2. Get employees involved and have them review their personnel files on a scheduled basis. Have employees formally acknowledge this review.
3. Be careful about personal data not directly related to job performance. Eliminate outdated information. Identify the purpose of each piece of data and who can have access to it.
4. Be careful about outside release. Have employees formally acknowledge what data can and cannot be released to which type of institution. It is the party that releases the information that is at risk, not the party that seeks the information.

Finally, the current dynamics of the employee-privacy issue preclude the statement of exacting positions that will eliminate risk in this sensitive area. However, this fluidity does not prevent personnel administrators from understanding general positions and trends in the area.

References

Introduction

1. M. E. Porter, *Competitive Strategy* (New York: Free Press, 1980).
2. W. Glueck, *Business Policy, Strategy Formulation and Management Action* (New York: McGraw-Hill, 1976).
3. Porter (1980).
4. R. E. Miles and C. C. Snow, *Organizational Strategy: Structure and Process* (New York: McGraw-Hill, 1978).
5. J. F. Rockart, "Chief Executives Define Their Own Data Needs," *Harvard Business Review,* March–April 1979.
6. C. V. Bullen and J. F. Rockart, "A Primer on Critical Success Factors" (Center for Information Systems Research [CISR] Working Paper #69, Sloan School of Management, MIT, June 1981).
7. A. Bernstein, "It's 1985. Do You Know What Your Information Management Policy Is?" *Business Computer Systems,* March 1985, pp. 70–76.

Chapter 1

1. A. M. Kantrow, "The Strategy-Technology Connection," *Harvard Business Review,* July–August 1980, pp. 6–21.
2. T. Levitt, "The Globalization of Markets," *Harvard Business Review,* May–June 1983, pp. 92–102.
3. Kantrow (July–August 1980).
4. M. E. Porter, *Competitive Strategy* (New York: Free Press, 1980).
5. G. L. Parsons, "Information Technology: A New Competitive Weapon," *Sloan Management Review,* Fall 1983, pp. 3–14; and F. W. McFarlan, "Linking I-S Strategy—Corporate Strategy" (Harvard Business School, Research Paper, 75th Anniversary Colloquium Series, July 10–13, 1983).
6. M. S. Scott Morton and J. F. Rockart, "Implications of Changes in Information Technology for Corporate Strategy" (CISR Working Paper #98, MIT, 1983).
7. See, for example, M. Gerstein and H. Reisman, "Creating Competitive Advantage with Computer Technology," *The Journal of Business Strategy,* Summer 1982, pp. 53–60; and H. C. Lucas, Jr., and J. A. Turner, "A Corporate Strategy for the Control of Information Processing," *Sloan Management Review,* Spring 1982, pp. 25–36.
8. Porter (1980), p. 2.
9. E. A. von Hippel, "Users as Innovators," *Technology Review,* January 1978.
10. J. L. Dionne, "Confronting the Communications Revolution," *The Journal of Business Strategy,* Summer 1983, pp. 74–77.

Chapter 2

1. Theodore Levitt, "Marketing Myopia," *Harvard Business Review,* November–December 1960, pp. 76–84.
2. Gregory L. Parsons, "Information Technology: A New Competitive Weapon," *Sloan Management Review,* Fall 1983, pp. 3–14.
3. F. Warren McFarlan, "Information Technology Changes the Way You Compete," *Harvard Business Review,* May–June 1984, pp. 98–103.
4. John F. Rockart and Adam D. Crescenzi, "Engaging Top Management in Information Technology," *Sloan Management Review,* Summer 1984, pp. 3–16.
5. Michael Porter, *Competitive Strategy* (New York: Free Press, 1980).
6. Rockart and Crescenzi (1984).

Chapter 3

1. *Wall Street Journal,* "Direct Data," 12 January 1983; *Wall Street Journal,* "Automated Self-Service Machines Spread after Their Success in Banks," July 21, 1983.
2. J. Dearden, "Will the Computer Change the Job of Top Management?" *Sloan Management Review,* Fall 1983, pp. 57–60.
3. L. M. R. Calingo, J. C. Camillus, P. Jenster, and T. S. Raghunathan, "Strategic Management and Organizational Action: A Conceptual Synthesis" (University of Pittsburgh: Working Paper Series, WP-527); and J. C. Camillus, "Strategic Management: Reflections on an Alternative Paradigm" (University of Pittsburgh: Working Paper Series, WP-476).
4. "SABRE—Realtime Benchmark Has the Winning Ticket," *Data Management,* September 1981, p. 26.
5. *Sun Oil Company (A) and (B)* (Boston: HBS Case Services #9-170-033/034, 1970).
6. W. R. King, "Strategic Planning for Management Information Systems," *MIS Quarterly,* March 1978, pp. 27–37; and *Business Week,* "Walden Books: Countering B. Dalton by Aping Its Computer Operations," October 8, 1979, p. 116.
7. Camillus (WP-476).
8. P. G. W. Keen and M. S. Scott Morton, *Decision Support Systems: An Organizational Perspective* (Reading, MA: Addison-Wesley, 1978).
9. H. A. Simon, *The New Science of Management Decision* (New York: Harper & Row, 1960).
10. Keen and Scott Morton (1978).
11. A. L. Lederer, "Going Outside or 'Why Buy a Programmer When You Can Rent One for Less?' " *Proceedings of the Eighteenth Annual Computer Personnel Research Conference of the ACM,* 1981, pp. 351–370.
12. D. McGregor, *The Human Side of Enterprise* (New York: McGraw-Hill, 1960).
13. J. C. Camillus, "Designing a Capital Budgeting System That Works," *Long Range Planning,* April 1984, pp. 57–60.
14. W. Glueck, *Business Policy, Strategy Formation and Management Action* (New York: McGraw-Hill, 1976); R. E. Miles and C. C. Snow, *Organizational Strategy: Structure and Process* (New York: McGraw-Hill, 1978); and M. E. Porter, *Competitive Strategy* (New York: Free Press, 1980).

Chapter 4

1. W. Hamilton and M. Moses, "A Computer-Based Corporate Planning System," *Management Science* (October 1974), pp. 148–159.
2. A. Kantrow, "The Strategies—Technology Connection," *Harvard Business Review,* July–August 1980, pp. 6–21.

3. "Market Research by Scanner," *Business Week,* May 5, 1980, pp. 113–114.
4. H. C. Lucas, Jr., and J. Moore, "A Multiple-Criterion Scoring Approach to Information Project Selection," *INFOR,* February 1976, pp. 1–12.
5. For further details of these plans, see J. Dearden and R. Nolan, "How to Control the Computer Resource," *Harvard Business Review,* November–December 1973, pp. 68–75.

Chapter 5

1. For a recent excellent experience-based effort toward explicating the role of the I/S executive today, see W. R. Synnott and W. H. Gruber, *Information Resource Management* (New York: John Wiley, 1981).
2. J. F. Rockart and L. S. Flannery, "The Management of End User Computing" (Proceedings of International Conference on Information Systems, December 1981).
3. J. F. Rockart, "Chief Executives Define Their Own Data Needs," *Harvard Business Review,* March–April 1979, p. 81.
4. D. R. Daniel, "Management Information Crisis," *Harvard Business Review,* September–October 1961, p. 111; and Rockart (March–April 1979).
5. C. V. Bullen and J. F. Rockart, "A Primer on Critical Success Factors" (CISR, Sloan School of Management, MIT, Working Paper #69, June 1981).
6. P. G. W. Keen and M. S. Scott Morton, *Decision Support Systems: An Organization Perspective* (Reading, MA: Addison-Wesley, 1978); G. A. Gorry and M. S. Scott Morton, "A Framework for Management Information Systems," *Sloan Management Review,* Fall 1971, p. 55; J. F. Rockart and M. E. Treacy, "Executive Information Support Systems" (CISR Working Paper No. 65, November 1980; Revised April 1981); and J. F. Rockart and M. E. Treacy, "The CEO Goes On-line," *Harvard Business Review,* January–February 1982, p. 82.
7. C. F. Gibson and R. L. Nolan, "Managing the Four Stages of EDP Growth," *Harvard Business Review,* January–February 1974, pp. 76–85.

Chapter 6

1. J. F. Rockart, "Chief Executives Define Their Own Data Needs," *Harvard Business Review,* March–April 1979, pp. 81–93.
2. R. D. Daniel, "Management Information Crisis," *Harvard Business Review,* September–October 1961, p. 111.
3. C. V. Bullen and J. F. Rockart, "A Primer on Critical Success Factors" (CISR Working Paper #69, Sloan School of Management, MIT, June 1981).
4. E. W. Martin, "Critical Success Factors of Chief MIS/DP Executives—An Addendum," *MIS Quarterly,* December 1982, pp. 79–81; and J. F. Rockart, "The Changing Role of the Information Systems Executive: A Critical Success Factors Perspective," *Sloan Management Review,* Fall 1982, pp. 3–13.
5. M. C. Munro, "An Opinion . . . Comment on Critical Success Factors Work," *MIS Quarterly,* September 1983, pp. 67–68.
6. M. C. Munro and B. R. Wheeler, "Planning Critical Success Factors, and Management's Information Requirements," *MIS Quarterly,* December 1980, pp. 27–38.
7. C. R. Anderson, *Management: Skills, Functions, and Organization Performance* (Dubuque, IA: William C. Brown, 1984).
8. C. R. Ferguson and R. Dickinson, "Critical Success Factors for Directors in the Eighties," *Business Horizons,* May–June 1982, pp. 14–18.
9. Munro (September 1983), pp. 66–68.
10. G. B. Davis, "Comments on the Critical Success Factors Method for Obtaining Management

Information Requirements in Article by John F. Rockart," *MIS Quarterly,* September 1979, pp. 57–58.

11. G. B. Davis, "Letter to the Editor," *MIS Quarterly,* June 1980, pp. 69–70.

12. W. R. King and R. W. Zmud, "Management Information Systems: Policy Planning, Strategic Planning, and Operational Planning," *Proceedings* (Second International Conference on Information Systems, Cambridge, MA, December 1982), pp. 299–308.

13. R. W. Zmud, *Information Systems in Organizations* (Glenview, IL: Scott, Foresman, 1983).

14. H. A. Simon, *The New Science of Management Decision* (New York: Harper & Row, 1979).

15. *Ibid.*

16. Davis (September 1979), pp. 57–58; Davis (June 1980), pp. 69–70.

Chapter 7

1. J. F. Rockart and M. S. Scott Morton, "Implications of Changes in Information Technology for Corporate Strategy," *Interfaces,* January–February 1984; "Foremost-McKesson: The Computer Moves Distribution to Center Stage," *Business Week,* December 7, 1981, pp. 115–122.

2. J. F. Rockart, "Chief Executives Define Their Own Data Needs," *Harvard Business Review,* March–April 1979, pp. 81–93; and C. V. Bullen and J. F. Rockart, "A Primer on Critical Success Factors" (CISR Working Paper #69, Sloan School of Management, MIT, June 1981).

3. R. A. Carpenter, "Designing and Developing Adaptive Information Systems," *Computer Technology Review,* Spring–Summer 1982, pp. 19–28.

4. The typology is taken from R. A. Anthony, *Planning and Control: A Framework for Analysis* (Cambridge, MA: Division of Research, Harvard Business School, 1965).

5. J. C. Henderson and M. A. Alavi, "An Evolutionary Strategy for Implementing a Decision Support System," *Management Science,* November 1981, pp. 1309–1323.

Chapter 8

1. One articulation of this idea, although it is by no means the first, appeared in 1974. See C. F. Gibson and R. L. Nolan, "Managing the Four Stages of EDP Growth," *Harvard Business Review,* January–February 1974, pp. 76–88.

2. IBM Corporation has produced considerable documentation on the BSP methodology and continues to teach the methodology to information systems professionals. Many consulting and accounting firms have produced variations on BSP. A good example of one of the extensions of the idea can be found in C. Finkelstein, *Principles of Information Engineering* (Englewood Cliffs, NJ: Prentice-Hall, 1982). For an overview of data-oriented planning methodologies, see J. Martin, *Strategic Data-Planning Methodologies* (Englewood Cliffs, NJ: Prentice-Hall, 1982).

3. The attempt to adapt SOG planning to a data-resource era may be found in R. L. Nolan, "Managing the Crises in Data Processing," *Harvard Business Review,* March–April 1979, pp. 115–126. For two introductions to IRM, see J. Diebold, "Information Resource Management: The New Challenge," *Infosystems,* June 1979, pp. 50–53; and J. Diebold, "IRM: New Directions in Management," *Infosystems,* October 1979, pp. 41–42. See also E. Truath, "Research-Oriented Perspective on Information Management," *Journal of Systems Management,* July 1984, pp. 12–17.

4. J. F. Rockart, "Chief Executives Define Their Own Data Needs," *Harvard Business Review,* March–April 1979; J. F. Rockart and M. E. Treacy, "Executive Information Support Systems" (Center for Information Systems Research Working Paper No. 65, November 1980;

revised April 1981); and C. V. Bullen and J. F. Rockart, "A Primer on Critical Success Factors" (CISR Working Paper #69, Sloan School of Management, MIT, June 1981).

5. An account of the study, excluding names of participating firms, is available as a research paper from the Information Technology Planning Corporation in Chicago.

6. The purpose of this article is to describe which kinds of planning, including architecture planning, work best in different systems environments. For a more complete introduction to, and treatment of, information technology architecture planning specifically, see C. H. Sullivan, "Rethinking Computer Systems Architecture," *Computerworld Extra,* 17 November 1982. An important element of this kind of planning is the process of modeling business requirements and technology capabilities.

Chapter 9

1. J. Naisbitt, *Megatrends* (New York: Warner Books, 1982).

2. L. Marion, "The Big Wallet Era," *Datamation,* September 1984, pp. 76–88.

3. L. F. Young, "The Information System as a Corporate Strategic Weapon," *Information Strategy: The Executive's Journal,* Fall 1984, pp. 21–25.

4. J. W. Verity, "1985 DP Budget Survey," *Datamation,* March 1985, pp. 74–78.

5. K. Mayo, "The VAR Option," *Business Computer Systems,* March 1985, pp. 60–66.

6. L. McCartney, "The New Info Centers," *Datamation,* July 1983, pp. 30–46.

7. R. A. Anthony, "Planning and Control: A Framework for Analysis" (Cambridge, MA: Harvard Business School, 1965).

8. J. Diebold, "John Diebold Talks about Information Management," *Computerworld,* December 6, 1982, pp. 2–28.

9. J. S. Mallory, "The Rising Tide of Information Management," *Computerworld,* November 8, 1982, pp. 2–14.

10. J. F. Rockart, "The Changing Role of the Information Systems Executive: A Critical Success Factors Perspective," *Sloan Management Review,* Fall 1982, pp. 3–13.

11. J. Diebold (December 6, 1982).

12. R. Youstra, "IBM NAO—Data Systems Support," *Washington Systems Center Technical Bulletin* (Gaithersburg, MD: IBM, April 1982).

13. R. Schneiderman, "Micro Managers' Becoming an Extension of MIS/dp," *Systems and Software,* April 1985, pp. 53–54.

14. R. M. Dickinson, "Telecom Management: An Emerging Art," *Datamation,* March 1984, pp. 121–130.

15. A. Bernstein, "It's 1985. Do You Know What Your Information-Management Policy Is?" *Business Computer Systems,* March 1985, pp. 70–76.

Chapter 10

1. American Bar Association, *Report on Computer Crime* (Washington, DC: American Bar Association, Computer Crime Task Force, White-Collar Crime Committee, Criminal Justice Section, June 1984).

2. H. H. Stevenson and J. Timmons, "Entrepreneurship Education in the 80's: What Do Entrepreneurs Say?" (Presented at Symposium on Entrepreneurship at Harvard Business School, July 6–8, 1983). Forthcoming in *Harvard Business School Colloquium Proceedings.*

Chapter 11

1. S. H. Nycum, "Legal Aspects of Computer Abuse," *Proceedings IEEE Computer Society International Conference,* February 1976, pp. 181–183.
2. K. S. Shankar, "The Total Computer Security Problem: An Overview," *Computer,* June 1977, pp. 50–73.
3. J. Martin, *Security, Accuracy, and Privacy in Computer Systems* (Englewood Cliffs, NJ: Prentice-Hall, 1973).
4. T. Alexander, "Waiting for the Great Computer Rip-off," *Fortune,* July 1974, pp. 143–150; C. F. Hemphill, Jr., and J. M. Hemphill, *Security Procedures for Computer Systems* (Homewood, IL: Dow Jones-Irwin, 1973); D. B. Hoyt, ed., *Computer Security Handbook* (New York: Macmillan Co., 1973); S. W. Leibholz and L. D. Wilson, *User's Guide to Computer Crime: Its Commission, Detection and Prevention* (Radnor, PA: Chilton, 1974); Martin (1973); D. Van Tassel, *Computer Security Management* (Englewood Cliffs, NJ: Prentice-Hall, 1972).
5. P. S. Browne and J. A. Cosenting, "I/O—A Logistics Challenge," *Proceedings 74 Eighth IEEE Computer Society International Conference,* February 1974, pp. 61–64.
6. IBM, *Data Security and Data Processing,* vol. 6, International Business Machines Corp., Data Processing Div., form no. G320-1376 (White Plains, NY, 1974).
7. B. R. Allen, "Embezzlement and Automation," *Proceedings IEEE Computer Society International Conference,* February 1976, pp. 187–188; J. Honig, "Company Security and Individual Freedom," *Datamation,* January 1974, p. 131.
8. R. H. Courtney, Jr., "Security Risk Assessment in Electronic Data Processing," *AFIPS Conference Proceedings* 46, National Computer Conference (1977), pp. 97–104; S. Glaseman, R. Turn, and R. S. Gaines, "Problem Areas in Computer Security Assessment," *AFIPS Conference Proceedings* 46, National Computer Conference (1977), pp. 105–112.
9. N. R. Nielsen, "Computers, Security, and the Audit Function," *AFIPS Conference Proceedings* 44, National Computer Conference (1975), pp. 947–954.
10. D. Clements and L. J. Hoffman, "Computer Assisted Security System Design," Electronics Research Laboratory, ERL-M468 (University of California, Berkeley, 1974).
11. IBM (vol. 3, pt. 2, form no. G 320-1373, 1974).
12. D. B. Parker, *Crime by Computer* (New York: Charles Scribner, 1976).
13. P. Hamilton, *Computer Security* (London: Associated Business Programmes, 1972).
14. E. Myers, "News in Perspective/Computer Criminal Beware," *Datamation,* December 1975, p. 105; Nielsen (1975); J. Wasserman, "Selecting a Computer Audit Package," *The Journal of Accountancy,* April 1974, pp. 30–34.
15. IBM (vol. 4, form no. G320-1374).
16. B. J. Walker and I. F. Blake, *Computer Security and Protection Structures* (Stroudsburg, PA: Dowden, Hutchinson & Ross, 1977).
17. IBM (vol. 6, form no. G320-1376).
18. "News in Perspective/Risk Managers Urged for Curbing Fraud," *Datamation,* June 1976, pp. 155–157; and D. Firnberg, "Your Computer in Jeopardy," *Computer Decisions,* July 1976, pp. 28–30.
19. A. Weissman, "Security—The Analyst's Concern," *Modern Data,* April 1974, p. 28; Nielsen (1975).

Additional Readings

L. J. Hoffman, *Modern Methods for Computer Security and Privacy* (Englewood Cliffs, NJ: Prentice-Hall, 1977).

D. K. Hsiao, D. S. Kerr, and S. E. Madnick, *Computer Security—Problems and Solutions* (New York: Academic Press, 1979).

IBM, *Data Security and Data Processing,* vols. 1–6, International Business Machines Corp., Data Processing Div., form nos. G320/1370–1376 (White Plains, NY, 1974).

E. Meyers, "News in Perspective/The Benefits of a Year Old Scandal: 'Everybody's Teaching EDP Auditing'," *Datamation,* March 1974, pp. 116–118.

N. R. Nielsen, D. H. Brandin, J. D. Madden, B. Ruder, G. F. Wallace, "Computer System Integrity Safeguards System Integrity Maintenance," Stanford Research Institute (Menlo Park, CA, 1976).

S. K. Reed, and D. K. Branstad, eds., "Controlled Accessibility Workshop Report," NBC/ACM Workshop (Rancho Santa Fe, CA, 1972).

Chapter 12

1. "SJC Outlines Rules on Employer Role in Workers' Privacy," *Boston Globe,* July 7, 1984. Decision upheld August 6, 1984, in U.S. Court of Appeals, First Circuit.
2. E. F. Stone, D. G. Gardner, H. G. Gueutal, and S. McClure, "A Field Experiment Comparing Information Privacy Values, Beliefs, and Attitudes across Several Types of Organizations," *Journal of Applied Psychology* 68 (1983), pp. 459–468.
3. J. Dewey, "The Public and Its Problems," in *Civil Liberties in American History,* ed. L. W. Levy (New York: Da Capo Press, 1941).
4. D. J. Duffy, "Privacy vs. Disclosure: Balancing Employee and Employer Rights," *Employee Relations Law Journal* 7 (1982), pp. 594–609.
5. *Ibid.*
6. Quinones v. United States, 492 F. 2d 1269 (3rd Cir., 1974); and W. Prosser and W. P. Keeton, *On Torts,* 5th ed. (St. Paul, MN: West, 1984), pp. 856–857.
7. Bulkin v. Western Kraft East, Inc., 422 F. Supp. 437 (E.D. Pa. 1976).
8. W. Prosser, "Privacy," *California Law Review* 48 (1960), p. 383.
9. Whalen v. Roe, 429 U.S. 589 (1977).
10. General Motors Corp. v. Director of NIOSH, 636 F. 2d 164 (6th Cir., 1980).
11. United States v. Allis-Chalmers Corp., 498 F. Supp. 1027 (E.D. Wis. 1980).
12. Detroit Edison Co. v. National Labor Relations Board, 440 U.S. 301 (1979).
13. Phillips v. Smalley Maintenance Services, 711 F. 2d 1524 (11th Cir., 1983), 435 So. 2d 705 (Ala. 1983).
14. Chambers v. Terex Corp., Cuyahoga County, Ohio, 8th District Court of Appeals, March 31, 1984.
15. R. W. Woodman, D. C. Ganster, J. Adams, M. K. McCuddy, P. D. Tolchinsky, and H. L. Fromkin, "A Survey of Employee Perceptions on Information Privacy in Organizations," *Academy of Management Journal* 25 (1982), pp. 647–663.
16. P. D. Tolchinsky, M. K. McCuddy, J. Adams, D. C. Ganster, R. W. Woodman, and H. L. Fromkin, "Employee Perceptions of Invasion of Privacy: A Field Simulation Experiment," *Journal of Applied Psychology* 66 (1981), pp. 308–313.
17. M. R. Fusilier and W. D. Hoyer, "Variables Affecting Perceptions of Invasion of Privacy in a Personnel Selection Situation," *Journal of Applied Psychology* 65 (1980), pp. 623–626.
18. E. F. Stone, D. G. Gardner, H. G. Gueutal, and S. McClure, "A Field Experiment Comparing Information Privacy Values, Beliefs, and Attitudes across Several Types of Organizations," *Journal of Applied Psychology* 68 (1983), pp. 459–468.
19. Duffy (1982), pp. 594–609; and A. Noel, "Privacy: A Sign of Our Times," *Personnel Administrator* 26 (1981), pp. 59–62.

Index

PRAISE FOR *BOYCOTT, DIVESTMENT, SANCTIONS*

"I have been to Palestine where I've witnessed the racially segregated housing and the humiliation of Palestinians at military roadblocks. I can't help but remember the conditions we experienced in South Africa under apartheid. We could not have achieved our freedom without the help of people around the world using the nonviolent means of boycotts and divestment to compel governments and institutions to withdraw their support for the apartheid regime. Omar Barghouti's lucid and morally compelling book is perfectly timed to make a major contribution to this urgently needed global campaign for justice, freedom, and peace."

—Archbishop Desmond Tutu

"I commend this excellent book by Omar Barghouti.... It challenges the international community to support the BDS campaign until the entire Palestinian people can exercise their inalienable rights to freedom and self-determination and until Israel fully complies with its obligations under international law. BDS is a call to refuse to be silent in the face of military occupation of the Palestinian people by the Israeli regime, apartheid, and colonialism. BDS is a nonviolent way in which each of us and our governments can follow our conscience and rightful moral and legal responsibility and act now to save Palestinian lives by demanding that the Israeli apartheid regime give justice and equality to all."

—Mairead Maguire, 1976 Nobel Peace Laureate

"This is a book about the political actions necessary to hinder and finally to stop the Israeli state machine that is operating every day to eliminate the Palestinian people. It is like an engineer's report, not a sermon. Read it, decide, and then act."

—John Berger, author

"When powerful governments will not act, ordinary people must take the lead.... Essential reading for all who care about justice and the plight of an oppressed people."

—Ken Loach, filmmaker

"The ABC for internationalist support for Palestine is BDS. And the boycott, divestment, and sanctions campaign against Israeli cruelty and injustice is gaining in significance and scope. Like the anti-apartheid movement against racist South Africa, BDS is helping to make a tremendous difference in what has been a most difficult struggle for human rights and the right of a colonized and dispossessed people to national self-determination. This inspiring book is a weapon in a noble struggle in which all right-thinking people can play a part."

—Ronnie Kasrils, author, activist, and
former South African government minister

"Once again Omar Barghouti delivers a conceptually lucid argument for the BDS movement that is difficult to refute. He offers a principled position accompanied by nuanced and thorough analyses, and though one may not agree with all of his claims, one is fully persuaded by the passionate clarity of his appeal. Barghouti reminds us what public responsibility entails, and we are lucky to have his relentless and intelligent analysis and argument. There is no more comprehensive and persuasive case than his for boycott, divestment, and sanctions to end the Israeli occupation and establish the ethical claim of Palestinian rights."

-Judith Butler, University of California at Berkeley

"Barghouti explains with lucidity, passion, and unrivaled intelligence... that bringing an end to apartheid in Palestine and seeing justice and equality for all the people who live there is not a distant dream but a reality we can bring about in the next few years using BDS."
—Ali Abunimah, author of *One Country* and cofounder of *Electronic Intifada*

"Barghouti is the future. He is intelligent, empowered, and nonviolent. He is completely impressive. It would help Americans to see such a picture of Palestinian political engagement when they have such a distorted image of who Palestinians are. Some day they will know him."

—Phillip Weiss, cofounder of Mondoweiss:
The War of Ideas in the Middle East

BDS: BOYCOTT, DIVESTMENT, SANCTIONS

THE GLOBAL STRUGGLE FOR PALESTINIAN RIGHTS

OMAR BARGHOUTI

Haymarket Books
Chicago, Illinois

First published by Haymarket Books in 2011
P.O. Box 180165
Chicago, IL 60618
773-583-7884
www.haymarketbooks.org
info@haymarketbooks.org

ISBN: 978-1-60846-114-1

Trade distribution:
In the US, Consortium Book Sales, www.cbsd.com
In Canada, Publishers Group Canada, www.pgcbooks.ca
In the UK, Turnaround Publisher Services, www.turnaround-uk.com
In Australia, Palgrave MacMillan, www.palgravemacmillan.com.au
All other countries, Publishers Group Worldwide, www.pgw.com

Cover design by Eric Ruder.

All the author's proceeds from this book will be donated to the Palestinian
Campaign for the Academic and Cultural Boycott of Israel, pacbi.org.

This book was published with the generous support of Lannan Foundation and
the Wallace Global Fund.

Printed in Canada by union labor on recycled paper containing 100 percent post-
consumer waste, in accordance with the guidelines of the Green Press Initiative,
www.greenpressinitiative.org.

Library of Congress Cataloging in Publication data is available.

10 9 8 7 6 5 4 3 2 1

CONTENTS

INTRODUCTION

Besiege your siege . . . there is no other way.

—Mahmoud Darwish

Since it is in a concrete situation that the oppressor-oppressed contradiction is established, the resolution of this contradiction must be objectively verifiable. Hence, the radical requirement—both for the individual who discovers himself or herself to be an oppressor and for the oppressed—that the concrete situation which begets oppression must be transformed.[1]

—Paulo Freire

First they ignore you, then they laugh at you, then they fight you, then you win.

—Mahatma Gandhi

Almost every day, the pale, slender woman complains to the ruthless, self-righteous ruffian about the miserable little shack she is confined to, not to mention the daily abuse she has to put up with. Sick of her endless whining, one day he brings in a goat to stay with them. Her complaints turn into desperate sobbing, quite expectedly, so he punches her

1

until she bleeds. She cries in silence, mourning for the day when she had more space, without the goat crowding the miserable shack.

After weeks of her begging, he gets rid of the goat. Now she feels she has her space again. Everything is finally back to normal—just the usual dose of abuse and exploitation. For a day she is content with her accomplishment, but the next morning she wakes up with an eruption of long-suppressed memories, erasing her forgetfulness and disturbing her "peace." She remembers when he first abducted her and forced her into slavery. She realizes how she has rationalized and internalized the battering as part of surviving, as the lesser evil. She could no longer care less about an extra few square feet here or there. She wants to feel whole again, and nothing less than her freedom—unmitigated, unconditional—would do. So she sets out to resist and calls out for support.[2]

For more than six decades Israel has enjoyed the best of both worlds, a free hand to implement its extremist colonial agenda of ethnically cleansing as many indigenous Palestinians from their homeland and grabbing as much of their land as possible and, simultaneously, a deceptive, mythical reputation for democracy and enlightenment. It has effectively succeeded in cynically exploiting the Nazi genocide of European Jewish communities, transforming the pain and guilt felt across the West into an almost invincible shield from censure and accountability. As Archbishop Desmond Tutu said: "I think the West, quite rightly, is feeling contrite, penitent, for its awful connivance with the Holocaust. The penance is being paid by the Palestinians. I just hope again that ordinary citizens in the West will wake up and say 'we refuse to be part of this.'"[3]

The collapse of the Soviet Union, the emergence of the United States as the sole superpower, and the ascension in Washington of a militarist neoconservative self-described "cabal" with uniquely strong ties to Israel[4]—and to warmongering Israeli leader Benjamin

Netanyahu in particular—all allowed Israel to maximize its gains and influence over decision-making processes in the United States.[5] Israel's power in the US Congress had been established for quite some time;[6] during the George W. Bush era the White House was subject to many of the same influences. The criminal attacks of September 11, 2001, created what Netanyahu saw as a golden opportunity to further consolidate Israel's already great influence over policy setting in Washington.[7] And starting a decade earlier, the sham "peace process" launched by Israel and the Palestine Liberation Organization (PLO) in Oslo in 1993 had rehabilitated Israel's diplomatic and, crucially, economic ties with dozens of countries across the world,[8] opening up badly needed markets for the state's expanding industrial, particularly military manufacturing, prowess.

Ironically, at the peak of its military, nuclear, economic, and political power, Israel started becoming more vulnerable.

The fact that the United States got mired in a seemingly indefinite "war on terror" (which should aptly be called "the mother of all terror," as it is the most egregious and immoral form of state terror, shedding any veneer of respect for international law, and simultaneously a *cause* of much terror by fanatic groups in many countries), causing death and destruction in Iraq and Afghanistan of genocidal proportions[9] and a significant loss of US soldiers' lives, has started to open some cracks in the otherwise iron wall of support for Israel in the US establishment. The 2008 defeat and democratic purge of the neocons helped widen those cracks.

John Mearsheimer, expert on the Israel lobby in the United States, describes the process of change, which has accelerated recently:

The combination of Israel's strategic incompetence and its gradual transformation into an apartheid state creates significant problems for the United States. There is growing recognition in both countries that their interests are diverging; indeed this perspective is even garnering attention inside the American Jewish community. *Jewish Week*, for example, recently published an article entitled "The Gaza Blockade: What Do You Do When U.S. and Israeli Interests Aren't in Synch?" Leaders in both countries are now saying that Israeli policy toward the Palestinians is undermining U.S. security. Vice President Biden and Gen. David Petraeus, the head of Central Command, both made this point recently, and the head of the Mossad, Meir Dagan, told the Knesset [Israel's parliament] in June, "Israel is gradually turning from an asset to the United States to a burden."

For decades, Israel's supporters have striven to shape public discourse in the United States so that most Americans believe the two countries' interests are identical. That situation is changing, however. Not only is there now open talk about clashing interests, but knowledgeable people are openly asking whether Israel's actions are detrimental to U.S. security.[10]

This context of relative change in the US establishment, accompanied by more radical change at the grassroots level in the United States and Europe in reaction to Israel's war crimes and other grave violations of international law in its bloody suppression of the second Palestinian intifada, provided fertile ground for a well-conceived, nonviolent citizens' movement for Palestinian rights to flourish.

On July 9, 2005, Palestinian civil society launched what is now widely recognized as a qualitatively different phase in the global struggle for Palestinian freedom, justice, and self-determination against a ruthless, powerful system of oppression that enjoys impunity and that is intent on making a self-fulfilling prophecy of the utterly racist, myth-laden foundational Zionist dictum of "a land without a people for a people without a land." In a historic moment of collective consciousness, and informed by almost a century of struggle against Zionist settler colonialism, the overwhelming majority in Palestinian civil society issued the Call for Boycott, Divestment and Sanctions (BDS) against Israel until it fully complies with its obligations under international law.[11] More than 170 Palestinian civil society groups, including all major political parties, refugee rights associations, trade union federations, women's unions, NGO networks, and virtually the entire spectrum of grassroots organizations, recalled how people of conscience in the international community have "historically shouldered the moral responsibility to fight injustice, as exemplified in the struggle to abolish apartheid in South Africa," calling upon international civil society organizations and people of conscience all over the world to "impose broad boycotts and implement divestment initiatives against Israel similar to those applied to South Africa in the apartheid era."

Since 2008, the BDS movement has been led by the largest coalition of Palestinian civil society organizations inside historic Palestine and in exile, the BDS National Committee (BNC).[12]

Peace, Justice, and Rights

Ngugi wa Thiong'o, one of Africa's most important contemporary writers, wrote in the introduction to his *Decolonising the Mind* about how imperialism presents the struggling peoples of the earth with the "ultimatum" that they must "accept theft or death," adding:

> The oppressed and the exploited of the earth maintain their defiance: liberty from theft. But the biggest weapon wielded and actually daily unleashed by imperialism against that collective defiance is the cultural bomb. The effect of a cultural bomb is to annihilate a people's belief in their names, in their languages, in their environment, in their heritage of struggle, in their unity, in their capacities and ultimately in themselves. It makes them see their past as one wasteland of non-achievement and it makes them want to distance themselves from that wasteland. . . . It even plants serious doubts about the moral

rightness of struggle. Possibilities of . . . victory are seen as remote, ridiculous dreams. The intended results are despair, despondency and a collective death-wish.[13]

Ngugi goes on to suggest that the most appropriate response by those struggling for freedom and justice is "to confront this threat with the higher and more creative culture of resolute struggle."

The BDS campaign is among the most important forms of such "resolute struggle" by the great majority of Palestinians, who resist the colonization of their land and minds and demand nothing less than self-determination, freedom, justice, and unmitigated equality. The BDS Call, anchored in international law and universal principles of human rights, adopts a comprehensive rights-based approach, underlining the fact that for the Palestinian people to exercise its right to self-determination, Israel must end its three forms of injustice that infringe international law and Palestinian rights by:

1. ending its occupation and colonization of all Arab lands [occupied in 1967] and dismantling the wall

2. recognizing the fundamental rights of the Arab-Palestinian citizens of Israel to full equality

3. respecting, protecting, and promoting the rights of Palestinian refugees to return to their homes and properties, as stipulated in UN Resolution 194

As South African archbishop emeritus Desmond Tutu once said: "I am not interested in picking up crumbs of compassion thrown from the table of someone who considers himself my master. I want the full menu of rights."[14]

For decades, but especially since the Oslo accords signed by Israel and the Palestine Liberation Organization (PLO) in 1993, Israel, with varying degrees of collusion from successive US administrations, the

European Union, and complacent Arab "leaders," has attempted to rede-fine the Palestinian people to include only those who live in Palestinian territory occupied in 1967. The main objective has been to deceptively reduce the question of Palestine to a mere dispute over some "contested" territory occupied by Israel since 1967, thus excluding the UN-sanctioned rights of the majority of the Palestinian people. In this context, peace de-void of justice becomes the objective, perpetuating injustice.[15]

The so-called international community, under the hegemonic in-fluence of the United States, the world's only superpower, has not only failed to stop Israel's construction of the wall and its settler colonies, both declared illegal by the International Court of Justice in 2004; it has colluded in undermining hitherto UN-sanctioned Palestinian rights. This has prompted Palestinian society to again surpass its "leadership" and reassert its basic rights. The BDS Call, with unprecedented near-consensus support among Palestinians in-side historic Palestine as well as in exile, reminded the world that the indigenous Palestinian people include the refugees forcibly dis-placed from their homeland—by Zionist militias and later the state of Israel—during the 1948 Nakba[16] and ever since, as well as the Palestinian citizens of Israel who remained on their land and now live under a regime of legalized racial discrimination.[17]

Ending the largely *discernible* aspects of the Israeli occupation while maintaining effective control over most of the Palestinian terri-tory occupied in 1967 "in return" for Palestinians' accepting Israel's annexation of the largest colonial blocs, with the most fertile lands and richest water resources; relinquishing the right of return; and ac-cepting Israel as an apartheid state—this has become the basic for-mula for the so-called peaceful settlement endorsed by the world's hegemonic powers and acquiesced to by an unelected, unrepresenta-tive, unprincipled, and visionless Palestinian "leadership." The entire spectrum of Zionist parties in Israel and their supporters in the West, with a few exceptions, ostensibly accept this unjust and illegal formula as the "only offer" on the table before the Palestinians—or else the menacing Israeli bludgeon. With the sharp rise of the ultraright in Israel, even this long-held Israeli formula no longer enjoys majority support in the Israel public.[18]

In fact, many Jewish Israelis are now vociferous in protesting what they see as a rise of "fascism" in the state, accompanied by an entrenchment in racism and rejection of any meaningful peace. The Jewish Telegraphic Agency (JTA) in a report titled *As Israel's Image Sinks, Whither Israeli PR?* explains a key reason behind what it viewed as Israel's failure in the battle for hearts and minds in the West despite its massive obsession with and substantial investments in "rebranding" its image: "The public face of Israel, the Netanyahu-Lieberman-Barak government, wins few points on the international stage. Prime Minister Benjamin Netanyahu is widely perceived as uninterested in making peace, Foreign Minister Avigdor Lieberman is seen as a racist bully, and Defense Minister Ehud Barak is seen as not doing enough to press for more peace-oriented policies."[19]

A *Haaretz* journalist, while typically reducing Israel's injustices to the 1967 occupation only, still succinctly explains Israel's loss of support at the international grassroots level thus:

Underlying the anger against Israel lies disappointment. Since the establishment of the state, and before, we demanded special terms of the world. We played on their feelings of guilt, for standing idle while six million Jews were murdered.

David Ben-Gurion called us a light unto the nations and we stood tall and said, we, little David, would stand strong and righteous against the great evil Goliath.

The world appreciated that message and even, according to the foreign press, enabled us to develop the atom bomb in order to prevent a second Holocaust.

> But then came the occupation, which turned us into the evil Go-
> liath, the cruel oppressor, a darkness on the nations. And now we are
> paying the price of presenting ourselves as righteous and causing dis-
> appointment: boycott.[20]

Coming on the heels of Israel's devastating war of aggression on
Lebanon (2006), its latest bloodbath in the Gaza Strip (2008–9), and
its multiyear illegal and immoral siege of the Strip have stimulated a
real transformation in world public opinion against Israeli policies.
The United Nations and leading human rights organizations have
amply documented the devastating consequences of the siege on the
health of the Palestinian population, especially children, among whom
stunted growth and anemia have become widespread. A May 2010 report by the BBC in fact reveals how Israel, through its siege, has allowed only the "minimum calorie intake needed by Gaza's million and
a half inhabitants, according to their age and sex," as a form of severe
collective punishment.[21] It has prevented not only candles, various
types of medicines, books, crayons, clothing, shoes, blankets, pasta,
tea, coffee and chocolate, but also musical instruments[22] from reaching
the 1.5 million Palestinians incarcerated in what has been called the
world's largest open-air prison and even a "prison camp," in the words
of British prime minister David Cameron.[23]

When the heart-wrenching images of Israeli phosphorus bombs
showering densely populated Palestinian neighborhoods and UN shelters in Gaza were beamed across the world during Israel's Operation
Cast Lead in 2008–9, they triggered worldwide outrage that translated
into boycotts and divestment initiatives in economic, academic, athletic, and cultural fields. Former president of the UN General Assembly
Father Miguel D'Escoto Brockmann, Archbishop Desmond Tutu, distinguished artists, writers, academics, and filmmakers, progressive Jewish groups, major trade unions and labor federations, church-affiliated

organizations, and many student groups have all endorsed, to varying degrees, the logic of boycott, convincing many that our "South
Africa moment" has finally arrived.

As the JTA news service put it: "The fear is that Israel is subject to a
growing tide of delegitimization that, if unchecked, could pose an existential threat. The nightmare scenario has the anti-Israel Boycott, Divestment and Sanctions (BDS) movement gaining more traction and
anti-Israel opinion moving from Western campuses to governments, followed by a lifting of the protective American diplomatic umbrella."[24] In
the same vein, in May 2009, at a policy conference of the American Israel
Public Affairs Committee (AIPAC), executive director Howard Kohr
warned that BDS was reaching the American mainstream and "laying the
predicate for abandonment [of Israel]." Kohr added, "This is a conscious
campaign to shift policy, to transform the way Israel is treated by its
friends to a state that deserves not our support, but our contempt; not
our protection, but pressure to change its essential nature."[25]

Despite massive investments of money and projection of intimidating power, the Israel lobby has largely failed, to date, to quell the
spread of support for BDS on US campuses as well as among faith-
based organizations, cultural figures, and even progressive and liberal
Jewish groups. Confronted with this failure to quash BDS in its infancy, Zionist groups everywhere, and especially in the United States,
have resorted to naked bullying, intimidation, and other increasingly
McCarthyesque measures, further alienating a fast-growing number
of Jewish Americans, especially the younger generation. At times one
feels that Zionist groups have lost their touch in playing the carrot-
and-stick game, so much so that they have forgotten what a carrot
even looks like. If a stick does not work, they use a thicker one.

Writing in the *New York Review of Books*, the influential Jewish American author and academic Peter Beinart considers this failure of the Jewish establishment in the United States as a foregone conclusion:

For several decades, the Jewish establishment has asked American Jews to check their liberalism at Zionism's door, and now, to their horror, they are finding that many young Jews have checked their Zionism instead.

Morally, American Zionism is in a downward spiral. If the leaders of groups like AIPAC and the Conference of Presidents of Major American Jewish Organizations do not change course, they will wake up one day to find a younger, Orthodox-dominated, Zionist leadership whose naked hostility to Arabs and Palestinians scares even them, and a mass of secular American Jews who range from apathetic to appalled.[26]

John Mearsheimer takes a different angle to explain the same phenomenon, the seemingly inexorable decline of the Israel lobby's ability to convince:

The lobby's unstinting commitment to defending Israel, which sometimes means shortchanging U.S. interests, is likely to become more apparent to more Americans in the future, and that could lead to a wicked backlash against Israel's supporters as well as Israel.

The lobby faces yet another challenge: defending an apartheid state in the liberal West is not going to be easy. Once it is widely recognized that the two-state solution is dead and Israel has become like white-ruled South Africa—and that day is not far off—support for Israel inside the American Jewish community is likely to diminish significantly.[27]

The most consequential achievement of the first five years of the BDS movement was indeed to expose the "essential nature" of Israel's regime over the Palestinian people as one that combines military occupation, colonization, ethnic cleansing, and apartheid.[28] Israel's mythical and carefully cultivated, decades-old image as a "democratic" state seeking "peace" may, as a result, have suffered irreparable damage.

The September 13, 2010, *Time* magazine cover story, "Why Israel Doesn't Care about Peace,"[29] may be the most prominent indicator yet of the growing feeling among many in the West, even in the environments most supportive of Israel's policies, that Israel truly has no interest in peace, particularly given that it is has not yet been compelled to pay a serious price for its belligerence and persistent violations of international law.

While analysts and legal experts continue to debate to what degree— or whether—the UN definition of apartheid applies to Israel's system of legalized racial discrimination, it has become more common in the mainstream Israeli media to read and hear the term *fascism* used by prominent figures to describe Israel. To cite one recent reason for increased usage of the term, the Israeli Supreme Court, in line with its long history of justifying racial discrimination and other violations of international law, sanctioned the planned construction of three apartment buildings for Jews only in the Jaffa neighborhood of Ajami, despite the fact that such a decision entails blatant racial discrimination.[30]

Hundreds of academics, artists, and other intellectuals signed a "Declaration of Independence from Fascism" right after the Israeli government overwhelmingly voted to adopt an amendment to the Citizenship Act, dubbed the "loyalty oath," whereby "non-Jews" applying for Israeli citizenship would have to pledge allegiance to Israel "as a Jewish democratic state."[31] Far-right Knesset member Michael Ben-Ari said following the vote, "Twenty years have passed since the assassination of Rabbi Kahane, and today Likud admits he was right. It's a refreshing change to see the Likud government, which persecuted the rabbi over his call to have Arabs sign a loyalty oath, admit today that what Kahane said 20 years ago was correct."[32] Meir Kahane was a fanatically racist rabbi elected to the Knesset in 1984. In 1988, Kahane's party, Kach, was banned for its incitement of racism. While in office, Kahane's legislative proposals included "revoking Israeli citizenship from non-Jews and banning Jewish-Gentile marriages or sexual intercourse."[33] He advocated ethnic cleansing and plotted acts of terrorism. While his views were regarded in the 1980s as extremist, mainstream Israeli parties today have adopted several of his most extreme positions.

In reaction to the loyalty oath, Israeli award-winning academic Gavriel Solomon went so far as to compare today's Israel to Germany in the 1930s: "The idea of Judenrein (Jew free zone) or Arabrein is not new.... Some might say 'how can you compare us to Nazis?' I am not talking about the death camps, but about the year 1935. There were no camps yet, but there were racist laws. And we are heading forward toward these kinds of laws. The government is clearly declaring our incapacity for democracy."[34]

The well-known Israeli writer Sefi Rachlevsky differed on the time frame of the comparison: "The struggle today is not between left and right but between democrats and fascists. . . Israel is becoming fascist and racist. In a sense you could say, we are not so much like the madness that was in Germany in 1933 but rather in 1944–45, when they were in danger of losing the war that madness prevented them from stopping."[35]

Israeli journalist and activist Uri Avnery has also compared the specter of fascism in Israel with the Nazi rise to power in Germany. He warns that fascism has started to take over the Israeli government and Knesset and that, unlike in the West where far-right groups are also growing in influence, "Israel's very existence is threatened by fascism. It can lead our state to destruction."[36]

After the Knesset took a significant step toward criminalizing any call for boycott of Israel or its institutions by citizens, residents, and even foreigners entering the country, Avnery wrote, "No doubt can remain that Kahanism—the Israeli version of fascism—has moved from the margin to center stage."[37] Reacting to the same development, the former chief editor of the influential Israeli daily *Haaretz*, David Landau, called for boycotting the Israeli Knesset "to stand against the wave of fascism that [has] engulfed the Zionist project."[38]

The by-now-customary calls by Israeli foreign minister Avigdor Lieberman, even from the podium of the UN General Assembly,[39] for ethnically cleansing Palestinian citizens of Israel and rejecting any peaceful settlement demanding a significant withdrawal of Israel from occupied Palestinian territory have only accelerated the spread of the view of Israel as a world pariah.[40]

A prominent Israeli academic commented thus on the far-right politics of Israeli cabinet ministers: "Israel is currently the only Western country whose cabinet includes the likes of Foreign Minister Avigdor Lieberman, Justice Minister Yaakov Neeman and Interior Minister Eli Yishai. The last time politicians holding views similar to theirs were in power in post–World War II Western Europe was in Franco's Spain."[41]

An Israeli BDS activist's mother, who lives in Tel Aviv, jokingly asked her son, "Has Lieberman been recruited to your [BDS] movement, too!"

This growing outcry about Israel "becoming fascist" reflects an unprecedented level of anxiety among "liberal" Zionists in Israel and elsewhere that Israel's system of colonial and racist repression, under which indigenous Palestinians have suffered since 1948, will now target Jewish Israeli dissenters as well.

The *facade* of democracy, not democracy itself, is what is truly collapsing in Israel, as democracy has never existed in any true form—nor could have existed—in a settler-colonial state like Israel.[42] Apartheid South Africa was a "democracy" for whites, after all, and the United States was a "democracy" when Southern states were still holding on to apartheid laws against African Americans and other non-whites. But when the facade of democracy and enlightenment collapses, the entire Israeli regime of apartheid, settler-colonialism, and occupation is put at serious risk of collapse as well, as it will be even less tolerated by the world and more likely to trigger even fiercer internal resistance to it.

In this context, the BDS movement has played a major role in intensifying the now public fear in Israel that Israel is becoming a world pariah, as apartheid South Africa was, with all the expected consequences. Witnessing exceptional growth, and winning over voices in the Western mainstream, BDS has produced an unmistakably loud alarm in Israel's highest political echelons.

Israeli prime minister Benjamin Netanyahu, for example, reacted angrily to a boycott call issued by prominent Israeli artists, supported by academics, in August 2010 against performing in Israel's illegal colonies: "The State of Israel is under an attack of delegitimization by elements in the international community. This attack includes attempts to enact economic, academic and cultural boycotts. The last thing we need at this time is to be under such an attack—I mean this attempt at a boycott—from within."[43]

The term *delegitimization* was first used by a shady Tel Aviv "think tank" that described the international boycott of Israel as "increasingly sophisticated, ripe and coherent," warning that the boycott is a "strategic threat," even a "potentially existential threat," to the state.[44] In a report presented to the Israeli government,[45] the organization partially—albeit implicitly—admitted what exactly the boycott movement was "delegitimizing": "A consistent and honest Israeli commitment to end its control over the Palestinians, advance human rights, and promote greater integration and equality for its Arab citizens is essential in fighting the battle against delegitimization. Such commitment must be reflected in a coherent and comprehensive strategy towards Gaza and the political process with the Palestinians."

While these recommended policy changes hardly meet the minimal rights of the Palestinian people, their mention indicates that the authors of the report realize that the boycott targets Israel *because of its denial of these basic rights*. Otherwise it would not make sense to prescribe recognizing them to combat the boycott. Indeed, BDS strives to delegitimize Israel's settler-colonial oppression, apartheid, and ongoing ethnic cleansing of the indigenous Palestinian people, just as the South Africa boycott was aimed at delegitimizing apartheid there.[46] In no other boycott against any state has the preposterous claim been made that this nonviolent tactic is intended to end the very physical existence of the target state.

The "delegitimization" scare tactic further failed to impress any reasonable person because its most far-reaching—and entirely unsubstantiated—claim against BDS is that the movement aims to "supersede the Zionist model with a state that is based on the 'one person, one vote' principle"[47]—hardly the most evil or disquieting accusation for anyone even vaguely interested in democracy!

In contrast to Israel, some leading legal experts have taken a far more sanguine attitude to the issue of legitimacy and delegitimization. UN special rapporteur for human rights in the Occupied Territories, Richard Falk, argues:

> At the present time I'm very sceptical [whether] inter-governmental diplomacy can achieve any significant result. And the best hope for the Palestinians is what I call a legitimacy war, similar to the [South African] anti-apartheid campaign in the late-1980s and 1990s that was so effective in isolating and undermining the authority of the apartheid government. I think that is happening now in relation to Israel. There's a very robust boycott, divestment and sanctions campaign all over the world that is capturing the political and moral imagination of the people, the NGOs and civil society and is beginning to have an important impact on Israel's way of acting and thinking.[48]

Besieging Israel's Siege[49]

BDS is perhaps the most ambitious, empowering, and promising Palestinian-led global movement for justice and rights. BDS has the capacity to challenge Israel's colonial rule and apartheid in a morally consistent, effective, and, crucially, intelligent manner.

Figures as diverse as Desmond Tutu, Jimmy Carter, and former Israeli attorney general Michael Ben-Yair have described Israel as practicing apartheid against the indigenous Palestinians.[50] Characterizing Israel's legalized and institutionalized racial discrimination as such does not attempt to equate Israel with South Africa under apartheid; despite the many similarities, no two oppressive regimes are identical. Rather, it stems from the argument that Israel's system of bestowing rights and privileges according to ethnic and religious identity fits the UN definition of the term as enshrined in the 1973 International Convention on the Suppression and Punishment of the Crime of Apartheid and in the 2002 Rome Statute of the International Criminal Court. The disingenuous or manifestly misinformed argument that rejects the apartheid charge on the basis that Jewish Israelis form a majority, unlike the whites in South Africa who were in the minority, ignores the fact that the universally accepted definition of apartheid has nothing to do with majorities and minorities. Rather, it is defined as "inhumane acts ... committed in the context of an institutionalized regime of systematic oppression and domination by one racial group over any other racial group or groups and committed with the intention of maintaining that regime."[51]

While Palestinian and other BDS advocates may support diverse solutions to the question of Palestinian self-determination and the colonial conflict with Israel, by avoiding the prescription of any particular political formula the BDS Call insists on the necessity of realizing the three basic, irreducible rights of the Palestinian people in *any* just solution. It presents a platform that not only unifies Palestinians everywhere in the face of accelerating fragmentation, but also appeals to international civil society by evoking the same universal principles of freedom, justice, and equal rights that animated the anti-apartheid movement in South Africa and the civil rights movement in the United States.

Since July 2005, there has never been a period with as many BDS achievements as after the Israeli massacre in Gaza in the winter of 2008–9 and the bloodbath on the Gaza-bound Freedom Flotilla in May 2010, which rudely awakened a long-dormant sense of international public outrage at Israel's exceptional status as a state above the law. People of conscience around the world seem to have crossed a threshold in challenging Israel's impunity through effective pressure, not appeasement or "constructive engagement."

"Besiege your siege," the haunting cry of Palestine's most celebrated poet, Mahmoud Darwish, suddenly acquires a different meaning in this context. Since attempts to convince a colonial power to give up its privileges and heed moral pleas for justice are at best delusional, many now feel the need to "besiege" Israel though boycotts, raising the price of its siege and apartheid. Rather than get bogged down in trying to convince Israel to recognize us as humans and then to win from it an emaciated set of our rights and bits and pieces of our dignity, the overwhelming majority of the Palestinian people have opted for this all-encompassing nonviolent civil resistance that counters the entire array of Israeli injustices.

Academic and Cultural Boycott of Israel Takes Off

Refusing to be complicit in whitewashing settler-colonial Jewish extremism did not start after Israel's flotilla attack or even its atrocities in Gaza. It actually started even before Israel was established on the ruins of Palestinian society. In February 1930, Zionist leaders asked Sigmund Freud, as an iconic Jewish figure, to contribute to a petition condemning the 1929 Palestinian riots against the intensifying Zionist colonization of Palestine.[52] Despite his outspoken Zionist tendency at the time, Freud refused to be complicit in what he regarded as the "baseless fanaticism" of Jewish colonial settlers, writing:

> Whoever wants to influence the [Jewish] masses must give them something rousing and inflammatory and my sober judgement of Zionism does not permit this. I certainly sympathise with its goals, am proud of our University in Jerusalem and am delighted with our settlement's prosperity. But, on the other hand, I do not think that Palestine could ever become a Jewish state, nor that the Christian and Islamic worlds would ever be prepared to have their holy places under Jewish care. . . .
> I concede with sorrow that the baseless fanaticism of our people is in part to be blamed for the awakening of Arab distrust.[53]

In the same spirit of rejecting complicity in Israel's violations of international law and Palestinian rights, British academics were the pioneers in launching international academic pressure campaigns against Israel. A petition initiated by Hilary and Steven Rose for a moratorium on EU funding of research collaboration with Israel was published in the *Guardian* in April 2002, with 130 signatures, triggering a singular backlash from Israel and its lobby groups but also giving birth to a new form of solidarity with Palestinian rights. Later, in response to the call by the Palestinian Campaign for the Academic and Cultural Boycott of Israel (PACBI),[54] the British Committee for Universities of Palestine (BRICUP) was formed and subsequently led several successful campaigns in British academic unions at the front of adopting the logic of a boycott of Israel.[55]

Established in 2009, USACBI, a US-based campaign for the academic and cultural boycott of Israel, recently announced having gained five hundred academic endorsements of its call, not to mention the hundreds of cultural figures who have also signed.[56]

Most recently, in October 2010, a Norwegian petition calling for an institutional cultural and academic boycott of Israel (in line with the

PACBI principles) has gathered one hundred impressive signatories—academics, writers, musicians, other cultural workers, and sports celebrities, including Egil "Drillo" Olsen, the coach of the Norwegian national soccer team.[57] Around the same time, the European Platform for the Academic and Cultural Boycott of Israel (EPACBI) was announced, with participation of boycott campaigns from across the continent, in full coordination with PACBI.[58]

Weeks earlier the Indian Campaign for the Academic and Cultural Boycott of Israel had been launched, with the endorsement of some of India's most famous writers and academics. In the campaign's statement, the signatories declared: "Just as it was in the case of the international call against South Africa in the apartheid years, we are confident that this boycott will be effective in contributing to international pressure on Israel to abandon its oppression and expulsion of the indigenous population based on military aggression, legal discrimination and persecution, and economic stranglehold."[59]

A South African petition issued in September 2010 calling on the University of Johannesburg to boycott Israel's Ben Gurion University was endorsed by 250 academics and prominent figures, including the heads of four South African universities, Archbishop Desmond Tutu, Breyten Breytenbach, John Dugard, Antjie Krog, Barney Pityana, and Kader Asmal. Invoking the moral weight of South Africa, the precedent-setting statement did not mince words in condemning the complicity of Israeli academic institutions in violations of international law: "While Palestinians are not able to access universities and schools, Israeli universities produce the research, technology, arguments and leaders for maintaining the occupation."[60]

Citing Nelson Mandela's caution not to be "enticed to read reconciliation and fairness as meaning parity between justice and injustice," Archbishop Tutu has defended the call to sever links with complicit Israeli institutions: "It can never be business as usual. Israeli Universities are an intimate part of the Israeli regime, by active choice." Reiterating his unwavering support for the Palestinian-led global campaign for boycott, divestment, and sanctions against Israel, he eloquently adds: "Together with the peace-loving peoples of this Earth, I condemn any form of violence—but surely we must recognise that people caged in, starved and stripped of their essential material and political rights must resist their Pharaoh? Surely resistance also makes us human? Palestinians have chosen, like we did, the nonviolent tools of boycott, divestment and sanctions."[61]

Most recently, and in a development that will be recorded as historic, artists in South Africa supporting the BDS Call against Israel issued a declaration titled "South African Artists against Apartheid." It stated:

> As South African Artists and Cultural Workers who have lived under, survived, and in many cases resisted apartheid, we acknowledge the value of international solidarity in our own struggle. It is in this context that we respond to the call by Palestinians, and their Israeli allies, for such solidarity.
>
> As artists of conscience we say no to apartheid—anywhere. We respond to the call for international solidarity and undertake not to avail any invitation to perform or exhibit in Israel. Nor will we accept funding from institutions linked to the government of Israel. This is our position until such time as Israel, in the least, complies with international law and universal principles of human rights. Until then, we too unite with international colleagues under the banner of "Artists Against Apartheid."[62]

Academic and cultural boycott campaigns have also spread to Canada,[63] France,[64] Italy,[65] and Spain.[66] In Canada, college student activists in Students Against Israeli Apartheid (SAIA) who are part of the Coalition Against Israeli Apartheid (CAIA)[67] pioneered in 2005 the largest campus BDS campaign around the world, Israeli Apartheid

Week,[68] which by now reaches dozens of international universities, including some of the most prestigious, spreading support for BDS and raising awareness about Israel's occupation and racial discrimination system.

Best-selling authors like Iain Banks, Alice Walker, and Henning Mankell have recently endorsed the boycott against Israel, and so did eminent scholar Ann Laura Stoler.[69] Top artists have shunned Israel due to its violation of international law and Palestinian rights. News of megastar Meg Ryan's canceling her visit to Israel and of concert cancellations by Elvis Costello, Gil Scott-Heron, Carlos Santana, The Pixies, and Faithless, among others, has finally put to rest skepticism about the potential of the campaign. World-renowned filmmakers from Jean-Luc Godard[70] and the Yes Men[71] to Mike Leigh have also heeded the boycott call and stayed away from Israeli festivals. Explaining his visit cancellation, Leigh addresses Israelis saying:

> As I watched the world very properly condemn [the Flotilla] atrocity, I almost canceled. I now wish I had, and blame my cowardice for not having done so. . . . Since then, your government has gone from bad to worse. . . . The resumption of the illegal building on the West Bank made me start to consider it seriously. . . . And now we have the Loyalty Oath. This is the last straw—quite apart from the ongoing criminal blockade of Gaza, not to mention the endless shooting of innocent people there, including juveniles. . . . But in any case, I am now in [an] untenable position, which I must confront according to my conscience.[72]

Even long before this latest swelling of support for the cultural boycott of Israel, renowned authors and cultural figures of the caliber of John Berger, Naomi Klein, Arundhati Roy, Ken Loach, John Greyson, and Judith Butler have supported BDS.[73]

In September 2010, in nothing less than a watershed in the cultural boycott, more than 150 US and British theater, film, and TV artists issued a statement,[74] initiated by Jewish Voice for Peace (JVP), supporting the spreading cultural boycott inside Israel of Ariel and the rest of Israel's colonial settlements, illegally built on occupied Palestinian territory (OPT), due to their violation of international law.[75] Frank Gehry, of Guggenheim fame, joined the supporters of this cultural boycott. While falling short of endorsing a comprehensive cultural boycott of Israel, this initiative broke a long-held taboo in the United States against calling for any pressure, let alone boycott, to be brought to bear against Israel in response to its ongoing violations of international law and war crimes. In the US context, where dissent from the two-party line that treats Israel as above the law of nations and, often, ahead of US interests,[76] may dearly cost an artist, a journalist, an elected official, an academic, or just about anyone else, this artists' statement is beyond courageous. Condemning Israel's colonial settlements and "ugly occupation," expressing "hope for a *just* and lasting peace" (emphasis added) in the region, and endorsing the logic of boycott as an effective and perfectly legitimate tool to end injustice, the statement is precedent-setting.

Countering the argument by anti-boycott groups that art, the academy, or any profession should be exempted from the boycott for being "above politics" despite evidence of being implicated in a very real political regime of oppression, Israeli British architect Abe Hayeem, who founded Architects and Planners for Justice in Palestine (APJP), holds up architecture as an example of complicity:

Architecture and planning are instruments of the occupation and constitute part of a continuing war against a whole people, whether as a minority within Israel's green line or in the occupied territories. Since this involves dispossession, discrimination and acquisition of land and homes by force, against the Geneva conventions, it can be classified as participation in war crimes.

What can one say about the Israeli architects who follow the state's policies and aims yet deny that their role is political? Despite all the evidence of illegality under international law and breaches of human rights in the land grabs, house demolitions and evictions, Israeli architects and planners continue their activities. They cannot claim that they do not know: there have been plenty of calls for them to stop. [77]

Sanctions, Divestment, and Economic Impact

Dismissing all the spectacular and concrete achievements of the still very young BDS movement as "largely symbolic," BDS opponents, including some who are widely seen in the West as supporters of—at least some—Palestinian rights, have argued that the boycott of Israel, unlike that waged against apartheid South Africa, is unrealistic and impractical, as it cannot possibly hurt Israel's formidable economic interests, protected by Western powers. Established analysts and leaders of the struggle against apartheid rule in South Africa who now support the Palestinian BDS movement against Israel recall how this same flawed and often disingenuous argument of economic unfeasibility was used against their struggle as well, often by liberals who ostensibly opposed apartheid but preferred "softer" tactics than boycott and divestment. Rejecting those softer tactics, a former South African cabinet minister and ANC leader, Ronnie Kasrils, who happens to be Jewish, writes in the *Guardian*:

> When Chief Albert Luthuli made a call for the international community to support a boycott of apartheid South Africa in 1958, the response was a widespread and dedicated movement that played a significant role in ending apartheid. Amid the sporting boycotts, the pledges of playwrights and artists, the actions by workers to stop South African goods from entering local markets and the constant pressure on states to withdraw their support for the apartheid regime, the role of academics also came to the fore....
>
> Almost four decades later, the campaign for boycott, divestment and sanctions is gaining ground again in South Africa, this time against Israeli apartheid.[78]

Durban-based economist Patrick Bond, in a lecture in Ramallah on September 26, 2010, cautioned his Palestinian audience not to fall for the insincere argument that the economic "invincibility" of Israel translates into the ultimate futility of BDS tactics. Seemingly unconquerable economic powers, he argued, have fallen much faster than many had thought possible. South Africa was no exception.[79]

While it is still too early to fairly expect BDS to have a considerable economic impact on Israel, in actual fact the movement has started to bite and, crucially, to empower activists worldwide, illuminating to them a path with great potential for raising the price of Israel's intransigence and disregard of international law.

Trade unions around the world, especially in the United Kingdom, Ireland, and South Africa, have endorsed boycotting Israel to end its impunity. The British Trades Union Congress, for instance, representing more than 6.5 million workers, unanimously passed a motion in September 2010, supported by the public-sector union Unison and the Fire Brigades Union as well as by the Palestine Solidarity Campaign (UK), calling for boycotting the products of and divesting from companies that profit from Israel's occupation of Palestinian territory.[80] The South African Municipal Workers Union (SAMWU) initiated a campaign to rid all municipalities in South Africa of Israeli products to make them "apartheid Israel free zones,"[81] a campaign that has started firing the imagination of BDS activists elsewhere.

Dockworkers' unions in Sweden, India, Turkey, South Africa, and the United States heeded, to various degrees, a unified appeal by all Palestinian trade unions and the BDS National Committee (BNC) for a boycott of loading and offloading Israeli ships to protest Israel's bloody flotilla attack.[82]

As early as April 2009, in the aftermath of the Israeli bloodbath in Gaza in the winter of 2008–9, the Israel Manufacturers Association reported that "21% of 90 local exporters who were questioned had felt a drop in demand due to boycotts, mostly from the UK and Scandinavian countries."[83]

A number of young, creative, well-conceived and -executed BDS campaigns, while not yet yielding any direct impact on the Israeli economy, are quite promising for the near future. Across the United States, especially on campuses, divestment and boycott campaigns are swelling as one campaign's success and lessons feed another. A national BDS conference of college students was held at Hampshire College in 2009,[84] months after BDS activists there succeeded in pressuring their school to divest from companies profiting from the Israeli occupation.[85] The sharing of experiences and best practices was invaluable for arguably the most important component of the BDS movement in the United States at present: campus-based groups.

Adalah-NY: The New York Campaign for the Boycott of Israel, was among the very first to innovate BDS tactics best suited for the New York setting. From parodies, music, and street dancing to meticulously researched and compelling press releases, they have scored a number of successes, inspiring many newer campaigns in several states and in many countries.[86]

The spectacular media triumph of the CodePink-led campaign—brilliantly named Stolen Beauty—against Israeli cosmetics company AHAVA, which manufactures in an illegal colony, had a distinctly inspiring effect on BDS campaigns across the Atlantic, particularly in France, the Netherlands, and the United Kingdom.[87]

In California, BDS activists and partners have launched one of the most ambitious BDS campaigns to date. With the slogan "Divest from Israeli Apartheid," they describe their initiative thus:

> If successful, the measure will appear on the next statewide ballot after March 2011.Then, if approved by a majority of voters, it will become California law. This means that the two public retirement systems, the

Public Employees' Retirement System (CalPERS) and the State Teachers' Retirement System (CalSTRS), would be required to engage in a divestment process with corporations providing equipment and services
to Israel that are used in the violation of human rights and international law, including but not limited to the building of the "Separation
Wall" and settlements.[88]

Another ambitious US-based divestment campaign that is exceptionally promising has been initiated by JVP,[89] with several partners,
and endorsed by the US Campaign to End the Israeli Occupation. The
TIAA-CREF campaign aims at convincing the large pension fund
manager to divest from companies implicated in Israel's occupation
and violations of international law.[90] The Palestinian leadership of the
BDS movement, the BNC, has warmly welcomed and endorsed the
TIAA-CREF campaign.[91]

Perhaps the most economically significant international BDS campaign to date is the one waged against the two French conglomerates,
Veolia and Alstom, due to their involvement in the so-called Jerusalem
Light Rail, a manifestly illegal project intended to cement Israel's colonial hold on occupied Jerusalem as well as on the colonies surrounding
it. Since the special BDS campaign targeting this project—named Derail Veolia/Alstom—was launched in November 2008 in Bilbao, Basque
Country (Spain), Veolia in particular has lost contracts worth billions
of dollars, largely due to intensive campaigning against the company in
several countries.[92]

Several campaigns spearheaded by the Irish Palestine Solidarity
Campaign are now being designed to target Israel's "blood diamonds."
Given the fact that Israel today is the world leader in exporting pol-
ished diamonds, with revenues reaching almost $20 billion in 2008[93]—
far larger than its lucrative and often scrutinized arms trade—I cannot
overemphasize the significance of effective BDS campaigns to raise

awareness about Israel's violations of human rights and international law and to convince diamond buyers to boycott Israeli diamonds.

Progressive lesbian, gay, bisexual, and transgender (LGBT) groups in the United States,[94] Canada,[95] and elsewhere have also challenged support for Israeli apartheid in LGBT communities in the West and joined the ranks of the global BDS movement. This was buoyed by the launch on June 27, 2010, of the Palestinian Queers for BDS initiative. Their statement reads:

> [W]e, Palestinian Queer activists, call upon the LGBTQI communities around the globe to stand for justice in Palestine through adopting and implementing broad boycott, divestment and sanctions (BDS) against Israel until the latter has ended its multi-tiered oppression of the Palestinian people, in line with the 2005 Palestinian civil society call for BDS.[96]

Following the Palestinian queer group's call, an Israeli LGBT call was announced, endorsing BDS.[97] In addition, several campaigns by LGBT groups have opposed "pink-washing" Israeli crimes by portraying it as a state that is tolerant of sexual diversity and gay rights.[98]

State-level sanctions against Israel have also been on the rise since the Israeli war of aggression on Gaza. Venezuela and Bolivia severed diplomatic relations with Israel.[99] The parliament of Chile voted in September 2010, with a large majority, to boycott Israeli products originating from the colonial settlements.[100] In September 2010 even the Netherlands, despite its long-standing foreign policy bias toward Israel, canceled a tour of the country by Israeli mayors because their group included representatives of colonial settlements.[101] The Dutch pension fund Pensioenfonds Zorg en Welzijn (PFZW), which has investments totaling 97 billion euros, has divested from almost all the Israeli companies in its portfolio.[102] The government of Spain, in September 2009, excluded an Israeli academic team from participating in an international university competition promoting sustainable architecture because the academics on the team represented the colony college of Ariel. The official statement explaining this decision, which came after intensive lobbying by Palestinian, Israeli, Spanish, and British civil society groups, asserted: "The decision has been taken by the Government of Spain based upon the fact that the University is located in the [occupied] West Bank. The Government of Spain is obliged to respect the international agreements under the framework of the European Union and the United Nations regarding this geographical area."[103]

The Court of Justice of the European Union, the highest legal authority mandated with interpreting EU laws, ruled in a landmark decision that may have significant consequences for the Israeli economy that Israeli products originating in colonies built in the occupied Palestinian territory "do not qualify for preferential customs treatment under the EC-Israel Agreement."[104]

In September 2009, Norway announced that its government pension fund, the third largest in the world, was selling its shares in a leading Israeli military manufacturer, Elbit Systems, because of the company's complicity in Israel's violations of international law. A year later, in September 2010, the Norwegian Department of Foreign Affairs (UD) also decided to ban testing German submarines built for Israel in Norwegian harbors and coastal waters. "We have extremely rigorous restrictions on exporting security goods and services … we don't export materials or services to states at war or in which there is a danger of war," said Norwegian foreign minister Jonas Gahr Støre.[105]

In March 2010, a major Swedish investment fund said it would eschew Elbit Systems shares on the same grounds. In August of the same year, the Norwegian pension fund divested from Africa Israel and its subsidiary Danya Cebus because of their involvement in constructing illegal colonial settlements.[106]

Also in 2010, Germany's biggest bank, Deutsche Bank, sold its 2 percent stake in Elbit Systems. Germany-based human rights groups Pax Christi and International Physicians for the Prevention of Nuclear War (IPPNW) had lobbied bank shareholders to vote against a routine motion of confidence in the board of directors because of its failure to divest from Elbit, while protesters outside the shareholders' meeting demanded divestment. In response, Deutsche Bank chair Josef Ackermann told the meeting, "Deutsche Bank is out of Elbit." Ackermann justified the decision based on the bank's commitment to voluntary codes of conduct such as the UN Global Compact, and he went as far as to deny that Deutsche Bank had ever held shares in Elbit—conflicting with figures published by NASDAQ, which showed that as of March 31, 2010, Deutsche Bank had still owned 2 percent of Elbit Systems and was the fifth largest investor in the company.[107] In January 2010, Danske Bank, the largest in Denmark, had also divested from Elbit and Africa Israel.[108]

Commenting on a small set of the above instances, a *Haaretz* economics reporter wrote: "The sums involved are not large, but their international significance is huge. Boycotts by governments give a boost to boycotts by non-government bodies around the world."[109]

Anticolonial Israeli Support for BDS

Significantly, the BDS Call, as it has come to be known, invites "conscientious Israelis to support this Call, for the sake of justice and genuine peace," thereby confirming that principled anticolonial Jewish Israelis who support the Palestinian people's inalienable right to self-determination, freedom, and equality in the pursuit of a just, comprehensive, and sustainable peace are partners in the struggle.

Principled Israeli anticolonialists committed to *full* Palestinian rights, such as Ilan Pappé, the late Tanya Reinhart, Rachel Giora, Haim Bresheeth, Moshe Machover, Oren Ben-Dor, Anat Matar, Michael

Warschawski, Kobi Snitz, Shir Hever, Dalit Baum, Yael Lerer, and Jonatan Stanczak, among many others, have truly been partners in this struggle for Palestinian rights. Many of them, aside from their un-equivocal commitment to Palestinian rights, realize that Israelis cannot possibly have normal lives without first shedding their colonial status and recognizing those Palestinian rights, paramount among them the right to self-determination.

Since 2009, Boycott! Supporting the Palestinian BDS Call from Within (or Boycott from Within, for short),[110] a growing movement in Israel, has fully adopted the Palestinian BDS Call and adhered to its principles, showing the way for genuine Israeli opposition to occupation and apartheid. Among the commendable principles that Boycott from Within has upheld is that progressive Israelis should focus most of their energies not on eating hummus with Palestinians in Ramallah, Bethlehem, or Jenin, or on sharing gestures of perceived "coexistence," but by working within *their* communities, the colonial oppressors, to educate and mobilize support for ending Israel's system of oppression and by supporting the Palestinian-led global BDS campaign.

Israeli groups that have endorsed the BDS Call include, among others, the Alternative Information Center (AIC),[111] the Israeli Committee Against House Demolition (ICAHD),[112] and Who Profits from the Occupation? (a project of the Coalition of Women for Peace),[113] all of which have played key roles in providing political, moral, and often logistical and information support to the BDS movement. For instance, Who Profits? keeps an updated database of Israeli and international corporations involved in the occupation. The list, available at www.whoprofits.org, is exceptionally useful and is often consulted by stockholders of pension funds, banks, and international institutions as well as activists to select their BDS targets and build their cases against them.

The spectacular growth of the Palestinian-initiated and Palestin-ian-led global BDS campaign against Israel, especially after the Israeli massacre in the besieged Gaza Strip, has also prompted some on the so-called Zionist left to abandon their long battle against the BDS movement (connected to their self-assigned role as gatekeepers for Palestinian aspirations and international solidarity) and adopt a wiser position. After the entry of BDS into the Western mainstream, some of these figures realized that reclaiming the limelight now demands flirting with BDS, even nominally adopting it, though they do not acknowledge its Palestinian leadership or frame of reference. Their new motto seems to be "If you can't beat it, hijack it!"

Rather than focusing on the true objectives of the BDS movement—realizing Palestinian rights by ending Israeli oppression against all three segments of the indigenous Palestinian people—members of the Zionist "left" often reduce the struggle to ridding Israel of "the occupation," presenting BDS as a "weapon" to *save Israel*, essentially as an apartheid, exclusivist state. They raise the slogan "Boycott the occupation, not Israel," or "We are against Israeli policies, not against Israel"—as if one could have opposed South African apartheid without being "against South Africa," or as if one could join a campaign against Saudi Arabian oppression of women, say, without being against Saudi Arabia! Only when it comes to Israel and safeguarding its exceptionalism, its exclusive, unquestionable "right" to exist as a racist state, do we read such insufferable nonsense. One would have understood if the argument had been, instead, that BDS targets Israel as a colonial state that violates international law and Palestinian rights but not the Israeli *people* per se; that would be more accurate in describing the BDS movement's goals.

While the BDS movement is not an ideological or centralized political party, it does have a Palestinian leadership, the BNC, and a well-thought-out and clearly articulated set of objectives that comprehensively and consistently address Palestinian rights in the context of upholding international law and universal principles of human rights. The heart of the BDS Call is not the diverse boycotting acts it urges but this rights-based approach that addresses the three basic rights corresponding to the main segments of the Palestinian people. Ending Israel's occupation, ending its apartheid, and ending its denial of the right of refugees to return together constitute the minimal requirements for justice and the realization of the inalienable right to self-determination. Endorsing BDS entails accepting these irreducible rights as the basis for a just peace.

Moreover, BDS is categorically opposed to all forms of racism and racist ideologies, including anti-Semitism. Individuals who believe that some are more human or deserve more rights than others based on differences in ethnic, religious, gender, sexual, or any other human identity attributes cannot belong to this consistently antiracist struggle for universal rights.[114]

At a practical level, after the principles in the Call are accepted, activists and solidarity groups set their own BDS targets and choose tactics that best suit their political and economic environment. Context sensitivity is the overriding principle for planning and implementing successful BDS campaigns.

BDS, as a distinctly Palestinian form of struggle that is rooted in a century of civil resistance against settler colonialism, inspired by the South African anti-apartheid struggle and the US civil rights movement, and supported by a global solidarity movement, is effective, flexible, and inclusive enough to welcome all those committed to the irreducible entitlement of all humans to equal rights.

Conclusion

Many around the world still lack the courage, moral consistency, or both to speak out against Israel's multi-tiered system of oppression. Despite all the compelling analyses showing the gradual decline of the power of the Israel lobby,[115] it still commands indisputable weapons in its arsenal that allow it to commit character assassination, to end careers of dissidents—whether members of the US Congress or other parliaments or artists or academics or trade unionists—and to muzzle serious debate about Israel's increasingly indefensible flouting of international law and basic human rights. Unfortunately, many still choose silence or toeing the line to avoid all this trouble.

Edward Said eloquently writes:

> Nothing in my mind is more reprehensible than those habits of mind in the intellectual that induce avoidance, that characteristic turning away from a difficult and principled position which you know to be the right one, but which you decide not to take. You do not want to appear too political; you are afraid of seeming controversial; you need the approval of a boss or an authority figure; you want to keep a reputation for being balanced, objective, moderate; your hope is to be asked back, to consult, to be on a board or prestigious committee, and so to remain within the responsible mainstream; someday you hope to get an honorary degree, a big prize, perhaps even an ambassadorship.
>
> For an intellectual these habits of mind are corrupting par excellence. If anything can denature, neutralize, and finally kill a passionate intellectual life it is the internalization of such habits. Personally I have encountered them in one of the toughest of all contemporary issues, Palestine, where fear of speaking out about one of the greatest injustices in modern history has hobbled, blinkered, muzzled many who know the truth and are in a position to serve it. For despite the abuse and vilification that any outspoken supporter of Palestinian rights and self-determination earns for him or herself, the truth deserves to be spoken, represented by an unafraid and compassionate intellectual.[116]

Heeding Said's memorable words, this book is an attempt to speak truth to power, to encourage others to speak truth to power, and to make a humble analytical, conceptual, and informative contribution to the most effective effort to date aimed at ending Israel's impunity and realizing Palestinian rights: the global BDS movement.

1

WHY NOW?

The current[1] grim reality on the ground in occupied Palestine makes a comprehensive boycott of Israel and its complicit institutions not only a moral obligation but also an urgent political necessity—first and foremost to avert genocide, and second, for those who may be oblivious to the moral argument and subscribe to what they perceive as a *realpolitik* approach, to head off a meltdown of the geopolitical system in the entire Arab / Middle Eastern region. Beyond preventing total, bloody chaos, the Palestinian civil society call for boycott, divestment, and sanctions (BDS)[2] aims to hold Israel accountable to international law and universal principles of human rights, in the pursuit of freedom, justice, self-determination, equality, and sustainable peace.

BDS is urgent because of the nightmarish conditions facing the Palestinian people and because the UN and the world's dominant states, led by the United States, have not only failed to hold Israel accountable to its obligations under international law but afforded it immunity, practically turning it into a state above the law of nations. This chapter focuses on the most serious of Israel's crimes against the

Palestinian people and why BDS promises to be an effective and potentially decisive response to them.

When the most stringent phase of Israel's ongoing siege of the occupied Gaza Strip started in June 2007, right after Hamas took over "power" there from a US-Israeli-backed faction of Fatah, few human rights and international law experts were able to accurately analyze the real motives and policy objectives behind Israel's patently illegal and immoral form of collective punishment. Even fewer had the insight to foretell the long-lasting consequences this siege would have on the 1.5 million Palestinians cramped in what was accurately described as the world's largest open-air prison. Richard Falk, a leading international law expert and the current UN special rapporteur for human rights in the occupied Palestinian territories, stood out among those few. In 2007 he wrote:

> Is it an irresponsible overstatement to associate the treatment of Palestinians with [the] criminalized Nazi record of collective atrocity? I think not. The recent developments in Gaza are especially disturbing because they express so vividly a deliberate intention on the part of Israel and its allies to subject an entire human community to life-endangering conditions of utmost cruelty. The suggestion that this pattern of conduct is a holocaust-in-the-making represents a rather desperate appeal to the governments of the world and to international public opinion to act urgently to prevent these current genocidal tendencies from culminating in a collective tragedy. If ever the ethos of "a responsibility to protect," recently adopted by the UN Security Council as the basis of "humanitarian intervention" is applicable, it would be to act now to start protecting the people of Gaza from further pain and suffering.[3]

Falk was not only diagnosing Israel's hermetic siege and its cruelty; he was actually predicting the slow genocide that has transpired as a result of the blockade and the December 2008–January 2009 Israeli war of aggression that aggravated it. Insightful indicators of the scale of the crime committed by Israel in Gaza were revealed in the report issued by UN Fact-Finding Mission on the Gaza Conflict, headed by the prominent South African judge Richard Goldstone, who happens to be a Zionist with ties to Israel. Among its damning findings, the Goldstone Report states:

1688. It is clear from evidence gathered by the Mission that the destruction of food supply installations, water sanitation systems, concrete factories and residential houses was the result of a *deliberate and systematic policy* by the Israeli armed forces. It was not carried out because those objects presented a military threat or opportunity but to make the daily process of living, and dignified living, more difficult for the civilian population.

1689. Allied to the systematic destruction of the economic capacity of the Gaza Strip, there appears also to have been an assault on the dignity of the people. This was seen not only in the use of human shields and unlawful detentions sometimes in unacceptable conditions, but also in the vandalizing of houses when occupied and the way in which people were treated when their houses were entered. The graffiti on the walls, the obscenities and often racist slogans all constituted an overall image of humiliation and dehumanization of the Palestinian population.

1690. The operations were carefully planned in all their phases. Legal opinions and advice were given throughout the planning stages and at certain operational levels during the campaign.

There were almost no mistakes made according to the Government of Israel. It is in these circumstances that the Mission concludes that what occurred in just over three weeks at the end of 2008 and the beginning of 2009 was a deliberately disproportionate attack designed to punish, humiliate and terrorize a civilian population, radically diminish its local economic capacity both to work and to provide for itself, and to force upon it an ever increasing sense of dependency and vulnerability.[4] (emphases added)

Although the UN report, adopted by the UN Human Rights Council with a comfortable majority despite hypocritical objections from the United States, the European Union, and Israel, calls on Israel—and the unrecognized Hamas government in Gaza—to "launch appropriate investigations that are independent and in conformity with international standards." It goes on to dampen any hope that Israel is capable, let alone willing, to do so:

1755. The Mission is firmly convinced that justice and respect for the rule of law are the indispensable basis for peace. The prolonged situation of impunity has created a justice crisis in the OPT that warrants action.

1756. After reviewing Israel's system of investigation and prosecution of serious violations of human rights and humanitarian law, in particular of suspected war crimes and crimes against humanity, the Mission found major structural flaws that in its view make the system inconsistent with international standards. With military "operational debriefings" at the core of the system, there is the absence of any effective and impartial investigation mechanism and victims of such alleged violations are deprived of any effective or prompt remedy. Furthermore, such investigations being internal to the Israeli military authority, do not comply with international standards of independence and impartiality.[5]

The necessity of holding Israel accountable by referring it to the International Criminal Court is the only logical conclusion one can reach from the above. This becomes more self-evident once the other, more fatal, long-term and genocidal aspects of Israel's war on and siege of Gaza are exposed.

The systematic Israeli targeting of Gaza's water and sanitation facilities has compounded an already "severe and protracted denial of human dignity," wrote Maxwell Gaylard, UN resident and humanitarian coordinator in the occupied palestinian territory, causing "a steep decline in standards of living for the [Palestinians] of Gaza, character-ized by erosion of livelihoods, destruction and degradation of basic infrastructure, and a marked downturn in the delivery and quality of vital services in health, water and sanitation."[6]

A 2009 report by Amnesty International on Israel's intentional and long-standing policy of denying Palestinian fair access to their water re-sources has shed light on a particularly fatal aspect of Israel's designs for the 1.5 million Palestinians in the occupied Gaza Strip. "In Gaza," the report affirms, "90–95 per cent of the water supply is contaminated and unfit for human consumption."[7] The report cites an earlier study by the UN Environmental Programme (UNEP), which correlates the widespread contamination of Gaza's water resources to the rise in ni-trate levels in the groundwater "far above the WHO accepted guideline," inducing a potentially lethal blood disorder in young children and new-borns called methemoglobinaemia, or the "blue babies" phenomenon. Some of the detected symptoms of this disease in Gaza infants include "blueness around the mouth, hands and feet," "episodes of diarrhea and vomiting," and "loss of consciousness." "Convulsions and death can occur" at higher levels of nitrate contamination, the report concludes.[8]

Contamination from Israel's assault and siege did not stop at Gaza's water resources; it dangerously polluted the soil as well. An in-dependent group of scientists and physicians from the New Weapons Committee, an Italy-based group that researches the effects of re-cently developed weapons on civilian populations in war zones, con-ducted a study on Israel's use of "non-conventional weapons" and their "middle-term effects" on the Palestinian residents of areas in Gaza that were bombed by the Israeli army on two separate occasions. "The 2006 and 2009 Israeli bombings on Gaza," the study shows, "left a high concentration of toxic metals in soil, which can cause tumours, fertility problems, and serious effects on newborns, like deformities and genetic pathologies."[9]

In a report tellingly titled *Rain of Fire: Israel's Unlawful Use of White Phosphorus in Gaza*, Human Rights Watch confirms Israel's deliberate targeting of civilians with devastating results. It states that the Israeli army's "repeatedly exploded white phosphorus munitions in the air over [densely] populated areas, killing and injuring civilians, and damaging civilian structures, including a school, a market, a humanitarian aid warehouse and a hospital," adding that the recurrent and indiscriminate use of this deadly weapon "indicates the commission of war crimes."[10]

Corroborating such findings by international human rights organizations and UN agencies on the impact of Israel's attacks on Gaza, on December 20, 2009, Al Dameer Association for Human Rights in Gaza published a position paper on the health and environmental problems caused by Israel's extensive use of proscribed radioactive and toxic materials throughout its assault on Gaza. Among the many grave, "long-lasting," and "tragic" effects of Israel's intentional choice of munitions and its indiscriminate and recurring targeting of densely populated civilian neighborhoods, schools, and even UN shelters, the paper gives special attention to the "dramatic" increase in the incidence of cancer—especially among children—as well as the rise in the number of birth defects and miscarriages, "particularly, in Jabalya, Biet Lahia, and Biet Hanoun as these areas witnessed the fiercest Israeli aggression." Drawing attention to the considerable "impact on men's fertility" that this radioactive and toxic weaponry is causing, the report warns that this wide deterioration in the health status of people in Gaza will "plague the future generation" and calls for "serious measures" toward "pressurizing Israel to lift the siege."[11]

The above, mostly ongoing, Israeli crimes do not occur in a vacuum; they are products of a culture of impunity, racism, and genocidal tendencies that has overtaken Israeli society, shaping its mainstream discourse and "commonsense" approach to the "Palestinian problem." Weeks after the end of Israel's attacks, for instance, testimonies of Israeli soldiers who participated in the commission of the Gaza massacre were published. Although the incidents they recount are merely the tip of the iceberg, these testimonies provide rare insight into prevailing Israeli thinking about the Palestinians and how best to "deal with them." The testimonies' significance is underscored by the fact that Israel's military remains a "people's army" based on mandatory service for men and women alike and, as a result, the army has long been regarded as the country's foremost melting pot and an accurate representation of a wide spectrum in Israeli society.

Explaining orders to indiscriminately shoot civilians in residential buildings and civilian neighborhoods, one solider says: "From above they said it was permissible because anyone who remained in the sector and inside Gaza City was in effect condemned, a terrorist, because they hadn't fled."

Another narrates how a well-reported incident of intentionally shooting and killing an elderly Palestinian woman took place: "A company commander saw someone coming on some road, . . . an old woman. She was walking along pretty far away, but close enough so you could take [her] out. . . . If she [was] suspicious, not suspicious—I don't know. In the end, he sent people up to the roof, to take her out with their weapons. From the description of this story, I simply felt it was murder in cold blood." When asked why they shot her despite recognizing her as an older woman who posed no threat, the soldier replies: "That's what is so nice, supposedly, about Gaza: You see a person on a road, walking along a path. He doesn't have to be with a weapon, you don't have to identify him with anything and you can just shoot him."

An honest soldier from an elite army brigade explains why a fellow sharpshooter who deliberately fired at a mother and her two children, killing all three, did not feel "too bad about it." He says: "After all, as far as he was concerned, he did his job according to the orders he was given. And the atmosphere in general, from what I understood from most of my men who I talked to . . . I don't know how to describe it. . . . The lives of Palestinians, let's say, [are] something very, very less important than the lives of our soldiers."[12]

Gideon Levy, a renowned Israeli journalist, contextualizes this phenomenon among soldiers as a "natural culmination" of killing thousands of Palestinians over the previous nine years, "nearly 1,000 of them children and teenagers." He writes:

> Everything the soldiers described from Gaza, everything, occurred during these blood-soaked years as if they were routine events. It was the context, not the principle, that was different. An army whose armored corps has yet to encounter an enemy tank and whose pilots have yet to face an enemy combat jet in 36 years has been trained to think that the only function of a tank is to crush civilian cars and that a pilot's job is to bomb residential neighborhoods.
>
> To do this without any unnecessary moral qualms we have trained our soldiers to think that the lives and property of Palestinians have no value whatsoever. It is part of a process of dehumanization that has endured for dozens of years, the fruits of the occupation.[13]

During the Israeli war on Gaza, fundamentalist Zionist rabbis played an unprecedented role in urging soldiers to "show no mercy" to any Palestinian in Gaza, citing popular, yet fanatic, interpretations of Jewish law as justifying genocide against Gentiles in the "Land of Israel" in any war of "revenge" or of necessity, as all Israeli wars are labeled by definition.[14] The late Israeli academic and human rights advocate Israel Shahak[15] was among the very first to expose this critical dimension, which had been intentionally overlooked by most analysts based on inexplicable sensitivities, as if Jewish fundamentalism were more benign or should be tolerated more than Islamic, Christian, Hindu, or any other fundamentalism.

It is crucial to note that fundamentalist interpretations of the Halacha, or Jewish law, openly justify massacres,[16] even genocide (as in mass murder of "non-Jewish" civilians, including children), in what is termed a "war of revenge" or a "necessary war." A war of necessity in fundamentalist teachings would be waged against the entire "enemy" population without sparing anyone. The only limit is on committing any act that might lead to *more* injury of the Jewish community in retribution. So if a massacre of, say, ten thousand Gentiles would cause damage to Israel that outweighed the "benefits," it should be avoided. This is the sole consideration that is allowed in such fanatical religious teachings, which have become dominant among the religious Zionist community in Israel and beyond and have seeped into the thinking of the general Israeli public in many ways.

And of course every war so far has been perceived by the absolute majority of Israeli Jews, including members of the traditional "peace movement," as a "war of necessity." This pattern was broken only after many days of the Lebanon 2006 war, specifically because the losses in the Israeli army far outweighed—in fundamentalist Jewish calculations, that is—the "benefits" of slaughtering Lebanese civilians and wantonly destroying the civilian infrastructure. Only then was there a substantial outcry against the war.

Gaza was different, though. Palestinian armed resistance could hardly put up a fight, especially given the condition of siege, against the far superior Israeli army, armed as it was with the United States' latest military technologies as well as diplomatic, financial, and political support. The extremely lopsided balance of fatalities on either side ensured overwhelming public support in Israel for the war. Many otherwise self-described liberals, even leftists, cheered their army while it was committing a live, televised massacre. While this was true in almost all sectors of Israeli society, one expression of racist fanaticism that stood out was popular army T-shirts.

Israeli army battalions and companies often compete in designing the most outrageously racist shirt that they can show off in front of the rest. The Israeli daily *Haaretz* published some examples and photographs of these T-shirts.[17] One T-shirt for infantry snipers "bears the inscription 'Better use Durex,'[18] next to a picture of a dead Palestinian baby, with his weeping mother and a teddy bear beside him." Another sharpshooters' shirt from the Givati Brigade's Shaked battalion "shows a pregnant Palestinian woman with a bull's-eye superimposed on her belly, with the slogan, in English, '1 shot, 2 kills.'"

Several prints depicted ruined, destroyed, or blown-up mosques, revealing a deeply entrenched Islamophobic tendency that is appallingly reminiscent of 1930s anti-Semitic cartoons in Europe. Another design shows a soldier raping a Palestinian girl, and underneath it says, "No virgins, no terror attacks."

Israeli sociologist Orna Sasson-Levy said that this phenomenon is "part of a radicalization process the entire country is undergoing, and the soldiers are at its forefront." She added: "There is a perception that the Palestinian is not a person, a human being entitled to basic rights, and therefore anything may be done to him."[19]

Was Israel simply "morally corrupted" by the occupation?

It's not uncommon for Israeli analysts from the Zionist "left" to try to explain the dominant racism and genocidal trends among Israelis as relatively new phenomena, departures from the good old days of liberalism and enlightenment, or signs of moral collapse. All such explanations have one thing in common: they betray the same symptoms of selective amnesia displayed by those on the right.

They ignore the fact that Israel's very establishment was a result of massive ethnic cleansing, massacres, rape, wanton destruction of hundreds of villages, and total denial of the most basic rights to the indigenous Palestinians who were dispossessed and exiled and those who remained despite all the attempts to annihilate their existence as a people with a distinct identity. During the Nakba, the massive campaign of ethnic cleansing by Zionist militias and later the Israeli army against the indigenous Palestinians, as Israeli historian Ilan Pappé, among others, has shown,[20] was premeditated, meticulously planned years in advance by Zionist leaders, including David Ben-Gurion, and executed systematically, brutally, and without compunction. As a result, over 800,000 Palestinians were dispossessed and uprooted and more than five hundred Palestinian villages were methodically destroyed to prevent the return of the refugees.

Today, refugees and internally displaced persons (IDPs) make up two-thirds of the Palestinian population. According to a survey by Badil Resource Center, a leading refugee rights advocacy group based in Bethlehem, "By the end of 2008, at least 67 percent (7.1 million) of the entire, worldwide Palestinian population (10.6 million) were forcibly displaced persons. Among them were at least 6.6 million Palestinian refugees and 455,000 internally displaced persons (IDPs)."[21]

Under the influence of Zionist ideology and decades of deceptive indoctrination, a great majority of Israelis today, including those in the Zionist "left camp," indulge in a convenient forgetfulness when it comes to recognizing that they, the colonial settlers, have always viewed the natives as *relative* humans[22] who are accordingly not entitled to the equal rights that only "full" humans can claim. Former deputy mayor of Jerusalem Meron Benvenisti commented in 2003 on the nature of this "conflict," saying:

> In the past two years I reached the conclusion that we are dealing with a conflict between a society of immigrants and a society of natives. If so, we are talking about an entirely different type of conflict. If so, we descend from the rational level to a completely basic, atavistic level that goes to the bedrock of personal and collective existence. Because the basic story here is not one of two national movements that are confronting each other; the basic story is that of natives and settlers. It's the story of natives who feel that people who came from across the sea infiltrated their natural habitat and dispossessed them.[23]

Israel's savagery in Gaza, whose population is 80 percent refugees, has gone well beyond dispossession, however. International law experts have debated whether Israel's crimes in Gaza, which largely conform to the UN definition of genocide, are committed with a clear intent—a necessary condition to consider these acts as constituting full-fledged genocide. Israel's most recent crimes in Gaza and ongoing medieval-style siege *can* accurately be categorized as acts of genocide, albeit slow. According to article II of the 1948 UN Convention on the Prevention and Punishment of the Crime of Genocide, the term is defined as

> any of the following acts committed with intent to destroy, in whole or in part, a national, ethnical, racial or religious group, as such:
>   (a) Killing members of the group;
>   (b) Causing serious bodily or mental harm to members of the group;
>   (c) Deliberately inflicting on the group conditions of life calculated to bring about its physical destruction in whole or in part . . .[24]

Clearly, Israel's hermetic siege of Gaza, designed to kill, cause serious bodily and mental harm, and inflict conditions of life calculated to bring about partial and gradual physical destruction, qualifies as an act of genocide, if not yet all-out genocide.[25]

While lawyers continue to argue, Palestinian "relative humans" are being subjected to what feels very much like slow genocide. Many Palestinian babies are still being born disfigured, "blue," or otherwise condemned to stunted growth, anemia, and a short, tormented life in the Gaza open-air prison camp. Palestinian soil and water are still being contaminated relentlessly, and not only in Gaza. Necessary sustenance requirements are still being denied to 1.5 million Palestinians there. Patients with chronic diseases as well as those suffering from a wide range of curable illnesses are dying a slow death, away from the mainstream media's radar. The forcible displacement of Palestinians has not stopped since the Nakba, with the latest campaigns in and around Jerusalem, as well as in the Naqab[26] (Negev), showing a clear intensification. Fragmentation of the Palestinian people in dozens of isolated communities to obliterate their national and social coherence and common identity is escalating.

In short, Palestinians cannot wait. Israel is no longer "just" guilty of occupation, colonization, and apartheid against the people of Palestine; as the evidence above suggests, it has embarked on what seems to be its final effort to literally disappear the "Palestinian problem." And it is doing so with utter impunity. The world cannot continue to watch. Thus BDS. Thus now.

Indeed, Israel's latest bloodbath in Gaza and its ongoing illegal and immoral siege of the Strip have stimulated a real transformation in world public opinion against Israeli policies. The heart-wrenching images, beamed across the world, of Israeli phosphorus bombs showering densely populated Palestinian neighborhoods and UN shelters triggered worldwide boycotts and divestment initiatives in economic, academic, athletic, and cultural fields of the kind that Palestinian civil society called for back in 2005.

The most inspiring and dramatic developments have taken place in South Africa and certain Western European countries. In February 2009, weeks after the end of Israel's assault on Gaza, the South African Transport and Allied Workers Union made history when it refused to offload an Israeli ship in Durban. In April, the Scottish Trade Union Congress followed the lead of the South African trade union federation, COSATU, and the Irish Congress of Trade Unions in adopting BDS. In May 2009, at its annual congress, the University and College Union (UCU), representing some 120,000 British academics, called for organizing an interunion BDS conference later this year to discuss effective, legal strategies for implementing the boycott.

Richard Falk commented on the seemingly inexorable spread of BDS across the world in an oral statement before the UN Human Rights Council on March 23, 2009:

> The public reaction to the Israeli military operations has led to a global reaction that has taken the form of an upsurge in civil initiatives that can be comprehended as part of a worldwide boycott and divestment campaign that has taken diverse forms; this development amounts to waging "a legitimacy war" against Israel on the basis of its failure to treat the Palestinian people in accord with international human rights law and international humanitarian law.[28]

2

WHY BDS?

The BDS (Boycott, Divestment and Sanctions) Call, launched in July 2005, was endorsed by an overwhelming majority of Palestinian civil society unions, political parties, and organizations everywhere. Rooted in a long tradition of nonviolent popular resistance in Palestine against Zionist settler-colonialism[1] and largely inspired by the anti-apartheid struggle in South Africa, it adopts a rights-based approach that is anchored in *universal* human rights, just as the US civil rights movement did. It resolutely rejects all forms of racism, including anti-Semitism and Islamophobia.

BDS unambiguously defines the three basic Palestinian rights that constitute the *minimal* requirements of a just peace and calls for ending Israel's corresponding injustices against all three main segments of the Palestinian people. Specifically, BDS calls for ending Israel's 1967 military occupation of Gaza, the West Bank (including East Jerusalem), and other Arab territories in Lebanon and Syria; ending its system of racial discrimination against its Palestinian citizens; and ending its persistent denial of the UN-sanctioned rights of Palestine refugees, particularly their right to return to their homes and to receive reparations.

Calling Israel an apartheid state does not imply that its system of discrimination is identical to apartheid South Africa's. It simply states that Israel's laws and policies against the Palestinians largely fit the UN definition of apartheid, which was adopted in 1973 and went into effect in 1976.[2]

For decades efforts to promote peace between Israel and the Palestinian people have categorically failed, further entrenching Israeli colonial hegemony and Palestinian dispossession. The main culprit is the insistence of Israel and successive US governments on exploiting the current massive power imbalance to impose a peace devoid of justice and human rights on the Palestinians, an unjust "solution" that fails to address our basic rights under international law and undermines our inalienable right to self-determination.

In parallel, official Western collusion manifested in unconditional diplomatic, economic, academic, and political support of Israel has further fed Israel's already incomparable impunity in violating human rights and spurred civil society worldwide to support boycotts against Israel as an effective, nonviolent form of struggle in the pursuit of peace based on justice and precepts of international law.

For too long, while nonviolence has been the mainstay of Palestinian resistance to settler-colonial conquest for decades, the term *nonviolence* has been associated among Palestinians with appeasement of Israel or submission to some of its unjust demands.[3] There are two main reasons for this negative connotation. First, many of those who advocated "nonviolence" in the past, and who received lavish Western media attention as a result, categorically vilified and denounced armed resistance, presented nonviolence as a substitute for it, and advocated only a minimal set of Palestinian rights, usually excluding or diluting the internationally recognized right of Palestinian refugees to repatriation and compensation, as well as ignoring the rights of Palestinian citizens of Israel. They therefore stood isolated from the Palestinian grass roots and virtually all respected civil society organizations. Second, Palestinian nonviolent campaigns were often funded, if not directed, by Western organizations, governmental or otherwise, with their own political agendas that conflicted with the *publicly* espoused Palestinian national agenda as expressed by the Palestine Liberation Organization (PLO). This entrenched association between nonviolence and a minimalist and seemingly "imported" political program made the term *nonviolence* subject to suspicion and antipathy among most Palestinians, particularly since armed resistance has been largely linked to a *maximalist* political program.

I beg to differ with this general characterization. While I firmly advocate nonviolent forms of struggle such as boycott, divestment, and sanctions to attain Palestinian goals, I just as decisively, though on a separate track, support a unitary state based on freedom, justice, and comprehensive equality as the solution to the Palestinian-Israeli colonial conflict. To my mind, in a struggle for equal humanity and emancipation from oppression, a correlation between means and ends, and the decisive effect of the former on the outcome and durability of the latter, is indisputable. If Israel is an exclusivist, ethnocentric, settler-colonial state, then its ethical, just, and sustainable alternative must be a secular, democratic state, ending injustice and offering unequivocal equality in citizenship and individual and communal rights *both* to Palestinians (refugees included) *and* to Israeli Jews. Only such a state can *ethically* reconcile the ostensibly irreconcilable: the inalienable, UN-sanctioned rights of the indigenous people of Palestine to self-determination, repatriation, and equality in accordance with international law and the *acquired* and internationally recognized rights of Israeli Jews to coexist—as equals, not colonial masters—in the land of Palestine.[4]

While individual BDS activists and advocates may support diverse political solutions, the BDS movement as such does not adopt any specific political formula and steers away from the one-state-versus-two-states debate, focusing instead on universal rights and international law, which constitute the solid foundation of the Palestinian consensus around the campaign. Incidentally, most networks, unions, and political parties in the BNC still advocate a two-state solution outside the realm of the BDS movement.

Starting with the collapse of the Soviet Union and the premature end of the first Palestinian intifada (1987–1991), through the launching of the Madrid-Oslo "peace process" and until a decade ago, the question of Palestine had been progressively marginalized, if not relegated to a mere nuisance factor, by the powers that be in the new unipolar world. Edward Said reflected on the "peace process" thus:

> What of this vaunted peace process? What has it achieved and why, if indeed it was a peace process, has the miserable condition of the Palestinians and the loss of life become so much worse than before the Oslo Accords were signed in September 1993? And why is it, as the *New York Times* noted on 5 November, that "the Palestinian landscape is now decorated with the ruins of projects that were predicated on peaceful integration"? And what does it mean to speak of peace if Israeli troops and settlements are still present in such large numbers? Again, according to RISOT, 110,000 Jews lived in illegal settlements in Gaza and the West Bank before Oslo; the number has since increased to 195,000, a figure that doesn't include those Jews—more than 150,000—who have taken up residence in Arab East Jerusalem. Has the world been deluded or has the rhetoric of "peace" been in essence a gigantic fraud?[5]

In quite a revealing turn of history, among the very first substantial consequences of this "new world order" was the UN General Assembly's 1991 repeal, under intense US pressure, of its 1975 "Zionism Is Racism" resolution,[6] thus removing a major obstacle on the course of Zionist and Israeli rehabilitation in the international community. This was followed by the PLO's formal recognition of Israel under the Oslo accords, which furthered the transformation of Israel's image from that of a colonial and inherently exclusivist state[7] into a *normal* member of the international community of nations, one that is merely engaged in a territorial dispute. After the establishment of the Palestinian Authority (PA), primarily, from Israel's perspective, to relieve Israel's colonial burdens in the West Bank and Gaza and to cover up its ongoing theft of Palestinian land to build Jewish-only settlements, Israel embarked on an ambitious public relations campaign in Africa, Asia, Latin America, and the Arab world, establishing diplomatic ties and opening new markets for its growing industries. Former sworn enemies suddenly warmed up to Israel, importing from it billions of dollars' worth of military hardware and other goods, and, convinced that the road to the US Congress passed through Tel Aviv, wooing it politically. As a result, Israel multiplied the number of states with which it holds diplomatic relations from a few dozen before Oslo to more than 160 at present.

Meanwhile, the election of George W. Bush in 2000 as the president of the United States and the rise of his neoconservative associates (erstwhile advisers to the far-right Israeli leader Benjamin Netanyahu) brought Zionist influence in the White House to unprecedented heights, finally matching its decades-old, almost unparalleled influence on Capitol Hill.

But shortly before the US presidential elections, in September 2000, after years of a sham "peace process" that served to disguise Israel's ongoing occupation and the enormous growth of its colonies in the occupied territories, the second Palestinian intifada broke out. As the uprising intensified, Israel's brutal attempts to crush it, through means described by Amnesty International and other human rights organizations as amounting to war crimes,[8] reopened—at least in intellectual circles—long-forgotten questions about whether a just peace can indeed be achieved with a colonial, ethnocentric, and expansionist Zionist state. It was against this background that the UN World Conference against Racism in Durban in 2001 revived the 1975 debate on Zionism.

Although, as expected, the official assembly failed to adopt a specific resolution on Israel's multitiered oppression of the Palestinian people due to direct threats from the United States and, to a lesser extent, powerful European states, the NGO Forum condemned Zionism as a form of racism and apartheid.[9] This was an expression of the views of thousands of civil society representatives from across the globe whose struggle against all forms of racism, including anti-Semitism, is mostly informed by humanist and democratic principles. Despite the official West's unwillingness to hold Israel to account, Durban confirmed that grassroots support, even in the West, for the justness of the Palestinian cause was still robust, if not yet channeled into effective forms of solidarity.

With the new intifada, boycott and sanctions were in the air. Campaigns calling for divestment from companies supporting Israel's occupation, for instance, spread to many US campuses,[10] initially causing panic among the ranks of the Israel lobby and its student arm. Archbishop Desmond Tutu of South Africa was among the earliest internationally renowned figures to support divestment from Israel.[11] The impromptu nature of these early, largely abortive efforts soon gave way to a higher degree of coordination and sharing of experience at a national level in the United States, culminating in the establishment of the Palestine Solidarity Movement and later the US Campaign to End the Israeli Occupation, a broad coalition of over three hundred groups working to change US foreign policy in favor of a just peace.[12] Across the Atlantic, particularly in the United Kingdom, calls for various forms of boycott against Israel started to be heard among intellectuals, academics, and trade unionists. These efforts intensified with the massive Israeli military reoccupation of Palestinian cities in spring 2002, with all the destruction and civilian casualties it left behind.

By 2004, academic associations, trade unions, and solidarity organizations in the United States and Europe calling for boycott had been joined by mainstream churches, which began to study divestment and other forms of boycott against Israel, similar in nature to those applied to South Africa during apartheid rule. The most significant development at that stage was the precedent-setting decision of the Presbyterian Church USA (PCUSA) in July 2004, in a resolution that was adopted by a resounding majority of 431 to 62, to start "a process of phased selective divestment in multinational corporations doing business in Israel." Unlike similar declarations adopted by student and faculty groups, the Presbyterian move could not be dismissed as "symbolic" or economically ineffective. Although PCUSA in 2006 dropped the term *divestment*, opting for "investment in peace" due to threats and intimidation by Israel lobby groups,[13] its initiative managed to inspire many faith-based organizations, especially, in the West to consider halting their investments in Israel as well.

A development of signal importance for these efforts was the historic advisory opinion issued by the International Court of Justice (ICJ) at The Hague on July 9, 2004, condemning as illegal both Israel's wall and the colonies built on occupied Palestinian land. Ironically, the PLO scored this momentous political, legal, and diplomatic victory at a time when it was least prepared to build on it. A similar advisory opinion by the ICJ in 1971, denouncing South Africa's occupation of Namibia, had triggered what became the world's largest and most concerted campaign of boycotts and sanctions directed against the apartheid regime, eventually contributing to its demise. Though the ICJ ruling on the wall did not prompt similar reaction, chiefly due to Palestinian structural and political powerlessness, it did fuel a revival of principled opposition to Israeli oppression around the world.

Days before the ICJ ruling, the Palestinian Campaign for the Academic and Cultural Boycott of Israel (PACBI), formed in April 2004, issued a call for the academic and cultural boycott of Israel endorsed by some sixty unions, organizations, and associations in the Palestinian occupied territories urging the international community to boycott all

Israeli academic and cultural *institutions* as a "contribution to the struggle to end Israel's occupation, colonization, and system of apartheid."[14] This call was greatly and qualitatively amplified on the first anniversary of the ICJ ruling, when more than 170 Palestinian civil society organizations and unions, including the main political parties, issued the Call for Boycott, Divestment and Sanctions (BDS) against Israel "until it fully complies with international law." After fifteen years of the so-called peace process, Palestinian civil society reclaimed the agenda, articulating Palestinian demands as part of the international struggle for justice long obscured by deceptive "negotiations." In a noteworthy precedent, the BDS Call was issued by representatives of the three segments of the Palestinian people—the refugees, the indigenous Palestinian citizens of Israel, and those under the 1967 occupation. It also directly "invited" conscientious Israelis to support its demands. The Palestinian boycott movement succeeded in setting new parameters and clearer goals for the growing international support network, sparking, or giving credence to, boycott and divestment campaigns in several countries.

A genuine concern raised by solidarity groups in the West regarding the calls for boycott has been the conspicuous absence of an *official* Palestinian body behind them. "Where is your ANC?" is a difficult and sometimes sincere question that faced Palestinian boycott activists everywhere. The PLO, in total disarray for years, has remained largely silent. The PA, with its circumscribed mandate and the constraints imposed upon it by the Oslo accords, is *inherently* incapable of supporting any effective resistance strategy, especially one that evokes injustices beyond the 1967 occupation. Indeed, with rare exceptions, the PA's role has actually been detrimental to civil society efforts to isolate Israel. This started to change in 2009, when the Sixth Conference of Fatah, the leading secular political party, adopted a political platform highlighting popular nonviolent struggle as the main form of resistance to the occupation.[15] Much criticism has been leveled at Fatah for holding its conference under occupation, accommodating Israeli demands, and, more substantively, transforming the Palestinian cause from a struggle for self-determination and comprehensive rights to what is seen by many pundits as a hollowed-out process of coexisting with Israeli injustices and denial of some of those basic rights.[16] Still, the enthusiasm for a strong commitment to nonviolent means of countering Israel's occupation and sprawling colonization eventually led the Fatah-dominated PA to adopt a—belated—policy of boycotting and calling on other states to boycott products of Israeli colonial settlements.[17] While many Palestinians saw this PA call for a partial boycott of Israel as "too little, too late," coming five full years after the great majority of Palestinian civil society had called for comprehensive BDS measures, there was a sense of vindication nonetheless. "Even" the PA, BDS leaders can now argue, eventually understood the immense power of boycott and popular resistance. It also has helped underline the consensus among Palestinians in support of boycott as a form of struggle against Israel's violations of international law.

As for "unofficial" Palestinian bodies, a tiny minority of them did not support the July 2005 BDS call. These were mostly smaller NGOs, ever attentive to donor sensitivities, that declined to endorse, some citing as "too radical" the clause on the right of refugee return (despite the fact that it is "stipulated in UN Resolution 194"). Some, bowing to pressure from their European "partners," feared that the term *boycott* would invite charges of anti-Semitism. Also, initially the largest Palestinian political factions, with their predominant decades-old focus on armed struggle, seemed unable to recognize the indispensable role of civil resistance, particularly in the unique—and certainly very different from South Africa's—colonial conditions of siege that the Palestinians had to resist.[18] By either inertia or reluctance to critically evaluate their programs in light of a changed international situation, these forces became addicted to the armed model of resisting the occupation, ignoring the troubling moral and legal questions raised by certain indiscriminate forms of that resistance and its failure to date to achieve concrete and sustainable results in an international environment dominated by Israel's main sponsor and enabler, the United States. Despite this initial reluctance, all major Palestinian political parties signed on to the BDS Call, widening the circle of consensus around it.

In order to realize Palestinian aspirations for self-determination, freedom, and equality and to pose a real challenge to Israel's dual strategy of on the one hand fragmenting, ghettoizing, and dispossessing Palestinians and on the other hand projecting a reduced image of the colonial conflict as a symmetrical dispute over rival claims and a diminished set of Palestinian rights, the PLO must be resuscitated and remodeled to embody the aspirations, creative energies, and national frameworks of the three main segments of the Palestinian people. The PLO's grassroots organizations need to be rebuilt from the bottom up with mass participation, inclusive of all political forces, and must be ruled by unfettered democracy through proportional representation.

In parallel, the entire Palestinian conceptual framework and strategy of resistance must be thoroughly and critically reassessed and transformed into a progressive action program capable of connecting the Palestinian struggle for self-determination and justice with the international social movement. The most effective and morally sound strategy for achieving these objectives is one based on gradual, diverse, context-sensitive, and sustainable campaigns of BDS—political, economic, professional, academic, cultural, athletic, and so on—and other forms of popular resistance, all aimed at bringing about Israel's comprehensive and unequivocal compliance with international law and universal human rights.

BDS will unavoidably contribute to the global social movement's challenge to neoliberal Western hegemony and the tyrannical rule of multi/transnational corporations. In that sense, the Palestinian boycott against Israel and its partners in crime becomes a small but critical part in an international struggle to counter injustice, racism, poverty, environmental devastation, and gender oppression, among other social and economic ills. Reflecting on this aspect of the BDS movement, and connecting it with the 2009 environmental international summit held in Denmark, John Pilger, the widely acclaimed journalist and writer, states:

> The farce of the climate summit in Copenhagen affirmed a world war waged by the rich against most of humanity. It also illuminated a resistance growing perhaps as never before: an internationalism linking justice for the planet with universal human rights, and criminal justice for those who invade and dispossess with impunity. And the best news comes from Palestine.
>
> ... To Nelson Mandela, justice for the Palestinians is "the greatest moral issue of the age." The Palestinian civil society call for boycott, disinvestment and sanctions (BDS) was issued on 9 July 2005, in effect reconvening the great, non-violent movement that swept the world and brought the scaffolding of [South] African apartheid crashing down."[19]

In this context, it is important to emphasize that it is not just Israel's military occupation and denial of refugee rights that must be challenged but the wider Zionist-Israeli system of racist exclusivism.[20] Jewish groups that historically stood in the front lines of the struggle for civil rights, democracy, equality before the law, and separation between church and state in many countries should find Israel's unabashedly ethnocentric and racist laws and its reduction of Palestinians to *relative* humans, whether in the occupied territories, in exile, or within Israel itself, to be politically indefensible and ethically untenable. Ultimately, then, successful nonviolent resistance requires transcending the fatally ill-conceived focus on the occupation alone to a struggle for justice, equality, and comprehensive Palestinian rights.

I am aware that reducing Palestinian demands to ending the occupation alone seems like the easiest and most pragmatic path to take, but I firmly believe that it is ethically and politically unwise to succumb to the temptation. The indisputable Palestinian claim to *equal humanity* should be the primary slogan raised, because it lays the proper moral and political foundation for effectively addressing the myriad injustices against all three segments of the Palestinian people. It is also based on universalist values that resonate with people the world over. While coalescing with diverse political forces is necessary to make this direction prevail, caution should be exercised in alliances with "soft" Zionists lest they assume the leadership of the BDS movement in the West, lowering the ceiling of its demands beyond recognition. On the other hand, principled Jewish voices—whether organizations or intellectuals consistently supporting a just and comprehensive peace—in the United States, Europe, and Israel[21] have courageously supported various forms of boycott, and this helps shield the nascent boycott movement from charges of anti-Semitism and the intellectual terror associated with them.

Supporting the UN-sanctioned rights of all segments of the Palestinian people does not, however, entail adopting BDS tactics that necessarily target all Israeli institutions. Tactics and the choice of BDS targets at the local level must be governed by the context particularities, political conditions, and the readiness (in will and capacity) of the BDS activists. In the United States, for instance, two of the most active and creative BDS groups, Adalah-NY[22] and CodePink,[23] endorse the 2005 BDS Call with its comprehensive rights-based approach and run effective campaigns that are very targeted and nuanced, focusing only on companies indisputably implicated in Israeli violations of international law in the occupied Palestinian territory. The same can be said of the largest BDS-related coalition in France, Coalition against Agrexco-Carmel.[24]

Besides the need to extend the struggle beyond ending the occupation, two other pertinent points in connection with BDS initiatives bear emphasizing. First, they should be guided by the principles of inclusion, diversity, gradualness, and sustainability. They must be flexibly designed to reflect realities in various contexts. Second, although the West, owing to its overwhelming political and economic power as well as its decisive role in perpetuating Israel's colonial domination, remains the main battleground for this nonviolent resistance, the rest of the world should not be ignored. Aside from South Africa and some beginnings elsewhere, the BDS movement has yet to take root in China, India, Malaysia, Brazil, and Russia, among other states that seek to challenge the West's monopoly on power. It is worth noting that Zionist influence in those states remains significantly weaker than in the West.

With the formation of the Palestinian BDS National Committee, BNC, in 2008,[25] it became the reference and guiding force for the global BDS movement, which was all along based on the Palestinian-initiated and -anchored BDS Call. The BNC is the coordinating body for the BDS campaign based on the Palestinian civil society BDS Call of 2005. Upholding civil and popular resistance to Israel's occupation, colonization, and apartheid, the BNC is a broad coalition of the leading Palestinian political parties, unions, coalitions, and networks representing the three integral parts of the people of Palestine: Palestinian refugees; Palestinians in the occupied West Bank (including Jerusalem) and Gaza Strip; and Palestinian citizens of Israel.

The BNC adopts a rights-based approach and calls for the international BDS campaign to be sustained until the entire Palestinian people can exercise its inalienable right to freedom and self-determination and Israel fully complies with its obligations under international law.

BDS is not only an idea. It is not merely a concept. It is not just a vision. It is not all about strategy. It is all those, for sure, but also much more. The Palestinian Civil Society Campaign for Boycott, Divestment and Sanctions against Israel is above everything else a deeply rooted yet qualitatively new stage in the century-old Palestinian resistance to the Zionist settler-colonial conquest and, later, Israel's regime of occupation, dispossession, and apartheid against the indigenous people of Palestine.

The global BDS campaign's rights-based discourse and approach decisively, almost irrefutably, exposes the double standard and exceptionalism with which the United States and most of the other Western states have to varying degrees treated Israel ever since its establishment through the carefully planned and brutally executed forcible displacement and dispossession of the majority of the Palestinian people in the 1948 Nakba.[26]

More crucially, the BDS movement has dragged Israel and its well-financed, bullying lobby groups into a confrontation on a battlefield where the moral superiority of the Palestinian quest for self-determination, justice, freedom, and equality neutralizes and outweighs Israel's military power and financial prowess. It is the classic right-over-might paradigm, with the right being recognized by an international public that is increasingly fed up with Israel's criminality and impunity and is realizing that Israel's slow, gradual genocide places a heavy moral burden on all people of conscience to act, to act fast, and to act with unquestionable effectiveness, political suaveness, and nuance, and above all else with consistent, untarnished moral clarity. Thus BDS.

3

THE SOUTH AFRICA STRATEGY FOR PALESTINE

In 2006, in an insightful and unprecedented exposé of the deep military and economic partnership, the shocking similarities, and the unmistakable sense of common destiny between Israel and apartheid South Africa, the *Guardian*'s award-winning Middle East correspondent Chris McGreal, who reported from Jerusalem for several years, wrote the following:

> Many Israelis recoil at the suggestion of a parallel because it stabs at the heart of how they see themselves and their country. . . . Some staunch defenders of Israel's policies past and present say that even to discuss Israel in the context of apartheid is one step short of comparing the Jewish state to Nazi Germany, not least because of the Afrikaner leadership's fascist sympathies in the 1940s and the disturbing echoes of Hitler's Nuremberg laws in South Africa's racist legislation. Yet the taboo is increasingly challenged.[1]

Whether it is legally accurate or politically astute to describe Israel as a state guilty of the crime of apartheid against the Palestinian people is of unquestionable importance and consequence. The significance to the Palestinian struggle for self-determination of the fact that international law considers apartheid a crime against humanity that therefore invites sanctions—similar in nature and breadth to those imposed on apartheid South Africa—cannot be overemphasized. The United Nations and the international community of states know well, from experience, how to deal with apartheid; all Palestinians and defenders of peace with justice have to do, then, is to prove beyond a doubt how Israel's own institutionalized and legalized system of racial discrimination, its denial of Palestinian refugee rights, and its two-tiered legal system in the occupied Palestinian territory constitute apartheid, among other serious crimes. The fact that Israel's regime of oppression is in fact worse than apartheid, as it encompasses ethnic cleansing, siege, and prolonged military occupation should not mitigate the need to also charge Israel with apartheid. If a proven serial rapist is also accused of a far more difficult to prove and more serious crime, like murder, forgoing the rape charge would be beyond irresponsible; it would be irrational. Winning a conviction on the easier-to-prove charge should help, not undermine, the case for the more elusive charge.

However, for the question whether Israel should be subjected to boycotts, divestment, and sanctions in response to its persistent and grave violations of international law and Palestinian rights, proving that Israel is guilty of apartheid is not necessary; it is not required. Those who oppose Israel's racist and colonial policies but reject the apartheid charge, whether they view Israel's regime over the Palestinian people as being worse or better than apartheid, should still be able to recognize that Israel's intensifying criminality and impunity as well as the world's—mainly Western—complicity in excusing it demand that citizens act to put an end to them. Without the "South African treatment" of global boycotts from outside supporting mass struggle inside, there is little hope of holding a state as powerful, belligerent, and increasingly fanatic as Israel accountable to international law. The fact that Israel is now seen by majorities in many countries in the world, including in most of the West, as the world's worst—or second worst—menace to international peace and security attests to the crucial need to stop Israel's warmongering and war crimes before it is too late.[2]

What could have stirred all this international moral indignation? one may wonder. The following representative samples of Israeli oppression of the three main sectors of the Palestinian people (under occupation, in exile, and in Israel) may help answer this question.

Israel's Occupation

Before the Israeli massacre in Gaza in the winter of 2008–9 inflicted massive destruction on Gaza's civilian infrastructure and the killing of more than 1,440 Palestinians, predominantly civilians (of whom 431 were children),[3] perhaps the most blatant testimony to Israel's willful disregard for international law and world courts is its colonial wall, which it continues to build, mostly on occupied Palestinian territory, in open defiance of the historic advisory opinion of the International Court of Justice (ICJ) at The Hague in July 2004, which condemned it—as well as the colonial settlements—as illegal.

Despite the wall's grave repercussions on Palestinian livelihood, environment, and political rights, a near total consensus exists among Israeli Jews in its support.[4] Former Israeli environment minister Yehudit Naot, however, did protest a specific aspect of the wall: "The separation fence severs the continuity of open areas and is harmful to the landscape, the flora and fauna, the ecological corridors and the drainage of the creeks. The protective system will irreversibly affect the land resource and create enclaves of communities that are cut off from their surroundings."[5] Likewise, even after irises were moved and passages for small animals were created, the spokesperson for the Israel Nature and National Parks Protection Authority complained: "The animals don't know that there is now a border. They are used to a certain living space, and what we are concerned about is that their genetic diversity will be affected because different population groups will not be able to mate and reproduce. Isolating the populations on two sides of a fence definitely creates a genetic problem."[6]

While so attuned to the welfare of wildflowers and little foxes, Israel treated Palestinian children as less worthy, even disposable, creatures. Professionally trained sharpshooters fatally targeted them in minor stone-throwing incidences. Medical sources[7] and human rights organizations, including Physicians for Human Rights, have documented in the first stage of the current Palestinian intifada a pattern of targeting the eyes and knees of Palestinian children with "clear intention" to harm.[8] The late Tel Aviv University professor Tanya Reinhart wrote, "A common practice [among sharpshooters] is shooting a rubber-coated metal bullet straight in the eye—a little game of well-trained soldiers, which requires maximum precision."[9]

And when there was no stone-throwing incident to hide behind, Israeli soldiers had to provoke one. The veteran American journalist Chris Hedges exposed how Israeli troops in Gaza had methodically provoked Palestinian children playing in the dunes of southern Gaza in order to shoot them. While the kids were playing soccer, a voice would bellow out from Israeli army Jeeps: "Come on, dogs. . . . Where are all the dogs of Khan Younis? Come! Come! . . . Son of a bitch!" Relating how the scheme would then unfold, Hedges writes:

> The boys—most no more than ten or eleven years old—dart in small packs up the sloping dunes to the electric fence that separates the camp from the Jewish settlement. They lob rocks toward two armored jeeps parked on top of the dune and mounted with loudspeakers. . . . A percussion grenade explodes. The boys . . . scatter, running clumsily across the heavy sand. They descend out of sight behind a sandbank in front of me. There are no sounds of gunfire.

The soldiers shoot with silencers. The bullets from the M-16 rifles tumble end over end through the children's slight bodies. Later, in the hospital, I will see the destruction: the stomachs ripped out, the gaping holes in limbs and torsos.

Yesterday at this spot the Israelis shot eight [boys]. . . . Children have been shot in other conflicts I have covered . . . but I have never before watched soldiers entice children like mice into a trap and murder them for sport.[10]

As outrageous as they are, Israeli violations of human rights in the occupied Palestinian territory are not the only form of oppression practiced against the Palestinians. Two other crucial dimensions of Israeli injustice and breaches of international law are no less important, if arguably less urgent—namely, Israel's denial of Palestinian refugee rights and its legalized and institutionalized system of racial discrimination against its own Arab Palestinian, or "non-Jewish," citizens. Palestinians cannot ignore either form of oppression.

Israel and Palestinian Refugee Rights

Far from admitting its guilt in creating the world's oldest and largest refugee problem, Israel has constantly evaded any responsibility for the Nakba, the catastrophe of Palestinian dispossession and uprooting around 1948. Most peculiar in the mainstream Israeli discourse about the "birth" of the state is the total denial of the fact that the state was created through the forcible displacement of a majority of the indigenous Palestinian population. In a unique case of inversion of truth, Israelis, with few bright exceptions, regard the Zionists' ruthless destruction of more than 500 Palestinian villages and their well-planned campaign of ethnic cleansing of more than 800,000 Palestinians as Israel's "independence." Even committed Israeli "leftists" often grieve over the loss of Israel's "moral superiority" *after* it occupied the

West Bank and Gaza in 1967, as if prior to that Israel had been a normal, civil, and law-abiding state.

But the truth that was literally buried under the rubble in 1948 was eventually unearthed, thanks in no small part to Israel's new historians.[11] Today, the refugee question irrefutably remains the most consequential and morally charged issue in this entire colonial conflict.

Manipulating the Holocaust,[12] Israel has premised its rejection of Palestinian refugee rights on the theory that Jews are unsafe among Gentiles and must therefore live in a state, a settler colony, with a dominant Jewish character that is to be maintained as sacrosanct, regardless of international law and irrespective of the human and political rights of the displaced indigenous population of the land on which this state was erected. No other country in the world today claims a similar sanctimonious right to ethno-religious supremacy. When the victims of the "super-victims" are portrayed as only relative humans,[13] as possessing inferior comparative worth, the portrayal is largely tolerated by the world's hegemonic powers.[14]

While denying Palestinian refugees their basic rights, particularly their right to return to their homes of origin and to receive reparations, as stipulated in UN General Assembly resolution 194, Jews in Israel and the West have scored numerous successes in their campaigns for Holocaust restitution and compensation, which often have included the right to return to Germany, Poland, and other countries from which Jewish refugees were expelled during World War II. But the quintessence of moral inconsistency is betrayed by the World Sephardic Federation's pressure on Spain to recognize the descendants of the Jews expelled from Andalusia more than five centuries ago as Spanish citizens and to rehabilitate them accordingly.[15]

The fact that refugees form an absolute majority of the Palestinian people and the fact of their decades-old suffering in exile make the recognition of the basic, UN-sanctioned rights of the Palestinian refugees *the litmus test of morality* for anyone seeking a just and enduring solution to the Palestinian-Israeli colonial conflict that is consistent with international law. Moral and legal rights aside, the denial of Palestinian refugee rights guarantees the perpetuation of conflict.[16]

Palestinian Citizens of Israel—Institutionalized Racism

Israel may not be unique, or even the most brutal, in racially discriminating[17] against an indigenous national minority, but it is certainly unique in its remarkable and sustained success—thus far—in getting away with it while projecting a false image of enlightenment and democracy. At the core of Israel's distinct form of apartheid[18] lies a deep-rooted view of the Palestinian citizens of the state not just as undesirable reminders of the "original sin"[19] but also as a demographic threat. Racial discrimination against them in every vital aspect of life has always been the norm. In fact, advocating comprehensive and unequivocal equality between Arabs and Jews in Israel has become tantamount to sedition, if not treason. An Israeli High Court justice once stated on record that "it is necessary to prevent a Jew or Arab who calls for equality of rights for Arabs from sitting in the Knesset or being elected to it."[20] To date, significant majorities of Jewish Israelis have consistently opposed full equality with the indigenous Palestinian citizens of Israel.[21]

Even in cancer research Israeli apartheid is strongly present. In June 2001, the Israeli Health Ministry published a map of the geographical distribution of malignant diseases in Israel during the years 1984–1999. Although the detailed report presents data about such diseases in communities with more than ten thousand residents, it excluded all Arab Palestinian communities in Israel, with the exception of Rahat in the Naqab (Negev) desert. When asked why, ministry officials resorted to the ubiquitous and quite absurd

excuse of "budgetary problems." This research is particularly important because in Israel only when a correlation is shown between the
presence of polluting sites and the incidence of malignant disease is
it possible to prevent installation of new hazards or to demand
tighter environmental controls. By intentionally omitting Palestinian towns and cities in its extensive cancer mapping, the Health Ministry has indirectly given a green light to polluters to relocate to those
towns. The results of such health apartheid are ominous. Between
1980 and 2010, the rate of malignant diseases in the Palestinian population *in Israel* rose by 97.8 percent among men and 123 percent
among women, as opposed to a rise of 39.8 percent for men and 24.4
percent for women in the Jewish population. A spokesperson for the
Center Against Racism commented: "The report has produced two
different groups. One, an overprivileged group, whose lives are dear
to the state and to the Health Ministry; a second, whose lives are of
no importance to the state."[22]

This systematic racial discrimination must be seen in the wider
context of Israel's perception of the Palestinians. Israeli politicians, intellectuals, academics, and mass media outlets often passionately debate how best to fight the country's demographic "war" with the
Palestinians. Racist walls have been erected in several localities inside
Israel where Jews and Palestinians live in close proximity. In Lydda,
Ramleh, and Caesaria, walls and barriers of various forms were built
to demographically separate the two communities.[23]

South African minister Ronnie Kasrils and British writer Victoria
Brittain addressed this rarely mentioned aspect of Israel's apartheid in
an article in the *Guardian*, where they wrote:

The desire for an ethnic-religious majority of Israeli Jews has seeped
across from the occupied territories to permeate the Israeli "national" agenda, which increasingly views Palestinian citizens of Israel

as a "demographic threat." . . . The Palestinian minority in Israel has for decades been denied basic equality in health, education, housing and land possession, solely because it is not Jewish. The fact that this minority is allowed to vote hardly redresses the rampant injustice in all other basic human rights. They are excluded from the very definition of the "Jewish state," and have virtually no influence on the laws, or political, social and economic policies. Hence their similarity to the black South Africans.[24]

Kasrils explains, "Apartheid was an extension of the colonial project to dispossess people of their land. That is exactly what has happened in Israel and the Occupied Territories—the use of force and the law to take the land. That is what apartheid and Israel have in common."[25]

And Kasrils isn't alone—even a few prominent Israeli politicians draw the connection between Israeli and South African apartheid. Former Israeli attorney general Michael Ben-Yair wrote in 2002:

We enthusiastically chose to become a colonial society, ignoring international treaties, expropriating lands, transferring settlers from Israel to the occupied territories, engaging in theft and finding justification for all these activities. Passionately desiring to keep the occupied territories, we developed two judicial systems: one—progressive, liberal— in Israel; and the other—cruel, injurious—in the occupied territories. In effect, we established an apartheid regime in the occupied territories immediately following their capture. That oppressive regime exists to this day. [26]

Echoing a popular view in Israel, Major General (reserve) Shlomo Gazit, a ranking academic with the Jaffee Center for Strategic Studies, preaches: "Democracy has to be subordinated to demography."[27] This once taboo, extreme-right slogan upheld by such fringe, racist figures as Rabbi Meir Kahane has now become part of the acceptable discourse about demography in the Israeli mainstream. Many Israelis from across the political spectrum now support various forms of ethnic cleansing of Palestinian citizens of Israel.[28]

The obsession with the Palestinian demographic "threat" has taken over Israel to the extent that it is overtly and frequently summoned to justify war crimes against the Palestinians, especially in the occupied Gaza Strip. For instance, on January 11, 2009, Reserve Colonel Yoav Gal, an Israeli Air Force pilot, told Army Radio during Operation Cast Lead:

> I believe that it should have been even stronger! Dresden! Dresden! The extermination of a city! After all, we're told that the face of war has changed. No longer is it the advancing of tanks or an organized military. . . . It is a whole nation, from the old lady to the child, this is the military. It is a nation fighting a war. I am calling them a nation, even though I don't see them as one. It is a nation fighting a nation. Civilians fighting civilians. I'm telling you that we . . . must know . . . that stones will not be thrown at us! I am not talking about rockets— not even a stone will be thrown at us. Because we're Jews. . . . I want the Arabs of Gaza to flee to Egypt. This is what I want. I want to destroy the city, not necessarily the people living within it.[29]

Similarly, in an interview with the *Jerusalem Post*, Israel's leading demographer, Arnon Soffer, who takes credit for the original idea of building a wall to surround Palestinian communities in the occupied Palestinian territory, stated:

> We will tell the Palestinians that if a single missile is fired over the fence, we will fire 10 in response. And women and children will be killed, and houses will be destroyed. After the fifth such incident, Palestinian mothers won't allow their husbands to shoot Qassams, because they will know what's waiting for them.
>
> Second of all, when 2.5 million people [*sic*] live in a closed-off Gaza, it's going to be a human catastrophe. Those people will become even bigger animals than they are today, with the aid of an insane fundamentalist Islam. The pressure at the border will be awful.

It's going to be a terrible war. So, if we want to remain alive, we will have to kill and kill and kill. All day, every day. . . . If we don't kill, we will cease to exist. . . . Unilateral separation doesn't guarantee "peace"—it guarantees a Zionist-Jewish state with an overwhelming majority of Jews.[30]

One conscientious Israeli who is revolted by all such language of demographic control is Dr. Amnon Raz-Krakotzkin of Ben-Gurion University, who says: "It's frightening when Jews talk about demography."[31]

By now, most Palestinians recognize Israel's entrenched system of colonialism, racism, and denial of basic human rights as including a form of apartheid. In fact, Palestinians are far from alone in holding this view of Israel; leading South African intellectuals, politicians, and human rights advocates subscribe to the same school of thought. In an article in the *Guardian* tellingly titled "Apartheid in the Holy Land," Archbishop Desmond Tutu writes: "I've been very deeply distressed in my visit to the Holy Land; it reminded me so much of what happened to us black people in South Africa. . . . Have our Jewish sisters and brothers forgotten their humiliation? Have they forgotten the collective punishment, the home demolitions, in their own history so soon?"[32]

In fact, many have not forgotten. Even inside Israel, some Jewish politicians and journalists have made clear analogies between Israel and South Africa. In 2005, Roman Bronfman, chair of the Democratic Choice faction in the Yahad Party, criticized what he termed "an apartheid regime in the occupied territories," adding, "The policy of apartheid has also infiltrated sovereign Israel, and discriminates daily against Israeli Arabs and other minorities. The struggle against such a fascist viewpoint is the job of every humanist."[33]

As early as 2005, former Israeli education minister Shulamit Aloni stated that Israel commits war crimes, "utilizes terror," and is "no different from racist South Africa." When asked how she viewed Israel's future, Aloni responded: "I can show you Mussolini's books about fascism. If you read them you'll reach the unequivocal conclusion that ministers in the current Israeli government are walking on the same path."[34]

Esther Levitan, the prominent Jewish South African grandmother once condemned to indefinite solitary confinement without trial in apartheid South Africa for her activism in the ANC, admitted in an interview with *Haaretz* that she considered Israel appallingly racist: "Israelis have this loathsome hatred of Arabs that makes me sick. . . . They will create a worse apartheid here."[35]

Brave Jewish South African leaders also made their voices heard against Israeli apartheid when they issued their famous Not in Our Names Declaration of Conscience, flatly condemning Israel's denial of Palestinian rights as the root cause of the conflict. The declaration, authored by then government minister Ronnie Kasrils and legislator Max Ozinsky, and signed by hundreds of other leading Jewish South Africans, states, "It becomes difficult, particularly from a South African perspective, not to draw parallels with the oppression experienced by Palestinians under the hand of Israel and the oppression experienced in South Africa under apartheid rule."[36]

More recently, even Knesset speaker Reuven Rivlin had this to say about Israel's "democracy": "The establishment of Israel was accompanied by much pain and suffering and a real trauma for the Palestinians. Many of them encounter racism and arrogance from Israel's Jews; the inequality in the allocation of state funds also does not contribute to any extra love."[37]

What's to Be Done, Then?

The abject failure of the international community in the last few decades to bring about Israel's compliance with international law has prompted people of conscience the world over to go beyond mere condemnation of Israeli crimes and human rights violations to explicitly endorse and advocate effective pressure on Israel, as was done with the apartheid regime in South Africa. In an article titled "Against Israeli Apartheid," Tutu states:

> Yesterday's South African township dwellers can tell you about today's life in the occupied territories. . . . The indignities, dependence and anger are all too familiar. . . . Many South Africans are beginning to recognize the parallels to what we went through. . . . If apartheid ended, so can the occupation, but the moral force and international pressure will have to be just as determined. The current divestment effort is the first, though certainly not the only, necessary move in that direction.[38]

This is precisely the conclusion reached by Palestinian civil society. What Palestinians everywhere have recognized after more than a decade of "peace talks" is that the Oslo process has only thickened their chains, intensified their dispossession, and entrenched the denial of their rights, while helping Israel to rehabilitate itself in the world and open new markets, propelling its economic growth to unprecedented levels. The only conclusion they could reach was that Israel's three-tiered system of oppression could not be seriously challenged by Palestinian resistance alone, in isolation from the world. The BDS movement, more than anything else, is the most ambitious drive yet launched by Palestinians to connect the struggle for Palestinian rights with global struggles for social and economic justice, freedom, sustainable development, environmental protection, and universal rights. Mass civil—and intelligent—resistance inside, coupled with effective and creative global solidarity from outside, is the recipe for success, the movement understands.

Support for boycotting Israel was strongest in South Africa. In October 2004, a call for a comprehensive boycott of Israel issued by solidarity groups in South Africa was endorsed by major South African organizations and unions, including the Congress of South

African Trade Unions (COSATU), Landless People's Movement, South African NGO Coalition, Anti-War Coalition, and Physicians for Human Rights.

So what is Palestinian civil society calling for exactly?

Based on the above described three-tiered Israeli system of oppression, the Palestinian BDS Call states:

> We, representatives of Palestinian civil society, call upon international civil society organizations and people of conscience all over the world to impose broad boycotts and implement divestment initiatives against Israel similar to those applied to South Africa in the apartheid era. We appeal to you to pressure your respective states to impose embargoes and sanctions against Israel. We also invite conscientious Israelis to support this Call, for the sake of justice and genuine peace.[39]

The BDS Call is modeled after the earlier call issued by the Palestinian Campaign for the Academic and Cultural Boycott of Israel (PACBI), which became the center of focus during the debate leading to and following the British Association of University Teachers' (AUT) boycott of selected Israeli universities back in April 2005. That historic decision was overturned in May of the same year, after an intensive and extraordinary intimidation and bullying campaign was waged against the AUT by Israel and pro-Israel lobbies in the United Kingdom and the United States. Though short lived, and some would say in hindsight premature, the unprecedented British academic boycott placed the boycotting of Israel on the agenda, inspiring many academics, artists, and other intellectuals around the world to start considering their moral obligation to help end complicity with an outlaw state and its institutions. The AUT showed in a concrete way that Israel could be brought down from the pedestal it has been placed on in the West, to borrow Archbishop Tutu's metaphor. The statement issued by PACBI to welcome the AUT decision to boycott remained largely valid even after the decision was rescinded. It said:

> Aside from passing the boycott motions, the debate itself about Israel's oppression and the collusion of Israeli academic institutions in it and the extensive media coverage that ensued have played a significant role in educating many around the world about the Palestinian struggle for freedom, self-determination and equality.
>
> The taboo has been shattered, at last. From now on, it will be acceptable to compare Israel's apartheid system to its South African predecessor. As a consequence, proposing practical measures to punish Israeli institutions for their role in the racist and colonial policies of their state will no longer be considered beyond the pale.

Indeed, throughout the process of debating, passing, rescinding, and debating again the British academic boycott of Israel, we witnessed a defining moment of transformation in the modus operandi of the solidarity movement from mostly raising awareness and issuing appeals or condemnations, as important as these forms of struggle are, to also applying effective sanctions to bring about justice and peace.

Main Arguments against BDS

Many arguments were raised against the Palestinian boycott calls. Even some distinguished supporters of the Palestinian cause have argued against applying South-Africa style boycotts to Israel for various reasons. I shall summarize here the least irrational and most frequently used among them, giving counterarguments, the key to which is the principle of moral consistency.

1. *Unlike South Africa, Israel is a democracy; persuasion and soft power are far more effective than boycotts in this case.* This assumes that Israel is essentially a democratic country with a vibrant and mostly progres-

sive civil society and a thriving peace movement, and therefore Israeli society deserves to be supported, not boycotted.

But how can an ethno-religious supremacy that is also a settler-colonial power ever qualify as a democracy? For instance, Tony Judt, the late New York University professor, calls Israel a "dysfunctional anachronism," categorizing it among the "belligerently intolerant, faith-driven ethno states."[40] And as far back as 1967 the famous Jewish-American writer I. F. Stone summed up the dilemma of Zionism thus: "Israel is creating a kind of moral schizophrenia in world Jewry. In the outside world, the welfare of Jewry depends on the maintenance of secular, non-racial, pluralistic societies. In Israel, Jewry finds itself defending a society in which mixed marriages cannot be legalized, in which non-Jews have a lesser status than Jews, and in which the ideal is racist and exclusivist."[41]

Henry Siegman, academic at the University of London and a former head of the American Jewish Congress, one of the main Israel lobby groups in the United States, argues:

> When a state's denial of the individual and national rights of a large part of its population becomes permanent—a permanence that has been the goal of Israel's settlement project from its very outset (and that many believe has been achieved)—that state ceases to be a democracy. When the reason for that double disenfranchisement is that population's ethnic and religious identity, the state is practicing a form of apartheid or racism. The democratic dispensation that Israel provides for its mostly Jewish citizenry cannot hide its changing (or changed) character. A political arrangement that limits democracy to a privileged class and keeps others behind military checkpoints, barbed-wire fences and separation walls does not define democracy. It defines its absence.[42]

In this context, the overused claim that Israeli academic, cultural, and other civil society institutions are "at the forefront" of the struggle against the occupation and must be supported, not ostracized, is increasingly being exposed as a fraud, an unfounded myth propagated and maintained mostly, but not exclusively, by some Zionist Israeli academics and intellectuals who count themselves on the "left." Recent research shows beyond doubt the depth of complicity of Israel's academic institutions in planning, executing, justifying, and whitewashing the state's myriad violations of international law and even war crimes.[43] The vast majority of Israelis, including academics and artists, serve in the army's reserve forces and therefore directly know of or participate in the daily crimes of occupation and apartheid. Moreover, with the exception of a tiny yet crucial minority, Israeli civil society is largely opposed to full equality of the Palestinians, is supportive of the state's colonial oppression, or is acquiescently silent about it.

A disingenuous argument raised by some opponents of boycotting Israel who supported boycotting apartheid South Africa is that, unlike in South Africa, the majority in Israel is opposed to boycott. Of all the anti-boycott arguments, this one reflects either surprising naiveté or deliberate intellectual dishonesty. Are we to judge whether to apply sanctions on a colonial power based on the opinion of the majority in the *oppressors'* community? Does the oppressed community count at all? Would those upholding this peculiar argument have withheld support for the South African boycott had the oppressed black population not been the majority? By this same skewed logic, should no one boycott any pariah state for oppressing its national or ethnic minorities anywhere in the world? Or does this "majority support" requirement apply only to Israel for some untold reason?

2. *Boycotting Israel is counterproductive, as it may harm the Palestinians more than help them.* The assumption here is that any party that endorses the boycott will lose the ability to influence Israel's possible path to peace; will radicalize the Israeli right, and undermine the left;

and will indirectly increase the suffering of Palestinians, as the vulnerable underdogs who stand to lose most, in terms of economic hardship and political repression at the hand of an even wilder, more isolated Israel.

On the point of influence, one cannot but wonder, *who* has real influence over Israeli policies? Europe hardly has any right now. The United States is the main sponsor, supporter, and protector of Israel, diplomatically, economically, militarily, and otherwise; its successive administrations have been, in fact, full partners in crime. Furthermore, the "Israelization" of US foreign policy, particularly in relation to the "Middle East," has reached new depths, effectively tying the hands of any prospective US pressure aimed at curtailing, not to mention ending, Israel's oppressive policies. The recent rebuffs of the Obama administration by the Netanyahu government when it rejected the US demand to extend the so-called freeze on colonial settlement construction in the occupied Palestinian territory were beyond humiliating; they reflected the entrenched power of the Israel lobby in shaping US foreign policy vis-à-vis Israel, the Palestinians, the Arab world, and far beyond.[44]

Given this, BDS presents an effective and empowering vehicle for grassroots movements to exert pressure on Israel to end its injustices as well as on the US administration to stop being an accomplice in, and sometimes instigator of, Israel's crimes.

In regard to undermining "the left," what left? Gideon Levy opines, justifiably, that the fact that "there were no significant protests during Operation Cast Lead" indicates that "there is no left to speak of."[45] In fact most of what passes as "left" in Israel are Zionist parties and groups that make some far-right parties in Europe look as moral as Mother Teresa, especially when it comes to recognizing Palestinian refugees' rights or demanding full equality for the "non-Jewish" citizens of the state. Entrenched colonial racism aside, the overwhelming majority of

Israelis are simply apathetic; they could not care less what their state and institutions are doing to the Palestinians so long as they can pursue as normal a life as possible without being bothered. This is the conclusion reached even in key mainstream publications not known to be remotely critical of Israel.[46]

On the other hand, the morally consistent, non-Zionist left is a principled but tiny group, whose members may inadvertently end up losing benefits and privileges as a result of boycott. This should compel us to nuance our boycott tactics to decrease the possibility of that. But as we all know, BDS is not an exact science (if any science is); we must emphasize the positive impact boycott can have on the overall struggle for human rights, equality, and real democracy even in Israel.

As for the counterproductiveness argument, one can only question how serious it is. If those who make it are indeed sincerely concerned about identifying the most productive and effective means of supporting the Palestinian struggle to attain justice and our inalienable rights under international law, then they must recognize that the Palestinian majority, which supports BDS, knows what is in its best interest far better than those who stand in solidarity with us. Usually the voices repeating the counterproductiveness argument fail to suggest any realistic and principled paths of struggle that could be more effective in attaining the same objectives. And if we scratch the surface, one quickly sees that they in fact reduce the objectives significantly and invariably prescribe goals that do not, and indeed cannot, empower or mobilize sustainable grassroots action. Regardless of the sincerity of their argument, it reveals an implicit colonial, patronizing attitude toward the Palestinians, as if its advocates know what is best for us more than we do. Moreover, Palestinians are well aware of the price we must pay if BDS is to succeed; but we are mature and rational enough to accept this price in our pursuit of freedom, equality, and self-determination. So were our South African comrades who fought for emancipation and equality against all odds.

Reflecting on the use of this same argument to undermine the South African anti-apartheid boycott, Archbishop Tutu writes:

> Consider for a moment the numerous honorary doctorates that Nelson Mandela and I have received from universities across the globe. During the years of apartheid many of these same universities denied tenure to faculty who were "too political" because of their commitment to the struggle against apartheid. They refused to divest from South Africa because "it will hurt the blacks" (investing in apartheid South Africa was not seen as a political act; divesting was).
>
> Let this inconsistency please not be the case with support for the Palestinians in their struggle against occupation.[47]

3. *Boycotting Israel is an expression of anti-Semitism, as it targets Israel for being a Jewish state.* Holocaust guilt is often used to buttress this argument, whereby an attempt is made to manipulate that guilt to win exceptional impunity for Israel and protection from censure or worse.

As the French philosopher Étienne Balibar says, "Israel should not be allowed to instrumentalize the genocide of European Jews to put [itself] above the law of nations."[48] Beyond that, by turning a blind eye to Israel's oppression, as the United States and most of official Europe have done, the West has in fact perpetuated the misery, the human suffering, and the injustice that have ensued since the Holocaust.

As to the anti-Semitism charge, it is patently misplaced and is clearly being used as a tool of intellectual intimidation. It is hardly worth reiterating that the Palestinian BDS Call does not target Jews, or even Israelis qua Jews; the call is strictly directed against Israel as a colonial and apartheid power that violates Palestinian rights and international law. The identity of the oppressors hardly matters; all that matters is the fact that they continue to oppress us, forcing us to resist them by all means in harmony with international law and human rights principles. Further, the growing support among progressive European, American, and Israeli Jews for effective pressure on Israel is one counterargument that is often suspiciously omitted in the arguments against BDS.[49]

How We Work—and Do Not Work—Together for Just Peace

BDS does not preclude joint Palestinian-Israeli cooperation projects so long as they recognize Palestinian rights, uphold the basic need for freedom and equality, and unambiguously aim to end Israel's colonial oppression of the Palestinian people.[50] The boycott campaign sets careful criteria for making such cooperation morally sound and politically effective. It is not enough to call for peace, for this word has become one of the most abused words in the English language, particularly when notorious and certified war criminals like Henry Kissinger and Menachem Begin are awarded the Nobel Peace Prize. Peace without justice is equivalent to institutionalizing injustice.

Peace projects that deliberately omit any mention of Israel's oppression of the Palestinians are nothing more than harmful and corrupt endeavors. Those who imagine they can wish away the conflict by suggesting some forums for rapprochement, détente, or "dialogue"—which they hope can somehow lead to authentic processes of reconciliation and eventually peace—without first recognizing the need to end injustice and uphold international law are clinically delusional or dangerously deceptive. Attempting, as many Western-funded projects do, to change and moderate the perception of the oppressed about "the conflict" rather than help end the system of oppression itself is an indicator of moral blindness and political short-sightedness. Prolonging oppression is not only unethical but pragmatically counterproductive as well, as it perpetuates the conflict.

Boycotts, divestment, and sanctions do not come in one size that fits all. If fundamental, inalienable Palestinian rights are recognized and the basic premise that Israel needs to be pressured in order to comply with international law and attain those rights is accepted, then diverse forms of BDS can be applied in accordance with specific contexts. Without principled and effective support for this minimal, civil, nonviolent form of resistance to oppression, international civil society organizations will be abandoning their moral obligation to stand up for right, justice, true peace, equality, and a chance to validate the prevalence of universal ethical principles.

ACADEMIC BOYCOTT

MORAL RESPONSIBILITY AND THE STRUGGLE AGAINST COLONIAL OPPRESSION

In the exercise of his rights and freedoms, everyone shall be subject only to such limitations as are determined by law solely for the purpose of securing due recognition and respect for the rights and freedoms of others and of meeting the just requirements of morality, public order, and the general welfare in a democratic society.

—Universal Declaration of Human Rights, Article 29(2)

The hurdles Palestinian Arab students face from kindergarten to university function like a series of sieves with sequentially finer holes. At each stage, the education system filters out a higher proportion of Palestinian Arab students than Jewish students.

—Human Rights Watch, "Second Class: Discrimination against Palestinian Arab Children in Israel's Schools," September 2001

Background note

In April 2005, the annual congress of the British academic union, Association of University Teachers (AUT), adopted a resolution calling for the boycott of two Israeli universities, Bar Ilan and Haifa, for various infringements, and asking AUT members to heed the call of the Palestinian Campaign for the Academic and Cultural Boycott of Israel (PACBI). In response, the American Association of University Professors (AAUP) issued a curt statement condemning academic boycotts. The statement declared that "since its founding in 1915, the AAUP has been committed to preserving and advancing the free exchange of ideas among academics irrespective of governmental policies and however unpalatable those policies may be viewed. We reject proposals that curtail the freedom of teachers and researchers to engage in work with academic colleagues, and we reaffirm the paramount importance of the freest possible international movement of scholars and ideas."[1]

Many boycott activists and academics criticized the AAUP statement, and some accused it of being misinformed and biased. The controversy over the academic boycott of Israel and AAUP's position against it prompted the association to announce its intention to organize an invitation-only debate on this issue in February 2006 at the Rockefeller Conference Center in Bellagio, Italy. After a concerted campaign of pressure by Israeli lobby groups against this meeting, the main financial sponsors were scared off, leading to the scuttling of the meeting.[2] Still, the AAUP resolved to publish the papers that were to be discussed so as to "present the viewpoints that would have been debated at the conference." The following is my contribution to the debate on the Palestinian Call for an Academic Boycott based on the papers that were published in the AAUP newsletter, *Academe*.

The American Association of University Professors ought to be commended for taking this timely and valuable initiative, promoting an open debate on academic boycotts and their bearing on the principle of academic freedom. Here I shall limit myself to critiquing the AAUP's position on academic boycotts and academic freedom as expressed in its Committee A on Academic Freedom and Tenure report "On Academic Boycotts."[3]

From my perspective, three sets of problems arise from the AAUP stance on this issue: in reverse order of importance, conceptual, functional, and ethical. Together, they pose a considerable challenge to the coherence of the AAUP's position on the academic boycott of Israel, and they call into question the consistency of this position with the organization's long-standing policies and modes of intervention—as delineated in the Committee A report—in cases where its principles are breached. Most important, by positing its particular notion of academic freedom as being of "paramount importance," the AAUP effectively, if not intentionally, sharply limits the moral obligations of scholars in responding to situations of oppression.

Conceptual Inadequacy

The AAUP's conception of threats to academic freedom appears to be restricted to intrastate conflicts, mainly "governmental policies" that suppress the "free exchange of ideas among academics." A governmental decree in China, say, institutionalizing censorship of academic publications, would fall under this category. This leaves out academics in contexts of colonialism, military occupation, and other forms of national oppression where "material and institutional foreclosures . . . make it impossible for certain historical subjects to lay claim to the discourse of rights itself," as philosopher Judith Butler eloquently argues.[4] Academic freedom, from this angle, becomes the exclusive privilege of some academics but not others. The role of the US occupation forces in suppressing academic freedom in Iraq, for instance, would present a serious challenge to AAUP's restricted formulation.

Moreover, by privileging academic freedom above all other freedoms, the AAUP's notion contradicts seminal international norms set by the United Nations. The 1993 World Conference on Human Rights proclaimed, "All human rights are universal, indivisible . . . interdependent and interrelated. The international community must treat human rights globally in a fair and equal manner, on the same footing, and with the same emphasis."[5] Finally, by turning the free flow of ideas into an absolute, unconditional value, the AAUP comes into conflict with the internationally accepted conception of academic freedom, as defined by the UN Committee on Economic, Social, and Cultural Rights (UNESCR), which states:

> Academic freedom includes the liberty of individuals to express freely opinions about the institution or system in which they work, to fulfill their functions without discrimination or fear of repression by the state or any other actor, to participate in professional or representative academic bodies, and to enjoy all the internationally recognized human rights applicable to other individuals in the same jurisdiction. The enjoyment of academic freedom carries with it *obligations*, such as the duty to respect the academic freedom of others, to ensure the fair discussion of contrary views, and to treat all without discrimination on any of the prohibited grounds.[6] (emphasis added)

When scholars neglect or altogether abandon such obligations, when they infringe on the "academic freedom of others," they can no longer claim what they perceive as their inherent right to this freedom. This rights-obligations equation is the general underlying principle of international law in the realm of human rights. It also was one of the foundations of the AAUP's initial view of academic freedom, as expressed in its 1915 *Declaration of Principles*, which conditioned this freedom upon "correlative obligations" to further the "integrity" and "progress" of scientific inquiry. Without adhering to a set of inclusive and evolving obligations, academic institutions and associations have little traction to discourage academics from engaging in acts or advocating views that are deemed bigoted, hateful, or incendiary.

Should a professor be free to write, "Among [Jews], you will not find the phenomenon so typical of [Islamic-Christian] culture: doubts, a sense of guilt, the self tormenting approach. . . . There is no condemnation, no regret, no problem of conscience among [Israelis] and [Jews], anywhere, in any social stratum, of any social position"? In fact, if we substitute for the words in brackets—in order—"Arabs," "Judeo-Christian," "Arabs," and "Muslims," the above becomes an exact quotation from a book by David Bukay of Haifa University.[7] A Palestinian student of Bukay's filed a complaint against him alleging racially prejudiced utterance. The university's rector exonerated Bukay of any wrongdoing, although Israel's deputy attorney general ordered an investigation of Bukay "on suspicion of incitement to racism."[8] In this case, the institution itself becomes implicated.

Criminal law aside, should an academic institution tolerate, under the rubric of academic freedom, a hypothetical lecturer's advocacy of the "Christianization of Brooklyn," say, or some "scientific" research explicitly intended to counter the "Jewish demographic threat" in New York? Arnon Soffer of Haifa University has worked for years on what is exactly the same, the "Judaization of the Galilee," and he is launching projects aimed at fighting the perceived "Arab demographic threat" in Israel.[9] In his university and in the Israeli academic establishment at large, Soffer is highly regarded and often praised.

Do academics who uphold Nazi ideology, deny the Holocaust, or espouse anti-Semitic theories enjoy the right to advocate their views in class? Should they? Does the AAUP notion of academic freedom have the competence to consistently address such thorny cases?

Operational Inconsistency

Throughout its report, the AAUP fails to maintain fairness and commensurability when dealing with Israeli academics and their Palestinian counterparts. According to the report, what provoked the AAUP's "prompt" condemnation of the AUT decision to apply academic boycott to Israeli academic institutions was the perceived violation of a specific aspect of Israeli scholars' academic freedom—their right to interact freely with international academics. The injustices that prompted the AUT's motion and that constituted, among various breaches of human rights, a much more radical and comprehensive denial of Palestinian academic freedom did not invite even censure from the AAUP. Indeed, when the AAUP report refers to these injustices at all, it reduces them to "what some see as the Israeli occupation's denial of rights to Palestinians," implying that most do not see military occupation as antithetical to the very claim to or exercise of freedom and rights.

It is worth mentioning that thirty-four days after adopting the academic boycott of Bar Ilan and Haifa Universities, the AUT was compelled to rescind it under enormous pressure from Israel lobby groups. In a statement issued just before the Special Congress of AUT decided to reverse the boycott policy, passed on April 22, 2005, PACBI attributed this inevitable reversal to three main factors:

(1) The extensive intimidation tactics used by organized Israeli and Zionist interest groups in the UK, Israel and even the US to vilify boycott leaders and to effectively suppress any rational debate[10] on Israel's oppression of the Palestinians, the main motive behind the boycott;

(2) The blanket media coverage given only to one side of the debate, that of the anti-boycott forces, with an almost complete preclusion of Palestinian voices;

(3) The appalling misinformation campaign waged by Israel and

its apologists, including some key figures in the Israeli "left," who joined the establishment chorus in this regard.[11]

While the AAUP report cited above asserts that the organization has approved numerous resolutions condemning "regimes and institutions that limit the freedoms of citizens and faculty," the organization, to the best of my knowledge, has never taken a public stand in response to Israel's military closure of Palestinian universities and schools for several consecutive years in the late 1980s and early 1990s and its simultaneous "criminalization" of all forms of alternative, "underground" education.[12] Despite ample documentation by major human rights organizations and UN organs as well as extensive media reports, Israel's current policy of hampering and often denying Palestinians access to their schools and universities—through its illegal colonial wall, its roadblocks, and "Israeli-only" roads—has also been ignored by the AAUP. The same can be said of the Israeli army's intentional shoot-to-harm policy against demonstrators, including schoolchildren.[13]

Another aspect of the violations of the Palestinian right to education that has eluded the AAUP censure system is Israel's contravention of the right to equality in education of its own Palestinian Arab citizens. A groundbreaking 2001 study by Human Rights Watch reached the following conclusions:

Discrimination at every level of the [Israeli] education system winnows out a progressively larger proportion of Palestinian Arab children as they progress through the school system—or channels those who persevere away from the opportunities of higher education. The hurdles Palestinian Arab students face from kindergarten to university function like a series of sieves with sequentially finer holes. At each stage, the education system filters out a higher proportion of Palestinian Arab students than Jewish students. . . . Although Israel's constitutional law does not explicitly recognize the right to education, its ordinary statutes effectively provide such a right. However, these laws, which prohibit discrimination by individual schools, do not specifically prohibit discrimination by the national government. And Israel's courts have yet to use either these laws or more general principles of equality to protect Palestinian Arab children from discrimination in education.[14]

Doesn't this institutionalized racial discrimination evoke parallels with South African apartheid? According to former Israeli education minister Shulamit Aloni, Israel is "no different from racist South Africa."[15] Also, Knesset member Roman Bronfman criticized what he termed "an apartheid regime in the occupied territories," adding, "The policy of apartheid has also infiltrated sovereign Israel, and discriminates daily against Israeli Arabs and other minorities."[16] Doesn't this call for a similar divestment initiative in response? It is worth mentioning that in the South African case, the AAUP expressly justified its call for sanctions as directed "against apartheid" in general, whereas in the Palestinian case, it restricted its interest to "violations of academic freedom."

Further, if calls for academic boycotts as a rule invite the AAUP's censure, did the organization condemn the American Library Association when it implemented an academic boycott against South Africa in the 1980s? What about the Anti-Defamation League's call for a counterboycott of British universities after the AUT boycott decision?[17]

Ethical Responsibility

The AAUP report "On Academic Boycotts" asks, "If there is no objective test for determining what constitutes an extraordinary situation, as *there surely is not*, then what criteria should guide decisions about whether a boycott should be supported?" (emphasis added). While "objective" criteria may indeed be an abstract ideal that one can strive for without ever reaching it, some ethical principles have

acquired sufficient universal endorsement to be considered relatively objective, at least in our era. Prohibitions against committing
acts of genocide and against murdering children are two obvious examples. The growing body of UN conventions and principles must
be considered the closest approximation to objective criteria to
guide us in adjudicating conflicts of rights and freedoms, particularly in situations of oppression.

UN norms and regulations may not be wholly consistent among
themselves, but they are mostly informed by the ultimate ethical principle of the equal worth of all human lives and the indivisibility and interdependence of human rights to which every human being has a
claim. Arguably, the violation of these principles was the strongest motivation behind the AAUP's laudable call for divestment from South
Africa during apartheid. This precedent is worth highlighting, as it
deals with criteria, implicit though they may be, for deciding what constitutes an "extraordinary situation" necessitating exceptional measures
of intervention.

The AAUP's support for a form of boycott against South Africa can
be interpreted or extrapolated to show that when a prevailing and
persistent denial of basic human rights is recognized, the ethical responsibility of every free person and every association of free persons,
academic institutions included, to resist injustice supersedes other
considerations about whether such acts of resistance may directly or
indirectly injure academic freedom. This does not necessarily mean
that academic freedom is relegated to a lower status among other
rights. It simply implies that in contexts of dire oppression, the obligation to help save human lives and to protect the inalienable rights of
the oppressed to live as free, equal humans acquires an overriding urgency and an immediate priority. This is precisely the logic that has
informed the call for boycott issued by the PACBI.

Misunderstanding the PACBI Call

Legitimate criticism from the AAUP and other organizations and individuals of the "exclusion clause"[18] in the Palestinian call for boycott, coupled with PACBI's resolute opposition to alleged "ideological tests" or "blacklisting," convinced the campaign to omit this clause altogether. The initial PACBI Call, issued in 2004, had a clause excluding from the proposed boycott measures against Israeli institutions "any conscientious Israeli academics and intellectuals opposed to their state's colonial and racist policies." Clearly, the presence of such an exclusion clause in a boycott call that is *institutional* in nature caused confusion, and PACBI concluded that it was unneeded and irrelevant. It was removed as a result. The intention of including it in the first place was not to draw up lists, but to nuance the call in order to address the inevitable gray-area situations where it is not clear whether academics or intellectuals are acting in their personal capacities or as representatives of institutions subject to boycott.

But overall, the AAUP largely misread the PACBI call. Since it is accustomed to dealing with violations of academic freedom perpetrated by governments or university administrations against academics, the AAUP report seems not to take account of possible institutional complicity of the academy itself in maintaining or furthering a system of oppression outside its gates, as is the case in Israel.

PACBI's call specifically targets Israeli academic institutions because of their complicity in perpetuating Israel's occupation, racial discrimination, and denial of refugee rights. This collusion takes various forms, from systematically providing the military-intelligence establishment with indispensable research—on demography, geography, hydrology, and psychology, among other disciplines—that directly benefits the occupation apparatus to tolerating and often rewarding racist speech, theories, and "scientific" research; institutionalizing discrimination against Palestinian Arab citizens; suppressing Israeli academic research on the Nakba,[19] the catastrophe of dispossession and ethnic cleansing of more than 750,000 Palestinians and the destruction of more than four hundred villages during the creation of Israel; and directly committing acts that contravene international law, such as the construction of campuses or dormitories in the occupied Palestinian territory, as Hebrew University has done, for instance.[20]

Accordingly, although the ultimate objective of the boycott is to bring about Israel's compliance with international law and its respect for Palestinian human and political rights, PACBI's targeting of the Israeli academy is not merely a means to an end but rather a part of that end. In other words, the boycott against Israel's academic institutions, which is one component of the general campaign for boycott, divestment, and sanctions against Israel, not only aims at *indirectly* undermining Israel's system of oppression against the Palestinians but also *directly* targets the academy itself as one of the pillars of this oppressive order.

Regardless of prevailing conditions of oppression, the AAUP has been consistent in opposing academic boycotts, preferring only economic boycotts and those only in extreme situations. In justifying its preference, the AAUP argues, among other points, that an academic boycott injures blameless academics. But doesn't an economic boycott hurt many more innocent bystanders, and not just in the academic community? Boycott is never an exact science, if any science *is* exact. Even when focused on a legitimate target, it invariably causes injury to others who cannot with any fairness be held responsible for the disputed policy. The AAUP-endorsed economic boycott of South Africa during apartheid certainly resulted in harming innocent civilians, academics included. But as in the South African boycott, rather than focusing on the "error margin," as important as it is, proponents of the boycott of Israel, while doing their utmost to reduce the possibility of inadvertently hurting innocent individuals, must emphasize the emancipating impact that a comprehensive and sustained boycott can have not only on the lives of the oppressed but also on the lives of the oppressors. As South African leader Ronnie Kasrils and British writer Victoria Brittain have argued, "The boycotts and sanctions ultimately helped liberate both blacks and whites in South Africa. Palestinians and Israelis will similarly benefit from this nonviolent campaign that Palestinians are calling for."[21] The Israel boycott, in this light, can be a crucial catalyst for processes of transformation that promise to bring us closer to realizing a just and durable peace anchored in the fundamental and universal right to equality.

Recommendations

Between 2006, when I wrote this critique of the AAUP's position, and the publication of this book in 2011, the AAUP policy on the matter has remained unaltered. So the recommendations made originally still stand. They are as follows:

a. Consistent with its long-standing principles and practices, the AAUP is urged to censure Israel for its systematic infringement of Palestinian rights, including academic freedom.

b. Following the model of its action in South Africa, the AAUP is urged to consider calling for divestment from companies that directly or indirectly prolong Israel's military occupation, colonization, and other forms of grave oppression of the Palestinians. UN standards similar to but more comprehensive than the Global Sullivan Principles of Corporate Social Responsibility ought to be the proper frame of reference guiding such divestment.

c. Recognizing the evolving centrality of the United Nations in establishing international principles in most situations affecting freedoms, rights, and conflict resolution, the AAUP is advised to revamp its notion of academic freedom and its principles of intervention in extraordinary situations to conform with international standards and to become more relevant globally and more responsive to situations of conflicting freedoms and rights. This would bring the AAUP's conception of academic freedom closer to the ideal evoked in the preamble quoted in my epigraph.

JUST INTELLECTUALS?

OPPRESSION, RESISTANCE, AND
THE PUBLIC ROLE OF INTELLECTUALS

"Your essay is great, but can you make it less 'intellectual,' less analytical, and more personal?" This was the reaction I received from an editor in New York after submitting an article on art and oppression she had solicited from me for publication in a collection of similar essays. Remarks like this—this was not the first time!—often betray a deep-seated perceived dichotomy, even among those committed to social justice, between intellectuals in the "global North" and their counterparts in the "global South," where the former are better equipped to think, analyze, reflect, create, and theorize while the latter are "naturally" (excuse the Aristotelian allusion) more predisposed to merely exist, experiencing corporal aspects of life and reacting to them.

The way most Israeli academics and intellectuals, particularly those self-defined as "leftists," reacted to the Palestinian call for an academic and cultural boycott of Israeli institutions[1] starkly embodied that dichotomy. Some screamed that they felt "betrayed" by the "ungrateful" Palestinians; others openly lectured us that such a boycott was "counterproductive" to our own interests; yet others resorted to innuendo and all sorts of deception and intellectual dishonesty to refute the strong case for boycott—inspired mainly by the anti-apartheid struggle in South Africa. Many were genuinely shocked that Palestinians would be so impertinent as to take the initiative and decide how best we want the world to help us resist Israel's own colonial and apartheid system. Having gotten used to their "self-appointed role as sole licensers of the form the anti-occupation struggle should take," these Israeli leftists, predominantly soft Zionists who publicly oppose the occupation but otherwise endorse the apartheid reality of Israel and stand firmly against Palestinian refugee rights, have "arrogated to themselves the exclusive right to arbitrate every issue dealing with the Palestinians."[2] It is as if they've created in their minds an unconsciously racist, static image of us, the native intellectuals, as servile followers or even *relative* humans[3] who lack the faculty of reason or, at best, possess it but lack the ability to put it to use for our own good.

Colonial patronizing aside, these Israeli "thought leaders," intentionally or otherwise, became effective instruments used by Israel and its Zionist backers abroad in fighting the spreading boycott, especially in Europe and the United States, through an immoral, protracted campaign of sheer intimidation, defamation, smearing, and all-out bullying.[4]

The claim most parroted by these self-styled progressives in numerous well-publicized columns in the mainstream Western media was that academic and cultural boycotts stifle the open exchange of ideas, hamper cultural dialogue, and infringe on academic freedom. Other than the hypocrisy of anyone who supported blanket boycotts of apartheid South Africa in the past and now moralizes about the "intrinsic" danger of boycott against Israel, there is a disturbing bias in this claim, because it regards only Israeli academic freedom as worthy of any consideration or concern. In addition, it invalidly privileges academic freedom as superior to other freedoms.[5]

Moreover, almost all of those who stood against the Palestinian-led academic and cultural boycott of Israel *on principle* and under the misleading pretense of defending academic/artistic freedom have by now endorsed the spreading academic and cultural boycott of institutions in Israel's colonial settlements built in the occupied Palestinian territory.[6] Regardless of the scope of their selective boycott, the point is that their earlier *categorical* rejection of boycott in the academic and cultural field has suddenly collapsed, giving way to acceptance of the tactic when it serves their narrower political agenda, "saving Israel from itself," not ending its myriad violations of international law and denial of fundamental Palestinian political and human rights.

But, some have questioned, shouldn't Palestinian intellectuals just focus on what they can do best, producing unadulterated, apolitical thought and art that can in their own right contribute much more substantially to the Palestinian cause? Isn't activism best left to activists? Admittedly, some of our own workers in the cultural and academic fields uphold similar ideas. One glaring problem in this line of argumentation is that it creates another, no less artificial dichotomy between thinkers and doers, intellectualism and activism, thereby drawing a static hierarchy that treats intellectuals as the patriarchs and activists as the hapless masses who are in desperate need of direction. While each group may have its own domain of action and creation, there are actually no solid, impermeable boundaries that separate the two. And there is a truly dialectical relationship between the two that ought not be dismissed or ignored.

Another serious flaw in the above argument is that it assumes that intellectuals in the context of colonial oppression can indeed just be intellectuals in the pure sense, if such a sense ever exists, who can and should distance themselves from the pressing and often depressing *political* reality of oppression to generate creative, high-quality *intellectual* works that might have potential for countering the oppressor's occupation of the mind—a far more dangerous and tenacious affliction than occupation of the land. Maintaining a distance from politics and focusing entirely on intellectual creation, the argument goes, can rekindle hope in the oppressed community, in the process nourishing self-development, particularly in the key cultural field. From my personal experience as an analyst and dance choreographer working in the midst of "conflict," I do not think that in a situation of oppression intellectuals have a choice of whether or not to reflect the impact of conflict on them and their society. Oppression, in a way, forces itself upon their work, their creative process. Their basic choice seems to be, then, whether to passively reflect it or to actively transcend it. Oppression, it seems, has its own way of touching everyone within its reach, irrespective of one's actual involvement in it or desire to be involved in it.

Anti-boycott writers would argue, in this case, why boycott and not engage "positively"? There are many more "constructive" ways of engaging in resisting oppression, the most potent of which is winning over substantial sectors of the oppressor community to your side through dialogue and joint projects in every field, the argument goes. With the lucrative funding available from European countries—bent on repenting for their Holocaust by sacrificing Palestinian rights under international law—and the prestige and personal gains that come with it, even some conscientious Palestinian intellectuals may acquiesce to shifting the focus of their work from resisting oppression to communicating with the oppressor, or a part of the oppressor community, to bring about change through persuasion, even if their own record shows dismal failure in this endeavor.

A joint Palestinian-Israeli dance work, for example, may be highly sought after as the ultimate model for promoting coexistence and mutual recognition between the "two sides." Such an agenda—for these projects more often than not stem from underhanded political agendas—essentially advocates a change in the "consciousness of the oppressed, not the situation which oppresses them,"[7] to cite Simone de Beauvoir's perceptive remark. Or worse, it aims at changing the world's perception of the conflict by giving the impression of symmetric, normal, even amiable relations between artists on the two sides of the divide. The inescapable implication is that all that is needed is to accumulate enough of such collaborations to eventually overcome the "hatred" embedded in this "conflict." With time, however, impression and image replace ending oppression as the ultimate objective sought in this peace business.

Those who think they can wish away a conflict by suggesting only some intellectual channels of rapprochement, détente, or "dialogue" are crucially seeking only an illusion of peace, and one that is devoid of justice at that. Striving for peace divorced from justice is as good as institutionalizing injustice, or making the oppressed submit to the overwhelming force of the oppressor, accepting inequality as fate.[8]

Boycott, on the other hand, remains one of the most morally sound nonviolent forms of struggle that can force the oppressors out of their oppression, thereby allowing true coexistence, equality, justice, and sustainable peace to prevail. South Africa attests to the potency and potential of this type of civil resistance.

Even if we forget the main political issues involved in the above arguments, is it possible to have equitable, mutually nourishing intellectual communication with members of the oppressor community? Of course, but not under all circumstances. A crucial problematic of interculturalism in a context of persistent oppression is *asymmetry*. Beyond all the complexities of cultural differences per se, asymmetry adds a whole new dimension, more vertical than horizontal. And because it has to do with stratification, it can be detrimental to an intercultural encounter if not addressed properly or sufficiently.

There is also the concern that the "weaker" side in such an asymmetric communication process may be exploited by the "stronger" party as an object, a tool, in an ostensibly progressive, considerate, and quite open atmosphere—with excellent intentions, but as a tool nonetheless.

This would negate any possibility of having a two-way bridge between the communicating sides; only a ladder could work!

At the core of this problem lies the relative worth attached by the stronger side, or even both, to the perceptions, wishes, and needs of the weaker side. If those are relegated to a comparatively lower status, the communication becomes another instrument of oppression, with the needs and objectives of the stronger party as the main driving force behind the process. Under these circumstances, dialogue is simply not possible. Any communication at this stage is within the realm of negotiation. Only after both sides have challenged preset attitudes and stereotypes and agreed a priori on the basic principles of justice that ought to govern their communication and common struggle can the relationship become more equitable, more balanced. Any relationship between intellectuals across the oppression divide must then be aimed, one way or another, at ending oppression, not ignoring it or escaping from it. Only then can true dialogue evolve, and thus the possibility for sincere collaboration.

In conclusion, in contexts of colonial oppression, intellectuals, especially those who advocate and work for justice, cannot be just—or mere—intellectuals in the abstract sense; they cannot but be immersed in some form or another of activism, to learn from fellow activists through real-life experiences, to widen the horizons of their sources of inspiration, and to organically engage in effective, collective emancipatory processes aimed at reaching justice without the self-indulgence, complacency, or ivory-towerness that might otherwise blur their moral vision. In short, to be *just* intellectuals, committed to justice as the most ethical and durable foundation of peace.

FREEDOM VERSUS "ACADEMIC FREEDOM"

DEBATING THE
BRITISH ACADEMIC BOYCOTT

*With Lisa Taraki**

On May 26, 2005, the Association of University Teachers (AUT) in Britain reversed its previous decision—taken on April 22 of that year—to boycott Israeli universities. Intimidation and bullying aside, no tool was as persistently used, abused, and bandied about as much as the claim that academic boycott infringes on academic freedom. Freedom to produce and exchange knowledge and ideas was deemed sacrosanct regardless of the prevailing conditions. There are two key faults in this argument. It is inherently biased because it regards as worthy only the academic freedom of Israelis; the fact that Palestinians are denied basic rights as well as academic freedom due to Israel's military occupation is lost on those parroting it. And its privileging of academic freedom as a super-value above all other freedoms is in principle antithetical to the very foundation of human rights. In situa-

---

*   Lisa Taraki teaches sociology at Birzeit University. With Omar Barghouti, she is a founding member of the Palestinian Campaign for the Academic and Cultural Boycott of Israel (PACBI).

tions of grave violation of human rights, the right to live and freedom from subjugation and colonial rule, to name a few, must be of more import than academic freedom. If the latter contributes in any way to suppression of the former, more fundamental rights, it must give way. By the same token, if the struggle to attain the former necessitates a level of restraint on the latter, then so be it. It will be well worth it.

But is there a compulsory trade-off? Is academic freedom mutually exclusive with basic human rights? In most cases, no; but in specific situations of persistent oppression and enduring breach of international law, supported—explicitly or implicitly—by academic institutions, the answer is a resounding yes. Toward the end of the apartheid era, when the world boycotted South African academics—as part of the overall regime of sanctions and boycotts endorsed by the United Nations at the time—a degree of violation of academic freedom was indeed entailed. That was accepted by the international community, though, as a reasonable price to pay in return for contributing to the defeat of apartheid and the attainment of more basic freedoms that had been denied black South Africans for generations. From an ethical perspective, freedom from racism and colonial subjugation was correctly perceived as more profound than the "unwanted side effects" caused to academic and other freedoms of individual academics opposed to apartheid. The march to freedom had to temporarily restrict a subset of freedom enjoyed by only a portion of the population.

And, upholding the principle of moral consistency, one cannot but view Israel in a similar light. As the South African Council of Churches, Archbishop Desmond Tutu, ANC leader and government minister Ronnie Kasrils, and hundreds of leading academics, trade unionists, and human rights activists in South Africa have publicly recognized, Israel's system of racial discrimination and colonial oppression is sufficiently similar to the defunct apartheid regime as to warrant Palestinian calls for sanctions similar to those declared against South

Africa in the past. The same trade-off accepted in the South African case will be encountered in the Palestinian struggle for freedom, justice, and peace.

However, it should be noted that in the Israeli context, what is being so valiantly defended by the opponents of the boycott is not only Israeli academics' unfettered access to the global community of scholars and participation in the "free exchange of ideas" but also the material and symbolic privileges of academic life. In this sense, rejecting academic boycotts in order to preserve Israeli academics' freedoms and privileges, while ignoring the more vital rights and freedoms of Palestinians—whether academics or not—is a blatant case of double standard.

It is also worth mentioning that the concept of academic freedom has been abused by opponents of the boycott and misunderstood by many others in this particular case. In democratic societies, the academy takes a grave view of scholars whose writings and activities can be interpreted as inciting to racial hatred. For example, academics in the United States and Europe who have denied that the Holocaust occurred, or who have challenged accepted facts about it, have faced harsh disciplinary measures from their universities and censure from colleagues and professional associations. In Israel, however, where racism against Palestinians and Arabs is a normal feature of everyday discourse and practice in the mainstream of society, the concept of academic freedom is so elastic as to include the freedom to propound racist theories and incite to hatred, ethnic cleansing, and worse.

Boycotts and sanctions are not exact sciences—if any science is. They affect real institutions providing jobs and services to real people, many of whom may not be directly implicated in the injustice that motivated those punitive measures in the first place. Any boycott, intended to redress injustice, will in the process harm some innocent people. That goes without saying. One must therefore resort to clear, morally consistent criteria of judgment to arbitrate whether the causes of the called-for boycott and its intended outcome adequately justify that unintended harm. In the case of Israeli universities, the weight of the causes cannot be more morally imperative or politically pressing.

Israel Boycott

For decades, Israeli academic institutions have been complicit in Israel's colonial and racist policies. Funded by the government, they have consistently and organically contributed to the military-security establishment and therefore to perpetuating its crimes, its abuse of Palestinian human rights, and its distinctive system of apartheid. Contrary to the false image—created and skillfully marketed by Israel and its apologists, academics included—of the Israeli academy as a "bastion of enlightenment" and a solid base for opposition to the occupation, this academy is in fact part of "the official Israeli propaganda," according to Ilan Pappé, one of the leading Israeli "New Historians" who exposed the systematic ethnic cleansing of Palestinians during the Nakba.[1]

Not only do most Israeli academics defend or justify their state's colonial narrative, but they play an active role in the process of oppression. Almost all of them obediently serve in the occupation army's reserve forces every year, thereby participating in, or at least witnessing in silence, crimes committed with impunity against Palestinian civilians. Despite decades of Israel's illegal occupation, very few of them have conscientiously objected to military service in the occupied territories. Likewise, those who have politically opposed the colonization of Palestinian land in any public forum have remained a depressingly tiny minority.[2]

Even the revered academic freedom on Israeli campuses that Israeli propaganda tries to project in the media is grossly exaggerated. It is well constrained within limits set by the Zionist establishment; dissenters who dare challenge those boundaries are fiercely ostracized and demonized. This is why another purpose of the proposed academic boycott is to "provide a means to transcend the publicly-sanctioned limits of debate," in the words of Oren Ben-Dor,[3] a British academic of Israeli origin. "Such freedom is precisely what is absent in Israel," he adds. From this angle, the boycott is seen as the means of *generating* true academic freedom. "The Zionist ideology which stipulates that Israel must retain its Jewish majority is a non-debatable given in the country—and the bedrock of opposition to allowing the return of Palestinian refugees. The very few intellectuals who dare to question this sacred cow are labeled 'extremists.'" Ben-Dor attacks those on the Israeli "left" who opposed the boycott as "sophisticated accomplices to the smothering of debate."

Irrespective of the individual accountability of Israeli academics, a judicious and methodical scrutiny of the culpability of Israeli academic institutions in the crimes perpetrated against the Palestinian people will reveal an abundance of incriminating evidence. Even Baruch Kimmerling, a renowned Israeli academic who is opposed to the academic boycott, writes: "I will be the first to admit that Israeli academic institutions are part and parcel of the oppressive Israeli state that has . . . committed grave crimes against the Palestinian people."[4] The facts presented below are only a small part of the evidence proving this institutional culpability. They are particularly pertinent in light of the misinformation propagated by some academics on the Israeli left who experienced nothing less than a moral collapse when they joined the establishment choir in spreading half-truths—or worse—to shield their academic institutions from international reproach.

Haifa University: Institutional Racism

Haifa University not only condones racist utterances and pronouncements by its faculty but also provides institutional sponsorship and thus legitimacy to the activities of academics engaged in scholarship that has been widely characterized as racist or inciting to racism and ethnic cleansing against the Palestinians of the occupied territories and the Palestinian citizens of Israel itself. This legitimacy is conferred by the university through its sponsorship of academic departments and research centers under whose aegis racist work is carried out.

Despite its substantial Arab Palestinian student population, Haifa University harbors, or at least tolerates, a culture of racism—against Arabs in general and Palestinians in particular—which manifests itself in the fact that members of its faculty espouse racist "theories," publish bigoted research papers, and advocate ethnic cleansing with impunity. The university has consistently and systematically failed to censure such academics or to properly investigate accusations regarding their racism.

The most notorious of these academics is Arnon Sofer (sometimes spelled Soffer), chair of geostrategy at Haifa University and vice chair of its Center for National Security Studies. Sofer is known in Israel as the prophet of the "Arab demographic threat." He takes credit for the route of the Israeli apartheid wall—declared illegal by the International Court of Justice in The Hague on July 9, 2004—saying, "This is exactly my map."[5]

Professor Sofer, who views the high birth rate of the Bedouin Palestinian citizens of Israel as a "tragedy" and has no patience for "democracy and pretty words,"[6] has for many years openly advocated "voluntary transfer"—or soft ethnic cleansing—of Palestinians in the occupied territories, as well as Palestinian citizens of Israel, in order to guarantee "a Zionist-Jewish state with an overwhelming majority of Jews." In one particularly telling prediction, Sofer says, "When 2.5 million [Palestinians] live in a closed-off Gaza, . . . those people will become even bigger animals than they are today, with the aid of an insane fundamentalist Islam. . . . So, if we want to remain alive, we will have to kill and kill and kill. All day, every day. If we don't kill, we will cease to exist. The only thing that concerns me is how to ensure that the [Jewish-Israeli] boys and men who are going to have to do the killing will be able to return home to their families and be normal human beings."[7]

Haifa University's promotion of the principles behind the infamous "Mitzpim Project," which aimed at "Judaizing" the Galilee in the 1970s and '80s, is another dark spot on its record of complicity in projects that espouse racial discrimination against Palestinian Arabs. A pamphlet examining the success of the project in reaching its goal, namely changing the demographic balance in that area in favor of Israeli Jews, is being distributed by Haifa University in high schools and academic institutions, thus "inculcating in future generations unacceptable norms that raise serious questions," according to *Haaretz*.[8] Sofer himself takes pride in having "an effect on where the Jewish hilltop communities [in Hebrew *mitzpim*] were later established."[9]

These mitzpim were designed, in the words of one of Sofer's colleagues, Avraham Dor, to increase the Jewish population in the Galilee and "to drive wedges between the blocs of Arab settlements, in order to block their ability to create a territorial continuity." Another goal was to make possible "a maximum distribution of [Jewish] settlement sites and the 'conquest' of the territory by means of access roads to them and by means of the permanent Jewish presence in the area." *Haaretz* comments on the project, saying, "Without mincing words, the study reveals that underlying the project were principles of ethnic discrimination, demographic phobia, and the concept that the country's Arab citizens are not equals but constitute a threat to its existence," and that "discrimination and inequality [against Arabs] are not a systemic failure but a deliberate intention."[10]

A more recent example of Haifa University's culpability in the advocacy of ethnic cleansing was the convening of a conference on May

17, 2005, titled "The Demographic Problem and Demographic Policy in Israel." Blessed by the rector of the university, this pseudo-academic forum for the purveyance of "demographic racism"—not innocently timed to coincide with the fifty-seventh anniversary of the Nakba—included almost all the academic and political luminaries of ethnic cleansing, such as Arnon Sofer, Yoav Gelber, Yitzhak Ravid, Brigadier-General Herzl Getz, General Uzi Dayan, and Yuval Steinetz. Ravid, a researcher at Rafael, the Israeli manufacturer of arms, has been an advocate of inhibiting the natural growth of the Palestinian population in Israel, claiming that "the delivery rooms in Soroka Hospital in Be'er Sheva have turned into a factory for the production of a backward population."[11]

Moreover, Haifa University's rector has recently "exonerated" Dr. David Bukay,[12] who teaches in the Department of Political Science, of any wrongdoing despite the fact that Israel's attorney general had ordered an investigation against him on suspicion of "racist incitement," upon receiving an official complaint filed by Mossawa—The Advocacy Center for Arab Citizens of Israel. Bukay made "unprecedented" racist remarks against Arabs and Muslims during his lectures, according to Mossawa. His publications, in which he defended his racist theories of "the Arab character," include titles such as "Mohammad's Monsters" and "The First Cultural Flaw in Thinking: The Arab Personality."[13]

Mossawa's lawyer wrote: "Dr. Bukay's statements listed above contain expressions of degradation, humiliation, hostility and violent incitement against a part of the population based on its national affiliation; and this, in our opinion, violates [the relevant Israeli law against incitement] of 1977 which prohibits racist incitement. In addition, the listed declarations, which contain admiration, sympathy, cheering and actual support for violence and terror, also constitute an infringement of [the law] of 1977." Mossawa argued that there is no room for "tolerating racist and inciting discourse" like Bukay's, which "hides behind the walls of 'academic freedom.'"

In a letter dated March 13, 2005, responding to Mossawa's complaint, deputy attorney general Shai Nizan wrote: "After studying the matter, I've decided to issue an order to the police to open an investigation of Dr. Bukay on the charge of racist incitement." But in a typical act of institutional cover-up, Haifa University's rector, Professor Yossi Ben Artzi, conducted his own "investigation" only to conclude that the remarks attributed to Bukay in the media "were not made in the way they were quoted and parts of sentences that were uttered in different contexts were yoked together by manipulation."[14]

Even Ken Jacobson, associate national director of the US-based Anti-Defamation League, was "shocked" after reading Bukay's article on "the Arab personality." Concurring with Mossawa's last point, he blames Haifa University's president for not censuring Bukay: "Naturally we respect academic freedom and understand that this is the only way academe can operate, but we believe that university presidents should condemn such things. It is not enough for a university president to say that his institution practices academic freedom. He must also say that such statements are obnoxious."[15]

The *Haaretz* reporter who covered the story and interviewed all parties involved wrote: "Something strange is happening at the University of Haifa. On the one hand, the Anti-Defamation League is 'very disturbed' by Bukay's article because of its 'destructive prejudices' and the attorney general has initiated an investigation against Bukay on suspicion of racist incitement. On the other hand, the university is conducting a disciplinary process against the student who accused Bukay of racism."[16]

Hebrew University: Colonial Land Grab

An indictment presented to the AUT executive by the Palestinian Federation of Unions of Universities' Professors and Employees against the Hebrew University exposes the following well-documented facts.

In 1968, more than one year after Israel's military occupation of Gaza and the West Bank (which includes East Jerusalem, according to UN Security Council resolutions), the Israeli occupation authorities confiscated 3,345 dunums of Palestinian land, justifying their action with reference to articles 5 and 7 of the Land (Acquisition for Public Purpose) Ordinance 1943. The decision was published in the official *Israeli Gazette*—the Hebrew edition—number 1425. Most of that land was (still is) privately owned by Palestinians living in that area.

A large part of the confiscated land was then given to the Hebrew University to expand its campus. The Palestinian landowners refused to leave their properties, arguing that the confiscation order of 1968 was illegal. In 1973, as expected, the Israeli court ruled in favor of the university and the state. The court decided that the Palestinian families must evacuate their homes and be offered alternative housing.

According to authoritative legal experts, the Hebrew University land confiscation deal is is illegal because this land is part of East Jerusalem, which is an occupied territory according to international law (numerous UN resolutions recognize East Jerusalem as an inseparable part of the occupied Palestinian territories). Israel's unilateral annexation of East Jerusalem, expropriation of Palestinian land, and efforts at forced eviction of its Palestinian owners in this area are illegal under the terms of International Humanitarian Law.[17] The annexation of occupied East Jerusalem into the state of Israel and the application of Israeli domestic law to this area have been repeatedly denounced as null and void by the international community, including the UN Security Council.[18]

By moving Israelis (staff and students) to work and live on occupied Palestinian land, the Hebrew University, like all Israeli settlements illegally established on occupied territories, is gravely violating article 49 of the Fourth Geneva Convention of 1949, which states,

"The occupying power shall not deport or transfer parts of its own civilian population into the territory it occupies."

Based on the above, the Hebrew University of Jerusalem *cannot invoke Israel's domestic law* in order to justify the oppressive and illegal measures it has been taking in order to evict the Palestinian families who under international law remain the legal owners of the land in question.

Given the multifaceted complicity of their institutions in oppressing Palestinians, Israeli academics should either mobilize to oppose what is done in their names, with their direct and indirect help, or stop complaining when conscientious academics around the world decide to take them to task.

REFLECTING ON THE CULTURAL BOYCOTT

Then there are occasions when merely having your name added to a concert schedule may be interpreted as a political act that resonates more than anything that might be sung and it may be assumed that one has no mind for the suffering of the innocent.

—Elvis Costello, May 15, 2010[1]

While having a "mind for the suffering of the innocent" may convince many to commit, often with fervor, to BDS (boycott, divestment, and sanctions) when it relates to boycotting Israeli products, calling on institutions to divest from companies profiting from Israel's occupation and apartheid, or even lobbying their elected representatives to exclude Israel from free trade and arms agreements, it is not immediately the case when people are asked to support the notion of a cultural or academic boycott of Israel. In a meeting I had with a prominent Jewish British actor in Ramallah, she confessed from the onset: "I completely agree with BDS, but it is the academic and cultural bit that concerns me. Honestly, this is the only aspect I cannot get myself to support."

I asked for the reason—almost sure of the response. Indeed, she replied, "As an artist, I cannot condone cutting off communication channels; we need to keep those open to convince, to argue, to debate. How else can we convince others of their wrongdoing?"

I told her, "As a dance choreographer myself, I cannot condone cutting off communication channels either; but where in the Palestinian call for the academic and cultural boycott of Israel do you see us calling for that?" I went on to explain how most objections to the academic and cultural boycott are in fact based on a wrong premise—that we are calling for ostracizing individual Israeli academics, writers, and artists.

PACBI (Palestinian Campaign for the Academic and Cultural Boycott of Israel) never issued *that* call.

The 2004 PACBI Call and all PACBI documents and speeches on record ever since have consistently called for an *institutional* boycott of Israel in the academic and cultural field, not a boycott of individuals. Unlike the South African academic and cultural boycott, which was a blanket action that targeted everyone and everything South African, the Palestinian boycott targets institutions only, due to their entrenched complicity in planning, justifying, whitewashing, or otherwise perpetuating Israel's violations of international law and Palestinian rights. As argued elsewhere, we have never targeted individual artists or academics—not because they tend to be more progressive or opposed to injustice than the rest of society, as is often mistakenly assumed, but because we are opposed *on principle* to political testing and blacklisting. If the United Nations eventually develops well-conceived and sufficiently justified lists based on widely accepted criteria of international law, as it did in the last stage of the struggle against apartheid in South Africa, then that will be fine; but the BDS movement, of which PACBI is a part, being a civil society movement, does not subscribe to drawing up lists to decide who is a good Israeli and who is not based on some arbitrary political criteria. A quick—or thorough—review of the PACBI guidelines for applying the international academic[2] and cultural[3] boycott will confirm the institutional nature of the Palestinian boycott against Israel.

Those who are now hesitant to support a boycott of Israel's academic and cultural institutions though in the past they endorsed or even struggled to implement a blanket academic or cultural boycott against apartheid South Africa are hard pressed to explain their inconsistency. Some in the Zionist "left" camp, for instance, who vehemently and angrily opposed the PACBI Call when it was first issued, citing the need to uphold "academic freedom" or "artistic communication channels," are now endorsing a full cultural boycott of the Israeli colonial settlement of Ariel and all other colonies built in the occupied Palestinian territory in contravention of international law. Suddenly the lofty language of rejecting boycott in the cultural field in the name of protecting free speech and dialogue disappears, and the boycott becomes not only legitimate but an absolute moral duty when it fits the narrow political agenda of that Zionist "left."[4]

A brief recollection of the history of the South Africa cultural boycott is quite enlightening in this context.

In 1965, the American Committee on Africa, following the lead of prominent British arts associations, sponsored a historic declaration against South African apartheid, signed by more than sixty cultural personalities. It read: "We say no to apartheid. We take this pledge in solemn resolve to refuse any encouragement of, or indeed, any professional association with the present Republic of South Africa, this until the day when all its people shall equally enjoy the educational and cultural advantages of that rich and beautiful land."[5] If one were to replace "Republic of South Africa" with "state of Israel," the rest should apply just as strongly, if not more.

A year before that, in 1964, the Irish Anti-Apartheid Movement issued a declaration signed by twenty-eight Irish playwrights who vowed not to permit their work to be performed before segregated audiences in South Africa.[6]

Israel today—sixty-plus years after its establishment through a deliberate and systemic process of ethnic cleansing of a large majority of the indigenous Palestinian population—still practices racial discrimination against its own "non-Jewish" citizens; it still maintains the longest military occupation in modern history; it still denies Palestinian refugees—uprooted, dispossessed, and expelled over the last six decades—their internationally recognized right to return to their homes and properties; and it still commits war crimes and violates basic human rights and international humanitarian law with utter impunity.

Israel has established a more sophisticated, evolved, and brutal form of apartheid than that of its South African predecessor, according to authoritative statements by South African anti-apartheid leaders like Archbishop Desmond Tutu and the country's past cabinet minister Ronnie Kasrils, who is Jewish. The Palestinian cause therefore deserves from all people of conscience around the world, particularly those who opposed South African apartheid, the same measures of solidarity and human compassion, through an effective application of BDS against Israel until it abides by international law and respects basic human rights.

Some may argue, though, that art should transcend political division, unifying people in their common humanity. They forget, it seems, that masters and slaves do not really share anything in common, least of all any notion of humanity. Rather than reinventing the wheel, I recall the wise words of Enuga S. Reddy, director of the UN Centre against Apartheid, responding in 1984 to criticism that the cultural boycott of South Africa infringed on freedom of expression:

> It is rather strange, to say the least, that the South African regime which denies all freedoms ... to the African majority ... should be-

come a defender of the freedom of artists and sportsmen of the world. We have a list of people who have performed in South Africa because of ignorance of the situation or the lure of money or uncon- cern over racism. They need to be persuaded to stop entertaining apartheid, to stop profiting from apartheid money and to stop serv- ing the propaganda purposes of the apartheid regime.[7]

It is worth noting that the United Nations General Assembly adopted a special resolution on the cultural boycott of South Africa in December 1980, almost two decades after civil society unions and as- sociations in Britain, Ireland, and later the United States, adopted such a boycott. That decision also heeded consistent appeals by black organizations in South Africa that effectively censured several foreign entertainers who violated the boycott.

Brand Israel

In a 2010 statement, Isaac Zablocki, director of the Israel Film Center in New York, said: "The goal of the center is to share with the public these amazing cinematic achievements coming out of a country that is normally only seen through news headlines. Through our viewing li- brary, screenings and promotion of films, we hope to share with the public a new slice of Israeli reality . . . an Israel filled with innocence, humor, and Ideals."[8] This strikingly echoed the logic of the official Brand Israel campaign, launched by the government of Israel as early as 2005 and intensified ever since, particularly at every juncture when Israel faces international fury after it has committed war crimes, as happened in 2006 in Lebanon, in the winter of 2008–9 in Gaza, and in the bloody 2010 attack on the humanitarian flotilla destined for Gaza.

Some projects that are not officially related to the Brand Israel campaign may still serve the same objectives of that Israeli propa- ganda campaign by adopting similar messaging, ignoring the reality of occupation and racial discrimination, and promoting the same false notions of Israel as a "democracy" or an "enlightened" member of the community of nations that is advanced in arts and sciences. What is essentially glossed over here is the inconvenient fact that Israel is a state practicing occupation, colonialism, and apartheid. One such project is the Other Israel Film Festival in New York. The festival director's own introduction of the project states:

> The Other Israel Film Festival was founded to be a vehicle for cultural change and social insights into the nature of Israel as a democracy and the complex condition of the lives of its minorities that are living in the Jewish state. . . . It is not about the conflict—it is not about taking sides—this festival is about people. . . .
>
> I care deeply about Israel and its future. Growing up in a democratic Jewish state has without any doubt shaped the cultural and national identity of all of its inhabitants and citizens—who know no other home. These films and artistic expressions are paving the way to co-existence and a new, more inclusive culture in the Middle East."[9]

In a statement exposing the festival's violation of the Guidelines for the International Cultural Boycott of Israel (Appendix 4), PACBI states:

> Describing Israel as a "democracy," endorsing the oxymoron notion of a "democratic Jewish state," and avoiding taking a position consistent with international law and human rights is a form of whitewashing Israel's colonial and apartheid reality, regardless of intentions. Instead of upholding equal rights for all, freedom, an end to the occupation, and speaking out against the institutionalized and legalized system of racial discrimination, that prevails in Israel, the OIFF website and project chose to cover up Israel's colonial and racist policies, portraying the state as a "democracy," albeit with some challenges.[10]

The Brand Israel campaign, which was agreed upon by the directors of Israel's three most powerful ministries, involved a new plan to improve Israel's image abroad "by downplaying religion and avoiding any discussion of the conflict with the Palestinians," as reported in *Forward* at the time.[11] Non-Jewish Americans in focus groups gathered for the purposes of this campaign "almost universally saw Israel only as 'militaristic' and 'religious,'" the report revealed. It went on to describe the campaign thus: "[This] is the latest manifestation of a growing movement—begun in America—to 're-brand' Israel, or to reinvent the country's image in the eyes of both Jews and non-Jews. The driving concept is that Israel will win supporters only if it is seen as relevant and modern rather than only as a place of fighting and religion." A former deputy director general of the Israeli ministry, Nissim Ben-Sheetrit, explained upon launching the Brand Israel campaign in 2005: "We are seeing culture as a *hasbara* [propaganda] tool of the first rank, and I do not differentiate between *hasbara* and culture."[12]

After the Israeli war of aggression against the besieged Gaza Strip, Israel's image took a further steep dip, prompting the government to throw more money into the Brand Israel campaign. One of the main figures in the campaign, Arye Mekel, deputy director general for cultural affairs in the Israeli foreign ministry, told the *New York Times*: "We will send well-known novelists and writers overseas, theater companies, exhibits. This way you show Israel's prettier face, so we are not thought of purely in the context of war."[13] And indeed Israel has been sending more and more dance companies, orchestras, poets, and films abroad, particularly after Operation Cast Lead. The greater the number of innocent victims of Israel's incessant brutality and belligerence, the more money it needs to spend, the argument goes, to whitewash its gruesome image.

This much is now well known. What is less known or discussed in the media is a hidden secret of the Brand Israel effort—a contract that obliges artists and writers, as "service providers" who receive state funding, to conform to and indeed promote state policies. Basically, the contract buys the artists' and writers' consciences, making a mockery of the "freedom of expression" mantra.

This contract was revealed in an article in *Haaretz* instructively titled "Putting Out a Contract on Art" by the famous Israeli writer Yitzhak Laor. Because of the exceptional importance of this contract for revealing the organic partnership between the state and the duly complacent and complicit intelligentsia, its most relevant excerpts are reproduced here:

> The service provider undertakes to act faithfully, responsibly and tirelessly to provide the Ministry with the highest professional services. The service provider is aware that the purpose of ordering services from him is to promote the policy interests of the State of Israel via culture and art, including contributing to creating a positive image for Israel. . . .
>
> The service provider will not present himself as an agent, emissary and/or representative of the Ministry. . . .
>
> The Ministry is entitled to terminate this contract, or a part thereof, immediately and at the Ministry's sole discretion, if the service provider does not provide the Ministry with the services and/or does not fulfill his obligations under this contract and/or does not provide the services and/or fulfill his obligations to the Ministry's full satisfaction, and/or provides the services in an inadequate fashion and/or deviates from the timetable, and/or if the Ministry does not need the services of the service provider for any reason and/or for budgetary, organizational or security and/or policy reasons, and the service provider will make no claim, demand or suit based on the termination of the contract by the Ministry.[14]

Dancing around Apartheid

A key clause in the PACBI Guidelines for the Cultural Boycott of Israel focuses on this aspect of cultural complicity:

The general principle is that an event or project carried out under the sponsorship/aegis of or in affiliation with an official Israeli body [or a Brand Israel type non-Israeli body] constitutes complicity and therefore is deserving of boycott. It is also well documented now that Israeli artists, writers and other cultural workers applying for state funding to cover the cost of their—or their cultural products'—participation in international events must accept to contribute to Israel's official propaganda efforts.

Accepting such conditioned funding, PACBI argues, transforms the touring artists or writers in question into "service providers" who willingly serve the propaganda agenda of the state and get paid handsomely for it, thereby forfeiting their disingenuous claim to "artistic freedom." Thus the boycott.

A glaring example of this "art in the service of Israeli propaganda" is the famous Israeli dance company Batsheva, whose tours are more often than not, especially lately, carefully planned to coincide with postmassacre efforts by Israel to cover up its crimes.

Adalah-NY: The New York Campaign for the Boycott of Israel and Artists against Apartheid's New York City chapter launched a protest campaign against Batsheva's September 2010 performance in New York, attended by Israeli president Shimon Peres and cosponsored by the Israeli consulate. The *New York Times*, quite uncharacteristically, covered the protest in its main review of the show. The reviewer wrote:

> I must say that the only distinction of real note [between the two Batsheva performances in New York] was the presence, on Saturday, of the Israeli president, Shimon Peres, accompanied by a considerable security detail and heckled by members of Adalah-NY: The New York Campaign for the Boycott of Israel.
>
> Adalah-NY has been protesting throughout Batsheva's run, picketing and handing out pamphlets criticizing Israeli policies toward Palestinians and urging a boycott of the company, which receives

substantial support from its government. Mr. Peres's arrival raised the ante: as audience members and passers-by were firmly herded to the end of the block by police and security officers and the protesters yelled "You're dancing around apartheid," Mr. Peres and his contingent swept into the theater.[15]

Batsheva artistic director Ohad Naharin said in an interview in 2005: "I continue to do my work, while 20 km from me people are participating in war crimes." But Batsheva is far from apathetic about war crimes; indeed, by affirming its relationship with the Brand Israel campaign, the group has been accused of planning some of its performances specifically to divert attention from those very war crimes. In their statement calling for boycotting Batsheva's performance, the two protest groups wrote: "Because of your ties to Brand Israel and in response to the Palestinian civil society call for the Academic and Cultural Boycott of Israel, we are calling for a local boycott of your performances."[16]

A slogan on a placard carried by one of the protesters outside the dance group's performance said: "Don't dance around apartheid. End it!"[17]

Hurting the Victims of Apartheid?

An argument often raised to counter the case for a cultural boycott of Israel is that such a boycott, if it entails refusing to show artworks in Israel, may actually hurt the state's victims, the Palestinians, more than it would hurt Israel itself. This general argument of "counterproductiveness" has been adequately rebutted elsewhere in this book, so I shall limit the discussion here to the *cultural* boycott and, again, the South African precedent.

US filmmaker Jonathan Demme, who with Martin Scorsese cofounded Filmmakers United against Apartheid to protest the racist regime in South Africa in the 1980s, was asked whether denying

American movies to all South African audiences would punish blacks as well as the white regime. He replied: "We believe the answer is no. Leaders of the (opposition) African National Congress have said they fervently want a boycott.... As far as denying the consciousness-raising among whites that American films could provide, the consensus is that it will take more than one movie or group of movies to raise the consciousness of the white rulers."[18]

Israeli cultural, as well as academic, institutions will always claim that a boycott would infringe upon their freedom and would punish artists and academics who are the most progressive and opposed to "the occupation" in Israeli society. In fact this argument, aside from being quite disingenuous, is intended to deflect attention from two basic facts: first, the Palestinian academic and cultural boycott of Israel targets institutions, not individuals; and second, those institutions, far from being more progressive than the average in Israel, are main pillars of the Israeli structure of colonial and apartheid oppression. Not only do the oppressed lose nothing when people of conscience boycott institutions that are persistently complicit in the system of oppression; in fact, they gain enormously from the ultimate weakening of this complicity that results from an effective and sustained boycott.

Archbishop Desmond Tutu reflected on this same argument recently while defending the call for the University of Johannesburg to sever ties with Ben-Gurion University of the Negev in Israel over its racist policies and complicity with the army:

> Consider for a moment the numerous honorary doctorates that Nelson Mandela and I have received from universities across the globe. During the years of apartheid many of these same universities denied tenure to faculty who were "too political" because of their commitment to the struggle against apartheid. They refused to divest from South Africa because "it will hurt the blacks" (investing in apartheid South Africa was not seen as a political act; divesting was).[19]

"Out of Israel" and into Complicity[20]

One of the largest "branding" efforts was organized in 2008 by the Israeli government for the so-called 60th Anniversary of the establishment of the state. Some of the most prominent artists, politicians, academics, and others were invited to celebrate with Israel. In response, PACBI, in cooperation with the Palestinian NGO Network (PNGO), took out a half-page advertisement in the *International Herald Tribune* titled "No Reason to Celebrate Israel at 60," after having collected dozens of endorsements from prominent international cultural figures, including the foremost poet in the Arab world, the late Palestinian Mahmoud Darwish, along with John Berger, Ella Shohat, Ken Loach, Augusto Boal, Roger Waters, André Brink, Judith Butler, Vincenzo Consolo, Nigel Kennedy, and many others. It stated:

> The creation of the state of Israel almost 60 years ago dispossessed and uprooted hundreds of thousands of Palestinians from their homes and lands. With their peaceful lives ruined, society fragmented, possessions pillaged and hope for freedom and nationhood dashed, Palestinian refugees held on to their dream of return, and Palestinians everywhere nourished their aspiration for freedom, dignified living, and becoming whole again.
>
> There is no reason to celebrate! Israel at 60 is a state that is still denying Palestinian refugees their UN-sanctioned rights, simply because they are "non-Jews." It is still illegally occupying Palestinian and other Arab lands, in violation of numerous UN resolutions. It is still persistently and grossly breaching international law and infringing fundamental human rights with impunity afforded to it through munificent US and European economic, diplomatic and political support.
>
> It is still treating its own Palestinian citizens with institutionalized discrimination.
>
> In short, celebrating "Israel at 60" is tantamount to dancing on Palestinian graves to the haunting tune of lingering dispossession and multi-faceted injustice.

There is absolutely no reason to celebrate! But there are myriad reasons to reflect, to engage, to work towards peace and justice.[21]

In the same year, and as part of the same effort, no doubt, two New York theaters hosted Israeli dance groups. The Joyce Theater featured an Israeli dance program by Emanuel Gat, and the 92nd Street Y presented "Out of Israel," a program featuring Israeli artists Saar Harari, Lee Sher, and Netta Yerushalmy. The two theaters effectively declared their acquiescence to partnering in rebranding Israel by helping it to cover up its persistent violation of international humanitarian law and to present a deceptive image of a normal, even "cultured," state.

But what does dance have to do with all this? one may ask. Shouldn't art be above politics?

Despite the obvious differences, was art above politics in the 1940s? Were German arts groups invited then to perform in London and New York, so that peers in these places could have a constructive dialogue with them and dissuade them from supporting the genocidal regime? Were Afrikaner dance groups given a platform in Europe or the United States in the 1980s? Of course not. But wasn't art above politics then? Why the double standard?

Aren't Israeli dance companies opposed to the occupation, though? In fact, no. None of them has ever issued a public condemnation of the occupation. While Ohad Naharin, arguably Israel's leading choreographer, has condemned—in his personal capacity, not as a representative of his company—"war crimes" by his country, he has never explicitly called for an end to the occupation. Nor has his group, for that matter. Moreover, Israeli dancers, artists, academics, and intellectuals, in harmony with the rest of Israeli society, apart from the occasional refusenik, obediently serve in the occupation army's reserve forces, oppressing Palestinians and participating in, or at the very least witnessing in disturbing silence, what Amnesty International has termed "war crimes." This makes them complicit.

In response to such charges of collusion, some in the Western mainstream media often attempt to justify Israel's oppression by citing Palestinian armed attacks against it. I have written openly and consistently, in Arabic and English, about the moral problems raised by any indiscriminate act of violence,[22] whether from the oppressor or oppressed, despite the immeasurable moral difference between the two. Even when it is in reaction to colonial violence, an indiscriminate attack on the civilian community of the oppressors is morally unjustifiable, in my opinion. But I can never accept any claim of parity between the oppressors and oppressed. Israel's decades-old state terrorism and its current acts of genocide in Gaza are far more lethal, immoral, and illegal than any act of Palestinian resistance. This is not only about body counts, which should always refer to human beings with names and faces on either side; it is about power asymmetry and the built-in moral asymmetry that goes with the territory, so to speak, when you have a colonial and apartheid regime like Israel's on one side and a colonized and dehumanized community on the other. Again, this does not in any way give Palestinians, or any other oppressed community, carte blanche to indiscriminately target civilians on the other side. International law does give nations under occupation the right to resist foreign occupation "by all means," including violent ones; but it never condones deliberate or criminally negligent attacks against civilians. I fully endorse that.

As the influential Brazilian educator Paulo Freire writes:

> Any situation in which "A" objectively exploits "B" or hinders his and her pursuit of self-affirmation as a responsible person is one of oppression. Such a situation in itself constitutes violence even when sweetened by false generosity; because it interferes with the individual's ontological and historical vocation to be more fully human.

With the establishment of a relationship of oppression, violence has *already* begun. Never in history has violence been initiated by the oppressed. How could they be the initiators, if they themselves are the result of violence? How could they be the sponsors of something whose objective inauguration called forth their existence as oppressed? There would be no oppressed had there been no prior situation of violence to establish their subjugation.[23]

The question, therefore, should be, why don't the Joyce Theater and the 92nd Street Y "do the right thing" and join the many prominent international cultural organizations and individual artists that have heeded the Palestinian calls for a boycott against Israel until it fully complies with its obligations under international law? Ken Loach, a distinguished Palme d'Or winner at Cannes, joined the growing boycott of Israel. The world-renowned British author and artist John Berger has issued his own boycott statement—endorsed by dozens of leading artists and intellectuals—supporting the Palestinian call for an institutional cultural boycott of Israel. One of the leading dance companies in Europe, Les Ballets C. de la B., of Belgium, issued a statement supporting the boycott.

It is quite ironic that in one of the Y's featured Israeli works, Netta Yerushalmy's *Bifocale*, a dance in which, according to the press release, two women "find themselves in a narrow, confined space," the choreographer resorted to extraordinary measures "to re-create the sense of confinement" needed for her theme. If she wanted real, genuine, and "natural" confinement, she might as well have set her dance in any Palestinian city or village, surrounded by a nine-meter-high wall and endless, suffocating military roadblocks.

Finally, inviting Israeli arts groups to any festival or theater in 2008, in particular, was a slap in the face to morality and civility, especially given Israel's rolling acts of genocide in Gaza and the celebration of its sixtieth "birthday" that was careful to ignore its dispossessed victims.

In this context, welcoming complicit Israeli dance companies, whether or not they are based in Israel, amounts to celebrating Israel at a time when those whose homes it is occupying—or demolishing—and whose lives it is decimating have precious little to celebrate. Conducting business as usual with Israel in any field, dance included, as if it were a normal country, not an apartheid state, is an egregious act of complicity, no less.

So You Think You Can Dance?

Some international dance groups that crossed the picket line of the Palestinian boycott and agreed to perform in Israel as part of its celebrations nevertheless got a taste of Israeli apartheid from the moment they entered the country. Security officers at Tel Aviv's Lydda (Ben-Gurion) Airport in September 2008 forced an African American member of the Alvin Ailey American Dance Theater—by far the best-known touring dance company in the United States—to perform twice for them in order to prove he was a dancer before letting him enter the country. Even after he complied, one of the officers suggested that Abdur-Rahim Jackson change his name. Jackson felt humiliated and "deeply saddened," according to an Ailey spokesperson, particularly because his Arab/Muslim-sounding first name, given to him by his Muslim father, was the reason that he was the only member of his company subjected to the ethnic profiling typical of Israeli society.

While still officially illegal in the United States, ethnic profiling, described as "racist" by human rights groups, is widespread in Israel at entrances to malls, public and private buildings, airports, and so forth. Israeli citizens and permanent residents with Arab names—or often just Arab accents—are commonly singled out for rough, intrusive, and painfully humiliating "security" checks. Even though I have an Israeli ID, whenever I travel through the Tel Aviv airport, for instance, stickers with the number 6 are stamped on my passport, luggage, and ticket. Israeli Jews, in comparison, usually get 1. A 6 leads to the most thorough and degrading check of luggage and person. The smaller figures, in contrast, mean you get whisked through security with just an x-ray scan of your luggage. A couple of years ago, people like me used to get a bright red sticker, while Israeli Jews got light pink or similarly "benign" colors. Some astute Israeli officials must have been alerted that color-coding passengers according to their ethnicity or religion was too overtly apartheid-like, so they switched to the supposedly "nuanced" number coding. No wonder Nobel Prize–winning Archbishop Desmond Tutu described Israeli practice as constituting a "worse" form of apartheid—it is more sophisticated than the original version.

The Alvin Ailey troupe was celebrating its fiftieth anniversary with a multicountry tour starting in Israel. Despite the above incident, the show went on as scheduled, and the company did nothing substantial to even protest the discriminatory policy to which one of its members had been subjected, notwithstanding artistic director Judith Jamison's statement to *Haaretz* that "we are here to irritate you, to make you think." This silence and business-as-usual attitude only enhances Israel's sense of impunity. More crucially, by the dance company's very performance in Israel, whether one of its members was targeted by Israeli ethnic profiling or not, the group has violated the 2004 Palestinian call for a cultural boycott of Israel due to that country's persistent violation of international law and fundamental human rights.[24]

More recently, the famous British dance and music group Faithless decided *not* to perform in Israel. Explaining the band's decision, Faithless front man Maxi Jazz unequivocally stated: "While human beings are being willfully denied not just their rights but their NEEDS for their children and grandparents and themselves, I feel deeply that I should not be sending even tacit signals that this is either 'normal' or 'ok.' It's neither and I cannot support it. It grieves me that it has come to this and I pray every day for human beings to begin caring for each other, firm in the wisdom that we are all we have."[25]

Humanity—and above all human dignity—is at the core of many of the works of Alvin Ailey. His company, and indeed all other artists and cultural entities that care about human rights and realize that art and moral responsibility should never be divorced, are called upon by their Palestinian colleagues and the public at large not to perform in Israel until justice, freedom, equality, and human rights are established for all, irrespective of ethnic, religious, gender, or any other form of identity. This is what the international arts and academic communities (Ailey codirects a degree program at Fordham University) did as their contribution to the struggle to end apartheid rule in South Africa. This is precisely what they can do to end injustice and colonial conflict in Palestine. Only then can dancers named Abdur-Rahim, Fatima, Paul, or Nurit be viewed and treated equally.

FIGHTING APARTHEID IN SOUTH AFRICA, CELEBRATING APARTHEID IN ISRAEL

OPEN LETTER TO NADINE GORDIMER

*With Haidar Eid**

Nadine Gordimer is a highly acclaimed liberal Jewish South African writer who won a Nobel Prize for Literature, among several other accolades. She vehemently opposed apartheid, and her work largely reflected and promoted the anti-apartheid struggle. Still, she insisted on violating the Palestinian cultural boycott by participating in a festival largely sponsored by the Israeli government.

April 28, 2008

In your response to our letters of concern[1] and protest over your planned visit to Israel to participate in a writers' festival largely endorsed by the Israeli government, you brush off our criticism, citing the role of literature in "opening up the human mind" and claiming that "whatever violent, terrible, bitter and urgent chasms of conflict lie between peoples, the only solution for peace and justice exist and

---

* Alongside Omar Barghouti, Haidar Eid is a member of the Palestinian Campaign for the Academic and Cultural Boycott of Israel (www.PACBI.org).

must begin with both sides talking to one another." So talking, in your opinion, has replaced resistance as the starting point for ending injustice and fighting apartheid and colonial rule? Is that what you and your fellow antiapartheid colleagues did in your struggle in South Africa—talk to the "other side"?

It is also worth reminding you that Palestinian writers in the occupied Palestinian territory (OPT), like all Palestinians under Israeli occupation, are denied their basic rights, including the "privilege" of freedom of expression that you—and all of us—so highly value. They are often denied their right to travel, sometimes even within the OPT; many are denied access to conferences and festivals where they could participate in a free exchange of ideas with their peers on an international level; and some are imprisoned, injured, or killed by the occupation forces. By attending this conference you are helping to perpetuate this special form of apartheid that denies us our human rights.

You start your letter asserting that you are "not invited to Israel by the Israeli Government." Is this accurate? Even if it is, is it relevant? You are invited, technically, by the International Writers Festival; but the festival itself is primarily funded, promoted, and sponsored by Israeli government sources. Hair-splitting aside, you are indeed invited by the Israeli government. Even if that festival were not at all supported by the government, does it in any way take a stand against the occupation, racism, and apartheid that essentially define the reality of Israel today?

Let us not forget, either, that those Israeli writers who invited you are themselves not exactly opposed to their state's key forms of racist and colonial oppression against the indigenous people of Palestine. They are virtually all Zionists who fully endorse and sometimes openly advocate, to varying degrees, the main pillars of the system of racial discrimination against Palestinian citizens within Israel, the denial of the Palestinian refugees' right to return, in accordance with international law, and even some aspects of the military occupation and colonization of the West Bank, especially in East Jerusalem. Imagine what your reaction would have been if a liberal international writer of your stature had accepted an invitation by some group of Afrikaner writers—most of whom did not oppose apartheid itself but supported only a subset of rights for blacks under apartheid—to a festival in apartheid South Africa that took no public position against the system of racial discrimination there.

Do you need to be reminded of how you, and the late Palestinian intellectual Edward Said, lobbied Susan Sontag to reject the Jerusalem Prize? As far as we know, your logic was that the involvement of the state, represented by Shimon Peres as a judge of the "literary" prize at the time, meant that Sontag and other writers should not participate.

In addition, we are utterly disappointed and saddened by your insulting attempt to "balance" your act of complicity by promising to visit a Palestinian university or some venue in Ramallah! Was visiting a bantustan ever a moral or rational excuse for participating in a largely pro-apartheid gathering in South Africa? Your participation simply violates the Palestinian Call for Academic and Cultural Boycott of Israel,[2] issued in 2004 and widely respected by progressive writers, academics, and cultural figures around the world.

And what about the timing? You know well that this festival, like all other cultural events scheduled to take place in Israel during this period, is planned to, and most likely will, promote the "Israel at 60" celebrations.[3] Regardless of your intentions, taking part in such an occasion that ignores the fundamental truth that Israel came into existence sixty years ago as a result of a systematic and brutal campaign of ethnic cleansing, what Palestinians refer to as the Nakba, that led to the dispossession and expulsion of more than 750,000 Palestinians is itself an act of collusion in whitewashing Israel's seminal crime. Doing so at this particular time, when Israel is committing war crimes and "acts of genocide," as international law expert Richard Falk characterizes them, in occupied Gaza is indicative of a regrettable crossover to the side of the oppressor and a betrayal of your principles in defense of the oppressed.

BETWEEN SOUTH AFRICA AND ISRAEL

UNESCO'S DOUBLE STANDARDS[1]

With Jacqueline Sfeir*

Palestinians can no longer understand or accept the fact that some United Nations organizations have started dealing with Israel as if it were just another liberal democracy, not the world's last surviving colonial bastion. We are particularly concerned about UNESCO's recent support for establishing a joint Palestinian-Israeli scientific organization, which in our view marks a serious setback for the cause of just peace in Palestine.

Under the noble aim of the World Science Day to "help focus the attention of young people on science and how its goals are congruent with their own aspirations," another message, which is subtle yet highly damaging politically, is being communicated. Through supporting the establishment of the Israeli-Palestinian Science Organization (IPSO), UNESCO is actually placing itself at odds with the decision of the Palestinian Council for Higher Education, which has repeatedly rejected "technical and scientific cooperation between Palestinian and Israeli universities." This move also conflicts with the Palestinian call for

---

*   Jacqueline Sfeir, an educator, is a member of the advisory board of the Palestinian Campaign for the Academic and Cultural Boycott of Israel (PACBI).

boycotting Israeli academic institutions, which was endorsed by dozens of the most important unions, associations, and organizations in the occupied West Bank and Gaza, including the Federation of Unions of Palestinian Universities' Professors and Employees.[2] Furthermore, by blessing IPSO, UNESCO is providing an international cover for a thinly veiled Israeli attempt to improve its image in the world and its status in UN organizations without having to comply with international law, which calls for an end to its illegal occupation, among other forms of its oppression of the people of Palestine.

Seemingly innocent activities with noble aims are increasingly used, sometimes with good intentions and often without, to give the impression that if Palestinians and Israelis jointly work on scientific, environmental, cultural, or health projects, they somehow make peace more possible or more attainable. Nothing could be further from the truth. Joint projects that claim to be "apolitical" are often the most blatantly politicized—and most readily deployed to defend an oppressive order—since they deliberately disregard the context of colonial oppression and deceivingly imply the possibility of achieving peace without addressing the root causes of conflict. Ostensibly apolitical collaborations actually substitute transient, superficial gestures of peace for the real struggle needed to achieve a just and lasting peace. Consequently, they fail to serve the cause of peace.

Normal relations between peoples can flourish only after oppression has ended, not before and not as a prelude to it. From our perspective, the only joint projects that ought to be encouraged in the process of addressing injustice are those that contribute to resisting this injustice. At the very least, any sincere joint project must be fundamentally based on the principle of equality and the rejection of military occupation and racial discrimination. Unfortunately, both essential elements are glaringly absent from the IPSO project description and UNESCO's endorsement of it. UNESCO's support for IPSO therefore legitimizes the attempt to convey a false perception of the possibility of peaceful coexistence and scientific cooperation despite oppression, rather than promoting all efforts to end this oppression.

Calling for sanctions under such circumstances is far from unique to Palestinians. During apartheid rule in South Africa, the United Nations established a regime of sanctions that eventually brought down the racist regime there and helped create democratic rule. South African scientists, athletes, artists, academics, and businesspeople were all subject to boycott then. As we all know, UNESCO played a distinguished and widely commended role in promoting sanctions and various forms of boycott against apartheid South Africa, by organizing no fewer than eight international conferences and seminars addressing a wide range of topics, including "solidarity," "resistance against occupation, oppression and apartheid," "sports boycott," "sanctions against racist South Africa," and the "educational needs of the victims of apartheid."[3] The most significant event that triggered sanctions in that case was the 1971 advisory opinion of the International Court of Justice (ICJ), which denounced South Africa's occupation of Namibia as illegal. When the ICJ issued a similar advisory opinion on July 9, 2004, condemning Israel's colonial wall and the entire occupation regime as violating international law, Palestinians, Arabs, and indeed all peace-loving people around the globe were hoping that the UN and its institutions would launch appropriate punitive measures against Israel to bring about its compliance with UN resolutions.

Some conscientious opinion leaders and organizations have endorsed various forms of such measures. Human-rights leader and Nobel Peace Prize winner Desmond Tutu has pointed out many similarities between Israel and apartheid South Africa, calling for boycotts against the former similar to those applied to the latter.[4] In 2005 the World Council of Churches urged its members to "give serious consideration to economic measures" against Israel to bring an end to its occupation of Palestinian territories.[5] It also praised the action of the Presbyterian Church USA, which started a process of "selective divestment" from companies linked to the illegal Israeli occupation. Several universities in the United States and Europe have started considering divesting from Israel or applying selective boycotts against its institutions. British celebrities and members of Parliament have launched a campaign against Israel's colonial wall, and some have gone so far as to call for outright sanctions against Israel.[6]

Alas, some UN organizations chose instead to overlook or undermine the gravity of Israel's own "occupation, oppression and apartheid," thereby encouraging its belligerent flouting of international law. UNESCO's support for joint Palestinian-Israeli projects that completely ignore the reality of occupation and oppression on the ground is inexplicable and disappointing.

Since Israeli academic institutions (mostly state controlled) and the vast majority of Israeli scientists and academics either have contributed directly to maintaining, defending, or otherwise justifying their state's oppression of the Palestinians or have been complicit in this oppression through their silence, we believe that the international community, led by the UN and its organizations, ought to call for boycotts and sanctions against Israeli academic and scientific institutions.

In the spirit of international solidarity, moral consistency, and resistance to injustice, we strongly feel that UNESCO ought to immediately withdraw its support for IPSO and any other similar effort that assists, cooperates with, or otherwise promotes Israeli scientific or cultural institutions until Israel desists from violating Palestinian human rights and fully complies with the pertinent precepts of international law and UN resolutions. Failing to do so would be further proof of UNESCO's double standards.

WHAT WE REALLY NEED!

A RESPONSE TO ANTI-BOYCOTT ARGUMENTS

Since the launch of the Palestinian boycott movement a few years ago, we have experienced an awkward phenomenon that demands urgent comment. Several Palestine solidarity organizations in the West that have been known for years—in some cases decades—for their tireless work for Palestinian rights have stood, for various reasons, firmly against the Palestinian civil society Call for Boycott, Divestment and Sanctions, BDS, since it was first issued on July 9, 2005. Some said that such tactics were "harmful" to the Palestinian struggle. Others opined that BDS would undermine the so-called Israeli peace movement. Still others stated that boycotting Israel would invite accusations of anti-Semitism and betrayal of Holocaust victims, thereby setting back Palestine solidarity work in a substantial way.

Many other anti-BDS arguments have been recorded in hundreds of articles over the years, but those were less significant or consequential, so I shall focus only on the above three.

Boycott Is Counterproductive?

Is it? Who is to judge? A call signed by more than 170 Palestinian political parties, unions, nongovernmental organizations, and networks, representing the entire spectrum of Palestinian civil society—under occupation, in Israel, and in the Diaspora—cannot be "counterproductive" unless Palestinians are not rational or intelligent enough to know or articulate what is in their best interest. This argument smacks of patronization and betrays a colonial attitude that we thought— hoped!—was extinct in the liberal West.

Pragmatically speaking, the BDS process has proved over the past few years that it is among the most effective forms of civil, nonviolent Palestinian resistance to the Israeli colonial and apartheid regime. The sheer breadth and depth of support this call has garnered among major trade unions, academic associations, church groups, and other grassroots organizations in such places as South Africa, the United Kingdom, Ireland, Canada, Norway, Sweden, and even the United States attest to the efficacy and enormous potential of this campaign in resisting Israeli injustice. For the first time in decades, many movements in Europe that have supported peace with justice in Palestine through demonstrations, public appeals, and—mostly marginal—media work discovered a process that they can actively and effectively contribute to and that promises to bring about concrete results on the ground, as proved to be the case in the struggle against apartheid struggle in South Africa. Judging by results so far, and as our South African comrades have told us repeatedly, our BDS campaign is moving at a faster pace than theirs ever did.

BDS Undermines the Israeli "Peace" Movement?

What Israeli peace movement? There is no such creature. The so-called peace groups in Israel largely work to improve Israeli oppression against the Palestinians, rather than eliminate it, with their chief objective being the guarantee of Israel's future as a "Jewish"—that is, exclusivist—state. The most radical Israeli "Zionist-left" figures and groups are still Zionist, adhering to the racist principles of Zionism that treat the indigenous Palestinians as lesser humans who are an obstacle or a "demographic threat" to be dealt with in order to maintain Israel's character as a colonial, ethnocentric, apartheid state. Specifically, they are opposed to the UN-sanctioned rights of the Palestinian refugees, ethnically cleansed during the establishment of the state and ever since, to return to their homes and lands, simply because they are the "wrong" type. For instance, celebrated Israeli writers A. B. Yehoshua and Amos Oz wrote: "We shall never be able to agree to the return of the refugees to within the borders of Israel, for the meaning of such a return would be the elimination of the State of Israel."[1]

The left-leaning former foreign minister Shlomo Ben-Ami acknowledged some justice in the Palestinian demand for this right, but quickly offered the Palestinian leadership a sobering choice between two options: "justice or peace."[2] From Ben-Ami's point of view, the two are mutually exclusive in the context of the Arab-Israeli colonial conflict.

Danny Rabinowitz suggested "dropping the definite article 'the'" before the phrase "right of return" in order to diminish that right and avoid the "maximalist" interpretation that is demanded by international law.[3] He later suggested limiting the right of return to only those Palestinian refugees born in Palestine before 1948, without their families, saying that: "There are about 200,000 people who fit that description, all of them over the age of 55, most of whom will not be having more children."[4]

Uri Avnery, while criticizing the mainstream Israeli left position on Palestinian refugee rights, especially as articulated by Yehoshua and Oz, censured then prime minister Ehud Barak for bringing it up at the Camp David II talks, "kicking the sleeping lion in the ribs" by insisting prematurely on "end of the conflict" language at Camp

David. Proposing an "annual quota of 50,000 for ten years" and keeping in mind Israel's annual absorption of 50,000 Jewish immigrants, Avnery meant to preserve the nation's "Jewish character" and maintain "the demographic picture." A large majority of Palestinian refugees, under Avnery's "generous" offer, would have to give up their right to return.[5] The underlying premise in all these proposals is that Israel somehow has a unique right to violate international law and to exist as a racist state that denies the indigenous population of Palestine, whether inside historic Palestine or in exile, their basic rights.

These same "leftists" also oppose ending the unique form of apartheid that dominates the entire state of Israel, where a decades-old system of institutionalized racial discrimination, enshrined in law, treats "non-Jewish" citizens of the state as second-class citizens who are not entitled to all the rights that Jewish citizens enjoy. Most of them unabashedly support ending Israel's 1967 occupation of the West Bank and Gaza *in order to* preserve Israel's character as a "Jewish state." If this is the Israeli "peace" movement, then no conscientious person should feel sorry about undermining it!

Israeli-British academic and political activist Moshe Machover commends the courageous actions by some of those Israeli self-described peace activists, but chastises them for contributing to Israel's propaganda. Machover writes:

[T]heir self-description as "peace activists" reveals a profound misapprehension as to the nature of the Israeli-Palestinian conflict and a delusion as to how it might be resolved.

The image it evokes is essentially symmetric: two sides, two nations, at war with each other, locked in a series of battles over a piece of disputed turf. To end the conflict, the two sides need to end the war, sit down together, and make peace.

In fact this is also the image promoted by Israeli *hasbarah* (propaganda). It likes to speak the symmetric language of "war" and "peace"....

The key to a proper understanding of the conflict is that it is an extremely asymmetric one: between settler-colonisers and the indigenous people. It is about dispossession and oppression.[6]

Those who claim that "most" Israelis simply are not aware of the crimes of the occupation and need to be talked to, not boycotted, are not only assuming wrong premises but also reaching a false conclusion. Most Israelis obediently serve in the occupation army without qualms or moral pangs, as part of the obligatory reserve duty. They know firsthand the occupation's crimes, since they either directly participate in committing them or watch in silence as they are perpetrated, thereby indirectly colluding in them. Besides, the Palestinian BDS was never a blanket boycott against individual Israelis. It is consistently institutional in nature, targeting all Israeli academic, cultural, economic, and political institutions, specifically because they are complicit in maintaining the occupation and other forms of racist and colonial oppression against the indigenous Palestinians. Finally, "talking" to Israelis, as in the flourishing "peace" industry's dialogue groups, not only has been misleading and terribly harmful to the struggle for a just peace, giving the false impression that coexistence can be achieved despite the Zionist oppression, but has also failed to bring about any positive shift in Israeli public opinion toward supporting justice as a condition for peace.[7] To the contrary, the Israeli-Jewish public is steadily and dangerously shifting to the fanatical right, with a growing majority supporting extremist solutions such as ethnic cleansing—called "transfer" in the sanitized Israeli mainstream jargon of the remaining indigenous Palestinians.

Dialogue and joint Palestinian-Israeli struggle can be justifiable, constructive, and conducive to just peace only if directed against the occupation and other forms of oppression and based on international law and basic human and political rights, particularly our inalienable right to self-determination.

Based on the above, the only true fighters for peace in Israel are those who support our three fundamental rights: the right of return for Palestinian refugees; full equality for the Palestinian citizens of Israel; and ending the occupation and colonial rule. These are our true partners. They all support various forms of BDS, not only out of principle but also because they realize that genuine, sustainable peace and security for all can never be achieved without justice, international law, universal human rights, and, most crucially, equality. BDS will only strengthen that true peace—with justice—movement in Israel and everywhere else.

European solidarity groups that consciously allow Zionist-left figures and movements to dictate their agendas, steering them away from coordinating with Palestinian civil society and understanding its real needs, away from committing themselves first and foremost to human rights and international law, hardly deserve the name "solidarity groups."

On the other hand, groups that for tactical reasons support only a subset of BDS, or a targeted boycott of specific products or organizations in Israel or supporting Israel, are still our partners. Boycott is not a one-size-fits-all type of process. To be most effective it must be customized to suit a particular context. What is important to agree on, though, is why we are boycotting and toward what ends. BDS is a rights-based approach with clear objectives that ought to form a common denominator for all groups in solidarity with Palestine. Ending the three main forms of Israeli injustice and advocating the corresponding Palestinian rights are the basic requirements for this international campaign to be effective and in harmony with the express needs and aspirations of Palestinian civil society.

BDS Promotes Anti-Semitism?

The anti-Semitism charge is patently misplaced and is wielded as a tool of intellectual intimidation. It is hardly worth reiterating that Palestinian calls for boycott, divestment, and sanctions do not target Jews or even Israelis *qua* Jews. Our calls are directed strictly against Israel as a colonial power that violates Palestinian rights and international law. The growing support among progressive European and American Jews for effective pressure on Israel is one counterargument that is not well publicized.

Moreover, characterizing actions and positions that target Israeli apartheid and colonial rule as anti-Semitic is *itself* anti-Semitic, for such arguments assume that Jews are a monolithic sum that Israel represents and can speak on behalf of and, moreover, that all Jews per se are somehow responsible for Israeli crimes, a patently racist assumption that belongs to the "collective responsibility" school of thought—criminalized at Nuremberg—and directly feeds anti-Semitism.

BDS is a civil form of struggle against Israel, regardless what religion most Israelis follow. It hardly matters what faith your oppressors belong to, really—whether they are Jewish, Christian, Muslim, or Hindu is irrelevant! The *only* thing that matters is that they are illegally, immorally oppressing you and that you want to be free and enjoy equal rights.

Projects supporting Palestinian steadfastness under occupation, whether in the health, education, social, or even political domain, are crucial and always needed. Many Palestinians, particularly the most vulnerable, cannot survive the cruelty of occupation without them. We appreciate the support for these projects tremendously—at least those of them that are not corrupt or corrupting, as many are. But this does not mean that we are for a moment convinced that such projects alone, plus token support for some abstract notion of "peace," can advance our struggle for freedom and justice. Only by ending the occupation and apartheid can we get there. And, experience tells us, the most reliable, morally justifiable way to do that is by treating Israel as apartheid South Africa was, by applying various context-sensitive and evolving measures of BDS against it. There is no better way to achieve just peace in Palestine and the entire region.

DERAILING INJUSTICE

PALESTINIAN CIVIL RESISTANCE TO THE "JERUSALEM LIGHT RAIL"

I believe that this [Jerusalem Light Rail] should be done, and in any event, anything that can be done to strengthen Jerusalem, construct it, expand it and sustain it for eternity as the capital of the Jewish people and the united capital of the State of Israel, should be done.

—Ariel Sharon, August 2005

"Swimming against the tide" is regarded by many cultures, including Arab culture, as unwise, if not altogether irrational and desperately futile; swimming against the tide and hoping to reach your desired destination would, then, defy common sense and call into question one's sanity. Taking such defiance to a new level, the Palestinian civil society campaign for Boycott, Divestment and Sanctions (BDS) and its international supporters in the solidarity movement have been contributing to resisting Israel's multifaceted oppression against the indigenous people of Palestine by mobilizing international civil society to apply effective, nonviolent, and sustained pressure against it until it fully complies with its obligations under international law and respects Palestinian rights.

The campaign against the "Jerusalem Light Rail" is a case in point that tellingly illustrates the potency and potential of such a struggle as well as the challenges stacked against it.

Realizing Herzl's Vision

According to its official brochure, the Jerusalem Light Rail (JLR) is intended to fulfill Theodore Herzl's vision of Jerusalem: "modern neighborhoods with electric lines, tree-lined boulevards . . . a metropolis of the 20th century."[1] The other crucial element of Herzl's Eurocentric vision for the entire land of Palestine as a Jewish state has been even more faithfully adhered to by the project planners.

While the professed goals of the JLR cite typical urban planning priorities such as relieving traffic congestion and renewal of the city center, the actual map of the JLR's planned route and stations reveals the unspoken underlying objective of the project: to irreversibly entrench the "Judaization" of Jerusalem[2] and perpetuate its current condition as a unified city with a predominantly Jewish population under Israeli control. By connecting its most significant colonies, or "settlement blocs," illegally built on the occupied Palestinian territory (OPT) including East Jerusalem,[3] in contravention of international law,[4] Israel hopes to use the JLR—as part of a comprehensive long-term strategy that includes the wall and other repressive measures[5]—to cement the integration of those blocs into an ever-wider-sprawling "Greater Jerusalem." Thus it will create the third most important fact on the ground, after the 1948 Nakba,[6] with the mass forcible displacement of hundreds of thousands of Palestinians that accompanied it, and the 1967 military occupation of the West Bank and Gaza.

The political and legal implications of the JLR cannot be fully appreciated unless they are seen within the context of Israel's strategic plans for Jerusalem, particularly the "secret plan" sponsored by the Israeli prime minister's office and the mayor of Jerusalem to "strengthen

Jerusalem as the capital of the State of Israel." This plan, exposed in *Haaretz* in 2009, aims at creating Israeli "hegemony" over the area around the Old City, "inspired by extreme right-wing ideology."[7] A recent Palestinian position paper on the JLR states, "The overarching policy framework for Jerusalem is illustrated most fully by the Master Plan 2020 document (2004) . . . , which outlines measures to prevent the growth of Palestinian communities and encourage the growth of Jewish settlements, with the goal of creating a 70:30 ratio of Jews to Palestinians, as stipulated by government decisions. Doing this involves ethnically cleansing Palestinian communities from Jerusalem through a variety of mechanisms, including the Wall and the revocation of identity papers."[8]

The JLR is the brainchild of the Jerusalem Transportation Master Plan, jointly administered by the Ministry of Transport and the Jerusalem Municipality. Its strategic role in Israel's colonial plans for Jerusalem stems from the fact that it purports to treat the increasing inadequacy of the existing Israeli road and mass transit system to meet the needs associated with the uncontrolled growth of Israel's illegal colonies in the occupied territory. After all, since the signing of the Oslo Peace Accords between Israel and the Palestine Liberation Organization in 1993, the population of Jewish settlers in the OPT has almost doubled. As the official route of the JLR reveals,[9] the tram's various routes are predominantly intended to serve Israel's illegal colonies in and surrounding occupied East Jerusalem, such as Atarot Airport, Neve Ya'kov, Pisgat Ze'ev, Ramot, Har Ha-Tzofim campus of the Hebrew University, and Gilo.

Perpetuating Injustice: The Legal Case against the JLR

Based on the Fourth Geneva Convention, numerous UN resolutions have condemned as illegal Israel's colonies (settlements) built on what is internationally recognized to be occupied Palestinian land. The most recent reaffirmation of this verdict of international law came from the International Court of Justice, which on July 9, 2004, issued an advisory opinion against Israel's wall and colonies in the OPT,[10] a ruling that is widely recognized as a legal and political watershed in the Palestinian struggle against Israel's occupation. Infrastructure and other projects that serve these colonies or act in any way to perpetuate their existence are, by extension, illegal. Not only does the JLR significantly contribute to Israeli designs to make its illegal annexation of occupied Palestinian territory irreversible; it also provides the colonies with a crucial service, connecting them to Israel. Accordingly, the JLR is considered an integral part of Israel's illegal colonial regime and thus a violation of international law that may amount to a war crime. Companies that participate in building and running the JLR, or in constructing, maintaining, and servicing Israeli colonies[11] more generally, can be regarded as "aiding and abetting" these crimes.

Citing the Hague Convention IV on Respecting the Laws and Customs of War on Land (October 18, 1907), the PLO's Negotiation Support Unit argues: "As an occupant, Israel has no sovereign rights or title to the OPT, including East Jerusalem. Consequently, it may only undertake changes in East Jerusalem and the rest of the OPT for the benefit of the occupied Palestinian population or for military necessity. As the Light Rail neither caters to the needs of Palestinian civilians nor serves any genuine military purpose, the Light Rail constitutes an illegal change to East Jerusalem and neighbouring West Bank areas."[12]

The above furnished the legal basis of a lawsuit in France against Veolia and Alstom, two of the companies involved in the consortium that signed the contract with the state of Israel to build and manage the JLR project. Both companies are French conglomerates involved in vast projects in dozens of countries around the world, mostly focusing on transportation, water, and sanitation. An unprecedented case brought before the Court of Nanterre, France, by the PLO and the Association France-Palestine Solidarité (AFPS) in 2007,[13] though still being deliberated, has made enough progress to inspire similar action elsewhere against companies implicated in the JLR project. In April 2009 the High Court of Nanterre (Tribunal de Grande Instance de Nanterre), according to an AFPS press statement, thwarted relentless efforts by Veolia and Alstom to have the case dismissed by declaring that it has jurisdiction to hear AFPS's legal claim against them regarding the construction and operation of East Jerusalem's light railway. Moreover, when Veolia and Alstom argued that the suit was invalid because the state of Israel enjoys sovereign immunity from being sued in foreign courts, the Nanterre court ruled that "apart from the fact that the state of Israel is not party to this action, this state could not seriously have standing in relation to disputed contracts in the guise of a sovereign state since this state is in fact an occupying power of the area in the West Bank where the light rail system is being built and where its exploitation is contentious, an area recognized by the international community and the International Court of Justice as being part of the Palestinian territory."[14]

In the United Kingdom, meanwhile, Daniel Machover, a prominent attorney and cofounder of Lawyers for Palestinian Human Rights, has adopted an innovative legal approach to challenge Veolia and other companies. Machover invokes UK 2006 Public Procurement Regulations, the British implementing measure of EU Directive 2004/18/EC,[15] to argue that a local authority may be subjected to legal challenge if it does not agree to exclude Veolia from a public bid as an economic operator. Specifically, he bases his case on article 45 of the EU Directive, which includes the provision that any economic operator "may be excluded from participation in a contract" if it "has been guilty of grave professional misconduct proven by any means which the contracting authorities can demonstrate."

Machover argues that this type of discretionary decision by a public body in the United Kingdom can be subject to a legal challenge in the High Court. It is expected that when local authorities are presented with hard evidence of Veolia's "grave professional misconduct," coupled with substantial public pressure and a credible threat of High Court involvement, they may opt to exclude Veolia to avoid the trouble. If this approach yields positive results, it is likely to be emulated across other EU states, where the same laws apply.

Derailing Veolia and Alstom

In October 2008 in partnership with Mewando, the leading Basque solidarity network, the Boycott, Divestment and Sanctions Campaign National Committee (BNC)[16] organized in Bilbao Europe's first civil society conference focusing on BDS. The main outcome of this effort was the Bilbao Initiative,[17] which endorsed BNC's groundbreaking, in-depth analysis of Israel's regime over the Palestinian people, "United against Apartheid, Colonialism and Occupation: Dignity and Justice for the Palestinian People,"[18] and focused on specific, practical BDS campaigns to be coordinated across Europe and beyond. The campaign against Veolia and Alstom was declared a top priority.

One of the earlier BNC efforts to counter JLR-implicated corporations was an appeal[19] sent to the Kingdom of Saudi Arabia by the Palestinian Grassroots Anti–Apartheid Wall Campaign and the Civic Coalition for Defending the Palestinians' Rights in Jerusalem, urging the Saudi government not to award Alstom a $2.5 billion contract to build a power plant. On top of presenting the legal, political, and moral arguments against Alstom, the document detailed Saudi Arabia's historic commitment to the Palestinian cause in general and the question of occupied Jerusalem in particular, concluding that awarding this lucrative contract to a company that is colluding in Israel's declared intent to further colonize and "Judaize" the Holy City would, for all intents and purposes, undermine these unique commitments, not to mention obligations under international law. Unfortunately the Saudi government has yet to respond to the appeal, let alone heed it. In fact, according to a recent report in the Dubai-based *Gulf News*, "Alstom is part of a consortium awarded a $1.8 billion (Dh6.6 billion) civil works contract in March for the Makkah-Madinah railway, the Haramain Express."[20] It is a bitter irony that Saudi Arabia is allowing the same company that is unapologetically complicit in colonizing Jerusalem, regarded by Islam as a holy city, to build a railway connecting Islam's two holiest cities, Mecca and Medina. This has prompted even the normally complacent Palestinian Authority to register an official complaint with the Saudis and try to convince them to scrap Alstom's involvement in the Haramain Express.[21]

In Europe, meanwhile, the scene was friendlier for the campaign against JLR partner companies. As part of the aforementioned Bilbao Initiative, human rights lawyers, activists, and trade unionists, in full coordination with the BDS National Committee, launched several focused BDS campaigns, targeting corporations and institutions that are unmistakably complicit in aspects of Israel's multifaceted system of oppression of Palestinians. Thus the "Derail Veolia" campaign was born, aiming to coordinate already existing efforts in several countries and launching new ones to pressure Veolia, as well as Alstom, to withdraw from the illegal project by threatening public boycott campaigns if it failed to do so.

Other significant local campaigns against the two French companies involved in the JLR project, detailed below, shed some light on the innovative and principled tactics used and the impressive achievements reached to date.

After a long pressure campaign initiated by one determined and resourceful human rights activist and eventually endorsed by influential civil society groups in the Netherlands, the Dutch bank ASN, which identifies itself as an "ethical bank" that upholds international law and human rights, decided in November 2006 to divest from Veolia Transport and other companies that benefit from Israel's occupation of Palestinian territory.[22] The decision followed months of meticulous research, networking, and public awareness efforts undertaken by the campaign organizers. United Civilians for Peace, a coalition of Dutch organizations advocating peace, human rights, and development, produced a well-researched document detailing the links between Dutch companies and the Israeli occupation of Palestinian territory. The Palestinian Grassroots Anti–Apartheid Wall Campaign was also involved in the campaign at various stages, providing empirical data and advice. Simultaneously, questions were raised in the Dutch Parliament about a specific Dutch company involved in the construction of the illegal wall. Veolia's initial claims that it was not aware that its involvement in the JLR was illegal ring hollow, given the fact that Amnesty International in France had issued a clearly worded document stating just that, months earlier,[23] and had warned Veolia's management not to get involved in this project.

Together, these developments led to extensive media coverage of the whole issue of the complicity as well as the legal and ethical responsibility of companies, which in turn raised the level of pressure on ASN Bank significantly, convincing it to start a process of investigation of Veolia's involvement in the objectionable project and, eventually, to end its investments in it.

A Swedish coalition of faith-based groups, led by Diakonia, was quick to follow suit. During Israel's atrocious war on Gaza, the Stockholm community council announced[24] that Veolia, which had been the operator of the Stockholm County metro for the previous ten years, had lost the contract for the next eight years. Worth 3.5 billion euros (approximately $4.5 billion), this contract is considered the largest ongoing public procurement process in Europe. And although the council stated that its decision was based solely on commercial considerations, the massive public campaign waged by Swedish groups against Veolia in the months leading up to the decision could not but have been a decisive factor for any politician hoping to get reelected.

Adri Nieuwhof, a human rights advocate who has played a leading role in exposing European corporate complicity in Israel's occupation, had this to say about the impressive Swedish public campaign against Veolia:

> Swedish activists informed the public about the role of companies in benefiting from the occupation through several actions. The Swedish non-governmental organization Diakonia's research on [the] Mul-T-Lock factory in the Barkan Industrial Park in a West Bank settlement led to the October 2008 decision of [factory] owner Assa Abloy to divest from the company. At that time Veolia was bidding for an eight-year, $4.5 billion contract to run the subway in Stockholm County. Swedish journalists questioned politicians about Veolia's role in an Israeli tramway project that links Israeli settlements and normalizes the illegal situation of the settlements. At the Give Veolia the Red Card event on 15 November 2008, passengers on the Stockholm subway were asked to attach a red card to their clothes to protest Veolia's involvement in the Jerusalem tramway on occupied Palestinian territory.[25]

Weeks after this meaningful defeat for Veolia in Sweden, its partner in the JLR project suffered just as momentous a setback when the Swedish national pension fund, AP7, decided to exclude Alstom from its investment portfolio.[26] Considering the size of the Swedish fund, $15 billion, this decision was bound to have serious consequences for Alstom and other companies in a similar situation. This time, however, the decision was explicitly justified on the grounds of Alstom's involvement in the illegal JLR project, reflecting the intensifying discontent in the Swedish public, especially after Gaza, with companies that profit from unethical and illegal Israeli projects and a determination to make them—literally—pay for it.

In March 2009, Palestine Solidarity Campaign (PSC) in the West Midlands, United Kingdom, celebrated another significant victory in the campaign against the JLR. The Sandwell Metropolitan Borough Council decided not to consider further Veolia's bid for the Waste Improvement Plan contract, which is worth about $1.5 billion over twenty years.[27] Again, the council insisted that the decision was commercial, not political. And again, the public pressure that was brought to bear before the decision looked too sweeping to ignore.

Elsewhere in the UK, several local campaigns have sprouted to derail Veolia from a number of large public works contracts. From Hampshire County to Liverpool to Camden to South Yorkshire, local authorities are facing mounting political, and sometimes legal, pressure from Palestine solidarity groups, mainly associated with PSC, to exclude Veolia from bidding for public projects.

Most recently, Veolia started feeling the heat right at home. The Greater Bordeaux local government announced that it was awarding—on commercial grounds, of course—a $1 billion contract for the biggest urban network in France to Veolia's competitor, despite intense lobbying by Veolia. La Plateforme BDS Bordeaux marked this achievement by saying, "Veolia's involvement in the situation of [Israeli] apartheid has already led to its loss of several contracts, and this is just the beginning."[28]

Artistic Resistance

In Australia, the campaign against Veolia's subsidiary Connex took on an entirely new shape. Award-winning visual artist Van Thanh Rudd created a stir in Melbourne with his installation *Economy of Movement:*

A Piece of Palestine. Rudd's installation, which looks like a museum display, shows a stone sitting on a glass base. A panel hanging behind it reads "The stone exhibited is from East Jerusalem (Occupied Palestinian Territory). It was thrown at an Israeli Defense Force (IDF) tank by a Palestinian youth." Another panel to the right reads "IDF tanks are protecting French companies Veolia (Connex) and Alstom as they conduct illegal operations on Occupied Palestinian Territory."

Rudd explained his motives saying, "I thought it would be a great opportunity to make artwork that would clearly outline Veolia's illegal operations on occupied Palestinian territory."[29]

Recent Developments: Veolia's Setbacks and Exposed Segregation

In an unexpected turn of events, after months of intensive lobbying and awareness-raising by the Derail Veolia and Alstom campaign, *Haaretz* reported that Veolia was "abandoning" the JLR and was even "trying to sell its 5% stake in Citypass, the light rail consortium." According to the report, "The organization based itself on an article in French law that allows the court to void business agreements, signed by French companies, that violate international law." However, it cites "political pressure" and the loss of "major projects in Europe because of its involvement in the Jerusalem job" as the "real reason" for Veolia's withdrawal from the JLR, according to unnamed observers.[30]

Reportedly due to contractual obligations, however, Veolia said it was unable to sell its share and instead embarked on a public relations campaign, conducting a survey, partially to try to show that Palestinians in occupied East Jerusalem are content with the JLR. The fact that the survey's scientific credibility was very much in doubt only confirmed the view that it was little more than Veolia's latest attempt to whitewash and deflect attention from the JLR's indisputable colonization and dispossession impact on the Palestinian people, especially in occupied Jerusalem. As Adri Nieuwhof reports: "The bad publicity around the [Veolia] survey—described as racist by even members of the Israeli government—is an ironic turn of events. . . . Veolia, which plays a key role in the rail project that strengthens Israel's grip on occupied East Jerusalem, has used dubious surveys of Palestinians in attempt to put a positive spin on its involvement in the project."[31]

The JLR consortium, CityPass, had asked Jerusalem residents whether they were comfortable with JLR stations in Palestinian neighborhoods of occupied East Jerusalem and whether they were bothered by both Jews and Arabs mounting freely "without undergoing a security check." In a letter to CityPass, Yair Maayan, Jerusalem's municipal director general, wrote: "We were flabbergasted to see how a private commercial consortium dared to address these subjects, which are none of its business whatsoever; to ask such racist questions and to arouse strife and contention in the city."[32]

Meanwhile Palestinians are affected by the JLR in various harmful ways, according to Nieuwhof's report:

> Two-thousand square meters of land belonging to Shuafat resident Mahmoud al-Mashni have been confiscated for the light rail project, and more of his land will be confiscated for the parking lot next to the station. "It is not good for us, it is good for the Jewish settlements," al-Mashni explained in a telephone interview with *The Electronic Intifada*. "We cannot afford to pay the fees. One ticket will cost 15 shekels [$4]. Our income is low. The bus to East Jerusalem costs us only four shekels [$1]." . . . According to al-Mashi, as the light rail uses half of the width of the main road that cuts through Shuafat, it is no longer possible to cross the road. Traffic is now restricted to two lanes in each direction, causing traffic jams when buses and cars stop at the shops along the road.[33]

In another scandal, Israeli TV revealed that the qualifications for a JLR control and operations management job included the requirement that candidates must have completed "full military/civic service." This blatantly discriminatory requirement, which echoes racist job requirements used for decades by Israeli public and private employers, automatically excludes the great majority of Palestinian citizens of Israel, who do not serve in the Israeli army. Despite reports that Veolia had retracted the ad, it is still prominently displayed on its website.[34]

While claiming "a clear, non-discriminatory policy based on free access for all parts of the population," the JLR is in fact entrenching the status quo of racial segregation that prevails in Jerusalem. CityPass spokesperson Ammon Elian told a Belgian researcher: "If Palestinians would want to make use of the light rail, both groups [Palestinians and Jewish Israelis] will not meet on the train, because of their different life patterns."[35]

Racial segregation is not the only form of discrimination condoned by Veolia. The company has also colluded in making some of the bus lines it operates gender segregated to appease Jewish fundamentalists. Nieuwhof writes:

> Meanwhile, Veolia Transport continues to operate the segregated bus service 322 from Tel Aviv to Ashdod. At the terminal for bus 322 in Tel Aviv, small posters promise eternal damnation for those who do not observe the rules of halacha, or Jewish religious law. On 8 April [2010] chairman of the municipal council in Tel Aviv Yael Dayan told the Swiss newspaper *Le Temps* that bus service 322 is a "kosher" bus route, meaning that gender segregation is practiced with the agreement of the authorities. Women enter through the rear of the vehicle and the men from the front. They cannot touch each other or sit next to one another. In some buses, a thick blanket is hung in the middle of the bus between the two sexes. "It's the return of the Middle Ages,"

Dayan told *Le Temps*. Veolia Transport confirmed in a phone call with Who Profits from the Occupation? that bus 322 is segregated.[36]

As a result of its ongoing involvement in such violations of international law and human rights, Veolia has suffered major setbacks in several places. The London-based Islamic Human Rights Commission recently reported that "Tehran's mayor scrapped plans for Veolia to have a key role in the city's urban transport system."[37] The BNC had sent a letter to the Iranian leadership last May through European NGOs in Geneva, during the UN Durban Review conference, reminding Tehran of its commitments and obligations to contribute to the defense of Jerusalem against Israel's colonial designs and urging it to exclude Veolia and Alstom from all Iranian public works contracts due to the companies' involvement in the illegal JLR project.

On May 10, 2010, the Dublin City Council unanimously passed a resolution calling on its city manager not to sign or renew any contracts with Veolia. The Irish Palestine Solidarity Campaign, which led the Derail Veolia/Alstom campaign in Ireland, expressed joy at this sweeping, hard-earned victory. IPSC spokesperson David Landy stated that this was "just the latest in a string of such defeats," adding, "Veolia has suffered as a result of their active participation in Israel's apartheid policies. . . . The IPSC once again urges Veolia to heed the Palestinian call for BDS and divest now from its Israeli operations in the occupied Palestinian territories. However, until it does so, the IPSC will continue to campaign for Veolia not to be granted contracts in Ireland."[38]

Following this inspiring victory in Ireland, the third in a row against Veolia, it was Wales's turn. On June 17, 2010, the Council of Swansea, the second largest city in Wales, set a precedent in the United Kingdom by voting to exclude Veolia from municipal contracts due to its complicity in violations of international law. The resolution states: "This Council therefore calls on the Leader & Chief Executive not to sign or allow to be signed any new contracts or renewal of any existing contracts with Veolia or any other company in breach of international law, so long as to do so would not be in breach of any relevant legislation."[39]

The Derail Veolia and Alstom Campaign will continue its civil pressure on both companies until they completely sever their links with all Israeli projects that are in violation of international law, not just the JLR. Specifically, Veolia is still involved in providing bus services that link Jerusalem with illegal colonies and in the dumping of waste from Israel and its settlements in the Tovlan landfill in the occupied Jordan Valley.[40]

Final Remarks

From Melbourne to Stockholm and from Bordeaux to Dublin and Swansea, companies implicated in the JLR project are not just facing symbolic protests by marginalized demonstrators; they are experiencing real, deep losses that are directly connected with their JLR involvement. What initially seemed like a desperate swim against the tide to reach the shores of justice is increasingly looking like a great wind that may well cause the tide itself to be reversed.

"BOYCOTTS WORK"

OMAR BARGHOUTI INTERVIEWED BY ALI MUSTAFA*

Why do you characterize Israel as an apartheid state, and how is it similar to or different from apartheid South Africa?

The most important point is that we don't have to prove that Israel is *identical* to apartheid South Africa in order to deserve the label *apartheid*. Apartheid is a generalized crime according to UN conventions, and there are certain criteria that may or may not apply in a given situation—so we judge a situation of institutionalized discrimination in a state on its own merits regarding whether it fulfills the conditions to be called an apartheid state. According to the basic conventions of the UN defining the crime of apartheid,[1] Israel satisfies the conditions to be assigned the label *apartheid*.

Beyond the clear racial separation in the occupied West Bank between Jews and "non-Jews" (indigenous Palestinians)—separate roads, separate housing, separate everything—apartheid is also alive and well *inside* Israel, despite deceptive appearances. Israel's version of apartheid is more sophisticated than South Africa's was; it's an evolved form.

---

*   Ali Mustafa is a freelance journalist, writer, and media activist. He is a member of the Coalition Against Israeli Apartheid (CAIA) and currently resides in Toronto.

South African apartheid was rudimentary, petty, primitive, so to speak—literally black and white, clear separation, no rights. Israel's apartheid is more hidden and covered up with a deceptive image of "democracy." Palestinian citizens of Israel (the indigenous population that survived the massive ethnic cleansing campaign of 1948 and remained put) have the right to vote, and that is a huge difference from South Africa; however, in every other vital domain they are discriminated against by law—not only by policy but by law. In addition, they are only allowed to vote for a system that enshrines apartheid! Any party that calls for dismantling Israel's racist laws, instituting unmitigated equality, and transforming the state into a real democracy as a state of all its citizens, cannot run for the Knesset.

Israel's system is a *legalized* and *institutionalized* system of racism that enables one racial group to persistently dominate another, and that's what makes it apartheid. Even successive US State Department reports on human rights have repeatedly condemned Israel's "institutional, legal and societal discrimination" against its "non-Jewish" minority.[2]

There is racism in Canada and other Western democracies as well, one may argue, but the difference is that it's not institutionalized and legalized, at least not any longer. The United States did have an apartheid situation in the Jim Crow South when there were different laws governing whites and nonwhites, but today we cannot say that about the United States in the legal sense, despite the prevalence of racism there in other, indirect forms.

A compelling case can be made, and indeed has been made, that Canada's and the United States' treatment of their respective indigenous populations, the first nations of the land, constitute institutionalized racism that is designed to deny them their right to self-determination on their ancestral lands and to receive reparations. Things are far more blatant in Israel, though.

There are basic laws, equivalent to constitutional laws in other countries (as Israel does not have a constitution), where there is clear-cut discrimination between Jews and non-Jews. The most important rights that are given to Jewish citizens and not to non-Jewish citizens are the rights to automatic citizenship *and* nationality for any Jewish immigrant who comes from abroad to Israel. By contrast, Palestinian refugees who were ethnically cleansed by Zionist militias and later Israel in 1948, and ever since, are not entitled to go back to their homes of origin, as stipulated in international law, simply because they are not Jewish. There is no officially recognized "Israeli" nationality, but there is "Jewish nationality"—Palestinians as citizens can never get nationality in Israel, because the Israeli establishment, including the High Court, does not recognize an Israeli nationality. This is the kind of apartheid we have in Israel.[3]

Another very important point is that almost all the land in Israel is by law off limits to the state's so-called non-Jewish citizens. As Chris McGreal writes in the *Guardian*: "Israeli governments reserved 93% of the land—often expropriated from Arabs without compensation—for Jews through state ownership, the Jewish National Fund and the Israeli Lands Authority. In colonial and then apartheid South Africa, 87% of the land was reserved for whites."[4] This is worse than South Africa—*93 percent of land* is for the benefit of Jewish citizens of the state of Israel and Jews around the world, and them alone. If this is not apartheid, I don't know what is.

Indeed many analysts would argue that Israel's occupation, colonization, and denial of refugee rights is much worse than anything South Africa had, and that is true. South Africa, unlike Israel, did not employ ethnic cleansing to expel most of the indigenous population out of the country, although they did transfer populations as a form of social engineering apartheid. In South Africa the overall plan was to exploit blacks not throw them out of the whole country. Israel's highest policy priority since its creation is getting rid of as many Palestinians as possible and grabbing as much of their land as practical, without inviting the full wrath of the world. South African apartheid force also never bombed bantustans with F-16s; they never reached Israel's level of sustained, massive, outright violence, medieval siege, and massacres. Of course there was Sharpeville, there were massacres in Soweto and so on, but it all pales in comparison to what Israel has been doing to the Palestinians, and this is according to testimonies from Desmond Tutu, former ANC leader and government minister Ronnie Kasrils, and other South African leaders.

One of the most contentious aspects of the BDS campaign is of course the academic boycott. Can you clarify exactly what this means and why Israeli academic institutions are, as you argue, such a fundamental extension of the Israeli state and state policy?

The academic boycott, which was called for by the Palestinian Campaign for the Academic and Cultural Boycott of Israel (PACBI) in July 2004, is an institutional boycott—so it's a call to every conscientious academic and academic institution to boycott *all* Israeli academic institutions because of their ongoing deep complicity in perpetuating Israel's occupation and other forms of oppression.[5] What do we mean by "complicity"? That's a very fluid term. Complicity of the academy in the case of Israel is different from academic complicity elsewhere. In Canada, for example, your biggest universities are certainly complicit in Canadian policy, especially because they're all state-funded institutions, exactly as in Israel (all universities in Israel are state funded). What's different is that in Israel they are in full, organic partnership with the security-military establishment, implicating them in war crimes and other grave violations of international law. Many weapons for the Israeli army are developed through the universities; most of the research used in planning, justifying, and whitewashing the oppression of the Palestinians and denial of Palestinian rights is done by academics in university programs; and major colonization projects that under international law are classified as war crimes have been produced by universities. There are many specific examples. The idea of the Israeli wall to be built on occupied Palestinian territory was produced in an academic environment, as was the wall's design. An academic at Haifa University claims that this is his brainchild—and there is no reason not to believe him, as he has produced other projects that were terribly involved in ethnic cleansing Palestinians even inside Israel. So at every level there is a very deep, entrenched complicity of the Israeli academia in the security-military establishment.

Also, nearly all Israeli academics, like other adult Israelis in a defined age group, serve in the occupation reserve army—that is, they serve as occupying soldiers—for three months each year. They leave academia, research, everything else, and serve at a military roadblock or a post that is even worse. During that service period, they're either participating in the commission of human rights violations and war crimes or watching them in apathy and silence. In either case they are complicit. The universities not only tolerate this reserve duty but promote it—it is part of the system. Omnipresent on campuses, the military-security establishment goes almost unnoticed, like any normal part of the academy.[6]

Despite this, we are not calling for boycotting individual academics but institutions. If our boycott is were focused on individuals, it would be McCarthyist—it would involve some form of McCarthyism or political testing: who is a good Israeli academic, who is bad, and, crucially, who decides and according to what criteria? We are opposed to that *on principle*. It's a very troubling prospect to impose political tests; that's why we have chosen an unambiguously *institutional* boycott.

One common argument against the BDS campaign is that dialogue is more constructive than boycotts. How would you respond?

That's a false argument, factually and logically. Factually, there have been so many attempts at "dialogue" since 1993 when the so-called peace process was launched at Oslo. Many grassroots dialogue organizations and initiatives were established; it became an industry—we call it the "peace industry." You could get rich and/or famous rather quickly by getting involved in one of those dialogue groups, plus you get to travel to Europe and stay in fancy hotels and get some other benefits as well. But otherwise it produces absolutely nothing on the ground in terms of advancing the cause of a just peace and ending oppression. The main reason is because this peace industry is morally flawed and based on a false premise: that this "conflict" is mainly due to mutual hatred and implies mutual responsibility, and thus you need some kind of therapy or dialogue between those two equivalent, symmetric, conflicting parties. Put them in a room, entice them—or force them—to talk to one another, and then they will fall in love, the hatred will go away, and you will have a Romeo and Juliet story. Of course, this is deceitful and morally corrupt because the conflict is a colonial conflict—it's not a domestic dispute between a husband and a wife in a culture of social equals. It's a colonial conflict based on ethnic cleansing, racism, settler colonialism, and apartheid. Without removing the root causes of the conflict, you cannot have any coexistence, at least not *ethical* coexistence.

There are many other issues related to this dialogue industry. Within it you don't have *dialogue* between asymmetric parties, you have lopsided *negotiations*. To have a dialogue you have to have a certain minimal-level common denominator, or a common vision for the ultimate solution based on freedom, equality, democracy, and ending injustice. If you don't have that common denominator, then it's *negotiation* between the stronger and weaker party. In such a situation, as I've written elsewhere, you can't have a bridge between them but only a ladder where you go up or down not across—because there is no across. I call this the master-slave type of coexistence. It's also a form of "peace": a master and a slave can reach an agreement where the enslavement is accepted as reality and the slave cannot challenge it but only make the best out of it. There is no war—no conflict, nobody is killing anybody—but the master remains master and the slave remains slave.

That is not the kind of peace that we, the oppressed, are seeking or can ever resign ourselves to. The minimal requirement for ethical coexistence is a peace based on justice and full respect for human rights. Only with justice can we have a sustainable peace. So dialogue between oppressor and oppressed cannot work when it is devoid of agreement on the basis for justice—it has not worked in reality and cannot work in principle.

Boycotts, on the other hand, work in reality and in principle, as was shown in the South African anti-apartheid struggle. There is absolutely no reason why they cannot work in our case too. Israel's total impunity, perpetuated through the official support it receives from the West in all fields (diplomatic, economic, cultural, academic, and so on), means that unless the price of its system of oppression is sufficiently raised through concerted civil-society pressure campaigns, it will never give it up; it will never concede on any of our inalienable, UN-sanctioned rights.

Of course there is the historical example of South African apartheid, but I am wondering whether there are any other historical forms of nonviolent resistance besides boycotts—that the PACBI and BDS campaigns draw their inspiration from.

Yes, we draw our inspiration and experience primarily from our rich Palestinian history of nonviolent, or civil, resistance. For a hundred years, well before the South African resistance movement's inspiration, our own history has had fertile roots of civil resistance against the settler-colonial conquest of Palestine. We have resisted mostly with *civil* resistance, not armed resistance, contra the common myth that Palestinian resistance is only armed. Palestinians from all segments of society have always resisted with social, political, cultural, and artistic popular resistance, strikes, demonstrations, tax boycotts, women's and trade union organizing, and so on. ... The majority of our people have always been involved in nonviolent resistance even before the inspiration of Gandhi, King, and Mandela.[7]

Many academics, even those generally sympathetic to the Palestinian cause, argue that any proposed academic boycott jeopardizes the principle of academic freedom.[8] Is there any truth to that claim?

The claim itself is quite biased in that it privileges Israeli academic freedom over any other freedom for the Palestinians. Those making this claim completely ignore that by denying Palestinians their basic rights—all our freedoms—Israel is infringing deeply on our academic freedom. That doesn't count, it seems.

The conception of academic freedom implied in the question is used primarily to muzzle serious debate about the complicity of the Israeli academy in planning, executing, and whitewashing Israel's occupation, colonization, and apartheid. It seems to be restricted to the suppression of the "free exchange of ideas among academics," leaving out the situation of academics in contexts of colonialism, military occupation, and other forms of national oppression, where "material and institutional foreclosures ... make it impossible for certain historical subjects to lay claim to the discourse of rights itself," as Judith Butler eloquently argues.[9] Academic freedom, from this perspective, becomes the exclusive privilege of some academics but not others.

We never heard those same liberal voices protest when Israel shut down Palestinian universities during the first intifada—Birzeit University, for example, was shut down for four consecutive years. We didn't hear much of an outcry among those liberals who are now shouting "Academic freedom!" Is academic freedom a privilege for "whites" only? Do we, global southerners, deserve academic freedom as well? Are we equally human or not?

Those who care about academic freedom only when it pertains to Jewish Israelis—perceived as "white," "European," "civilized"—and not when it pertains to us brown Palestinians are hypocritical, to put it mildly. Moreover, the academic boycott that PACBI is calling for and that all our partners are adopting is *institutional*, targeting academic institutions due to their entrenched complicity. It does not infringe on the rights and privileges of Israeli academics to go out and participate in conferences and so on, so long as this is not the product of an institutional link. We are calling for cutting all *institutional* links, not for cutting off visits by individual academics, artists, or cultural figures to participate in events. It is, then, quite inaccurate and politically motivated to call the institutional academic boycott of Israel a form of infringement on academic freedom.

Some have actually claimed that such an academic boycott would *enhance* the academic freedom of Israeli academics. Could you elaborate on that a little bit?

Yes. Professor Oren Ben-Dor, for instance, who is an Israeli British philosopher supporting the boycott, argued this in an article a few years ago.[10] He wrote that one of the purposes of the proposed academic boycott is to "provide a means to transcend the publicly sanctioned limits of debate," adding, "Such freedom is precisely what is absent in Israel." The academic boycott, from this viewpoint, is credited for "generating," not repressing, academic freedom. "The Zionist ideology which stipulates that Israel must retain its Jewish majority," Ben-Dor says, "is a non-debatable given in the country—and the bedrock of opposition to allowing the return of Palestinian refugees. The very few intellectuals who dare to question this sacred cow are labeled 'extremists.' "

My next question is along these lines. Another common argument made by critics of the BDS campaign is that only after Hamas ceases launching rockets into Israel will peace be possible. How would you respond to this claim?

OK, where do I start? Well, let's start with the occupied West Bank. In the West Bank you have a largely obedient Palestinian Authority (PA) that acts mainly as a subcontractor for the Israeli occupation, serving its "security" needs and relieving it of its civic burdens of running the education, health, sanitation, and other systems for the Palestinian population in most of the occupied territory. Israel gets indispensable support from the Palestinian Authority in Ramallah, which lacks any democratic mandate from the Palestinian people under occupation. The PA has not succeeded in stopping Israel's construction of the wall (which is illegal according to the 2004 advisory opinion of the International Court of Justice at The Hague), or the construction of colonial settlements (which are also illegal—fitting the definition of war crimes under the Fourth Geneva Convention), or the checkpoints (there are more than six hundred roadblocks and checkpoints that severely curtail Palestinian freedom of movement), or the confiscation of land, or the indiscriminate killings (including of children), or house demolitions (the collective punishment of choice in occupied Jerusalem), or the incarceration of political prisoners, or any of the other repressive occupation measures that are designed to ethnically cleanse the indigenous Palestinians in a very slow and gradual, but persistent, manner, especially in and around Jerusalem. We have not seen any difference between Israel's repression in the West Bank and its repression in Gaza, prior to the siege and the latest war of aggression of course. In other words, with or without Hamas, Israel's multifaceted colonial oppression hardly changes. Its master plan is to get rid of us or as many of us as politically possible, no matter who "rules" us. In the West Bank there is no Hamas in power—it's the US- and Israel-backed PA—but still Israel continues with its policies of colonization and racism. It's irrelevant whether or not Hamas accepts Israel's so-called right to exist as a Jewish state (read: an apartheid state)[11] or accepts the '67 borders—totally irrelevant. Israel will never accept our rights as a people unless it is compelled to.

No colonial settler regime, from Northern Ireland to Algeria to South Africa, ever gave up power voluntarily or through persuasion, history teaches us, without effective, persistent, and ever-evolving resistance, coupled with massive and sustained international solidarity, the oppressed have little hope in ending injustice and achieving real peace. Our sixty-two years of experience with Zionist colonial oppression and apartheid have shown us that unless we resist by all means that are harmonious with international law—particularly civil resistance—in order to force Israel into a pariah status in the world, like that of South Africa in the 1980s, there is no chance of advancing the prospects for a just peace.

Finally, you have argued numerous times in your published works that ultimately you would like to see in historic Palestine a binational, secular, democratic state . . .

Not a *binational* state! I am completely against "binationalism" in our context. A secular, democratic state yes, but not binational. There is a big difference.

OK, so maybe you can clarify that for me—a secular, democratic state in which Palestinians and Israeli Jews can live together with equal rights under the law. Israeli policy that has rendered a viable two-state solution unlikely and the so-called international consensus aside, what exactly is the sentiment on the ground in Palestine on this question?

OK, first I must clarify that the BDS movement takes no position on the shape of the political solution. It adopts a rights-based, not a solution-based, approach. In other words, the BDS movement is neutral on the one-state, two-state debate. It is largely a consensus movement among Palestinians, focusing on our three fundamental rights, which very few Palestinians disagree with.

On a personal level, not as a representative of the BDS movement, I have for over twenty-five years consistently supported the secular democratic unitary state solution in historic Palestine, based on justice and full equality. I am categorically against binationalism as a solution for the question of Palestine, for several moral and logical reasons that would take me too long to explain.[12] Let me just give a primary reason. The binational model assumes that there are two nations with equal and competing moral claims to the land, and therefore we have to accommodate both national rights.

I prefer to stick to the model I support, which is a secular, democratic state: one person, one vote—regardless of ethnicity, religion, nationality, gender, and so on and so forth—full equality under the law with the inclusion of the refugees (this must be based on the right of return for Palestinian refugees to their homes of origin, per UN resolutions). In other words, I am calling for a secular, democratic state that can reconcile our *inalienable* rights as indigenous Palestinians with the *acquired* rights of Israeli Jews as colonial settlers, once they've shed their colonial character and privileges and accepted justice and international law.

Why do I see this as the most moral and sustainable solution? It's ethically superior, in my view, because it treats people as equal humans. The two-state solution is not only impossible to achieve now—

Israel has made it an absolute pipe dream that cannot happen—but also, crucially, an *immoral* solution. At best, it would address some of the rights of Palestinians in the occupied West Bank and Gaza, a mere one-third of the Palestinan people, while ignoring the majority of Palestinians—those in exile, the refugees, as well as the Palestinian citizens of Israel. There are three segments of the Palestinian people; unless the basic requirements of justice for all three segments are guaranteed, as the BDS Call and entire campaign insists, we shall not have exercised our right to self-determination. The only way that we can exercise our right to self-determination, without imposing unnecessary injustice on our oppressors, is to have a secular, democratic state where nobody is thrown into the sea, nobody is sent back to Poland, and nobody is left suffering in refugee camps. We can coexist ethically with our inalienable rights given back to us, and everyone's and every community's rights are safeguarded and promoted.

Now on the ground—back to your question—there is no political party in Palestine now or among Palestinians in exile calling for a secular, democratic state solution. Despite this, polls in the occupied West Bank and Gaza in the last few years have consistently shown some 25–30 percent support for a secular, democratic state.

Two polls in 2007 showed two-thirds majority support for a single-state solution in all flavors—some of them think of a purely Palestinian state without Israelis, for example. In exile, the percentage of support for one state is much higher, because the main issue is that refugees in particular, and people fighting for refugee rights as I am, know that you cannot practically reconcile the right of return for refugees with a *negotiated* two-state solution, as Israel will never accede to it. It must be *compelled* to accept applying international law in this regard, as apartheid South Africa was. That is the big elephant in the room, and people are ignoring it. Realizing the UN-stipulated right of return and reparation for Palestinian refugees would radically transform Israel from an ethnocentric, racist Jewish state to a true democracy based on justice and equality. The right of return is a basic individual and collective right that cannot be given away and is not voided by the passing of time; it's inalienable.

A two-state solution was never moral, and it's no longer practically attainable either—it's impossible with all the Israeli colonies and structures of control. So we need to move on to the more moral solution that treats everyone as equal under the law, whether they are Jewish Israelis or Palestinians.

You hear a lot of academics and public intellectuals—including those opposed to the occupation—saying that the two-state solution represents the "international consensus," and that the one-state solution of the kind you speak of is unrealistic. How do you respond?

The siege of Gaza is also an expression of "international consensus" of sorts, a consensus of the world's hegemonic powers, not the peoples'; still, that doesn't make it right. It's an international conspiracy of complicity and silence; it is a war crime, indeed a crime against humanity, despite support from the US-controlled UN and all the powers that be around the world. It's quite peculiar—and unfortunate—for activists, and public intellectuals who are counted as activists, to support the international consensus when they like to and oppose it on every other account. Opposing the Indonesian occupation of East Timor and calling for its independence from it at a time when there was an international consensus supporting Indonesia is a case in point. Progressive intellectuals the world over are not supposed to be fettered by some illusion of "international community," which effectively means the United States, the European Union, and their satellites.

So "international consensus" often means that the main powers agree to perpetuate an unjust order because it fits their interests. That doesn't mean we have to accept that; we have to struggle to change it, and the way we do that is on the ground. By proposing the more moral solution, we are saying that this can mobilize universal support from around the world—except from those who are keen to maintain Israel as a racist, ethnocentric state, or an evolved apartheid.

BOYCOTTING ISRAELI SETTLEMENT PRODUCTS

TACTIC VERSUS STRATEGY

A spate of news reports in 2008 on international companies moving out of the occupied Palestinian territory (OPT) to locations inside pre-1967 Israeli borders gave the impression that boycotting products originating in illegal Israeli colonies is on its way to becoming mainstream, handing the growing Boycott, Divestment and Sanctions (BDS) movement a fresh, substantial victory. While this development should indeed be celebrated by BDS activists everywhere, caution is called for in distinguishing between advocating such a targeted boycott as a *tactic*, leading to the ultimate goal of boycotting all Israeli goods and services, and advocating such a targeted boycott as the ultimate *strategy*. While the former may be necessary in some countries as a convenient and practical tool to raise awareness and promote debate about Israel's colonial and apartheid regime, the latter, despite its lure, would be in direct contradiction with the stated objectives of the Palestinian boycott movement.

In 2008, the Swedish company Assa Abloy heeded appeals from the Church of Sweden and other prominent Swedish organizations[1] and decided to move its Mul-T-Lock door factory from the industrial zone of the illegal Israeli colony of Barkan in the occupied West Bank to an as yet unannounced location inside Israel. In a thinly veiled warning, the Swedish NGO Diakonia, which led civil society efforts to bring about Assa Abloy's abandonment of the Barkan industrial colony, had stated that "international humanitarian and human rights laws primarily set out obligations for state actors. Under the principle of individual criminal responsibility, however, individuals—also CEOs of companies—can be held individually responsible for certain grave violations of international law, including war crimes."

Assa Abloy actually followed the lead of Barkan Wineries, a partially Dutch-owned company that had already left Barkan to Kibbutz Hulda.[2] The fact that part of this kibbutz sits on top of an ethnically cleansed Palestinian village (whose name, Khulda, the kibbutz had—typically—appropriated) was apparently not viewed as worthy to be mentioned in the documents that had initially accused the wine maker of wrongdoing under international law and some nevertheless welcomed its rectification of that infringement when it moved to the kibbutz.[3] This inconsistency raises serious questions about the commitment of some human rights and other civil society organizations to the *comprehensive* application of international law, not its selective application only to convenient cases that are acceptable to the—usually Western—funders, with their restrictive political agendas.

Moreover, in a noteworthy precedent, the *Independent* reports that the British government has angered Israeli officials by its decision to "crack down on exports from Israeli settlements," based on the fact that Israel has persistently violated its trade agreements with the European Union, which provide tariff exemptions only for goods produced within Israel, not those produced in the occupied Palestinian territory (OPT).[4] Conforming to UN resolutions and international law, the United Kingdom and its EU partners, along with almost the entire so-called international community, consider Israeli settlements illegal, even a war crime, according to the Fourth Geneva Convention, and therefore ostensibly refuse to extend any tariff privileges to their products.

In reality, though, EU countries have for decades looked the other way while Israel exported its colonies' products as produce of Israel.

According to an article in *Haaretz* on the background to this unfolding trade row between Israel and the United Kingdom—and potentially the whole European Union—Israel had agreed, in past disputes with the European Union, to indicate on products exported to the EU countries the geographic origin of its goods. Britain, however, charges that "Israeli companies located in settlements try to get around the agreement by registering company offices within the Green Line,"[5] effectively obfuscating the lines distinguishing settlement products from other Israeli products and thereby breaching clauses in its agreements with the EU that specifically target the former.

Following intensive pressure from British and Palestinian human rights groups as well as from a fast-spreading—and quite promising—boycott campaign against Israel in the United Kingdom that reached the ivory tower of the academy as well as the largest trade unions, it seems that the British government is finally taking note of Israel's most obvious and unmistakable illegal practices and trying—albeit still lukewarmly—to work with its partners to put an end to them.

This evolving, commendable British policy, actually a belated recognition of the need to respect and implement a long-approved European policy, shows that the position advocated by the Palestinian Boycott, Divestment and Sanctions (BDS) campaign to boycott *all* Israeli products is not only morally but also pragmatically sound. At a most basic level, the BDS campaign's ceiling of demands should aim to be rather higher than that of the British government.

In fact, while the Palestinian BDS movement has consistently expressed its deep appreciation for every effort to treat Israel as apartheid South Africa was, it views the approach of focusing on banning only settlement products as the ultimate goal—rather than as a first, convenient step toward a general Israeli products boycott—as problematic, practically, politically, and morally.

At a practical level, as argued above, Israel has made it extremely difficult to differentiate between settlement and other Israeli products, simply because the majority of parent companies are based inside Israel or because colony-based companies have official addresses there. Most organic Israeli products, for instance, are produced in the illegal colonies in the OPT, but are labeled as products of Israel since the companies that *sell* them are based inside Israel, and that's where the final packaging (the last phase of the production process) is often done. This type of deception is common, especially since Israel is well aware that it is violating the EU-Israel trade agreement and is doing its best to get around the restrictions included in it. The only reason Israel has managed to get away with such blatant violation for so long is not technical but political: shameful—and, unfortunately, quite typical—EU official complacency and treatment of Israel as a state above the law of nations.

Still, some genuine supporters of Palestinian rights may argue, it is much easier to continue to target settlement products with boycotts, as there is a consensus of sorts on the illegality of the settlements, whereas the same cannot be said about other Israeli injustices that would motivate a more comprehensive boycott, as urged in the Palestinian BDS Call. Even if one were to accept this pragmatic argument, the fact that Israel has failed to distinguish between settlement products and other Israeli products should justify—at a tactical level—advocating a boycott of all Israeli products and services, at least until Israel adequately complies with the EU requirement of labeling settlement products clearly and accurately.

Politically speaking, though, and even if distinguishing between produce of settlements and produce of Israel were possible, activists who on principle—rather than out of convenience—advocate a boycott of *only* the former may argue that they are merely objecting to the Israeli military occupation and colonization of 1967 and have no further problems with Israel. In other words, the fact that Israel is a state that practices apartheid, or institutionalized racial discrimination, against its own "non-Jewish" citizens and denies Palestinian refugee rights, sanctioned by the UN, does not raise their interest or burden their conscience. They seem content with supporting most of the rights of a mere one-third of the Palestinian people, ignoring the basic rights of the other two-thirds. Even if one ignores those other grave injustices committed by Israel, and irrespective of what solution to this entire oppression any of us may uphold, one cannot but recognize the inherent flaws in this argument.

When a state X occupies another "state" Y and persistently violates UN resolutions calling for an end to this occupation, the international community often punishes X and not some manifestation of X's occupation. Governments aside, international civil society organizations have repeatedly boycotted entire states implicated in prolonged belligerent occupation, apartheid, or other severe human rights violations, and not just parts of those states. Was there ever a movement calling for boycotting the bantustans alone in South Africa? Are there calls for boycotting only the Sudanese army, or government officials and companies present in Darfur today? Did any of the free-Tibet activists ever call for boycotting only those Chinese products made in Tibet?

As far as the legal dimension is concerned, the state of Israel, without doubt, bears full legal responsibility for its persistent infringements of international law. The eminent international law expert—and current UN special rapporteur for human rights in the occupied Palestinian territories—Professor Richard Falk lucidly makes this point.

> From an international law perspective the broader view of Israel's responsibility for violations of international law is also beyond serious

debate. In this respect, to single out the settlements has no particular relevance from the perspective of international law. The comprehensive blockade maintained by Israel in relation to Gaza since mid-2007 or the recurrent practice of house demolitions are shocking instances of collective punishment in direct violation of Geneva Convention IV, Article 33, and arguably of a more serious character from a humanitarian perspective and carried out directly by the Israel Occupation Forces or other official instruments of the Israeli government. The Government of Israel is clearly responsible for such practices, and many others, and should be held accountable under international law. For a civil society campaign to seek a boycott of Israeli official institutions or divestment from corporations doing profitable business in Israel, especially if in some way related to the occupation, is entirely appropriate, and arguably, is a civic duty supportive of the implementation of international law. . . .

The prevailing [legal] view is that all such [BDS] activities are consistent with international law and the legal positions repeatedly adopted by the United Nations. In light of the persistence and severity of the Israeli violation of fundamental Palestinian rights for a period of over sixty years, and given the failure of the United Nations and the governments of the world to implement Palestinian rights, it is politically and morally appropriate, as well as legally correct, to accord maximum support to the BDS campaign.[6]

Forgetting for the moment the fact that Israel was born out of ethnic cleansing of a majority of the Palestinian people and the systematic destruction of the indigenous Palestinian society, Israel is the state, the legal entity, that built and is fully responsible for maintaining the illegal Jewish colonies. Why should anyone punish the settlements and not Israel? This hardly makes any sense, politically speaking. Despite their noble intentions, people of conscience supporting peace and justice in Palestine who accept this distinction are effectively accommodating Israeli exceptionalism, or Israel's status as a state above the law.

Finally, and most crucially, there is a moral problem that must be addressed in this approach. Ignoring Israel's denial of refugee rights and its system of racial discrimination against its "non-Jewish" citizens, the two other fundamental injustices listed in the BDS Call, is tantamount to accepting these two grave—certainly not any less evil—violations of human rights and international law as givens, or things that "we can live with." Well, *we* cannot. Why should the European civil society that fought apartheid in South Africa accept apartheid in Israel as normal, tolerable, or unquestionable? Holocaust guilt cannot morally justify European complicity in prolonging the suffering, bloodshed, and decades-old injustice that Israel has visited upon Palestinians and Arabs in general, using the Nazi genocide as pretext.

This whole paradigm needs to be challenged, not accepted as common wisdom.

Therefore, wherever necessary in a particular context, advocating a boycott of settlement produce should be only a first, relatively easy step toward a full boycott of all Israeli products and services. It cannot be the final goal of activists committed to international law and human rights in a morally consistent way.

14

OUR SOUTH AFRICA MOMENT HAS ARRIVED

As Israel shifts steadily to the fanatic, racist right, as 2009 parliamentary election results have shown, Palestinians under its control are increasingly being brutalized by its escalating colonial and apartheid policies, designed to push them out of their homeland to make a self-fulfilling prophecy out of the old Zionist canard "a land without a people." In parallel, international civil society, according to numerous indicators, is reaching a turning point in its view of Israel as a pariah state acting above the law of nations and in its effective action, accordingly, to penalize and ostracize Israel as it did to apartheid South Africa.

Palestinian communities in Jerusalem, Jaffa, Hebron, the Jordan Valley, and the Naqab (Negev), among others, have been recently subjected to some of the worst ongoing Israeli campaigns of gradual ethnic cleansing intended to "Judaize" their space.[1] Qalqilya is suffocated by the colonial apartheid wall that surrounds it almost from all sides, while Nablus is often subjected to prolonged siege. In October 2008 the Palestinian community in Acre was brutally attacked by Jewish-Israeli fundamentalists and xenophobes in one of the worst pogroms witnessed by Palestinians inside Israel in recent memory.[2]

Still, Gaza today stands out as *the* test of our common humanity and of our indispensable morality. A thorough analysis of the role played by Western and some Arab governments in relation to Israel's criminal war of aggression against Gaza will demonstrate a resounding failure on both accounts. Throughout the atrocious assault, the official West, the governments of Egypt and Saudi Arabia, the Ramallah-based Palestinian Authority leadership, and the obsequious UN leadership[3] were willing accomplices in Israel's grave violations of international law and basic human rights.

In words that can quite accurately be used to describe Israel, Robert Kagan, a leading neoconservative ideologue, once justified US hegemonic tendencies as a prerogative of the mightiest: "The United States remains mired in history, exercising power in the anarchic Hobbesian world where international laws and rules are unreliable and where true security and the defense and promotion of a liberal order still depend on the possession and use of military might."[4] True to this paradigm, Israel has for decades maintained a regime of occupation, colonization, and apartheid over the indigenous people of Palestine through the "possession and use of military might," in addition to the requisite collusion of Western powers, whose unconditional largesse has for six decades enabled Israel to maintain and develop its multifaceted system of colonial oppression against the Palestinian people.

By contributing to Israel's illegal blockade of Gaza and its criminal war against it, the European Union and other Western states have reached a qualitatively different stage of complicity, becoming, more blatantly than ever, full partners in the US-Israeli policy of undermining the rule of law and espousing in its stead the law of the jungle, thereby promoting the Bush–Bin Laden self-fulfilling prophecy of a dichotomous world divided surgically into good and evil, with each side regarding the other as evil.

In response to this fatal alliance of savage capitalism in the West with Israeli racism, exclusion, and colonial subjugation, the global movement for boycott, divestment, and sanctions (BDS) against Israel presents not only a progressive, antiracist,[5] sophisticated, sustainable, moral, and effective form of civil nonviolent resistance but also a real chance of becoming the political catalyst and moral anchor for a strengthened, reinvigorated international social movement capable of reaffirming the rights of all humans to freedom, equality, and dignity and the right of nations to self-determination.

Gaza: The West's Complicity in War Crimes

As early as 2007, Richard Falk, a prominent international law expert at Princeton University and the current UN special rapporteur for human rights in the occupied Palestinian territories (OPT), called the Western-supported Israeli siege of Gaza a prelude to "genocide"[6] and, later, "a Holocaust in the making."[7] Falk, who happens to be Jewish, argued that the siege is especially disturbing because it vividly expresses "a deliberate intention on the part of Israel and its allies to subject an entire human community to life-endangering conditions of utmost cruelty."[8]

Using more discreet language, Sara Roy, a Harvard University expert on development in the OPT, accuses the European Union, along with the United States, of complicity in a deliberate Israeli policy of "de-development" of the OPT, killing any possibility of creating an independent and sovereign Palestinian state. By providing the Palestinians with "tangible benefits such as higher income and improved infrastructure," Roy argues, the European Union was hoping to buy Palestinian support for substantial concessions in the so-called peace negotiations. She concludes, "The logic of international law was abandoned in the interest of maintaining a failed political process."[9]

An examination of the Israeli siege of Gaza, most of whose population are refugees forcibly displaced[10] by Zionist militias—and later
the state of Israel—during the 1948 Nakba, can elucidate this "de-
development" policy, which amounts to collective punishment, as
most legal experts agree. During this ongoing siege, which started as
early as 2006, more than 80 percent of the 1.5 million Palestinians
caged within the world's "largest open-air prison" have been pushed
into poverty and dependency on international humanitarian assistance;[11] the entire economic infrastructure has been systematically
decimated, with more than 95 percent of the factories forced to shut
down,[12] driving poverty and unemployment above sub-Saharan
African levels; educational institutions have been unable to function
properly due to lack of fuel and electricity for prolonged periods, as
well as the lack of construction material needed to build schools to
meet the rising demand, a fact that has denied forty thousand Gaza
students enrollment in the UN school system for the school year
2010–11;[13] the health care system is on the verge of collapse, and
hundreds of patients in need of critical health care, particularly cancer and kidney patients, have died after being denied access to medical facilities outside Gaza.

The longer-term effects of the siege are even more daunting.[14] According to the World Health Organization, chronic malnutrition and
dietary-related diseases have alarmingly increased, resulting in rampant low birth weights; anemia in more than two-thirds of all children
of age one year and younger; and stunted growth among children
under age five, reaching 30 percent in parts of northern Gaza.[15] Moreover, preventable diseases, caused by polluted water and inadequate
sewage processing, started spreading wildly. Thousands, mainly children, have suffered "anxiety attacks, bedwetting, muscle spasms, temporary loss of hearing and breathing difficulties," according to a UN
report, due to Israel's concentrated use of sonic booms for weeks on

end, a policy described by a senior Israeli army intelligence source as "intended to break civilian support for armed Palestinian groups."[16]

A whole generation of Palestinian children in Gaza will suffer severe developmental and psychological disorders for many years to come, authoritative health studies have shown.[17] Field reports also point to a significant increase in the already-high rate of incidences of cancer and other deadly diseases directly related to Israeli-inflicted pollution and health care denial.

Reacting to the devastating impact of Israel's siege, Karen Koenig AbuZayd, the commissioner-general of the United Nations Relief and Works Agency for Palestine Refugees in the Near East (UNRWA), warned:

> Gaza is on the threshold of becoming the first territory to be intentionally reduced to a state of abject destitution with the knowledge, acquiescence and—some would say—encouragement of the international community. . . . Humanitarian and human development work was never meant to function in an environment devoid of constructive efforts to resolve conflict or to address its underlying causes. Indeed, humanitarian work is profoundly undermined in a context where there is implicit or active complicity in creating conditions of mass suffering.[18]

It is this aspect of the siege, the processes leading to the slow death of masses of people and to inhibiting the development of a generation of Palestinian children, that prompted Falk's eye-opening description of Israel's siege as constituting acts of genocide.

Former Israeli education minister Shulamit Aloni warned years ago of exactly that. As early as 2003, she condemned an Israeli atrocity that pales in comparison with the Israeli massacres just committed in Gaza, saying: "So it's not yet genocide of the terrible and unique style of which we were past victims. And as one of the smart [Israeli] Generals told me, we do not have crematoria and gas chambers. Is anything less than that consistent with Jewish ethics? Did he ever hear how an entire people said that it did not know what was done in its name?"[19]

And that was before Operation Cast Lead, Israel's rolling massacre in Gaza.

According to respected human rights organizations active in the field, Israel's twenty-three-day military offensive starting on December 27, 2008, led to the deaths of more than 1,400 Palestinians, approximately 83 percent of whom are civilians,[20] and to the partial or complete destruction of thousands of homes; the leading university; forty-five mosques; the Palestinian Legislative Council and several ministries, including those of education and justice;[21] scores of schools;[22] a Red Crescent Hospital and dozens of ambulances[23] and clinics; and thousands of factories and small businesses. Several massacres were committed and well documented.[24] The International Committee of the Red Cross accused Israel, in an unusually sharp tone, of failing to provide medical care to the injured and impeding medical relief from reaching them, thereby causing their bleeding to death, both severe violations of international humanitarian law.[25] More than 430 Palestinian children were killed in the three-week-long Israeli bombing,[26] some due to burns caused by Israel's illegal use of phosphorous bombs.

On the opening day of its assault on Gaza, the Israeli military caused massive destruction of civilian infrastructure and massacred close to two hundred Palestinian civilians, many of whom were noncombatant police trainees, while no Israeli civilians were reportedly killed. Nevertheless, Western leaders were quick to issue statements expressing concern about the loss of life and suffering "on both sides," blaming the Palestinian resistance for provoking the atrocities, and absolving Israel of any responsibility under the pretext of its "right to defend itself."

Leading international jurists, however, categorically rejected Israel's self-defense argument, accusing it of committing war crimes.[27] The UN

Human Rights Council and the UN secretary general have called for impartial, independent war crimes investigations. Amnesty International,[28] Human Rights Watch,[29] even the main Israeli human rights organization,[30] B'Tselem,[31] the International Federation for Human Rights (FIDH), Oxfam, and the Euro-Mediterranean Human Rights Network,[32] among many others, have similarly accused Israel of committing war crimes, effectively refuting its self-defense claim—particularly since it was Israel that first violated the June 2008 ceasefire with Hamas on November 4, when it attacked and killed six resistance fighters without any provocation.[33]

Gerald Kaufman, a senior Jewish Labor Party member of the British Parliament, compared some Israeli actions to those of Nazis.[34] So did Noam Chomsky[35] and Holocaust survivor and senior academic Hajo Meyer,[36] of A Different Jewish Voice in the Netherlands. Echoing Kaufman, Chomsky, and Meyer, prominent Jewish British intellectuals and academics compared Gaza to the Warsaw Ghetto in a letter to the *Guardian*,[37] as did the International Jewish Anti-Zionist Network (IJAN) on Holocaust Remembrance Day in 2009.[38]

Israel's Other Colonial and Apartheid Policies

Gaza aside, Palestinian civil society and a growing number of influential human rights advocates recognize that Israel's regime over the indigenous people of Palestine constitutes occupation, colonization, and apartheid. Specifically, Israel's decades-old oppression takes three basic forms, which were at the core of the Palestinian BDS Call:

1. the prolonged occupation and colonization of Gaza and the West Bank, including East Jerusalem, and other Arab territories

2. the legalized and institutionalized *system* of racial discrimination against Palestinian citizens of Israel

3. the persistent denial of the UN-sanctioned rights of Palestinian refugees, paramount among which is their right to reparations and to
   return to their homes of origin, in accordance with UNGA Resolution 194

Palestinian civil society has expressed its belief that ending these three forms of oppression is the minimal requirement to achieve a just peace in our region.

The most important of all three injustices is without a doubt Israel's denial of the right of Palestinian refugees to return. The core of the question of Palestine has always been the plight of the refugees who were ethnically cleansed during the Nakba. The fact that refugees form a majority of the Palestinian people, coupled with their sixty-plus-year suffering in exile, makes the recognition of their basic rights, including their right to reparations and return to their homes of origin, *the litmus test of morality* for anyone suggesting a just and enduring solution to the Palestinian-Israeli conflict. Moral and legal rights aside, the denial of Palestinian refugee rights guarantees the perpetuation of conflict.[39]

Israel's repressive and racist policies in the 1967-occupied Palestin-ian territory have been recognized as constituting apartheid by a host of opinion leaders such as Archbishop Desmond Tutu, former US president Jimmy Carter, and former UN special rapporteur for human rights John Dugard. In the same vein, former Israeli attorney general Michael Ben-Yair wrote in a 2002 *Haaretz* article describing Israel's regime in the OPT, "We enthusiastically chose to become a colonial society, ignoring international treaties, expropriating lands, transferring settlers from Israel to the occupied territories, engaging in theft and finding justification for all these activities. . . . In effect, we established an apartheid regime in the occupied territories."[40]

However, the applicability of the crime of apartheid as defined in UN conventions to Israel itself has, for the most part, been either in-advertently glossed over or intentionally ignored as an explosive subject that has every potential to invite the vengeful wrath of powerful pro-Israel lobbies. Regardless, one cannot but examine the facts and analyze Israel's system of governance accordingly.

The strongest argument given by—sometimes well-meaning—experts who dismiss the *apartheid* label for Israel is that the "analogy" between Israel and South Africa is not exact and in many respects Israel's oppression is even more severe, demanding a different designation altogether. The problem with this argument is that it assumes, incorrectly, that apartheid is a South African trademark and therefore that every regime accused of practicing apartheid must be shown to be identical to South Africa's apartheid regime of yesteryear. Apartheid, however, although brought to world attention and given its name by the racist regime in South Africa, has for decades been recognized by the United Nations as a generalized crime with a universal definition.

The Convention on the Suppression and Punishment of the Crime of Apartheid that went into force in 1976 defines apartheid as "similar policies and practices of racial segregation and discrimination as practised in southern Africa" which have "the purpose of establishing and maintaining domination by one racial group of persons over any other racial group of persons and systematically oppressing them, in particular by means such as segregation, expropriation of land, and denial of the right to leave and return to their country, the right to a nationality and the right to freedom of movement and residence" (article 2).[41] The similarity to South Africa is cited not as a condition but in recognition of its status as a historic precedent. Furthermore, the 2002 Rome Statute of the International Criminal Court defines the crime of apartheid as "inhumane acts . . . committed in the context of an institutionalized regime of systematic oppression and domination by one racial group over any other racial group or groups and committed with the intention of maintaining that regime."[42]

As a 2008 in-depth strategic position paper published by the Palestinian BDS National Committee (BNC) states, Israel's origins, laws, and policies against the Palestinian people fit to a large extent the definition of apartheid.[43] The conceptual origins of Israel's unique form of apartheid are found in political Zionism, a racist European ideology that was adopted by the dominant stream of the Zionist movement (World Zionist Organization, Jewish Agency, Jewish National Fund, among others) in order to justify and recruit political support for its colonial project of establishing an exclusive Jewish state in historic Palestine. Political Zionists dismissed the indigenous population of Palestine as nonexistent, as expressed in the famous Zionist slogan describing Palestine as "a land without a people"; making this a self-fulfilling prophecy, starting toward the end of 1947, Zionist forces and later the state of Israel forcibly displaced between 750,000 and 900,000 Palestinians from their homeland and destroyed hundreds of the depopulated Palestinian villages in an operation termed "cleaning the landscape" that lasted until 1960.[44]

Israel's regime over the Palestinian people amounts to apartheid precisely because it displays many of the main features of the crime as defined by international law:

1. Racial discrimination against the indigenous Palestinian people who became citizens of the state of Israel was formalized and institutionalized through the creation by law of a "Jewish nationality" that is distinct from Israeli citizenship. No "Israeli" nationality exists in Israel, and the Supreme Court has persistently refused to recognize one, as it would end the system of Jewish supremacy in Israel. The 1950 Law of Return entitles all Jews—and only Jews—to the rights of nationals, namely the right to enter "Eretz Yisrael" (Israel and the OPT) and immediately enjoy full legal and political rights. "Jewish nationality" under the Law of Return is extraterritorial in contravention of

international public law norms pertaining to nationality. It includes Jewish citizens of other countries, irrespective of whether they wish to be part of the collective of "Jewish nationals," and excludes "non-Jews" (i.e., Palestinians) from nationality rights in Israel.

2. The 1952 Citizenship Law[45] has created a discriminatory two-tier legal system whereby Jews hold nationality and citizenship while indigenous Palestinian citizens hold only citizenship.[46] Under Israeli law the status of Jewish nationality is accompanied with first-class rights and benefits not granted to Palestinian citizens.

3. The Israeli Status Law of 1952 authorizes the World Zionist Organization / Jewish Agency and its subsidiaries, including the Jewish National Fund, to control most of the land in Israel for the exclusive benefit of Jews. In 1998 the Committee on Economic, Social and Cultural Rights (CESCR) expressed grave concern about this law and stated that large-scale and systematic confiscation of Palestinian land and property by the state and the transfer of that property to these agencies constitute an institutionalized form of discrimination, because these agencies by definition would deny the use of these properties to non-Jewish citizens of the state.[47]

4. The return of Palestinian refugees and internally displaced persons (IDPs), as required by international law, has been prevented by means of force and legislation on racist grounds. Simply because they are not Jews, Palestinian refugees were excluded from entitlement to citizenship in the state of Israel under the 1952 Citizenship Law. They were "denationalized" and turned into stateless refugees in violation of the law of state succession. Their land and other property were confiscated by the state. The approximately 150,000 Palestinians who remained in Israel after the 1948 Nakba were placed under a military regime (1948–66) similar to the regime currently in place in the OPT.

For decades, racial discrimination against Palestinian citizens of Israel in every vital aspect of life has been the norm. From land ownership to education to health to jobs to housing, the indigenous Palestinians have been denied equality by the state's laws and policies. For instance, they are not allowed to buy or rent land in about 93 percent of the state lands of Israel.[48] To date, polls consistently show overwhelming majorities of Israeli Jews standing in opposition to full equality with the indigenous Palestinians in the state.[49] The fact that those Palestinians can vote, unlike their black African counterparts under South African apartheid, becomes almost a formality, a tokenism of sorts, clearly designed to project a deceptive image of democracy and fend off well-justified accusations of apartheid.[50]

The complicity of Western governments in these horrific and persistent violations of international law and basic human rights has led many analysts to view the role of the West as profoundly flawed, both morally and legally. The entrenched impunity enjoyed by Israel has allowed it to project itself and to act as an uncontrollable "mad dog"—an image advocated by Moshe Dayan decades ago and endorsed most recently by Israeli military historian Martin Van Creveld[51]—in an attempt to make the Palestinians submit to its colonial will, to accept slavery as fate.

This criminal impunity and categorical denial of rights, more than anything else, were the main motivation behind the Palestinian BDS campaign. Israel's state terrorism in Gaza, enabled by virtually unlimited support from the United States and from Western governments in general, was a key catalyst in spreading and deepening BDS around the world, leading advocates of Palestinian rights to feel that our South Africa moment has finally arrived. Israel is now widely perceived, at a grassroots level, as an international pariah that commits war crimes with impunity and that needs to be held accountable to international law and basic principles of human rights.

The few weeks following Cast Lead witnessed some of the most significant indicators of the spectacular spread of BDS. Part of the Canadian Union of Public Employees (CUPE), Ontario's University Workers Coordinating Committee (OUWCC) at its annual conference last February endorsed a boycott of Israeli academic institutions.[52] The Fédération autonome du collégial (FAC), Quebec College Federation, also joined the BDS campaign.[53] In Durban, South Africa, the COSATU (Congress of South African Trade Unions)–affiliated dockworkers' union, SATAWU (South African Transport and Allied Workers' Union), refused in early February to offload an Israeli cargo ship,[54] reminding us of similar sanctions taken against South African ships during the apartheid era. An Australian dockworkers' union and a group of American progressive union leaders endorsed the South African BDS action. In the United States, Hampshire College set a historic precedent by announcing its divestment from six companies profiting from the Israeli occupation.[55] Significantly, Hampshire was also the first US college to divest from apartheid South Africa in the 1970s. In Wales, Cardiff University acceded to demands by students and decided to divest from companies supporting the occupation.[56] Even in France, where BDS had faced an uphill struggle for several years, a statement was issued by leading academics explicitly endorsing BDS to end Israel's impunity.[57]

The latest spectacular entrenchment of the BDS campaign, especially since the Israeli aggression against Gaza, gives us hope that one day Israel's impunity and Western, UN, and Arab collusion with it will come to an end, allowing a genuine, just peace to flourish in Palestine and the entire region. Only thus can ethical coexistence have a real chance to be realized.

In his poem "Message to the Living" Henk van Randwijk, a Dutch poet of resistance against the Nazis, wrote:

> *A people giving in to tyrants*
> *will lose more than body and goods*
> *the light will be extinguished*

On Saturday, January 24, 2009, merely days after the end of Israeli hostilities and despite all the death, devastation, and trauma, hundreds of thousands of Gaza's children almost literally rose from under the rubble that most of Gaza was reduced to and walked eagerly to their damaged schools, carrying their torn bags, scarred books, and injured souls. Their agony was deep, their anger deeper, but their eyes were still shining with defiance, ambition, and hope for emancipation. BDS empowers Palestinians and supporters of just peace worldwide to nourish and eventually realize that hope.

Based on a presentation given at Canadian universities as part of Israeli Apartheid Week in 2009.

AFTER THE FREEDOM FLOTILLA ATROCITY: BDS TAKES OFF

Moshe Dayan, Israel's most celebrated general, once said, "Israel must be like a mad dog, too dangerous to bother."[1] Israel has indeed achieved that peculiar status of deterrence at the level of states; but with its bloodbath on the Gaza-bound Freedom Flotilla on May 31, 2010, it is increasingly being perceived in international public opinion as too menacing and lawless to ignore. Calls for holding Israel accountable, including by applying punitive measures, have risen sharply.

What was dubbed Israel's "Flotilla Massacre" of humanitarian relief workers and peace activists was not only categorically immoral and patently illegal but undeniably irrational too. It is swelling the global ranks of those who support boycott, divestment, and sanctions against Israel until it respects international law and basic human rights. International civil society's tolerance of Israel's impunity, criminality, and "mad dog" deterrence seems to have grown quite thin.

Since July 9, 2005, when the historic Call for Boycott, Divestment and Sanctions (BDS) against Israel was launched by an overwhelming majority of Palestinian unions, political parties, community networks, and NGOs, there has never been a period with as many BDS achievements as the few months following the attack on the flotilla, which rudely awakened a long-dormant sense of international moral responsibility for Israel's exceptional status for decades as a state above the law. World-renowned legal experts, literary giants, top performing artists, major church groups, large trade unions, and many more international civil society organizations, especially in the West, crossed a threshold in their view of Israel and, crucially, in their commitment to challenge its impunity and counter, in diverse forms, its perceived menace to world security.

Israel's subsequent announcement that it would "ease" its siege of the occupied Gaza Strip was met with universal skepticism and outright demands to end the siege altogether. After the flotilla attack, the siege, a form of collective punishment that constitutes a war crime, is seen as unacceptable, unsustainable, or both by almost all world governments. A damning—and rare—report by the International Committee of the Red Cross about the devastating impact of Israel's blockade on the health, environmental, economic, and general developmental conditions of Palestinians in Gaza highlighted the urgency of pressuring Israel to lift the siege completely.[2] News reports on June 25 of Israel's seizing Norwegian-donated life-saving oxygen machines destined for Palestinian hospitals in Gaza as well as the occupied West Bank cannot help but exacerbate international suspicions of Israel's definition of "easing" the siege.[3]

The fact that the flotilla attack was illegal, immoral, and unjustifiable; that it targeted civilian ships in international waters; that it led to the murder and injury of dozens of humanitarian relief workers and civilian activists from many countries; that among the siege-breaking activists were prominent intellectuals, a Nobel Peace laureate, a Holocaust survivor, European and other parliamentarians, a former senior US diplomat, and representatives of international media—all triggered mass anger around the world and unprecedented mainstream calls for treating Israel as a pariah state, including through applying boycotts.

After years of the global BDS campaign's awareness-raising about Israel's multitiered system of oppression and the movement's call for creative practical action to contribute to justice and peace,[4] moral indignation at Israel's latest bloodbath was bound to be channeled into pressure measures that are more effective than the same old demands that have been ignored again and again by Israel and its hegemonic partners. Mahmoud Darwish's famous cry "Besiege your siege" suddenly acquired an entirely different meaning. Since any attempt to convince a colonial power to heed moral pleas for justice or voluntarily give up its privileges is, at best, delusional, many people of conscience felt it was time to end Israel's deadly siege by "besieging" it, by adopting BDS measures to isolate it as a world pariah, thus drastically raising the price of its siege, occupation, and apartheid policies.

Henry Siegman, once a leading figure in the US Jewish establishment, indignantly reacted to the flotilla attack writing in the Israeli daily *Haaretz* newspaper, "A million and a half civilians have been forced to live in an open-air prison in inhuman conditions for over three years now, but unlike the Hitler years, they are not Jews but Palestinians. Their jailers, incredibly, are survivors of the Holocaust, or their descendants. Of course, the inmates of Gaza are not destined for gas chambers, as the Jews were, but they have been reduced to a debased and hopeless existence." Despite the obvious differences between both situations, Siegman argues, "the essential moral issues are the same."[5]

Echoing the same parallels, Israeli academic and human rights advocate Jeff Halper wrote, "In a policy [frighteningly] reminiscent of other dark regimes in which Jews suffered from controlled malnutrition, our government has imposed a regime of 'counting calories' on the Gaza population—imposing a 'minimal dietary regime' on a million and a half people who receive as little as 850 calories a day, less than half the recommended daily intake." Halper cites Dov Weisglass, Ariel Sharon's chief of staff, who joked about this policy: "It's like a meeting with a dietitian. We need to make the Palestinians lose weight, but not to starve to death."[6] Examinations of Israel's attack on the basis of international law have only fueled world anger. Ben Saul, who served on the International Criminal Tribunal for the former Yugoslavia, published an authoritative legal analysis of the flotilla attack. According to the 1988 Rome Convention for the Suppression of Unlawful Acts against the Safety of Maritime Navigation, "One cannot attack a ship and then claim self-defence if the people on board resist the unlawful use of violence." He adds, "Legally speaking, government military forces rappelling onto a ship to illegally capture it are treated no differently than other criminals. The right of self-defence in such situations rests with the passengers on board: a person is legally entitled to resist one's own unlawful capture, abduction and detention." Saul concludes: "This latest sad and shocking episode is a reminder of Israel's recklessness towards the lives of others, its utter disregard for international opinion, and its incivility as an outlaw of the international community."[7] Prominent British legal scholars reached the same conclusion in a letter published in the *Times* of London,[8] and so did leading Dutch international law professors in a letter to *NRC Handelsblad*.[9]

The United Nations response was uncharacteristically firm. The Human Rights Council voted by an overwhelming majority (32–3) to strongly condemn Israel's actions against the flotilla and to organize an independent, international probe into violations of international law resulting from it. Only Italy and the Netherlands joined the United States in voting *against* this simple measure of accountability.[10] Usually cautious not to denounce Israel lest it irk the United States, UN Secretary General Ban Ki-Moon and his top assistants condemned the attack and called on Israel to immediately end its illegal siege of Gaza.[11] But, as expected, the clearest and most principled voice in the UN officialdom was that of the special rapporteur for human rights in the occupied Palestinian territories, Richard Falk, who stated, "It is essential that those Israelis responsible for this lawless and murderous behavior, including political leaders who issued the orders, be held criminally accountable for their wrongful acts." He added, "The worldwide campaign of boycott, divestment, and sanctions against Israel is now a moral and political imperative, and needs to be supported and strengthened everywhere."[12]

At the official sanctions level, several governments reacted swiftly to the attack. Nicaragua suspended its diplomatic relations with Israel.[13] South Africa recalled its ambassador to Tel Aviv.[14] Turkey recalled its ambassador to Tel Aviv for "consultations,"[15] while the Turkish parliament voted *unanimously* to "revise the political, military and economic relations with Israel" and to "seek justice against Israel through national and international legal authorities"[16]—a move that alarmed Israel considerably given Turkey's status as the second largest importer of Israeli weapons, after India. Norway's minister of education and head of the Socialist Left Party, Kristin Halvorsen, reconfirmed Norway's arms ban on Israel and called all other states to "follow the Norwegian position which excludes trading arms with Israel."[17]

The Palestinian BDS National Committee (BNC), the largest coalition of Palestinian civil society forces supporting the Israel boycott, called on June 1 for intensifying BDS, arguing as follows:

> Israel's impunity is the direct result of the international community's failure to hold it accountable for its ongoing occupation, colonization and apartheid against the Palestinian people. Israel's most recent war crimes committed in Gaza and documented in the Goldstone report as well as crimes committed in 2006 against the Lebanese people did not trigger any UN or official sanctions, entrenching Israel's feeling of being above the law. In fact, Israel's grave violation of international law was recently rewarded when the OECD voted unanimously to accept its membership. The BNC urges international civil society to end this deep and fatal complicity.[18]

Inspired by the historic February 2009 example set by the South African Transport and Allied Workers Union (SATAWU) in Durban when it refused to offload an Israeli ship,[19] the BNC and, a few days later, the entire Palestinian trade union movement called on transport and dockworkers' unions around the world to "block Israeli maritime trade in response to Israel's massacre of humanitarian relief workers and activists aboard the Freedom Flotilla, until Israel complies with international law and ends its illegal blockade of Gaza."[20]

The response from trade unions surpassed all expectations.

SATAWU called upon its members "not to allow any Israeli ship to dock or unload" and urged fellow trade unionists "not to handle them."[21] The Swedish Dockworkers' Union decided to blockade all Israeli ships and cargo to and from Israel[22] and started implementing that week-long boycott on June 23.[23] Indian and Turkish dockworkers' unions followed suit.[24]

The South African trade union federation COSATU, which had played a key role in abolishing apartheid in South Africa, called for "greater support for the international boycott, divestment and sanction campaign against Israel," urging "all South Africans to refuse to buy or *handle* any goods from Israel or have any dealings with Israeli businesses."[25] The South African Municipal Workers Union (SAMWU) unanimously endorsed a motion to immediately work toward making every municipality in South Africa an "Apartheid Israel free zone,"[26] an idea that has begun to inspire BDS activists in Europe and elsewhere.

In the United Kingdom, a key market for Israeli goods, the largest trade union, Unite, at its first policy conference in Manchester unanimously passed a BDS motion to boycott *all* Israeli companies.[27] Unison, the second largest union, reportedly adopted in its 2010 annual conference similar boycott measures, including the suspension of bilateral ties with Histadrut, the Israeli labor entity that justified Israel's flotilla attack just as it had the war of aggression on Gaza earlier.[28] The

British academic union UCU, representing 120,000 members, issued a strong condemnation of the Israeli attack, demanding that "the UK government . . . not change the rules on universal jurisdiction to impede bringing the people responsible for these murders to justice." It is worth mentioning that just a day before the flotilla attack, the UCU had made BDS history when it voted by an overwhelming majority to sever all links with Histadrut.[29]

LO, Norway's largest trade union federation, comprising almost one-fifth of the entire Norwegian population, called on the state pension fund, the third largest sovereign fund in the world, to divest from all Israeli companies.[30] A poll taken after the attack showed more than 42 percent of all Norwegians supporting a comprehensive boycott of Israeli goods.[31]

In the port of Oakland, California, union members and community activists set a historic precedent by blocking the offloading of an Israeli ship for twenty-four hours.[32]

At its annual conference, the Northern Illinois Conference (NIC) of the United Methodist Church (UMC) voted to "divest all holdings in three international corporations that profit from the occupation of Palestine," explaining that "this action is in response to a plea by Palestinian Christians for action, not just words."[33]

With a 79.5 percent majority of the student body supporting it, Evergreen State College in the United States decided to divest[34] from companies that profit from the Israeli occupation, following the precedent-setting decision by Hampshire College[35] in February 2009, in the aftermath of the Israeli atrocities in Gaza.

In the cultural domain the reaction to Israel's attack was no less decisive. Cartoon artist Martin Rowson expressed the shock shared by millions in a cartoon in the *Guardian*. Rowson depicted intimidating, heavily armed Israeli commandos commandeering Noah's ark, incarcerating all the frightened animals, with one of the soldiers cruelly crushing a dead peace dove—olive branch and all—and justifying it to a devastated Noah by saying, "[The dove] was clearly intent on pecking innocent civilians."[36]

Endorsing the widely popular cultural boycott of Israel[37] called for by the Palestinian Campaign for the Academic and Cultural Boycott of Israel (PACBI)[38] since 2004, world-renowned British writer Iain Banks stated in the *Guardian* that the best way for international artists, writers, and academics to "convince Israel of its moral degradation and ethical isolation" is "simply by having nothing more to do with this outlaw state."[39] Stéphane Hessel, coauthor of the Universal Declaration of Human Rights, Holocaust survivor, and former French diplomat, endorsed Banks's position in a *Huffington Post* opinion piece.[40]

The world-renowned Swedish writer, Henning Mankell, who was on the Freedom Flotilla when attacked, called for South Africa–style global sanctions against Israel in response to its brutality.[41]

Drawing on the US civil rights struggle and the boycott against the Montgomery bus company that was triggered by Rosa Parks and championed by Martin Luther King Jr., bestselling author Alice Walker called for wide endorsement of BDS against Israel as a moral duty in solidarity with Palestinians, "to soothe the pain and attend the sorrows of a people wrongly treated for generations."[42]

Dozens of British literary and academic figures published a letter in the *Independent* that said, "We . . . appeal to British writers and scholars to boycott all literary, cultural and academic visits to Israel sponsored by the Israeli government, including those organised by Israeli cultural foundations and universities."[43]

BDS also reached mainstream Western papers. *Aftonbladet*, Sweden's largest tabloid, called on various occasions for a boycott of Israel.[44] A main editorial in the Irish *Sunday Tribune* stated, "The power of a people's movement lies in its ability to challenge national or international policies that are inherently unjust. A boycott of Israeli goods by Irish people may seem like gesture politics, but it could achieve two aims. It would show solidarity with the people of Gaza and it would also register collective displeasure at what the Israelis are doing."[45]

In the high-visibility realm of performing arts, famous bands reacted to the flotilla attack by canceling scheduled gigs in Israel, triggering more introspection among the Israeli public—almost all of which supports the attack and the siege of Gaza—than any other boycott development to date. The Klaxons and Gorillaz Sound System withdrew first,[46] followed by the Pixies.[47] Another cancellation came from US singer-songwriter Devendra Banhart. While holding on to the ill-conceived and historically discredited notion that in a situation of grave violations of human rights, a musician can simply entertain the oppressor community and "share a human not a political message" with them, Banhart justified his withdrawal by saying, "It seems that we are being used to support views that are not our own."[48] Israeli media outlets had tried to portray his scheduled gig as a political message in solidarity with Israel in a time of increasing isolation. A *Washington Post* article titled "Israel's Feeling of Isolation Is Becoming More Pronounced" captured the mood in Israel well.[49] Another article, this time in the leading music-industry publication *Billboard*, also highlighted the growing controversy surrounding performing in Israel in light of the flotilla attack.[50]

In the weeks before the flotilla attack, artists of the caliber of Elvis Costello, Gil Scott-Heron, and Carlos Santana had all canceled scheduled performances in Israel after receiving appeals from Palestinian and international BDS groups.[51] Increasingly Tel Aviv is being compared to the South African resort Sun City, which was boycotted by world artists during apartheid. Today Palestinians and supporters of just peace around the world view any musician who performs in Israel today just as those who violated the boycott against apartheid South Africa, as motivated by personal gain far more than by moral principles. Israel, it is worth noting, offers large sums of money to lure international performers as part of its "Brand Israel" campaign, designed explicitly to hide its violations of human rights and international law under a deceptive guise of artistic and scientific glamour.[52]

Despite the promise of lucrative remuneration, many top artists refuse to perform in Israel. The *Forward,* the leading Jewish daily in New York, cites a "music insider saying that in recent months he had approached more than 15 performing artists with proposals to give concerts in Israel. None had agreed. The contracts offered high levels of compensation. He called them 'extreme, big numbers that could match any other gig.'"[53]

Many cultural figures, well before the flotilla attack, explicitly supported the Palestinian cultural boycott of Israel. A statement by 500 Artists against Apartheid in Montreal is the latest, perhaps most impressive of these efforts.[54] But earlier, in 2006, the famous British author and artist John Berger issued a statement explicitly endorsing the cultural boycott of Israel, collecting ninety-three endorsements from prominent writers and artists.[55] Intellectuals and artists who have endorsed BDS include Ken Loach, Judith Butler, Naomi Klein, the Yes Men, Sarah Schulman, Aharon Shabtai, Udi Aloni, Adrienne Rich, John Williams, and Arundhati Roy, among others.

Some cultural figures have refused to participate in Israel's official celebrations and festivals without explicitly adopting the boycott. In 2008, for instance, countering Israel's "60th Anniversary" celebrations, PACBI collected dozens of signatures of prominent artists and authors for a half-page advertisement that was published in the *International Herald Tribune.*[56] The list included luminaries like Mahmoud Darwish, Augusto Boal, Roger Waters, André Brink, Vincenzo Consolo, and Nigel Kennedy. Some of the signatories on that ad later adopted the boycott explicitly.

A third category is artists who accept invitations to play in Israel and then cancel after being approached by PACBI and its partners around the world, including the Israeli group Boycott from Within, which plays a significant role in convincing performers to stay away from Israel due to its violation of Palestinian rights.[57] This category includes Bono, Björk, Jean-Luc Godard, Snoop Dogg, and others.

Whether in culture, academia, business, or mere image, Israel is feeling the heat as never before. Years of a fast-spreading BDS campaign have caused fury in Israel, prompting twenty-five members of Knesset, including from ruling and opposition parties, to put forth a bill that would criminalize advocating, justifying, or supporting the boycott by Palestinian, Israelis, and internationals alike.[58] This sign of desperation, more than anything else, proves beyond a shadow of doubt that Israel fears the global reach and effectiveness of a well-argued, civil, nonviolent campaign of resistance, especially one based on international law and universal human rights. In many ways it confirms that the "South Africa moment"[59] has arrived for Palestine.

LEADERSHIP, REFERENCE, AND THE ROLE
OF ISRAELI ANTICOLONIALISTS

OMAR BARGHOUTI INTERVIEWED
BY MAXINE KAUFMAN-LACUSTA

Even before I completed the interviews for the collection *Refusing to Be Enemies*, it was clear that the BDS campaign had really taken off. Several interviewees emphasized its importance, some saying it was one of the most important, if not *the* most important, form of support especially for internationals to take up in one form or another. I asked my interviewees in January if they agreed with this point of view (they all did, Palestinian and Israeli alike), though they didn't necessarily all subscribe to the same form of BDS.

From what I heard you say in 2007 in Bil'in and read subsequently, I had the (very positive) impression that although you favor a full response to the original 2005 call, including support for the Palestinian right of return and a very broadly defined boycott of Israel and Israeli enterprises/institutions/cultural events, you also welcome support that is less sweeping. For example, you said in your speech: "To be in effective solidarity with Palestine today is to actively support some form of BDS. This is what the overwhelming majority of Palestinian civil society is calling for. Boycott, divestment, and sanctions, however, do not come in 'one size that fits all.' If the basic premise that Israel needs to be pressured is accepted, then various forms of boycott, divestment, and sanctions can be adapted according to the specific context in each country."

More recently, in an article on the *CounterPunch* website, you stated even more explicitly: "The only true fighters for peace in Israel are those who support our three fundamental rights: the right of return for Palestinian refugees; full equality for the Palestinian citizens of Israel; and ending the occupation and colonial rule. Those are our true partners. They *all* support various forms of BDS. . . . On the other hand, groups that, for tactical reasons, support only a subset of BDS, or a targeted boycott of specific products or organizations in Israel or supporting Israel, are also our partners, of course. Boycott is not a one-size-fits-all type of process. It must be customized to suit a particular context to be most effective. What is important to agree on, though, is why we are boycotting and towards what ends."[1]

So my question to you is whether you still feel this way, or whether you have become more strict in your interpretation of what support for BDS should consist of. Could you clarify?

Context sensitivity is a key principle of the BDS movement that the movement's leadership, the Palestinian BDS National Committee (BNC), takes to heart. BDS is not an ideology or run by a political party; it is a wide movement that brings together groups and individuals of diverse ideological and political backgrounds that converge on the utmost respect for international law and the morally consistent application of human rights to the question of Palestine.

Regarding the BDS movement, it is key to recognize that it is led by Palestinians—the BNC specifically. The BNC is the largest coalition of Palestinian civil society unions, NGOs, political parties, and networks, representing Palestinians in the OPT, inside Israel, and, crucially, Palestinians in exile, who are the majority of the Palestinian people. It is also essential to recognize that the 2005 Palestinian Civil Society Call for BDS is *the* reference for the global BDS movement. Thus the principles, the three basic rights, upon which the movement is based are the same; they constitute the minimal requirements for realizing the Palestinian people's right to self-determination. What differs from location to location according to the political and organizational context is the specific target of the BDS campaign and the tactics used in the local work.

Some allies in BDS campaigns in the West are not fully on board with the BDS Call itself. However, they are active in specific BDS campaigns, and they refrain from contradicting or undermining the BDS Call. We consider them allies in the movement but not yet full strategic partners. The latter need to agree with us, in the BNC, on our principles and comprehensive rights, regardless what action or campaign they undertake to help us achieve them. As I've jokingly said in my talks, even if a partner adopts the BDS Call and then decides to launch a campaign targeting Israeli tomatoes only, we'll gladly view them and work with them as strategic partners. CodePink is a good example of that. They've endorsed the BDS Call and chosen to focus their creative energies on boycotting AHAVA, the Israeli cosmetics company that manufactures in the OPT. Many campaigns in Europe also have a narrow focus in their BDS targets, and that's perfectly fine.

Where we have problems is when any group tries to appropriate the right to set the movement's goals or parameters instead or on behalf of the Palestinians. We view that as a colonial and patronizing attitude that we reject, just as much as our South African anti-apartheid comrades did in the past when similar situations presented themselves. Solidarity with the oppressed primarily means understanding and recognizing what the oppressed need, and what the Palestinian people need is to exercise our inalienable right to self-determination and achieving freedom, justice, and unmitigated equality. Trying to impose on the oppressed objectives and frameworks that stem from narrow political agendas is more often than not indicative of a colonial attitude, whether recognized as such or not.

In the period covered by [*Refusing to be Enemies*] (basically 2003–7) I witnessed and heard about an exciting trend toward the spread of what some refer to as the

"Bil'in model" of joint struggle—that is, with Israelis and internationals very much integrated in the local struggles, and with Israeli activists working side by side with the popular committees, although in a supporting role, under Palestinian leadership. In 2010 I encountered a variety of responses, some suggesting that Israelis were no longer welcome, others that this wasn't the case but that some Palestinian organizations had become disillusioned because of the Israeli left's diminished influence on its government's policies, and basically didn't want to waste time with them anymore (I'm not exactly quoting anyone here).

Do you have any comments on this situation?

Two points are worth mentioning in this context.

Number one, a few Israeli and international activists have a tendency to make the struggle Israel-centric, arguing that *ending the occupation is good for Israel, above everything else,* as if that should be the overriding concern for anyone seeking justice and human rights. We totally reject that "save Israeli apartheid" view. I am intentionally referring to this trend as one that aims to save Israeli apartheid because striving to end the occupation alone, without addressing the UN-sanctioned right of the great majority of the Palestinian people, the refugees, to return to their homes and receive reparations, and omitting any mention of the need to end Israel's legalized and institutionalized system of racial discrimination, or apartheid, against the indigenous Palestinians—"non-Jews"—who hold Israeli citizenship, cannot be interpreted except as an attempt to *maintain Israeli apartheid.* This school of thought even seeks, often quite overtly, to strengthen apartheid by demographically getting rid of some four million Palestinians (in the OPT), thus maintaining Israel's character as an ethnocentric, racist, and exclusivist state for decades longer.

This is not a symmetrical struggle where "both sides" are in conflict or progressives from "both sides" are partnering to better their mutual destiny. This is a case of occupation, colonization, and apartheid by one side over the other. The struggle is, therefore, one for freedom, justice, and self-determination *for the oppressed*, above everything else. Only by ending oppression can there be any real potential for what I call ethical coexistence, one that is based on justice and full equality, not the master-slave type of coexistence that many in the peace industry advocate.

Second, the boycott criteria adopted by Palestinian civil society and advocated by the BNC set two conditions without which relations between a Palestinian side and an Israeli side would be regarded as constituting normalization. Normalization in the Arab—including Palestinian—context is defined as joint relations and projects with an Israeli side that give the false impression of normalcy despite the continuation of colonial oppression. Such projects and relations, by definition and by effect, attempt to normalize the abnormal: Israel's colonial and racist oppression. The two conditions to guarantee a normalization-free relationship, as set by PACBI and adopted by the great majority of Palestinian civil society since November 2007, are these: first, the Israeli side must recognize the internationally sanctioned and inalienable rights of the Palestinian people, including the right to self-determination; second, the project itself, regardless what its nature may be (cultural, academic, environmental, medical, feminist, etc.), must have as one of its main objectives *resisting* the occupation and/or apartheid.

A joint artistic project, for instance, that ignores the oppressive colonial reality and calls for people from "both sides" to engage in some artistic endeavor, as if art were "above politics," is cynically politicizing art and presenting a deceptive image of normal relations or "coexistence" *despite* oppression. A joint project that satisfies the first condition above *and* condemns the occupation, advocating in diverse forms for its end, on the other hand, is not normalization. Nothing in the boycott criteria opposes such projects.

Whether or not these projects are useful is up to activists in each particular project to decide. It is not intuitively true that Israeli involvement in any Palestinian struggle is invariably welcome or has positive effects. But that is a pragmatic consideration that has nothing to do with whether the project is itself a violation of the boycott criteria that almost all Palestinian organizations observe and respect.

Finally, a favorite approach of mine, as you can see from my epilogue especially, is noncooperation from within the oppressive society. However, with the notable exceptions of military refusal and some of the actions of groups like New Profile, and of course support for BDS inside Israel—noncooperation with the oppressive regime (refusal to carry out demolition orders, refusal to enforce travel restrictions, and so on—the kind of bureaucratic undermining of the regime that one sees described, for example, in Gene Sharp's works) not only were not happening to any significant degree but weren't seen as feasible on the whole. I wonder if you have any ideas about this.

At first, the colonial society bands together against perceived external threats of isolation that can lead to a pariah status. The prospects for the struggle from within to challenge the structures of colonialism and apartheid seem at that stage improbable, at best, if not altogether dreamy. But when the Palestinian-led and conscientious-Israeli-supported struggle inside associated with the struggle from outside start producing sustainable pressure that considerably raises the price of oppression, this seemingly invincible or garrison-oriented unity starts to crack. The courageous Israeli BDS group Boycott from Within is acutely aware of this equation, which we all know to be true from the struggles across the world, particularly in South Africa, France during the Algerian liberation struggle, the United States in Vietnam, and even now in Iraq, and so on.

Are you saying specifically that once pressure generated by the BDS campaign (and other sources of political/economic pressure) starts to really be felt, the BDS movement inside Israeli will become much stronger? Or are you suggesting a broader effect: at that point more Israelis will be willing to withhold their co-operation from various aspects of the oppressive regime?

I meant both. When Israel's oppression is met with substantial resistance, primarily from the Palestinian people, the Arab world, and the world at large, particularly in the form of sustainable BDS campaigns leading to comprehensive UN sanctions, as was the case in the struggle against South African apartheid, the Israeli economy will suffer tremendously and the BDS movement inside Israel will gain considerable momentum. At that stage, ordinary, apolitical Israelis will start rethinking whether they want to continue "living by the sword," as a world pariah in a state that lacks economic prospects and that is shunned, loathed, and widely boycotted by international civil society and eventually by states. Then, under severe and daunting pressure from within and without, the natural human quest for normalcy, for a peaceful, dignified, and economically viable life, will lead many of those Israelis to withdraw their support for Israeli apartheid and occupation. Many may even join movements that aim to end both. Collapse of the multitiered Israeli system of oppression then becomes a matter of time. Again, despite the obvious differences, we've seen it all before in South Africa.

CONCLUSION

IF NOT NOW, WHEN?

The great Brazilian educator Paulo Freire wrote in his iconic *Pedagogy of the Oppressed*: "One of the gravest obstacles to the achievement of liberation is that oppressive reality absorbs those within it and thereby acts to submerge human beings' consciousness. Functionally, oppression is domesticating. To no longer be prey to its force, one must emerge from it and turn upon it. This can be done only by means of the praxis: reflection and action upon the world in order to transform it."[1]

The people of Palestine have once more emerged from their oppressive reality, reflected, and acted upon it, calling upon international civil society to shoulder the moral responsibility to fight Israeli injustices, as it fought South Africa's in the struggle to abolish apartheid. The Palestinian BDS Campaign has almost all the ingredients for success in ending Israel's occupation, colonization, and apartheid:

- a comprehensive rights-based approach, rooted in a century of popular and civic Palestinian struggle against settler colonialism, that addresses the three fundamental rights corresponding to the main components of the indigenous people of Palestine and accordingly enjoys a solid consensus among Palestinians everywhere, inside historic Palestine and in exile

- a morally compelling message anchored in unmitigated equality, freedom, universal human rights, firmly antiracist principles, and compliance with international law

- an empowering strategy of nonviolent, creative civil resistance to injustice and oppression—a strategy to which people of conscience all over the world can contribute[2]

- A massive civil society coalition supported by near consensus leading and constantly evolving the struggle

An important component in the BDS Call that is often overlooked is the unambiguous invitation to conscientious Israelis to support the call, recognizing the important role anticolonialist, antiracist—that is, anti-Zionist—Israelis can and ought to play in ending Israel's criminal impunity, colonialism, and apartheid. Even as the BDS movement advocates diversity and ingenuity in designing and implementing BDS campaigns in various settings, the Palestinian BDS Call with its comprehensive emphasis on Palestinian rights remains the movement's frame of reference. A fast-growing group of principled Israeli (predominantly Jewish) supporters of BDS fully recognizes this Palestinian reference.[3] However, a few on the Zionist "left"—and their supporters in Western countries—who have recently jumped on the BDS "bandwagon," so to speak, just as the movement started breaking ground in the mainstream, have attempted, perhaps unintentionally, to invent or suggest an alternative reference for the international BDS movement that perpetuates their Israel-centered perspective, unwarranted agency, inflated sense of entitlement, and entrenched colonial privilege. In their persistent attempts to divert BDS from its inclusive and broad rights-based principles to a narrow focus on the occupation or even the colonial settlements alone, some of those voices have openly adopted a "save Israel" agenda that essentially aims at ridding Israel of four million Palestinians in Gaza and the West Bank, including East Jerusalem, in order to strengthen its apartheid existence as a "Jewish state." It seems some have yet to overcome their age-old patronizing attitudes toward the Palestinians, whom they apparently perceive as "irrational natives."

As in the struggle against South African apartheid, genuine solidarity movements are those that recognize and follow the lead of the oppressed,[4] who are in turn not passive objects but active, rational subjects who are asserting their aspirations and rights and their strategy to realize them. Solidarity groups advocating BDS tactics are guided by the principles and overall strategy defined by the BDS National Committee, the BNC, which is the largest alliance of Palestinian civil society political parties, unions, mass organizations, NGOs, refugee-rights networks, and professional associations, representing the main segments of the indigenous people of Palestine.

Another strength of the BDS movement lies in the fact that it is, above everything else, a quest for justice, freedom, and equal rights. Its agenda, like its South African precursor's, cannot be easily dismissed as some dogmatic or fanatic ideology, because of its grounding in universal principles of human rights and international law that ought to appeal to liberals as well as progressives of diverse ideological backgrounds, religious and secular alike.

Whereas moral consistency and commitment to universal human rights are the overriding principles of the global BDS movement, operationally BDS is based on three basic principles: context sensitivity, gradualness, and sustainability. Accordingly, conscientious academics, intellectuals, human rights advocates, "peace with justice" activists, and civil society organizations in any given country know best how to apply BDS most effectively in their particular circumstances, taking into consideration their respective political realities, organizational capacities, and appropriate tactics. The following BDS campaign priorities are recommendations that reflect the collective experiences in the BDS movement since its inception in 2005:[5]

1. Promoting a general boycott of all products and services of Israeli companies (especially those producing diamonds and military products) as well as international companies implicated in profiting from or otherwise supporting Israel's violations of international law and Palestinian rights until Israel fully complies with its obligations under international law and ends its multitiered oppression of the Palestinian people.

2. Promoting a boycott of all Israeli academic,[6] cultural, athletic, and tourist institutions that are complicit in maintaining the Israeli regime of occupation, apartheid, and denial of the UN-sanctioned refugee rights. By the same token, the boycott should extend to all academic, cultural, and other events and activities that receive funds from Israel or any of its complicit institutions, or that cover up and whitewash Israel's violations of international law, as in the Brand Israel campaign and similarly deceptive initiatives. This demands raising awareness among academics, students, artists, cultural workers, and athletes about the role these institutions have played in perpetuating injustice and colonial oppression. Crossing the Palestinian BDS picket line, so to speak, by violating the widely endorsed Palestinian boycott criteria and guidelines[7] should be denounced in the same firm language used in the past against those who played Sun City or otherwise failed to respect the anti-apartheid boycott against South Africa. Heeding the boycott guidelines is the minimum that any conscientious academic or cultural worker must do in the face of Israel's persistent and intensifying oppression.

3. Promoting ethical investment by trade unions, faith-based organizations,[8] local councils, private investment funds, and national pension funds, among others, by divesting from Israeli bonds and from all companies, banks, and other financial institutions that profit from or are otherwise complicit in maintaining Israel's occupation, denial of Palestinian refugee rights, or apartheid system

of racial discrimination against the indigenous Palestinian citizens of Israel.

4. Promoting ethical *corporate* responsibility leading to divestment from and a boycott of products of companies—whether Israeli or international—that are implicated in Israel's violations of international law and human rights, such as Elbit Systems, Veolia, Alstom, Eden Springs, Agrexco-Carmel, AHAVA, Lev Leviev Diamonds, Motorola, Northrop Grumman, and Caterpillar.

5. Working to expel Israel and its complicit institutions from international and interstate academic, cultural, sporting (such as the Olympics and FIFA), environmental, financial, trade, and other forums until it fully complies with its obligations under international law.

6. Promoting ethical pilgrimage to the Holy Land by directly benefiting Palestinian hotels, restaurants, coach services, guides, and the like, denying Israel, its airlines, its complicit travel agencies, and its other apartheid institutions the lucrative revenues that accrue from such pilgrimage. Alternative Palestinian tourism should also be considered.[9]

7. Applying public pressure to ostracize the Jewish National Fund, JNF, and to deny it its current legal status in most Western countries as a tax-exempt "charitable" organization.[10]

8. Lobbying local councils and regional governments to strictly apply domestic and international laws that urge the preclusion from public contracts of companies involved in "grave misconduct" (as EU regulations stipulate, for instance), especially at the human rights level.

9. Applying effective pressure on public officials and political parties to heed Amnesty International's call for an immediate arms

embargo on all parties to the Middle East "conflict." Despite valid criticisms of Amnesty's morally and legally untenable equation between the occupying power and the people under occupation, to whom international law grants the right to resist, this call largely pertains to banning arms trade with Israel and the shipment of arms to it through any country's ports, airspace, and sovereign territory, including territorial waters.[11] Such a ban should require third-party and end-user conformity to international law and human rights principles as well.

10. Calling for an immediate suspension of all free-trade[12] and other preferential trade agreements with Israel until it comprehensively and verifiably ends its violations of international law and Palestinian rights.

11. Holding Israel and complicit partner states, as the case may be, legally accountable for fully compensating the Palestinian people for all the illegal, wanton destruction it has wreaked upon Palestinian society and economy, as well as private and public property, in its siege, attacks, and wars of aggression against the Palestinian people, especially the 2009 war on Gaza and past invasions and military offensives in the occupied West Bank.

12. Applying pressure for immediate and unconditional implementation of the recommendations included in the Goldstone Report, adopted by the UN Human Rights Council, the UN General Assembly, and almost all leading international human rights organizations, to hold Israel and all colluding parties accountable for committing war crimes and crimes against humanity and to prosecute accused war criminals, among other legal actions.

In challenging Israel's oppression, the global BDS campaign does not call for Israel to be treated according to standards that are higher or lower than those that apply to any other state committing similar crimes and violations of international law. The crucial demand is for

Israel to be taken off the lofty pedestal on which it has been placed by the same Western powers that sponsored and justified its creation on the ruins of Palestinian society and that have largely sustained its three-tiered system of oppression against the Palestinian people. Although Israel is by no means the most atrocious offender in the world, it is the only persistent wrongdoer that has constantly been treated as an honorary member of the Western club of "democracies," with the Holocaust cynically—and quite irrelevantly—summoned as a smoke-screen to cover up this collusion. The virtually unparalleled state of exceptionalism and impunity that Israel enjoys today allows it to pursue its apartheid, ethnic cleansing, and slow-genocide agenda against the indigenous people of Palestine without any regard to international law or concern about possible punitive measures for violating it.

It is worth repeating in this context that Palestinians—and Arabs more generally—bear no responsibility whatsoever for the Holocaust, a European genocide committed against mostly European communities of Jews, Roma, and Slavs, among others. It is therefore not incumbent upon Palestinians to pay in our lives, land, and livelihoods the price for relieving Europe's conscience of its collective guilt over the Holocaust. Holocaust guilt should never be used as a means to justify or tolerate Israel's horrific injustices against the people of Palestine. And as some progressive Jewish intellectuals have stated recently, "Never again!" must always be understood to mean *never again to anyone*,[13] a call echoed by Archbishop Desmond Tutu in his defense of BDS against Israeli injustices.[14]

Western civil society, in particular, carries a unique responsibility to hold Israel accountable to international law, due to Western governments' particularly persistent and shameful role in buttressing Israel's system of colonial and racial oppression through vast diplomatic, economic, academic, cultural, and political support—all in the name of Western citizens and using their tax money without their consent.

Deep complicity engenders profound moral responsibility. This complicity, though, should not be reduced to merely a function of Holocaust guilt; while the Holocaust is utilized to rationalize the West's indefensible and blatant support for Israel's crimes and acts of genocide, this support fundamentally stems from the Western establishments' hegemonic economic interests, lingering colonial racism, and belligerent crusade to preserve a system of privilege and exploitation, based on might and a monopoly on the tools of mass devastation, coercion, and intimidation. Maintaining Israeli colonial hegemony and apartheid, as was the case with the South African predecessor, has become the Western establishment's most critical frontier in its endless imperial wars against the rest of humanity.

Collusion and moral duty aside, the responsibility to promote and support the BDS campaign against Israel also derives from common interest. While the United States and other Western states fund Israel's ongoing belligerence and system of apartheid to the tune of billions of dollars every year, millions of children in parts of the West are still left behind in substandard housing, inadequate or nonexistent health care, pathetic education, and, when they grow up, an establishment that consciously and bureaucratically prevents them from effectively and actively participating in the democratic political process. At the same time that the oil, military, homeland security, and banking industries are aggrandizing their colossal wealth, nourishing fear and xenophobia to maintain the "health" of the market, most working people in the West are seeing their civil rights and economic well-being erode before their very eyes. A progressive transformation in US and EU priorities for their great human and material resources, from investment in wars and imperial hegemony to investing in universal health care, dignified housing, school systems conducive to critical and contextual learning and development, decent jobs, and environmental repair, would not only be good for the peoples of the West; it would also be great for the world—for Iraq, Afghanistan, South Asia, Latin America, Africa, Lebanon, and, most certainly, Palestine. With such a transformation, Israel's regime of oppression against the Palestinian people would become untenable—and other regimes would find it harder to carry out similar atrocities and violations of international law elsewhere in the world.

John Dugard, leading South African international law expert and former UN special rapporteur on human rights in the occupied Palestinian territory (OPT), wrote in 2007:

> The West cannot expect the rest of the world to take issues it regards as important seriously if it persists in its present attitude to the [Israeli occupation]. For the rest of the world the issue of Palestine has become the litmus test for human rights. If the West fails to show concern for human rights in the OPT, the rest of the world will conclude that human rights are a tool employed by the West against regimes it dislikes and not an objective and universal instrument for the measurement of the treatment of people throughout the world.[15]

The global BDS movement for Palestinian rights presents a progressive, antiracist, sophisticated, sustainable, moral, and effective form of nonviolent civil resistance. It has become one of the key political catalysts and moral anchors for a strengthened, reinvigorated international social movement capable of ending the law of the jungle and upholding in its stead the rule of law, reaffirming the rights of all humans to freedom, equality, and dignified living.

Our South Africa moment has finally arrived!

CALL FOR THE ACADEMIC AND CULTURAL BOYCOTT OF ISRAEL

Whereas Israel's colonial oppression of the Palestinian people, which is based on Zionist ideology, comprises the following:

- Denial of its responsibility for the Nakba—in particular the waves of ethnic cleansing and dispossession that created the Palestinian refugee problem—and therefore refusal to accept the inalienable rights of the refugees and displaced stipulated in and protected by international law;

- Military occupation and colonization of the West Bank (including East Jerusalem) and Gaza since 1967, in violation of international law and UN resolutions;

- The entrenched system of racial discrimination and segregation against the Palestinian citizens of Israel, which resembles the defunct apartheid system in South Africa;

Since Israeli academic institutions (mostly state controlled) and the vast majority of Israeli intellectuals and academics have either contributed directly to maintaining, defending or otherwise justifying the above forms of oppression, or have been complicit in them through their silence,

Given that all forms of international intervention have until now failed to force Israel to comply with international law or to end its repression of the Palestinians, which has manifested itself in many forms, including siege, indiscriminate killing, wanton destruction and the racist colonial wall,

In view of the fact that people of conscience in the international community of scholars and intellectuals have historically shouldered the moral responsibility to fight injustice, as exemplified in their struggle to abolish apartheid in South Africa through diverse forms of boycott,

Recognizing that the growing international boycott movement against Israel has expressed the need for a Palestinian frame of reference outlining guiding principles,

In the spirit of international solidarity, moral consistency and resistance to injustice and oppression,

We, Palestinian academics and intellectuals, call upon our colleagues in the international community to *comprehensively and consistently boycott all Israeli academic and cultural institutions* as a contribution to the struggle to end Israel's occupation, colonization and system of apartheid, by applying the following:

1. Refrain from participation in any form of academic and cultural cooperation, collaboration or joint projects with Israeli institutions;

2. Advocate a comprehensive boycott of Israeli institutions at the national and international levels, including suspension of all forms of funding and subsidies to these institutions;

3. Promote divestment and disinvestment from Israel by international academic institutions;

4. Work toward the condemnation of Israeli policies by pressing for resolutions to be adopted by academic, professional and cultural associations and organizations;

5. Support Palestinian academic and cultural institutions directly without requiring them to partner with Israeli counterparts as an explicit or implicit condition for such support.

Endorsed by (2004):

Palestinian Federation of Unions of University Professors and Employees; Palestinian General Federation of Trade Unions; Palestinian NGO Network, West

Bank; Teachers' Federation; Palestinian Writers' Federation; Palestinian League of Artists; Palestinian Journalists' Federation; General Union of Palestinian Women; Palestinian Lawyers' Association; and tens of other Palestinian federations, associations, and civil society organizations.

BDS CALL

PALESTINIAN CIVIL SOCIETY CALLS FOR BOYCOTT, DIVESTMENT AND SANCTIONS AGAINST ISRAEL UNTIL IT COMPLIES WITH INTERNATIONAL LAW AND UNIVERSAL PRINCIPLES OF HUMAN RIGHTS

9 July 2005

One year after the historic Advisory Opinion of the International Court of Justice (ICJ) which found Israel's Wall built on occupied Palestinian territory to be illegal, Israel continues its construction of the colonial Wall with total disregard to the Court's decision. Thirty-eight years into Israel's occupation of the Palestinian West Bank (including East Jerusalem), Gaza Strip and the Syrian Golan Heights, Israel continues to expand Jewish colonies. It has unilaterally annexed occupied East Jerusalem and the Golan Heights and is now de facto annexing large parts of the West Bank by means of the Wall. Israel is also preparing—in the shadow of its planned redeployment from the Gaza Strip—to build and expand colonies in the West Bank. Fifty-seven years after the state of Israel was built mainly on land ethnically cleansed of its Palestinian owners, a majority of Palestinians are refugees, most of whom are stateless. Moreover, Israel's entrenched system of racial discrimination against its own Arab-Palestinian citizens remains intact.

In light of Israel's persistent violations of international law, and

Given that, since 1948, hundreds of UN resolutions have condemned Israel's colonial and discriminatory policies as illegal and called for immediate, adequate and effective remedies, and

Given that all forms of international intervention and peace-making have until now failed to convince or force Israel to comply with humanitarian law, to respect fundamental human rights and to end its occupation and oppression of the people of Palestine, and

In view of the fact that people of conscience in the international community have historically shouldered the moral responsibility to fight injustice, as exemplified in the struggle to abolish apartheid in South Africa through diverse forms of boycott, divestment and sanctions;

Inspired by the struggle of South Africans against apartheid and in the spirit of international solidarity, moral consistency and resistance to injustice and oppression,

We, representatives of Palestinian civil society, call upon international civil society organizations and people of conscience all over the world to impose broad boycotts and implement divestment initiatives against Israel similar to those applied to South Africa in the apartheid era. We appeal to you to pressure your respective states to impose embargoes and sanctions against Israel. We also invite conscientious Israelis to support this Call, for the sake of justice and genuine peace.

These non-violent punitive measures should be maintained until Israel meets its obligation to recognize the Palestinian people's inalienable right to self-determination and fully complies with the precepts of international law by:

1. Ending its occupation and colonization of all Arab lands and dismantling the Wall;

2. Recognizing the fundamental rights of the Arab-Palestinian citizens of Israel to full equality; and

3. Respecting, protecting and promoting the rights of Palestinian refugees to return to their homes and properties as stipulated in UN resolution 194.

Endorsed by:

The Palestinian political parties, unions, associations, coalitions and organizations below represent the three integral parts of the people of Palestine: Palestinian refugees, Palestinians under occupation and Palestinian citizens of Israel:

Unions, Associations, Campaigns

1. Council of National and Islamic Forces in Palestine (coordinating body for the major political parties in the Occupied Palestinian Territory–OPT)

2. Palestinian Independent Commission for Citizen's Rights (PICCR)

3. Palestinian NGO Network, West Bank–Gaza Strip (PNGO)

4. Union of Arab Community Based Associations (ITTIJAH), Haifa

5. Forum of Palestinian NGOs in Lebanon

6. Palestinian General Federation of Trade Unions (PGFTU)

7. General Union of Palestinian Women (GUPW)

8. General Union of Palestinian Teachers (GUPT)

9. Federation of Unions of Palestinian Universities' Professors and Employees

10. Consortium of Professional Associations

11. Union of Palestinian Medical Relief Committees (UPMRC)

12. Health Work Committees–West Bank

13. Union of Agricultural Work Committees (UAWC)

14. Union of Palestinian Agricultural Relief Committees (PARC)

15. Union of Health Work Committees–Gaza (UHWC)

16. Union of Palestinian Farmers

17. Occupied Palestine and Syrian Golan Heights Advocacy Initiative (OPGAI)

18. General Union of Disabled Palestinians

19. Palestinian Federation of Women's Action Committees (PFWAC)

20. Palestinian Campaign for the Academic and Cultural Boycott of Israel (PACBI)

21. Palestinian Grassroots Anti-Apartheid Wall Campaign

22. Union of Teachers of Private Schools

23. Union of Women's Work Committees, Tulkarem (UWWC)

24. Dentists' Association–Jerusalem Center

25. Palestinian Engineers Association

26. Lawyers' Association

27. Network for the Eradication of Illiteracy and Adult Education, Ramallah

28. Coordinating Committee of Rehabilitation Centers–
    West Bank

29. Coalition of Lebanese Civil Society Organizations
    (150 organizations)

30. Solidarity for Palestinian Human Rights (SPHR), Network of
    Student-Based Canadian University Associations

Refugee Rights Associations/Organizations

1. Al-Ard Committees for the Defense of the Right of Return, Syria

2. Al Awda–Palestine Right-to-Return Coalition, U.S.A.

3. Al-Awda Toronto

4. Aidun Group–Lebanon

5. Aidun Group–Syria

6. Alrowwad Cultural and Theatre Training Center,
   Aida refugee camp

7. Association for the Defense of the Rights of the Internally Displaced
   (ADRID), Nazareth

8. BADIL Resource Center for Palestinian Residency and Refugee
   Rights, Bethlehem

9. Committee for Definite Return, Syria

10. Committee for the Defense of Palestinian Refugee Rights, Nablus

11. Consortium of the Displaced Inhabitants of Destroyed Palestinian
    Villages and Towns

12. Filastinuna–Commission for the Defense of the Right of Return,
    Syria

13. Handala Center, 'Azza (Beit Jibreen) refugee camp, Bethlehem

14. High Committee for the Defense of the Right of Return, Jordan
    (including personal endorsement of seventy-one members of parlia-
    ment, political parties, and unions in Jordan)

15. High National Committee for the Defense of the Right of Return,
    Ramallah

16. International Right of Return Congress (RORC)

17. Jermana Youth Forum for the Defense of the Right of Return, Syria

18. Laji Center, Aida camp, Bethlehem

19. Local Committee for Rehabilitation, Qalandia refugee camp, Jerusalem

20. Local Committee for Rehabilitation of the Disabled, Deheishe refugee camp, Bethlehem

21. Palestinian National Committee for the Defense of the Right of Return, Syria

22. Palestinian Return Association, Syria

23. Palestinian Return Forum, Syria

24. Palestine Right-of-Return Coalition (Palestine, Arab host countries, Europe, North America)

25. Palestine Right-of-Return Confederation–Europe (Austria, Denmark, France, Germany, Italy, Netherlands, Norway, Poland, Sweden)

26. Palestinian Youth Forum for the Right of Return, Syria

27. PLO Popular Committees–West Bank refugee camps

28. PLO Popular Committees–Gaza Strip refugee camps

29. Popular Committee–al-'Azza (Beit Jibreen) refugee camp, Bethlehem

30. Popular Committee–Deheishe refugee camp, Bethlehem

31. Shaml–Palestinian Diaspora and Refugee Center, Ramallah

32. Union of Women's Activity Centers–West Bank Refugee Camps

33. Union of Youth Activity Centers–Palestine Refugee Camps, West Bank and Gaza

34. Women's Activity Center–Deheishe refugee camp, Bethlehem

35. Yafa Cultural Center, Balata refugee camp, Nablus

Organizations

1. Abna' al-Balad Society, Nablus

2. Addameer Center for Human Rights, Gaza

3. Addameer Prisoners' Support and Human Rights Association, Ramallah

4. Alanqa' Cultural Association, Hebron

5. Al-Awda Palestinian Folklore Society, Hebron

6. Al-Doha Chilren's Cultural Center, Bethlehem

7. Al-Huda Islamic Center, Bethlehem

8. Al-Jeel al-Jadid Society, Haifa

9. Al-Karameh Cultural Society, Um al-Fahm

10. Al-Maghazi Cultural Center, Gaza

11. Al-Marsad Al-Arabi, occupied Syrian Golan Heights

12. Al-Mezan Center for Human Rights, Gaza

13. Al-Nahda Cultural Forum, Hebron

14. Al-Taghrid Sociey for Culture and Arts, Gaza

15. Alternative Tourism Group, Beit Sahour (ATG)

16. Al-Wafa' Charitable Society, Gaza

17. Applied Research Institute Jerusalem (ARIJ)

18. Arab Association for Human Rights, Nazareth (HRA)

19. Arab Center for Agricultural Development (ACAD)

20. Arab Center for Agricultural Development–Gaza

21. Arab Education Institute (AEI)–Pax Christi Bethlehem

22. Arab Orthodox Charitable Society–Beit Sahour

23. Arab Orthodox Charity–Beit Jala

24. Arab Orthodox Club–Beit Jala

25. Arab Orthodox Club–Beit Sahour

26. Arab Students' Collective, University of Toronto

27. Arab Thought Forum, Jerusalem (AFT)

28. Association for Cultural Exchange Hebron–France

29. Assocation Najdeh, Lebanon

30. Authority for Environmental Quality, Jenin

31. Bader Society for Development and Reconstruction, Gaza

32. Bisan Center for Research and Development, Bethlehem

33. Canadian Palestine Foundation of Québec, Montréal

34. Center for the Defense of Freedoms, Ramallah

35. Center for Science and Culture, Gaza

36. Chamber of Commerce and Industry, Ramallah—Al-Bireh District

37. Child Development and Entertainment Center, Tulkarem

38. Committee for Popular Participation, Tulkarem

39. Defense for Children International–Palestine Section, Ramallah (DCI/PS)

40. El-Funoun Palestinian Popular Dance Troupe

41. Ensan Center for Democracy and Human Rights, Bethlehem

42. Environmental Education Center, Bethlehem

43. FARAH–Palestinian Center for Children, Syria

44. Ghassan Kanafani Society for Development, Gaza

45. Ghassan Kanafani Forum, Syria

46. Gaza Community Mental Health Program, Gaza (GCMHP)

47. Golan for Development, occupied Syrian Golan Heights

48. Halhoul Cultural Forum, Hebron

49. Himayeh Society for Human Rights, Um al-Fahm

50. Holy Land Trust–Bethlehem

51. Home of Saint Nicholas for Old Ages–Beit Jala

52. Human Rights Protection Center, Lebanon

53. In'ash al-Usrah Society, Ramallah

54. International Center of Bethlehem (Dar An-Nadweh)

55. Islah Charitable Society–Bethlehem

56. Jafra Youth Center, Syria

57. Jander Center, al-Azza (Beit Jibreen) refugee camp, Bethlehem

58. Jerusalem Center for Women, Jerusalem (JCW)

59. Jerusalem Legal Aid and Human Rights Center (JLAC)

60. Khalil Al Sakakini Cultural Center, Ramallah

61. Land Research Center, Jerusalem (LRC)

62. Liberated Prisoners' Society, Palestine

63. Local Committee for Social Development, Nablus

64. Local Committee for the Rehabilitation of the Disabled, Nablus

65. MA'AN TV Network, Bethlehem

66. Medical Aid for Palestine, Canada

67. MIFTAH–Palestinian Initiative for the Promotion of Global Dialogue and Democracy, Ramallah

68. Muwatin–The Palestinian Institute for the Study of Democracy
69. National Forum of Martyr's Families, Palestine
70. Near East Council of Churches Committee for Refugee Work–Gaza Area
71. Network of Christian Organizations–Bethlehem (NCOB)
72. Palestinian Council for Justice and Peace, Jerusalem
73. Palestinian Counseling Center, Jerusalem (PCC)
74. Palestinian Democratic Youth Union, Lebanon
75. Palestinian Democratic Union, Palestine
76. Palestinian Farmers' Society, Gaza
77. Palestinian Hydrology Group for Water and Environment Resources Development–Gaza
78. Palestinian Prisoners' Society–West Bank
79. Palestinian Society for Consumer Protection, Gaza
80. Palestinian University Students' Forum for Peace and Democracy, Hebron
81. Palestinian Women's Struggle Committees
82. Palestinian Working Women Society for Development
83. Popular Art Centre, Al-Bireh
84. Prisoner's Friends Association–Ansar Al-Sajeen, Majd al-Krum, Israel
85. Public Aid Association, Gaza
86. Ramallah Center for Human Rights Studies
87. Saint Afram Association–Bethlehem
88. Saint Vincent De Paule–Beit Jala
89. Senior Citizen Society–Beit Jala
90. Social Development Center, Nablus
91. Society for Self-Development, Hebron
92. Society for Social Work, Tulkarem
93. Society for Voluntary Work and Culture, Um al-Fahm
94. Society of Friends of Prisoners and Detainees, Um al-Fahm
95. Sumoud–Political Prisoners Solidarity Group, Toronto
96. Tamer Institute for Community Education, Ramallah
97. TCC–Teacher's Creativity Center, Ramallah

98. Wi'am Center, Bethlehem

99. Women's Affairs Technical Committee, Ramallah and Gaza (WATC)

100. Women's Studies Center, Jerusalem (WSC)

101. Women's Center for Legal Aid and Counseling, Jerusalem (WCLAC)

102. Yafa for Education and Culture, Nablus

103. Yazour Charitable Society, Nablus

104. YMCA–East Jerusalem

105. Youth Cooperation Forum, Hebron

106. YWCA–Palestine

107. Zakat Committee–al-Khader, Bethlehen

108. Zakat Committee–Deheishe camp, Bethlehem

APPENDIX 3

PACBI GUIDELINES
FOR THE INTERNATIONAL
ACADEMIC BOYCOTT OF ISRAEL

(Revised August 2010)

Since its founding in 2004, PACBI has advocated a boycott of Israeli academic and cultural institutions, based on the premise that these institutions are complicit in the system of oppression that has denied Palestinians their basic rights guaranteed by international law. This position is in line with the authoritative call by the Palestinian Council for Higher Education (CHE) for "non-cooperation in the scientific and technical fields between Palestinian and Israeli universities."[1] Academic institutions in particular are part of the ideological and institutional scaffolding of the Zionist settler-colonial project in Palestine, and as such are deeply implicated in maintaining the structures of domination and oppression over the Palestinian people. Since its founding, the Israeli academy has cast its lot with the hegemonic political-military establishment in Israel, and notwithstanding the efforts of a handful of principled academics, is deeply implicated in supporting and perpetuating the status quo.

Aside from the CHE boycott call, the first civil society efforts for an academic boycott of Israel can be traced to 2002, the year in which Israel launched its destructive assault upon Palestinian cities, towns, refugee camps and villages, targeting the institutions of Palestinian society and wreaking havoc on communities, residential neighborhoods, and urban infrastructure. The April 2002 statement by 120 European academics and researchers urging the adoption of a moratorium on EU and European Science Foundation support for Israel was followed by a number of pro-boycott initiatives in the same year by academics in the USA, France, Norway, and Australia. Particularly noteworthy have been the annual congresses of UK academics' unions, where boycott-related resolutions have been debated and passed since 2002. PACBI's key partner in the UK, BRICUP,[2] has been instrumental in the ongoing struggle to popularize the academic boycott in the union movement in the UK and beyond.

In October 2003, the first Palestinian Call for Boycott was issued by a group of Palestinian academics and intellectuals in the diaspora and the occupied Palestinian territory. Building on all previous boycott initiatives, PACBI issued its Call for an Academic and Cultural Boycott of Israel in Ramallah in 2004, providing the Palestinian reference for a steadily growing and sustainable institutional academic boycott effort throughout the world. The lethal Israeli assault on the Gaza Strip in December 2008–January 2009 served as a catalyst for further activism, and the period since then has witnessed a tremendous growth of initiatives in the spirit of BDS and targeting Israeli academic institutions. Such efforts have come from Australia, Canada, Ireland, Norway, Egypt, Sweden, Scotland, Lebanon, Spain, the United States, Italy and France, among others. Particularly encouraging has been the founding of the US Campaign for the Academic and Cultural Boycott of Israel (USACBI), inspired by PACBI and basing itself upon the PACBI Call.

Palestinian student and youth organizations, particularly in Gaza, endorsed the PACBI Call in the aftermath of Israel's war of aggression on the occupied and besieged Gaza Strip.[3]

During six years of intensive work with partners in several countries to promote the academic boycott against Israel, PACBI has examined many academic projects and events, assessing the applicability of the boycott criteria to them and, accordingly, has issued open letters, statements or advisory opinions on them. Based on this experience and in response to the burgeoning demand for PACBI's specific guidelines on applying the academic boycott to diverse projects, from conferences to exchange programs and research efforts, the Campaign lays out below unambiguous, consistent and coherent criteria and guidelines that specifically address the nuances and particularities of the academy.

These guidelines are mainly intended to assist conscientious academics and academic bodies around the world in adhering to the Palestinian call for boycott, as a contribution towards establishing a just peace in our region. Similar guidelines for the cultural boycott have been issued by PACBI.[4]

Academic Boycott Guidelines

Inspired by the anti-apartheid struggle in South Africa as well as the long tradition of civil resistance against settler-colonialism in Palestine, the PACBI Call[5] urges academics and cultural workers "to comprehensively and consistently boycott all Israeli academic and cultural institutions as a contribution to the struggle to end Israel's occupation, colonization and system of apartheid, by applying the following:

1. Refrain from participation in any form of academic and cultural cooperation, collaboration or joint projects with Israeli institutions;

2. Advocate a comprehensive boycott of Israeli institutions at the national and international levels, including suspension of all forms of funding and subsidies to these institutions;

3. Promote divestment and disinvestment from Israel by international academic institutions;

4. Work toward the condemnation of Israeli policies by pressing for resolutions to be adopted by academic, professional and cultural associations and organizations;

5. Support Palestinian academic and cultural institutions directly without requiring them to partner with Israeli counterparts as an explicit or implicit condition for such support."

Before discussing the various categories of academic activities that fall under the boycott call, and as a general overriding rule, it is important to stress that all Israeli academic institutions, unless proven otherwise, are complicit in maintaining the Israeli occupation and denial of basic Palestinian rights, whether through their silence, actual involvement in justifying, whitewashing or otherwise deliberately diverting attention from Israel's violations of international law and human rights, or indeed through their direct collaboration with state agencies in the design and commission of these violations. Accordingly, these institutions, all their activities, and all the events they sponsor or support must be boycotted. Events and projects involving individuals explicitly representing these complicit institutions should be boycotted, by the same token. Mere institutional *affiliation* to—as opposed to *representation* of—the Israeli academy is therefore not a sufficient condition for applying the boycott.

An increasing number of Palestinian civil society institutions are no longer willing to host international academics and cultural workers who insist on visiting or working with boycottable Israeli institutions, thereby violating the Palestinian boycott. Hosting those who cross our boycott "picket lines," many Palestinian organizations now recognize, can only undermine the boycott by presenting a false symmetry" or "balance" between the colonial oppressor and the colonized.

Although visits to the occupied Palestinian territory by international supporters and advocates of Palestinian rights have always been viewed by Palestinians as a source of encouragement and inspiration, PACBI and many Palestinian institutions believe that solidarity also entails respecting the boycott guidelines.

While an individual's academic freedom should be fully and consistently respected in this context, an individual academic, Israeli or not, cannot be exempt from being subject to boycotts that conscientious citizens around the world (beyond the scope of the PACBI boycott criteria) may call for in response to what is widely perceived as a particularly offensive act or statement by the academic in question (such as direct or indirect incitement to violence; justification—an indirect form of advocacy—of war crimes and other grave violations of international law; racial slurs; actual participation in human rights violations; etc.). At this level, Israeli academics should not be automatically exempted from due criticism or any lawful form of protest, including boycott; they should be treated like all other offenders in the same category, not better or worse.

The following guidelines may not be completely exhaustive and certainly do not preempt, replace or void other, common-sense rationales for boycott, particularly when a researcher, speaker, or event is shown to be explicitly justifying, advocating or promoting war crimes, racial discrimination, apartheid, suppression of fundamental human rights and serious violations of international law.

Based on the above, PACBI urges academics, academics' associations/unions and academic institutions around the world, where possible and as relevant, to boycott and/or work towards the cancellation or annulment of events, activities, agreements, or projects that promote the normalization of Israel in the global academy, whitewash Israel's violations of international law and Palestinians rights, or violate the boycott.

Specifically, the Palestinian academic boycott against Israel applies to the following events, activities, or situations:

1. Academic events (such as conferences, symposia, workshops, book and museum exhibits) convened or co-sponsored by Israeli institutions. All academic events, whether held in Israel or abroad, and convened or co-sponsored by Israeli academic institutions or their departments and institutes, deserve to be boycotted on institutional grounds. These boycottable activities include panels and other activities sponsored or organized by Israeli academic bodies or associations at international conferences outside Israel. Importantly, they also include the convening in Israel of meetings of international bodies and associations.

2. Institutional cooperation agreements with Israeli universities or research institutes. These agreements, concluded between international and Israeli universities, typically involve the exchange of faculty and students and, more importantly, the conduct of joint research. Many of these schemes are sponsored and funded by the European Union (in the case of Europe), and independent and government foundations elsewhere. For example, the five-year EU Framework programs, in which Israel has been the only non-European participant, have been crucial to the development of research at Israeli universities. European academic activists have been campaigning for the suspension of the EU-Israel Association Agreement since 2002; under this Agreement, Israeli and European universities exchange academic staff and students and engage in other activities, mainly through the Erasmus Mundus and Tempus schemes.[6] It should be noted that Israel is in violation of the terms of this Agreement, particularly of the second article.[7]

3. Study abroad schemes in Israel for international students. These programs are usually housed at Israeli universities and are part of the Israeli propaganda effort, designed to give international students a "positive experience" of Israel. Publicity and recruitment for these schemes are organized through students' affairs offices or academic departments (such as Middle East and international studies centers) at universities abroad.

4. Addresses and talks at international venues by official representatives of Israeli academic institutions such as presidents and rectors.

5. Special honors or recognition granted to official representatives of Israeli academic institutions (such as the bestowal of honorary degrees and other awards) or to Israeli academic or research institutions. Such institutions and their official representatives are complicit and as such should be denied this recognition.

6. Palestinian/Arab-Israeli collaborative research projects or events, especially those funded by the various EU and international grant-giving bodies. It is widely known that the easiest route to securing a research grant for a Palestinian academic is to apply with an Israeli partner. This is a case of politically motivated research par excellence, and contributes to enhancing the legitimacy of Israeli institutions as centers of excellence instead of directly and independently strengthening the research capacity of Palestinian institutions. The argument that "science is

above politics" is often used to justify such collaborations. In PACBI's view, no normal collaboration between the institutions of the oppressor and the oppressed, or indeed between the academics of the oppressor and oppressed can be possible while the structures of domination remain in place. In fact, such projects do nothing to challenge the status quo and contribute to its endurance. As an example, Palestinian/Arab-Israeli research efforts in the field of water and environment take as given the apartheid reality; tackling Palestinian/Arab and Israeli water and environmental "problems" as commensurate, without recognizing the apartheid reality, only contributes to the continuation of that reality.

As in the cultural field, events and projects (such as those involving educators, psychologists, or historians) involving Palestinians and/or Arabs and Israelis that promote "balance" between the "two sides" in presenting their respective narratives or "traumas," as if on par, or are otherwise based on the false premise that the colonizers and the colonized, the oppressors and the oppressed, are equally responsible for the "conflict," are intentionally deceptive, intellectually dishonest and morally reprehensible. Such events and projects, often seeking to encourage dialogue or "reconciliation between the two sides" without addressing the requirements of justice, promote the normalization and perpetuation of oppression and injustice. All such events and projects that bring Palestinians and/or Arabs and Israelis together, unless based on unambiguous recognition of Palestinian rights and framed within the explicit context of opposition to occupation and other forms of Israeli oppression of the Palestinians, are strong candidates for boycott. Other factors that PACBI takes into consideration in evaluating such events and projects are the sources of funding, the design of the project or event, the objectives of the sponsoring organization(s), the participants, and similar relevant factors.

7. Research and development activities in the framework of agreements or contracts between the Israeli government and other governments or institutions. Researchers in such projects are based at American, European or other universities. Examples include the United States–Israel Binational Science Foundation (BSF), an institution established by the US and Israeli governments in 1972 to sponsor research by Israelis and Americans, and the "Eureka Initiative," a European inter-governmental initiative set up in 1985 that includes Israel as the only non-European member.

8. Research and development activities on behalf of international corporations involving contracts or other institutional agreements with departments or centers at Israeli universities.

9. Institutional membership of Israeli associations in world bodies. While challenging such membership is not easy, targeted and selective campaigns demanding the suspension of Israeli membership in international forums contribute towards pressuring the state until it respects international law. Just as South Africa's membership was suspended in world academic—among other—bodies during apartheid, so must Israel's.

10. Publishing in or refereeing articles for academic journals based at Israeli universities, or granting permission to reprint material published elsewhere in such journals. These journals include those published by international associations but housed at Israeli universities. Efforts should be made to re-locate the editorial offices of these journals to universities outside Israel.

11. Granting permission for the use of copyrighted or non–publicly available material, such as artwork and audiovisual products, at or by Israeli universities and other boycottable institutions, regardless of the purposes of such use.

12. Advising on hiring or promotion decisions at Israeli universities through refereeing the work of candidates,[8] or refereeing research proposals for Israeli funding institutions. Such services, routinely provided by academics to their profession, must be withheld from complicit institutions.

PACBI
www.pacbi.org
pacbi@pacbi.org

PACBI GUIDELINES
FOR THE INTERNATIONAL
CULTURAL BOYCOTT OF ISRAEL

(Revised October 2010)

Since April 2004, PACBI has called upon intellectuals and academics worldwide to "comprehensively and consistently boycott all Israeli academic and cultural institutions as a contribution to the struggle to end Israel's occupation, colonization and system of apartheid."[1]

In 2006, a decisive majority of Palestinian cultural workers, including most filmmakers and artists, supported by hundreds of international cultural workers, appealed to all international artists and filmmakers of good conscience to join the institutional cultural boycott against Israel.[2] In response, the renowned British artist and writer John Berger issued a statement that was backed by dozens of prominent international artists, writers and filmmakers calling on their colleagues everywhere to endorse the Palestinian cultural boycott call.[3]

In the spirit of this cultural boycott and consistent with its logic, on 8 May 2008, in a half-page advertisement in the *International Herald Tribune* under the banner "No Reason to Celebrate," tens of leading international cultural figures—including Mahmoud Darwish, Augusto Boal, Ken Loach, Andre Brink, Ella Shohat, Judith Butler, Vincenzo Consolo, Ilan Pappé, David Toscana and Aharon Shabtai—signed a statement responding to worldwide celebrations of Israel's "60th anniversary" saying:

> There is no reason to celebrate! Israel at 60 is a state that is still denying Palestinian refugees their UN-sanctioned rights, simply because they are "non-Jews." It is still il-

legally occupying Palestinian and other Arab lands, in violation of numerous UN resolutions. It is still persistently and grossly breaching international law and infringing
fundamental human rights with impunity afforded to it through munificent US and
European economic, diplomatic and political support. It is still treating its own
Palestinian citizens with institutionalized discrimination.[4]

The cultural boycott campaign against apartheid South Africa has been a major
source of inspiration in formulating the Palestinian boycott calls and their criteria.
In that context, the key argument put forth by the South African apartheid regime
and its apologists around the world against the anti-apartheid cultural and sports
boycott—that boycotts violate the freedom of expression and cultural exchange—
was resolutely refuted by the director of the United Nations Centre Against
Apartheid, Enuga S. Reddy, who in 1984 wrote:

> It is rather strange, to say the least, that the South African regime which denies all
> freedoms ... to the African majority ... should become a defender of the freedom of
> artists and sportsmen of the world. We have a list of people who have performed in
> South Africa because of ignorance of the situation or the lure of money or unconcern
> over racism. They need to be persuaded to stop entertaining apartheid, to stop prof-
> iting from apartheid money and to stop serving the propaganda purposes of the
> apartheid regime.[5]

Similarly, the Palestinian boycott call targets cultural institutions, projects and
events that continue to serve the purposes of the Israeli colonial and apartheid
regime.

During years of intense work with partners in several countries to promote the
cultural boycott of Israel, PACBI has thoroughly scrutinized tens of cultural projects and events, assessing the applicability of the boycott criteria to them and, accordingly, has issued open letters, statements or advisory opinions on them. The
two most important conclusions reached in this respect were: (a) many of these
events and projects fall into an uncertain, grey area that is challenging to appraise,
and (b) the boycott must target not only the complicit institutions but also the inherent and organic links between them which reproduce the machinery of colonial subjugation and apartheid. Based on this experience and in response to the
burgeoning demand for PACBI's specific guidelines for applying the cultural boycott to diverse projects, from film festivals to art exhibits to musical and dance performances to conferences, the Campaign lays out below unambiguous, consistent
and coherent criteria and guidelines that specifically address the nuances and particularities of the field of culture.

These guidelines are mainly intended to help guide cultural workers and organizers around the world in adhering to the Palestinian call for boycott, as a contribution towards establishing a just peace in our region.

Cultural Boycott Guidelines

Before discussing the various categories of cultural products and events and as a general overriding rule, virtually all Israeli cultural institutions, unless proven otherwise, are complicit in maintaining the Israeli occupation and denial of basic Palestinian rights, whether through their silence or actual involvement in justifying, whitewashing or otherwise deliberately diverting attention from Israel's violations of international law and human rights. Accordingly, these institutions (mainly major state and public entities), all their products, and all the events they sponsor or support must be boycotted. By the same token, international artists and cultural workers are urged not to exhibit, present, or showcase their work (e.g., films, installations, literary works) or lecture at complicit Israeli institutions or events, or to grant permission for the publication or exhibition of such work by such institutions. Events and projects involving individuals *explicitly representing* these complicit institutions should be boycotted, likewise.

International cultural workers who fail to heed the call for boycott and attempt to visit Palestinian institutions as a "balancing act" are assuming "parity between justice and injustice," which Nelson Mandela has warned against. Although visits to the occupied Palestinian territory by international supporters and advocates of Palestinian rights have always been viewed by Palestinians as a source of encouragement and inspiration, Palestinians increasingly believe that solidarity entails respecting the boycott call and not combining a visit to Palestinian institutions with visits to or attending conferences and other events at boycottable Israeli institutions. International visitors who insist on including Israeli cultural institutions in their itinerary, in violation of the boycott, should not expect to be welcomed by Palestinian cultural institutions.

In all the following, "product" refers to cultural products such as films and other art forms; "event" refers to film festivals, conferences, art exhibits, dance and musical performances, tours by artists and writers, among other activities.

The following criteria may not be completely exhaustive and certainly do not preempt, replace or void other, common-sense rationales for boycott, particularly when a cultural product or event is shown to be explicitly justifying, advocating or promoting war crimes, racial discrimination, apartheid, suppression of fundamental human rights and serious violations of international law.

Based on the above, the Palestinian cultural boycott
of Israel applies in the following situations:

*(1) Cultural product is commissioned by an official Israeli body or non-Israeli
institution that serves Brand Israel or similar propaganda purposes[6]*

All cultural products commissioned by an official Israeli body (e.g., government
ministry, municipality, embassy, consulate, state or other public film fund, etc.) or
an Israel rebranding effort or organization, whether Israeli or international, deserve to be boycotted on institutional grounds, as they are commissioned and thus
funded by the Israeli state or colluding institutions specifically to help the state's
propaganda or "rebranding" efforts aimed at diluting, justifying, whitewashing or
otherwise diverting attention from the Israeli occupation and other violations of
Palestinian rights and international law. However, this level of explicit complicity
is difficult to ascertain quite often, as information on such direct commissioning
may not be readily available or may even be intentionally concealed.

*(2) Product is funded by an official Israeli body, but not commissioned
(no political strings)*

The term "political strings" here specifically refers to those conditions that obligate
a fund recipient to directly or indirectly serve the Israeli government's or a complicit institution's "rebranding" or propaganda efforts. Products funded by official
Israeli bodies—as defined in category (1) above—but not commissioned, therefore not attached to any political strings, are not *per se* subject to boycott. Individual cultural products that receive state funding as part of the individual cultural
worker's entitlement as a tax-paying citizen, without her/him being bound to
serve the state's political and PR interests, are not boycottable, according to the
PACBI criteria. Accepting such political strings, on the other hand, would clearly
turn the cultural product or event into a form of complicity, by contributing to Israel's efforts to whitewash or obscure its colonial and apartheid reality, and would
render it boycottable, as a result.

While an individual's freedom of expression, particularly artistic expression,
should be fully and consistently respected in this context, an individual artist, filmmaker, writer, etc., Israeli or not, cannot be exempt from being subject to boycotts
that conscientious citizens around the world (beyond the scope of the PACBI boycott criteria) may call for in response to what is widely perceived as a particularly offensive act or statement by the cultural worker in question (such as direct or indirect

incitement to hatred and violence; justification—an indirect form of advocacy—of war crimes and other grave violations of international law; racial slurs; actual participation in human rights violations; etc.). At this level, Israeli cultural workers should not be automatically exempted from due criticism or any lawful form of protest, including boycott; they should be treated like all other offenders in the same category, not better or worse.

(3) Event is partially or fully sponsored or funded by an official Israeli body or a complicit institution

The general principle is that an event or project carried out under the sponsorship/aegis of or in affiliation with an official Israeli body or a complicit institution constitutes complicity and therefore is deserving of boycott. The same may apply to support or sponsorship from non-Israeli institutions that serve brand Israel purposes. It is also well documented now that Israeli artists, writers and other cultural workers applying for state funding to cover the cost of their—or their cultural products'—participation in international events must accept to contribute to Israel's official propaganda efforts. To that end, the cultural worker must sign a contract with the Israeli Foreign Ministry binding her/him to "undertake to act faithfully, responsibly and tirelessly to provide the Ministry with the highest professional services. The service provider is aware that the purpose of ordering services from him is to promote the policy interests of the State of Israel via culture and art, including contributing to creating a positive image for Israel."[7]

(4) Product is not funded or sponsored by an official Israeli body or complicit institution

Unless violating any of the above criteria, in the absence of official Israeli or other complicit institutional sponsorship, the individual product of an Israeli cultural worker *per se* is not boycottable, regardless of its content or merit.

(5) Event or project promotes false symmetry or "balance"

Cultural events and projects involving Palestinians and/or Arabs and Israelis that promote "balance" between the "two sides" in presenting their respective narratives, as if on par, or are otherwise based on the false premise that the colonizers and the colonized, the oppressors and the oppressed, are equally responsible for the "conflict," are intentionally deceptive, intellectually dishonest and morally reprehensible.

Such events and projects, often seeking to encourage dialogue or "reconciliation between the two sides" without addressing the requirements of justice, promote the normalization of oppression and injustice. All such events and projects that bring Palestinians and/or Arabs and Israelis together, unless the Israeli side is explicitly supportive of the inalienable rights of the Palestinian people and unless the project/event is framed within the explicit context of joint opposition to occupation and other forms of Israeli oppression of the Palestinians, are strong candidates for boycott. Other factors that PACBI takes into consideration in evaluating such events and projects are the sources of funding, the design of the program, the objectives of the sponsoring organization(s), the participants, and similar relevant factors.

PACBI
www.pacbi.org
pacbi@pacbi.org

NOTES

INTRODUCTION

1. Paulo Freire, *Pedagogy of the Oppressed* (New York: Continuum, 2006), 50.
2. An adaptation of the classic tale "The Rabbi and the Goat."
3. Reuters, "Tutu: World Doesn't Criticize Israel Because of the Holocaust," September 18, 2008, http://www.haaretz.com/hasen/spages/1022535.html.
4. Seymour Hersh, "Selective Intelligence," *New Yorker*, May 12, 2003, http://www.newyorker.com/archive/2003/05/12/030512fa_fact.
5. Craig Unger, "From the Wonderful Folks Who Brought You Iraq," *Vanity Fair*, May 2007, http://www.vanityfair.com/politics/features/2007/03/whitehouse200703.
6. According to a *Haaretz* report, newly revealed US State Department documents on the last phase of the Vietnam War and transcripts of Golda Meir's war cabinet during the 1973 Arab-Israeli War demonstrate the massive influence of the Israel lobby over Congress during that critical era. When the war broke out, Israeli leaders were chiefly concerned about US aid in materiel and diplomacy, given the competing demands of the US-client South Vietnamese government facing the daunting threat of the communist-controlled North. "Without this aid," the report says, "Israel would have been exhausted and defeated in a long war; with it, Israel developed total dependence on Washington." It adds, "Fortunately for Israel, Washington does not only consist of the White House, the Pentagon and the State Department, but also Congress. Thanks to Israel's power in Congress, it has fared better than other, smaller allies, like South Vietnam. In the absence of congressional support, [the South Vietnamese] did not win the administration's affection; this is why Saigon fell and Jerusalem hasn't." Amir Oren,

"Vietnam and Yom Kippur Wars Were Closely Connected, Newly Released U.S. Documents Reveal," *Haaretz*, October 17, 2010, http://www.haaretz .com/print-edition/features/vietnam-and-yom-kippur-wars-were-closely -connected-newly-released-u-s-documents-reveal-1.319467.

7.   US journalist and editor John Sugg writes: "Former Israeli Prime Minister Benjamin Netanyahu, when asked what 9/11 would mean for American-Is-raeli relations, responded: 'It's very good.' Realizing his maladroit gaffe, he then added: 'Well, it's not good, but it will generate immediate sympathy' for Israel from the United States. The fact that no Palestinian had anything to do with 9/11 is a mountain-size distinction intentionally overlooked by Ne-tanyahu." John Sugg, "Judith Miller and Me: 'Playing Fast and Loose with the Facts,'" *Counterpunch*, October 25, 2005, http://www.counterpunch.org/ sugg10252005.html. In April 2008 Netanyahu echoed his earlier sentiment, telling an audience at Bar Ilan University: "We are benefiting from one thing, and that is the attack on the Twin Towers and Pentagon, and the American struggle in Iraq," reportedly adding that these events "swung American public opinion in our favor." Haaretz Service and Reuters, "Re-port: Netanyahu Says 9/11 Terror Attacks Good for Israel," *Haaretz*, April 16, 2008, http://www.haaretz.com/news/report-netanyahu-says-9-11-terror -attacks-good-for-israel-1.244044.

8.   Israel established or renewed diplomatic relations with at least sixty-eight countries since the beginning of the Madrid peace talks. Israel Ministry of Foreign Affairs, "Israel's Diplomatic Missions Abroad: Status of Relations," updated August 2010, http://www.mfa.gov.il/MFA/About+the+Ministry/ Diplomatic+missions/Israel-s+Diplomatic+Missions+Abroad.htm.

9.   Martin Shaw, "Afghanistan and Iraq: Western Wars, Genocidal Risks," openDemocracy: free thinking for the world, July 27, 2009, http://www .opendemocracy.net/article/afghanistan-and-iraq-western-wars-genocidal -risks.

10. John Mearsheimer, "Sinking Ship," *American Conservative*, August 2010.

11. Global BDS Movement, "Palestinian Civil Society Calls for Boycott, Divest-ment and Sanctions against Israel Until It Complies with International Law and Universal Principles of Human Rights," July 9, 2005, http://bdsmovement .net/?q=node/52.

12. Global BDS Movement, "The Boycott, Divestment & Sanctions Campaign National Committee (BNC)," n.d., http://bdsmovement.net/?q=node/126.

13. Ngugi wa Thiong'o, *Decolonising the Mind: The Politics of Language in African Literature* (London: James Currey; Portsmouth, NH: Heinemann, 1986), 3.

14. Desmond Tutu on *Today* (NBC TV), January 9, 1985, Desmond Tutu Peace Foundation, http://tutu-foundation-usa.org/exhibitions.html.

15. For more on justice as a requirement for genuine peace, see Omar Bargh-

outi, "Peace with Justice," in *Encyclopedia of the Israeli-Palestinian Conflict*, ed. Cheryl A. Rubenberg (Boulder, Lynne Rienner, 2010).

16. For more on the planned and systematically executed Zionist campaign to dispossess and uproot the Palestinian people, see Ilan Pappé, *The Ethnic Cleansing of Palestine* (Oxford: Oneworld, 2006).

17. There are at least twenty Israeli laws, including Basic Laws (equivalent to constitutional laws), that legalize and institutionalize the system of racial discrimination against Palestinian citizens of the state for being "non-Jews." See Adalah, "Major Findings of Adalah's Report to the UN Committee on the Elimination of Racial Discrimination," presented in Geneva, March 1998, http://www.adalah.org/eng/intladvocacy/cerd.htm#major.

18. A poll by Dahaf Polling Institute published in the mass circulation Israeli daily *Yedioth Ahronoth* on September 14, 2010, found that 48 percent of Israelis opposed, while only 45 percent supported, the following outline of a "peace" agreement with the Palestinians, which fails to meet the minimal requirements of international law: "There is a plan stipulating that in the framework of a peace agreement in which the Palestinians recognize Israel as a Jewish state, Israel will concede most of the territories in Judea and Samaria but the settlement blocs will remain in Israeli hands, in exchange for which Israel will return to the Palestinians territory of comparable size from within the State of Israel. Do you support such a plan or are you opposed?" "Poll: Majority Opposed to Moratorium," *Yediot*, September 14, 2010, quoted in "*Yediot* to Abe Foxman: Are We Anti-Semitic Too?" *Coteret* blog, September 14, 2010, http://coteret.com/2010/09/14/yediot-to-abe-foxman-are-we-anti -semitic-too/#more-2833.

19. Leslie Susser, "As Israel's Image Sinks, Whither Israeli PR?" JTA, July 6, 2010, http://www.jta.org/news/article/2010/07/06/2739921/as-israels-image-sinks -wither-israeli-pr.

20. Nehemia Shtrasler, "Anti-Israel Economic Boycotts Are Gaining Speed," *Haaretz*, September 5, 2010, http://www.haaretz.com/print-edition/business/ anti-israel-economic-boycotts-are-gaining-speed-1.312210.

21. Tim Franks, "Details of Gaza Blockade Revealed in Court Case," BBC News, May 3, 2010, http://news.bbc.co.uk/2/hi/8654337.stm.

22. "Guide: Gaza Under Blockade," BBC News, last updated July 6, 2010, http://news.bbc.co.uk/2/hi/middle_east/7545636.stm.

23. "Cameron Calls Gaza 'Prison Camp,'" CNN World, July 27, 2010, http:// articles.cnn.com/2010-07-27/world/cameron.gaza_1_aid-flotilla-gaza-strip -turkish-mavi-marmara?_s=PM:WORLD.

24. Susser, "As Israel's Image Sinks."

25. Howard Kohr, address to AIPAC Policy Conference, May 3, 2009, http:// www.aipac.org/Publications/SpeechesByAIPACLeadership/HowardKohr.pdf.

26. Peter Beinart, "The Failure of the American Jewish Establishment," *New York*

Review of Books, June 10, 2010, http://www.nybooks.com/articles/archives/2010/jun/10/failure-american-jewish-establishment/.

27. Mearsheimer, "Sinking Ship."

28. For a thorough study of Israel's three-tiered system of oppression, see Palestinian Civil Society, *United against Apartheid, Colonialism and Occupation: Dignity and Justice for the Palestinian People*, October 2008, position paper for Durban Review Conference, April 20–24. 2009, http://bdsmovement.net/files/English-BNC_Position_Paper-Durban_Review.pdf,

29. Karl Vick, "Why Israel Doesn't Care About Peace," *Time*, September 13, 2010, http://www.time.com/time/covers/0,16641,20100913,00.html.

30. Noah Kosharek, "Supreme Court Okays Jewish-only Buildings in Jaffa," *Haaretz*, November 8, 2010, http://www.haaretz.com/print-edition/news/supreme-court-okays-jewish-only-buildings-in-jaffa-1.323474.

31. Uri Misgav, "Fascism in Jewish State?," *Ynetnews*, October 21, 2010, http://www.ynetnews.com/articles/0,7340,L-3972908,00.html.

32. Attila Somfalvi, "Government Approves Loyalty Oath Bill," *Ynetnews*, October 10, 2010, http://www.ynetnews.com/articles/0,7340,L-3967149,00.html.

33. Rabbi Meit David, "Kahane," in *Encyclopedia of the Israeli-Palestinian Conflict*, ed. Cheryl A. Rubenberg (Boulder, Lynne Rienner, 2010).

34. Gavriel Solomon, quoted in Stephen Lendman, "Israel on a Fast Track to Despotism," *Baltimore Chronicle and Sentinel*, October 12, 2010, http://baltimorechronicle.com/2010/101210Lendman.shtml.

35. http://www.ynet.co.il/articles/0,7340,L-3967389,00.html (Hebrew).

36. Uri Avnery, "Weimar in Jerusalem: Israel on the Footsteps of Nazi Germany," Al-Jazeerah: Cross-Cultural Understanding, October 25, 2010, available at http://tinyurl.com/2dawq9b.

37. Uri Avnery, "A Parliamentary Mob," Gush Shalom, July 17, 2010, http://zope.gush-shalom.org/home/en/channels/avnery/1279370237.

38. David Landau, "Boycott the Knesset," *Haaretz*, July 16, 2010, http://www.haaretz.com/print-edition/opinion/boycott-the-knesset-1.302259.

39. In his September 28, 2010, speech before the UNGA, Lieberman stated: "Thus, the guiding principle for a final status agreement must not be land-for-peace but rather, exchange of populated territory. Let me be very clear: I am not speaking about moving populations, but rather about moving borders to better reflect demographic realities." The full text of his speech is available at Israel Ministry of Foreign Affairs http://www.mfa.gov.il/MFA/Government/Speeches+by+Israeli+leaders/2010/FM_Liberman_Addresses_UN_General_Assembly_28-Sep-2010.htm.

40. The veteran British journalist Robert Fisk describes Lieberman thus: "Israelis have exalted a man . . . who out-Sharons even Ariel Sharon. A few Palestinians [have said] the West will see the 'true face' of Israel. [He's] talked

of drowning Palestinians in the Dead Sea or executing Israeli Palestinians who talked to Hamas. [His] incendiary language [promotes] executions . . . drownings . . . hell and loyalty oaths." Fisk, "Why Avigdor Lieberman Is the Worst Thing That Could Happen to the Middle East," *Independent*, March 18, 2009, http://www.independent.co.uk/opinion/commentators/fisk/robert -fisk-why-avigdor-lieberman-is-the-worst-thing-that-could-happen-to-the -middle-east-1647370.html.

41. Zeev Sternhell, "The Obligation of a True Patriot," *Haaretz*, February 19, 2010, http://www.haaretz.com/print-edition/opinion/the-obligation-of-a -true-patriot-1.263621.

42. For an insightful critique of the Zionist "left" initiated "Declaration of Independence from Fascism," see Gabriel Ash, "On the Loyalty Oath and the Wretched Zionist 'Left,'" *Jews sans Frontieres* blog, November 1, 2010, http:// jewssansfrontieres.blogspot.com/2010/11/on-loyalty-oath-and-wretched -zionist.html.

43. Benjamin Netanyahu, quoted in Rebecca Anna Stoil, "PM Blasts Artists Boycotting Ariel Culture Center," *Jerusalem Post*, August 29, 2010, http://www .jpost.com/Home/Article.aspx?id=186333.

44. Reut Institute, "The Delegitimization Challenge: Creating a Political Firewall," February 14, 2010, http://www.reut-institute.org/Publication.aspx ?PublicationId=3769.

45. Barak Ravid, "Think Tank: Israel Faces Global Delegitimization Campaign," *Haaretz*, February 12, 2010, http://www.haaretz.com/print-edition/news/ think-tank-israel-faces-global-delegitimization-campaign-1.265967.

46. South Africa–based economist Patrick Bond writes: "It was only by fusing bottom-up pressure with top-down international delegitimization of white rule that the final barriers were cleared for the first free vote, on April 27 1994." Bond, "Palestine Liberation Recalls Anti-Apartheid Tactics, Responsibilities and Controversies," ZSpace, October 13, 2010, http://www.zcommunications .org/palestine-liberation-recalls-anti-apartheid-tactics-responsibilities-and -controversies-by-patrick-bond.

47. Reut Institute, "Delegitimization Challenge."

48. Richard Falk, interview by C. Gouridasan Nair, *Hindu*, September 24, 2010, http://www.thehindu.com/news/resources/article793269.ece.

49. Some of the following is based on Omar Barghouti, "Besieging Israel's Siege," *Guardian*, August 12, 2010, http://www.guardian.co.uk/commentisfree/2010/ aug/12/besieging-israel-siege-palestinian-boycott.

50. Michael Ben-Yair wrote: "We enthusiastically chose to become a colonial society, ignoring international treaties, expropriating lands, transferring settlers from Israel to the occupied territories, engaging in theft and finding justification for all these activities. . . . In effect, we established an apartheid regime in

the occupied territories." Ben-Yair, "The War's Seventh Day," *Haaretz*, March 3, 2002, http://www.haaretz.com/hasen/pages/ShArt.jhtml?itemNo=136433.

51. Rome Statute of the International Criminal Court, http://untreaty.un.org/cod/icc/statute/99_corr/cstatute.htm.

52. While the term *colonization* may be currently considered controversial in describing the Zionist conquest of Palestine, Zionist leaders before the 1948 Nakba used it openly and regularly. In 1940, for example, Joseph Weitz, head of the Jewish Agency's Colonization Department, bluntly confessed, "Between ourselves it must be clear that there is no room for both peoples together in this country. We shall not achieve our goal if the Arabs are in this small country. There is no other way than to transfer the Arabs from here to neighboring countries—all of them. Not one village, not one tribe should be left." From Joseph Weitz, "A Solution to the Refugee Problem," *Davar*, September 29, 1967, cited in Uri Davis and Norton Mezvinsky, eds., *Documents from Israel, 1967–1973: Readings for a Critique of Zionism* (London: Ithaca Press, 1975), 21.

53. Sigmund Freud, letter to the Keren Hajessod (Dr. Chaim Koffler), February 26, 1930, http://www.freud.org.uk/education/blog/40082/the-arab-israeli-conflict/.

54. Palestinian Campaign for the Academic and Cultural Boycott of Israel (PACBI), "Call for Academic and Cultural Boycott of Israel," July 6, 2004, http://www.pacbi.org/etemplate.php?id=869.

55. British Committee for the Universities of Palestine, "EPACBI—the European Platform for the Academic and Cultural Boycott of Israel Launched," n.d., http://www.bricup.org.uk/.

56. U.S. Campaign for the Academic and Cultural Boycott of Israel, "Endorse Our Call to Boycott," n.d., http://usacbi.wordpress.com/.

57. "Call for an Academic and Cultural Boycott of the State of Israel," http://www.akulbi.net/index_en.php.

58. PACBI, "European Platform for the Academic and Cultural Boycott of Israel (EPACBI) Brings Boycott Movement to a Higher Level in Europe," October 12, 2010, http://www.pacbi.org/etemplate.php?id=1382.

59. "Indian Call for the Academic and Cultural Boycott of Israel," July 2010, http://pacbi.org/etemplate.php?id=1309.

60. "SA Academics Call for UJ to Terminate Relationship with Israeli Institution," www.UJpetition.com.

61. Desmond Tutu, "Israeli Ties: A Chance to Do the Right Thing," *Times Live*, September 26, 2010, http://www.timeslive.co.za/world/article675369.ece/Israeli-ties—a-chance-to-do-the-right-thing.

62. South African Artists Against Apartheid, "A Declaration," http://www.southafricanartistsagainstapartheid.com/2010/11/declaration.html.

63. PACBI, "PACBI Salutes Canadian Academic Trade Unionists," February 25, 2009, http://www.pacbi.org/etemplate.php?id=954.

64. Association des Universitaires pour le Respect du Droit International en Palestine, http://www.aurdip.fr/.

65. L'appello italiano per il boicottaggio accademico e culturale, http://sites .google.com/site/icacbi/04-l-appello-italiano-per-il-boicottaggio-accademico -e-culturale.

66. Comissió Universitària Catalana per Palestina (CUNCAP), "Col·laboració amb xarxes europees: No a l'acord EU-Israel," April 30, 2010, http://cuncap .wordpress.com/.

67. Coalition Against Israel Apartheid, http://www.caiaweb.org/.

68. Israeli Apartheid Week, http://apartheidweek.org/.

69. Ann Laura Stoler, "By Colonial Design," September 10, 2010, http://www .pacbi.org/etemplate.php?id=1361.

70. Matthew B. Zeidman, "Jean-Luc Godard Cancels Trip to Tel Aviv Student Film Festival," *Hollywood Today*, June 3, 2008, http://www.hollywoodtoday .net/2008/06/03/jean-luc-godard-cancels-trip-to-tel-aviv-film-festival/.

71. "For Once, the Yes Men Say No," letter from the Yes Men to the Jerusalem Film Festival, July 3, 2009, http://www.pacbi.org/etemplate.php?id=1031 &key=the%20yes%20men.

72. Hannah Brown, "Mike Leigh Cancels Visit over 'Israeli Policies,'" *Jerusalem Post*, October 17, 2010, http://www.jpost.com/Israel/Article.aspx?ID=191708 &R=R1&utm_source=twitterfeed&utm_medium=twitter.

73. See various reports at www.pacbi.org.

74. "Making History: Support for Israeli Artists Who Say NO to Normalizing Settlements," Jewish Voice for Peace, http://jvp.org/campaigns/making-history-support-israeli-artists-who-say-no-normalizing-settlements-4.

75. Chaim Levinson and Or Kashti, "150 Academics, Artists Back Actors' Boycott of Settlement Arts Center," *Haaretz*, August 31, 2010, http://www .haaretz.com/print-edition/news/150-academics-artists-back-actors-boycott -of-settlement-arts-center-1.311149.

76. In their book *The Israel Lobby and US Foreign Policy* (New York: Farrar, Straus and Giroux Paperbacks, 2008), John Mearsheimer and Stephen Walt make a compelling and well-documented argument that Israel's influence over the decision-making apparatus is not necessarily a factor of shared interests with the United States but rather a result of its lobby's massive power. Without denying the almost unparalleled influence the Israeli lobby has in designing and shaping US policy in the Middle East and beyond, I wish to make a clear distinction here between the interest of the majority of the people in the United States versus that of the military-oil-security complex. The latter has a record of supporting war, including Israeli militarism and expansionism.

77. Abe Hayeem, "Architects against Israeli Occupation," *Guardian*, October 4, 2010, http://www.guardian.co.uk/commentisfree/2010/oct/04/architects-settlement -freeze-israel.

78. Ronnie Kasrils, "South Africa's Israel Boycott," *Guardian*, September 29, 2010, http://www.guardian.co.uk/commentisfree/2010/sep/29/south-africa-boycott-israel.

79. From notes I took at this lecture.

80. "TUC Votes for Campaign of Boycott and Disinvestment to Free Palestine," press release posted on Palestinian Solidarity Campaign website, n.d., http://www.palestinecampaign.org/index7b.asp?m_id=1&l1_id=4&l2_id=24 &Content_ID=1493.

81. "SAMWU Declares, Every Municipality an Apartheid Israel Free Zone!" press release, June 4, 2010, http://www.samwu.org.za/index.php?Itemid=1&id=621 &option=com_content&task=view.

82. Greg Dropkin, "Dockworkers, Worldwide, Respond to Israel's Flotilla Massacre and Gaza Siege," *Counterpunch*, July 13, 2010, http://www.counterpunch.org /dropkin07132010.html.

83. Rachel Shabi, "Israeli Exports Hit by European Boycotts after Attacks on Gaza," *Guardian*, April 3, 2009, http://www.guardian.co.uk/world/2009/ apr/03/israel-gaza-attacks-boycotts-food-industry.

84. Adam Horowitz and Philip Weiss, "The Boycott Divestment Sanctions Movement," *Nation*, June 28, 2010, http://www.thenation.com/article/boycott -divestment-sanctions-movement.

85. "Hampshire College First University to Divest from Israel," *News One*, February 12, 2009, http://newsone.com/nation/news-one-staff/hampshire-college -first-university-to-divest-from-israel/.

86. Adalah-NY: The New York Campaign for the Boycott of Israel, http:// adalahny.org/.

87. Stolen Beauty Campaign, http://www.stolenbeauty.org/.

88. Home page of Israel Divestment Campaign (IDC), http://www .israeldivestmentcampaign.org/.

89. Though it has not yet endorsed the Palestinian Civil Society Call for BDS, JVP coordinates closely with the BDS National Committee (BNC) in its BDS-related campaigns.

90. Jewish Voice for Peace, "TIAA-CREF: Divest from the Occupation," http://www.jewishvoiceforpeace.org/campaigns/tiaa-cref-divest-occupation.

91. Global BDS Movement, "TIAA-CREF: Divest from Injustice," October 4, 2010, http://bdsmovement.net/?q=node/775.

92. For more on this, see chapter 11.

93. Sean Clinton, "Israel's Blood Diamonds," *Electronic Intifada*, March 29, 2010, http://electronicintifada.net/v2/article11170.shtml.

94. Queers Undermining Israeli Terrorism (QUIT), http://www.quitpalestine.org/.

95. Queers Against Israeli Apartheid (QuAIA), http://queersagainstapartheid.org/.

96. Palestinian Queers for BDS, http://pqbds.wordpress.com/.

97. Israeli Queers for Palestine, http://israeliqueersforpalestine.wordpress.com/.

98. In response to Israel's attempts to win over queer activists worldwide by presenting itself as a "free society," and in the aftermath of a terror attack by an Israeli gunman against Israeli queer teenagers at a Tel Aviv LGBT association where a counselor and a teenager were killed and several teenagers wounded, Israeli academic Aeyal Gross asks: "Can we speak of a free society and continue to rule millions of dispossessed Palestinians? And are the two issues unrelated?," adding, "[T]he obvious question is whether in a society where shooting at children of the 'other' is the norm, we should be surprised that GLBT children become the target of similar violence." Aeyal Gross, "Harvey Milk Was Here," *Zeek*, n.d. http://www.zeek.forward.com/articles/115761.

99. Israel Ministry of Foreign Affairs, "Israel's Diplomatic Missions Abroad: Status of Relations," updated August 2010, http://www.mfa.gov.il/MFA/About+the +Ministry/Diplomatic+missions/Israels+Diplomatic+Missions+Abroad.htm.

100. Shtrasler, "Anti-Israel Economic Boycotts."

101. Jonathan Lis, "Netherlands Cancels Tour by Israeli Mayors over Settlers' Presence," *Haaretz*, September 19, 2010, http://www.haaretz.com/news/ diplomacy-defense/netherlands-cancels-israeli-mayors-tour-1.314620.

102. Adri Nieuwhof and Guus Hoelen, "Major Dutch Pension Fund Divests from Occupation," *Electronic Intifada*, November 12, 2010, http://electronicintifada .net/v2/article11621.shtml.

103. Architects and Planners for Justice in Palestine (APJP), "Spain excludes Israeli Settlement University from International Solar Decathlon Europe 2010 to Be Held in Madrid," press release, September 21, 2009, http:// www.pacbi.org/etemplate.php?id=1105.

104. Court of Justice of the European Union, "Products Originating in the West Bank Do Not Qualify for Preferential Customs Treatment under the EC-Israel Agreement," press release, Luxembourg, February 25, 2010, http://europa.eu/ rapid/pressReleasesAction.do?reference=CJE/10/14&format=HTML&aged=0 &language=EN&guiLanguage.

105. "Norway Bans Testing of Israel-bound Submarines," Homeland Security Newswire, October 1, 2010, http://homelandsecuritynewswire.com/norway -bans-testing-israel-bound-submarines.

106. Shtrasler, "Anti-Israel Economic Boycotts."

107. According to NASDAQ website as of March 31, 2010, http://www.nasdaq .com/asp/holdings.asp?symbol=ESLT&selected=ESLT.

108. Nicolai Raastrup, "Israel Uforstående over for Danske Bank," *Business.dk*, January 25, 2010, http://www.business.dk/finans/israel-uforstaaende-over -danske-bank.

109. Shtrasler, "Anti-Israel Economic Boycotts."

110. Boycott! Supporting the Palestinian BDS Call from Within, http://boycottisrael
     .info/.

111. The Alternative Information Center Palestine/Israel, http://www
     .alternativenews.org/english/.

112. "About ICAHD," Israeli Committee Against House Demolitions, http://
     www.icahd.org/?page_id=68.

113. Who Profits? Exposing the Israeli Occupation Industry, http://www.
     whoprofits.org/.

114. The BDS Call's Palestinian initiators and sponsors have never minced words
     about how the Palestinian people at large view the central and indispensable
     role of Zionism in Israel's system of colonial oppression. The BNC's strategic
     position paper states: "The sources of Israel's regime [of oppression] are
     found in the **racist ideology of late 19th century European colonialism**
     which was adopted by the dominant stream of the Zionist movement (World
     Zionist Organization, Jewish Agency, Jewish National Fund, a.o.) in order to
     justify and recruit political support for its **colonial project of an** *exclusive*
     Jewish state in Palestine (i.e. in the area of current Israel and the OPT). Thus,
     secular political Zionism translated ancient religious-spiritual notions of
     Jews as 'a chosen people' and of 'Eretz Israel' **into an aggressive and racist,
     political colonial program,** which—**based on the doctrine that Jews were a
     nation in political terms with superior claims to Palestine**—called to 're-
     deem' Palestine, which was declared to be 'a land without people.' " (Palestin-
     ian Civil Society, "United against Apartheid, Colonialism").

115. M. J. Rosenberg, "AIPAC: Fighting for Survival," *Aljazeera.net*, November 20,
     2010, http://english.aljazeera.net/indepth/2010/11/2010112083231771111.html.

116. Edward Said, *Representations of the Intellectual: The 1993 Reith Lectures*
     (New York: Vintage, 1994), p. 11.

CHAPTER 1: WHY NOW?

1. The time of writing is in September 2010.

2. For the text of the historic 2005 call issued by nearly two hundred Palestinian
    civil society organizations, see http://www.bdsmovement.net/?q=node/52.

3. Richard Falk, "Slouching towards a Palestinian Holocaust," Transnational
    Foundation for Peace and Future Research, June 29, 2007, http://www
    .transnational.org/Area_MiddleEast/2007/Falk_PalestineGenocide.html.

4. "Human Rights in Palestine and Other Occupied Arab Territories: Report of
    the United Nations Fact-Finding Mission on the Gaza Conflict," September
    25, 2009, http://www2.ohchr.org/english/bodies/hrcouncil/docs/12session/
    A-HRC-12-48.pdf.

5. Ibid.

6. Maxwell Gaylard, quoted in "Humanitarian Organisations Deeply Concerned about the Ongoing Water and Sanitation Crisis in Gaza; Call for an Immediate Opening of Gaza's Crossings," Association of International Development Agencies press statement, August 2009, http://www.ochaopt.org/documents/hc_aida_statement_gaza_watsan_20090803_english.pdf.

7. Amnesty International, "Troubled Waters—Palestinians Denied Fair Access to Water," October 2009, http://www.amnesty.org/en/library/asset/MDE15/027/2009/en/e9892ce4-7fba-469b-96b9-c1e1084c620c/mde150272009en.pdf.

8. UNEP, "Environmental Assessment of the Gaza Strip Following Hostilities in December 2008–January 2009," September 2009, http://postconflict.unep.ch/publications/UNEP_Gaza_EA.pdf.

9. Newweapons Committee, "Gaza Strip, Soil Has Been Contaminated Due to Bombings: Population in Danger," press release, December 17, 2009, http://www.newweapons.org/?q=node/110.

10. Human Rights Watch, *Rain of Fire: Israel's Unlawful Use of White Phosphorus in Gaza*, March 2009, http://www.hrw.org/sites/default/files/reports/iopt0309web.pdf.

11. Al Dameer Human Rights Association, December 2009, http://www.aldameer.org/en/index.php?pagess=main&id=138

12. Amos Harel, "Shooting and Crying," *Haaretz*, March 20, 2009, http://www.haaretz.com/hasen/spages/1072475.html (accessed May 27, 2009).

13. Gideon Levy, "IDF Ceased Long Ago Being 'Most Moral Army in the World,'" *Haaretz*, March 22, 2009, http://www.haaretz.com/hasen/spages/1072821.html.

14. Amos Harel, "IDF Rabbinate Publication during Gaza War: We Will Show No Mercy on the Cruel," *Haaretz*, January 26, 2009, http://www.haaretz.com/hasen/spages/1058758.html.

15. Israel Shahak and Norton Mezvinsky, *Jewish Fundamentalism in Israel* (London: Pluto, 1999); Israel Shahak, *Jewish History, Jewish Religion: The Weight of Three Thousand Years* (London: Pluto, 2002).

16. For more on this, see Omar Barghouti, "Israel's Latest Massacre in Qana: Racist Jewish Fundamentalism a Factor," *Electronic Intifada*, July 30, 2006, http://electronicintifada.net/v2/article5338.shtml.

17. Uri Blau, "Dead Palestinian Babies and Bombed Mosques: IDF Fashion 2009," *Haaretz*, March 20, 2009, http://www.haaretz.com/hasen/spages/1072466.html.

18. Durex is a brand of condoms that is popular in Israel.

19. Blau, "Dead Palestinian Babies."

20. Ilan Pappé, *The Ethnic Cleansing of Palestine* (Oxford: Oneworld, 2006).

21. Badil Resource Center, "2008 Survey Summary of Statistical Findings (Number & Distribution of Displaced Palestinians)," June 20, 2009, http://www.badil.org/en/documents/category/23-population?download=442%3A2008-survey-summary-of-statistical-findings-number-distribution-of-displaced

      -palestinians.
22.   Omar Barghouti, "Relative Humanity: The Essential Obstacle to a Just
      Peace in Palestine," *Counterpunch*, December 13–14, 2003, http://www
      .counterpunch.org/barghouti12132003.html.
23.   Ari Shavit, "Cry the Beloved Two-State Solution," *Haaretz*, August 10, 2003.
24.   UN Convention on the Prevention and Punishment of the Crime of Geno-
      cide, 1948, http://www2.ohchr.org/english/law/genocide.htm.
25.   International lawyers insist that intention must be proved without doubt
      before such crimes can be condemned as full-fledged genocide. Systematic
      announcements and threats by key political, religious, and cultural leaders
      in Israel to visit mass death on Gaza "in response" to attacks emanating
      from the Strip can be regarded as consistent declarations of intent.
26.   A recent example is the Israeli forces' bulldozing, five consecutive times in a few
      weeks, the "unrecognized" Bedouin Palestinian village Araqib (Arakib) in the
      Naqab (Ilana Curiel, "Bedouin Village Razed for 5th Time," *Ynetnews*, Septem-
      ber 13, 2010, http://www.ynetnews.com/articles/0,7340,L-3953174,00.html).
      For more context see "Bedouins in Israel Call upon Obama to Intervene, End
      Violation of Their Most Basic Rights," Alternative News Information Center,
      September 2, 2010, http://www.alternativenews.org/english/index.php/
      topics/news/2844-bedouins-in-israel-call-upon-obama-to-intervene-end-
      violation-of-their-most-basic-rights-.
27.   International Court of Justice, "Legal Consequences of the Construction of
      a Wall in the Occupied Palestinian Territories," press release, July 9, 2004,
      http://www.icj-cij.org/docket/index.php?pr=71&code=mwp&p1=3&p2=4
      &p3=6&case=131&k=5a.
28.   Richard Falk, Statement on Gaza to the Human Rights Council, March
      23, 2009, http://www.transnational.org/Area_MiddleEast/2009/Falk
      _OralStatement_Gaza.html.

CHAPTER 2: WHY BDS?

1.   Ann Laura Stoler, a renowned US scholar of colonialism, has recently de-
      scribed Israel as "a colonial state committed to replacing and displacing a
      Palestinian population" ("By Colonial Design," Palestinian Campaign for
      the Academic and Cultural Boycott of Israel, September 10, 2010, http://
      www.pacbi.org/etemplate.php?id=1361).
2.   For an in-depth analysis of Israeli apartheid and the colonial system, see the
      strategic position paper published by the BDS National Committee (BNC),
      "United Against Apartheid, Colonialism and Occupation," October 2008,
      http://bdsmovement.net/files/English-BNC_Position_Paper-Durban_Review.pdf.

3.   The following section is based on a previously published article: Omar Bargh-
     outi, "Putting Palestine Back on the Map: Boycott as Civil Resistance," *Journal
     of Palestine Studies* 35, no. 3 (Spring 2006), http://www.palestine-studies
     .org/journals.aspx?id=6804&jid=1&href=fulltext.

4.   For my analysis of the one-state solution, see Omar Barghouti, "Re-imagin-
     ing Palestine: Self-Determination, Ethical De-colonization and Equality,"
     ZNet, July 29, 2009, http://www.zmag.org/znet/viewArticle/22158.

5.   Edward Said, "Palestinians under Siege," *London Review of Books* 22, no. 24
     (December 14, 2000), http://www.lrb.co.uk/v22/n24/edward-said/palestinians
     -under-siege. For a more detailed study of the failure of the "peace process," see
     Edward Said, *The End of the Peace Process* (New York: Pantheon Books, 2000).

6.   UN Resolution 3379 (XXX), "Elimination of All Forms of Racial Discrim-
     ination," November 10, 1975, http://unispal.un.org/UNISPAL.NSF/0/
     761C1063530766A7052566A2005B74D1.

7.   For more on the application of the term *apartheid* to Israel, see chapter 13.

8.   Reuters, "Amnesty Slams Israel for Role in Mideast Violence," November 1,
     2000.

9.   WCAR NGO Forum Declaration, September 3, 2001, http://www.africaresource
     .com/war/vol3.1/ngo_declare.pdf.

10. University of California Berkeley Students for Justice in Palestine launched
     its first divestment drive in 2001, inspiring groups on many other cam-
     puses across the United States: Cal Divest From Apartheid, http://www
     .caldivestfromapartheid.com/2010/05/29/bds-at-uc-berkeley-the-campaign
     -the-vote-and-the-veto-by-youmna-derby-and-dina-omar/. The Columbia
     University divestment campaign started in 2002 ("Statement to the Commu-
     nity Hearing, Advisory Committee on Socially Responsible Investing, Colum-
     bia University," http://www.columbiadivest.org/press2.html), and so did
     Harvard's (Ewen MacAskill, "Harvard Insists Israeli Shares Sale Not Driven by
     Boycott," *Guardian*, http://www.guardian.co.uk/world/2010/aug/16/harvard
     -israeli-shares-sale-boycott).

11. Desmond Tutu, "Of Occupation and Apartheid: Do I Divest?" *Counter-
     punch*, October 17, 2002, http://www.counterpunch.org/tutu1017.html.

12. US Campaign to End the Israeli Occupation, http://www.endtheoccupation
     .org/.

13. Alan Cooperman, "Israel Divestiture Spurs Clash: Jewish Leaders Condemn
     Move by Presbyterian Church," *Washington Post*, September 29, 2004, http://
     www.washingtonpost.com/wp-dyn/articles/A58039-2004Sep28.html; Nathan
     Guttman, "Church Adopts Compromise Resolution on Israel," *Jerusalem Post*,
     June 19, 2006, http://www.jpost.com/International/Article.aspx?id=25377
     and "Disinvestment from Israel," *Wikipedia*, http://en.wikipedia.org/wiki/
     Disinvestment_from_Israel (last modified October 11, 2010).

14. PACBI's 2004 Call for Boycott can be read at http://www.pacbi.org/etemplate .php?id=869.

15. AP, "Fatah Backs Two-State Solution, Sharpening Rift with Hamas," *Haaretz*, October 8, 2009, http://www.haaretz.com/print-edition/news/ fatah-backs-two-state-solution-sharpening-rift-with-hamas-1.281694.

16. Palestinian academic and political analyst Haidar Eid, for instance, accused Fatah of moving "into the post-colonial condition without achieving independence." "The Pitfalls of Palestinian National Consciousness," *Electronic Intifada*, August 25, 2009, http://electronicintifada.net/v2/article10728.shtml.

17. Ethan Bronner, "Palestinians Try a Less Violent Path to Resistance," *New York Times*, April 6, 2010, http://www.nytimes.com/2010/04/07/world/ middleeast/07westbank.html?_r=1.

18. Palestinian analyst Nadia Hijab convincingly argues that while armed resistance is legal under international law, if it abides by its precepts it is "the least effective source of power available to the Palestinians." "More Than One *S* in Resistance," Middle East Online, August 10, 2009, http://www .middle-east-online.com/english/?id=33649.

19. John Pilger, "For Israel, a Reckoning," *New Statesman*, January 2010, http://www.newstatesman.com/international-politics/2010/01/pilger-israel -palestinian-gaza.

20. A 2010 poll of Jewish-Israeli teens, for instance, reveals that half of them do not want Arab students in their classrooms (Or Kashti, "Poll: Half of Israeli Teens Don't Want Arab Students in Their Class," *Haaretz*, June 9, 2010, http://www.haaretz.com/news/national/poll-half-of-israeli-teens-don-t-want -arab-students-in-their-class-1.312479#article_comments). In another example, the Carmel Academic Center in Haifa canceled an accounting course because a majority of the students applying were Palestinian citizens of Israel, it was revealed in a news item reported on Israeli news Channel 10 on May 24, 2010 (see Alternative Information Center, May 27, 2009, http://www .alternativenews.org/english/index.php/topics/news/1950-carmel-academic -center-closes-academic-track-as-too-many-palestinian-students-registered-).

21. Supporting the Palestinian BDS Call from Within, http://boycottisrael.info/.

22. Adalah-NY: The New York Campaign for the Boycott of Israel, http:// adalahny.org/.

23. Stolen Beauty, http://www.codepink4peace.org/section.php?id=415.

24. Campagne Agrexco/Carmel, http://www.bdsfrance.org/index.php?option =com_content&view=article&id=19&Itemid=21.

25. BNC Statements, http://bdsmovement.net/?q=node/126.

26. For more on the systematic forcible displacement of the Palestinians, see Ilan Pappé, *The Ethnic Cleansing of Palestine* (Oxford: Oneworld, 2006).

CHAPTER 3: THE SOUTH AFRICA STRATEGY FOR PALESTINE

1. Michael Ben-Yair, "The War's Seventh Day," *Haaretz*, March 3, 2002, http://www.haaretz.com/print-edition/opinion/the-war-s-seventh-day-1.51513.

2. In a 2003 poll published on the BBC website, "Nearly 60% of Europeans said yes when asked in the Eurobarometer survey if Israel presents a threat to peace, putting it ahead of Iran, North Korea, and the United States, each of which polled 53%" ("Israeli Anger over EU "Threat" Poll," November 3, 2003, http://news.bbc.co.uk/2/hi/middle_east/3237277.stm). In a poll carried out toward the end of 2008, the largest number of countries—nineteen out of twenty-one—gave negative ratings to Israel, rated most negatively, along with Iran and Pakistan ("Views of China and Russian Decline in Global Poll," June 2, 2009, http://www.bbc.co.uk/pressoffice/pressreleases/stories/2009/02_february/06/poll.shtml). A major poll of public opinion in six "moderate" Arab states carried out by the authoritative Zogby International revealed that 95 percent of Arabs view Israel as the "biggest threat" to them (Jim Lobe, "Israel, US Greatest Threats to Middle East," *Electronic Intifada*, April 15, 2008, http://electronicintifada.net/v2/article9458.shtml)-.

3. United Nations Office for the Coordination of Humanitarian Affairs, "Field Update on Gaza from the Humanitarian Coordinator," February 6–9, 2009, http://www.ochaopt.org/documents/ocha_opt_gaza_humanitarian_situation_report_2009_02_09_english.pdf.

4. "A Fence along the Settlers' Lines," editorial, *Haaretz*, October 3, 2003.

5. Mazal Mualem, "Old Habitats Die Hard," *Haaretz*, June 20, 2003.

6. Ibid.

7. Dr. Aghlab Khouri of St. John Eye Hospital in Jerusalem explains in his affidavit to a human rights organization the effect of the impact of a rubber-coated metal bullet to the eye: "The cases that I [have] treated during the clashes were cases of direct shots to the eyes with rubber coated metal bullets. This kind of bullet does not have a sharp end but has a piece of metal inside; they hit the eye with great speed, creating an impact that shatters the eye." The Palestinian Society for the Protection of Human Rights and the Environment (LAW), "Israel's Excessive and Indiscriminate Use of Force: Eye Injuries," November 2, 2000.

8. Physicians for Human Rights, "Evaluation of the Use of Force in Israel, Gaza and the West Bank," November 3, 2000, http://www.phrusa.org/research/forensics/israel/Israel_force_2.html.

9. Tanya Reinhart, "Don't Say You Didn't Know," Indymedia, November 6, 2000.

10. Chris Hedges, "A Gaza Diary," *Harper's Magazine*, October 2001.

11. Leon Hadar, "New Historians Laying Foundations for New Realities," *Washington Report on Middle East Affairs*, (November–December 1994), http://

www.washington-report.org/backissues/1194/9411016.htm.

12. "Survivors of the Holocaust are entitled to feelings that are irrational," ADL national director Abraham Foxman recently told the *New York Times* in one blatant example of such manipulation. Referring to families who lost loved ones on 9/11, Foxman continued, "Their anguish entitles them to positions that others would categorize as irrational or bigoted." Foxman is essentially saying that you can be a racist if you are a survivor—and of course not just of the Holocaust but also of 9/11. Obviously, Foxman has not stopped to consider what this logic—that the victims of an injustice have the right to be bigots—might mean if applied to Palestinians who have suffered the Nakba and ongoing ethnic cleansing at the hands of Zionists (Michael Barbaro, "Debate Heats Up about Mosque near Ground Zero," *New York Times*, July 30, 2010, http://www.nytimes.com/2010/07/31/nyregion/31mosque.html?_r=1&pagewanted=2).

13. For more on the concept of "relative humanity," see Omar Barghouti, "Relative Humanity: The Fundamental Obstacle to a One-State Solution in Historic Palestine," *Electronic Intifada*, January 6, 2004, http://electronicintifada.net/v2/article2325.shtml.

14. For more on this argument, refer to Omar Barghouti, "The Spirit of Auschwitz," *Al-Ahram Weekly Online*, May 2–8, 2002.

15. Deutsche Presse Agentur (DPA), "Sephardi Jews Demand Recognition from Spanish Government," *Haaretz*, October 15, 2002.

16. For more details on this, refer to Omar Barghouti, "On Refugees, Creativity and Ethics," *ZNet*, September 28, 2002.

17. According to Adalah: The Legal Center for Arab Minority Rights in Israel, "Israel never sought to assimilate or integrate the Palestinian population, treating them as second-class citizens and excluding them from public life and the public sphere. The state practiced systematic and institutionalized discrimination in all areas, such as land dispossession and allocation, education, language, economics, culture, and political participation." "Historical Background," http://www.adalah.org/eng/backgroundhistory.php.

18. The application of the internationally accepted definition of apartheid to Israel is discussed in more detail in chapter 14.

19. Israeli writer Benjamin Beit-Hallahmi says, "Israelis seem to be haunted by . . . the curse of the original sin against the native Arabs. How can Israel be discussed without recalling the dispossession and exclusion of non-Jews? This is the most basic fact about Israel, and no understanding of Israeli reality is possible without it. The original sin haunts and torments Israelis: it marks everything and taints everybody. Its memory poisons the blood and marks every moment of existence." Benjamin Beit-Hallahmi, *Original Sins: Reflections on the History of Zionism and Israel* (New York: Olive Branch, 1993), 216.

20. Edward Herman, "Israeli Apartheid and Terrorism," *Z Magazine*, April 29, 2002.

21. *Haaretz*, May 22, 2003.

22. Eli Ashkenazi, "Budget for Cancer Mapping Doesn't Extend to Arab Sector," *Haaretz*, March 28, 2005.

23. Lily Galili, "Long Division," *Haaretz*, December 19, 2003.

24. Ronnie Kasrils and Victoria Brittain, "Both Palestinians and Israelis Will Benefit from a Boycott," *Guardian*, May 25, 2005.

25. Ibid.

26. Ibid.

27. Lily Galili, "A Jewish Demographic State," *Haaretz*, July 1, 2002.

28. Yulie Khromchenco, "Poll: 64% of Israeli Jews Support Encouraging Arabs to Leave," *Haaretz*, June 22, 2004.

29. Amnesty International, "Israel and the Occupied Territories (OPT): Update of the Briefing to the Committee against Torture," 2009, http://www2 .ohchr.org/english/bodies/cat/docs/ngos/AI_Israel_Gaza42.pdf.

30. Ruthie Blum, "It's the Demography, Stupid," *Jerusalem Post*, May 21, 2004.

31. Galili, "Jewish Demographic State."

32. Desmond Tutu, "Apartheid in the Holy Land," *Guardian*, April 29, 2002, http://www.guardian.co.uk/israel/comment/0,10551,706911,00.html.

33. Roman Bronfman, "The Hong Kong of the Middle East," *Haaretz*, May 20, 2005, http://www.haaretz.com/hasen/pages/ShArt.jhtml?itemNo=578338 &contrassID=2&subContrassID=4&sbSubContrassID=0&listSrc=Y.

34. Roee Nahmias, "Israeli Terror Is Worse," *Ynetnews*, July 29, 2005, http://www.ynetnews.com/articles/0,7340,L-3119885,00.html.

35. Thomas O'Dwyer, "Parts and Apartheid," *Haaretz*, May 24, 2002.

36. Jon Jeter, "South African Jews Polarized over Israel," *Washington Post*, December 19, 2001.

37. Zvi Zrahiya and Haaretz Service, "Israel Official: Accepting Palestinians into Israel Better Than Two States," April 29, 2010, http://www.haaretz.com/ hasen/spages/1166300.html.

38. Desmond Tutu and Ian Urbina, "Against Israeli Apartheid," *Nation*, July 15, 2002.

39. Palestinian Civil Society's Call for Boycott, Divestment and Sanctions (BDS) can be read in full at www.PACBI.org.

40. Tony Judt, "Israel: The Alternative," *New York Review of Books* 50, no. 16 (October 23, 2003), http://www.nybooks.com/articles/16671.

41. I. F. Stone, "Holy War," *New York Review of Books*, August 3, 1967, http:// www.nybooks.com/articles/12009.

42. Henry Siegman, "Is Israel's Legitimacy under Challenge?" *Huffington Post*, August 16, 2010, http://www.huffingtonpost.com/henry-siegman/is-israels-legitimacy-und_b_682989.html.

43. For more on this, see Uri Yacobi Keller, "The Economy of the Occupation: Academic Boycott of Israel," Alternative Information Center, October 2009, http://www.alternativenews.org/images/stories/downloads/Economy_of_the _occupation_23-24.pdf; and SOAS Palestine Society, "Tel Aviv University— A Leading Israeli Military Research Centre," February 2009, http://www .electronicintifada.net/downloads/pdf/090708-soas-palestine-society.pdf.

44. Without delving into the debate on whether the tail (the Israeli lobby) wags the dog(US foreign policy) or not, one can deduce that both sides of the debate concur that the tail and the dog are organically connected. With the current power structure in the United States, the declared foreign policy objectives tend to reflect the great influence of the Israeli lobby in the US Congress as well as in key parts of the White House; this influence has reached the stage of becoming an organic part of the system. The recent in-your-face Israeli dismissal of the simplest US demands will undoubtedly fuel the question of who exactly shapes US foreign policy in the region. Stephen Walt argues that Obama has acted as any other US president would have in an election year, bowing to the wishes of the lobby: "Settling for More Settlements," *Stephen Walt Foreign Policy* blog, September 27, 2010, http://walt. foreignpolicy.com/posts/2010/09/27/settling_for_more_settlements.

45. Johan Hari, "Is Gideon Levy the Most Hated Man in Israel or Just the Most Heroic?" *Independent*, September 24, 2010, http://www.independent.co.uk/ news/world/middle-east/is-gideon-levy-the-most-hated-man-in-israel-or -just-the-most-heroic-2087909.html.

46. A September 2, 2010, cover article in *Time* by Karl Vick, interestingly titled "Why Israel Doesn't Care about Peace," reveals the level of apathy that prevails among Israelis: http://www.time.com/time/world/article/0,8599 ,2015602-1,00.html. A *New York Times* columnist concludes, "So long as this attitude [of apathy] prevails, the far right [in Israel] will have veto power over policy in the occupied territory. For a peace deal to happen, Israel's centrists need to get jarred out of their indifference. Someone needs to scare these people." He goes on to suggest to the oppressed Palestinians persistent nonviolent action and demands for equal rights (Robert Wright, "A One-to-Two-State Solution," New York Times.com, *Opinionator* blog, September 28, 2010, http://opinionator.blogs.nytimes.com/2010/09/28/a-one -to-two-state-solution/?hp). Not quite endorsing BDS, but very close.

47. Desmond Tutu, "Israeli Ties: A Chance to Do the Right Thing," *Times Live* (South Africa), September 26, 2010, http://www.timeslive.co.za/world/ article675369.ece/Israeli-ties—a-chance-to-do-the-right-thing.

48. Étienne Balibar, "A Complex Urgent Universal Political Cause," address at conference of Faculty for Israeli-Palestinian Peace (FFIPP), Université Libre de Bruxelles, July 4, 2004.

49. For a more detailed refutation of the anti-Semitism smear, see chapter 10.

50. For a fuller discussion of guidelines and criteria for working with Israeli anticolonial activists and groups, see chapter 16.

CHAPTER 4: ACADEMIC BOYCOTT: MORAL RESPONSIBILITY AND THE STRUGGLE AGAINST COLONIAL OPPRESSION

1. AAUP (American Association of University Professors), "The AAUP Rejects Academic Boycotts (2005)," May 3, 2005. http://www.aaup.org/AAUP/comm/rep/A/opposeboy.htm.

2. Editorial, "Sponsors Quash Boycott Debate," *Mail and Guardian Online*, February 18, 2006. http://www.pacbi.org/etemplate.php?id=143.

3. AAUP, Committee A on Academic Freedom and Tenure, "On Academic Boycotts," *Academe*, September-October 2006, http://www.aaup.org/AAUP/pubsres/academe/2006/SO/Boycott/OnAcademicBoycotts.htm.

4. Judith Butler, "Israel/Palestine and the Paradoxes of Academic Freedom," *Radical Philosophy* 135 (January-February 2006): 8–17.

5. United Nations World Conference on Human Rights, "Vienna Declaration and Program of Action," July 12, 1993, http://www.unhchr.ch/huridocda/huridoca.nsf/(Symbol)/A.CONF.157.23.En?OpenDocument.

6. UN Committee on Economic, Social and Cultural Rights, "The Right to Education (Art. 13)," December 8, 1999, http://www.unhchr.ch/tbs/doc.nsf/(Symbol)/ae1a0b126d068e868025683c003c8b3b?Opendocument.

7. David Bukay, "The First Cultural Flaw in Thinking: The Arab Personality," in Bukay, *Arab-Islamic Political Culture: A Key Source to Understanding Arab Politics and the Arab-Israeli Conflict* (Shaarei Tikva, Israel: Ariel Center for Policy Research, 2003).

8. Meron Rapoport, "In the Name of Truth," *Haaretz*, April 28, 2005.

9. For more on this point, see Esther Zandberg, "Unacceptable Norms," *Haaretz*, September 26, 2004; and Lily Galili, "A Jewish Demographic State," *Haaretz*, July 1, 2002.

10. For more on the need to promote open rational debate in North America about Israel's policies and Western complicity, see PACBI Statement, "Upholding Debate as a Necessary Component of Academic Freedom," September 2, 2007, http://www.pacbi.org/etemplate.php?id=592.

11. PACBI's statement, "Boycotting Israel Put High on the Agenda," May 25, 2005, is available at http://www.pacbi.org/etemplate.php?id=48.

12. Birzeit University's Public Relations Office, "The Criminalization of Education: Academic Freedom and Human Rights at Birzeit University during the Palestinian Uprising," December 1989, 2.

13. Tel Aviv University professor Tanya Reinhart wrote at the beginning of the 2000 intifada that "a common practice [among Israeli sharpshooters] is shooting a rubber-coated metal bullet straight in the eye—a little game of well-trained soldiers, which requires maximum precision." *Zspace*, November 8, 2000, http://www.zcommunications.org/dont-say-you-didnt-know -by-tanya-reinhart. See Physicians for Human Rights, "Evaluation of the Use of Force in Israel, Gaza and the West Bank," October 2000, http://physiciansforhumanrights.org/library/report-useofforce-israel.html.

14. Human Rights Watch, "Second Class: Discrimination against Palestinian Arab Children in Israel's Schools," September 2001, http://www.hrw.org/reports/2001/israel2.

15. Shulamit Aloni, quoted in Roee Nahmias, "Israeli Terror Is Worse," *Yedioth Ahronoth*, July 29, 2005.

16. Roman Bronfman, "The Hong Kong of the Middle East," *Haaretz*, May 20, 2005.

17. Yair Sheleg, "ADL's Boss Threatens Boycott of UK Academe," *Haaretz*, May 18, 2005.

18. The PACBI statement ("The Palestinian Call for Academic Boycott Revised: Adjusting the Parameters of the Debate," January 28, 2006) can be read in full at http://www.pacbi.org/etemplate.php?id=117.

19. Prof. Ilan Pappé, author of *The Ethnic Cleansing of Palestine* and a supporter of Teddy Katz, an Israeli graduate student who revealed evidence of an Israeli massacre during 1948, was subjected to undue pressure and threats from his own institution, Haifa University, as well as from his colleagues, and eventually was convinced to leave Israel altogether for the United Kingdom. For more on this, see Zalman Amit, "Tantura, Teddy Katz and Haifa University," *Counterpunch*, May 11, 2005, http://www.counterpunch.org/amit05112005.html; and Oren Ben-Dor, "To Create It, an Academic Boycott Is Needed: Academic Freedom in Israel Is Central to Resolving the Conflict," *Counterpunch*, May 21–22, 2005, http://www.counterpunch.org/bendor05212005.html.

20. Oren Ben-Dor argues that one of the purposes of the proposed academic boycott is to "provide a means to transcend the publicly sanctioned limits of debate," adding, "Such freedom is precisely what is absent in Israel." Ben-Dor, "Academic Freedom in Israel Is Central."

21. Ronnie Kasrils and Victoria Brittain, "Both Palestinians and Israelis Will Benefit from a Boycott," *Guardian*, May 25, 2005.

CHAPTER 5: JUST INTELLECTUALS? OPPRESSION,

RESISTANCE, AND THE PUBLIC ROLE OF INTELLECTUALS

1.   The PACBI call for an academic and cultural boycott of Israel can be found at http://www.pacbi.org/etemplate.php?id=869.

2.   See Omar Barghouti and Lisa Taraki, "Academic Boycott and the Israeli Left," *Electronic Intifada*, April 15, 2005.

3.   See Omar Barghouti, "Relative Humanity—the Fundamental Obstacle to the One State Solution," *ZNet*, December 16, 2003.

4.   PACBI has recently issued two important statements dealing with the role of Zionist "left" academics and cultural figures in undermining the Palestinian BDS Call: http://www.pacbi.org/etemplate.php?id=1175 and http://www.pacbi.org/etemplate.php?id=1350.

5.   For more on this, see chapter 6.

6.   Dan Williams, "Israeli Actors Boycott Theatres in Settlements", *Reuters AlertNet*, August 29, 2010, http://www.alertnet.org/thenews/newsdesk/LDE67S04H.htm; Chaim Levinson and Or Kashti, "150 Academics, Artists Back Actors' Boycott of Settlement Art Center," *Haaretz*, August 31, 2010, http://www.haaretz.com/print-edition/news/150-academics-artists-back-actors-boycott-of-settlement-arts-center-1.311149.

7.   Cited in Paulo Freire, *Pedagogy of the Oppressed* (New York: Herder and Herder, 1972).

8.   See Omar Barghouti, "The Morality of a Cultural Boycott of Israel," *OpenDemocracy*, September 20, 2005.

CHAPTER 6: FREEDOM VERSUS "ACADEMIC FREEDOM": DEBATING THE BRITISH ACADEMIC BOYCOTT

1.   Meron Rappaport, "Alone on the Barricades," *Haaretz*, May 6, 2005.

2.   Ilan Pappé states: "The boycott reached academia because academia in Israel chose to be official, national. Prof. Yehuda Shenhav checked into it and found that out of 9,000 members of academia in Israel, only 30-40 are actively engaged in reading significant criticism, and a smaller number, just three or four, are teaching their students in a critical manner about Zionism and so on" (quoted in ibid.).

3.   Oren Ben-Dor, "The Boycott Should Continue," *Independent*, May 30, 2005.

4.   Baruch Kimmerling, "The Meaning of Academic Boycott," *ZNet*, April 26, 2005.

5.   Meron Rappaport, "A Wall in Their Heart," *Yedioth Ahronoth*, May 23, 2003, reproduced at http://www.gush-shalom.org/archives/wall_yediot_eng.html.

6.   *Haaretz*, February 25, 2003.

7.   *Jerusalem Post* weekend supplement "Up Front," May 21, 2004.

8.   *Haaretz*, September 26, 2004.

9.   *Jerusalem Post*, July 20, 2004.

10. *Haaretz*, September 26, 2004.

11. Arjan El Fassed, "Racism Thrives at Israel's Herzliya Conference," Palestinian Return Centre, January 2004, www.prc.org.uk/data/aspx/d2/332.aspx.

12. *Haaretz*, April 28, 2005.

13. The following examples (all from the above cited *Haaretz* article) of Bukay's writings and utterances in class give a representative sample:

     1. "Among Arabs, you will not find the phenomenon so typical of Judeo-Christian culture: doubts, a sense of guilt, the self-tormenting approach. . . . There is no condemnation, no regret, no problem of conscience among Arabs and Muslims, anywhere, in any social stratum, of any social position."

     2. "Palestinian Terrorists should be shot in the head in front of their families as a deterrent. . . . A whole house should be demolished with the occupants inside."

     3. "Arabs are nothing but alcohol and sex."

     4. "The Arabs are stupid and have contributed nothing to humanity."

14. *Haaretz*, April 28, 2005.

15. Ibid.

16. Ibid.

17. In particular, the Fourth Geneva Convention relative to the Protection of Civilian Persons in Time of War (1949), part 3, section 3, article 47, states: "Protected persons who are in occupied territory shall not be deprived, in any case or in any manner whatsoever, of the benefits of the present Convention by any change introduced, as the result of the occupation of a territory, into the institutions or government of the said territory, nor by any agreement concluded between the authorities of the occupied territories and the Occupying Power, nor by any annexation by the latter of the whole or part of the occupied territory."

18. UN Security Council Resolution 252 (May 21, 1968) considers that "all legislative and administrative measures and actions taken by Israel, including expropriation of land and properties thereon, which tend to change the legal status of Jerusalem are invalid and cannot change that status . . . and urgently calls upon Israel to rescind all such measures already taken and to desist forthwith from taking any further action which tends to change the status of Jerusalem." Also UNSC Resolution 478 (August 20, 1980) determines that "all legislative and administrative measures and actions taken by Israel, the occupying Power, which have altered or purport to alter the character and status of the Holy City of Jerusalem, and in particular the recent 'basic law' on Jerusalem, are null and void and must be rescinded forthwith."

CHAPTER 7: REFLECTING ON THE CULTURAL BOYCOTT

1. Part of Elvis Costello's statement after canceling a concert in Israel over its "intimidation, humiliation or much worse [of] Palestinian civilians in the name of national security," May 5, 2010, http://www.elviscostello.com/news/it-is-after-considerable-contemplation/44.

2. Palestinian Campaign for the Academic and Cultural Boycott of Israel (PACBI), "PACBI Guidelines for the International Academic Boycott of Israel," October 1, 2009, http://www.pacbi.org/etemplate.php?id=1108.

3. PACBI, "PACBI Guidelines for the International Cultural Boycott of Israel," July 20, 2009, http://www.pacbi.org/etemplate.php?id=1047.

4. For more on the inconsistencies of the Zionist "left" in dealing with the boycott of Israel, see PACBI, "Boycotting Ariel: Missing the Forest for the Trees," September 2010, http://www.pacbi.org/etemplate.php?id=1350, and PACBI, "Boycott 'Ariel' and the Rest! All Israeli Academic Institutions Are Complicit in Occupation and Apartheid," February 10, 2010, http://www.pacbi.org/etemplate.php?id=1175.

5. Nomazengele A. Mangaliso, "Cultural Boycotts and Political Change," cited in Neta C. Crawford and Audie Klotz (eds.), *How Sanctions Work: Lessons from South Africa* (London: Macmillan Press, 1999), p.233.

6. Gregory Houston, "International Solidarity: Introduction," *Road to Democracy*, Vol. 3, March 31, 2008, http://www.sadet.co.za/docs/RTD/vol3/vol3_chapter%201.pdf.

7. Enuga S. Reddy, "Statement," January 11, 1984, http://www.anc.org.za/6847?t=United%20Nations.

8. Isaac Zablocki, "Announcing New (and Enormous) Database of Israeli Films Is Now Live," *Culture Shuk*, July 7, 2010, http://cultureshuk.com/2010/07/07/announcing-new-and-enormous-database-of-israeli-films-is-now-live/.

9. "About Us," The Other Israel Film Festival, http://www.otherisrael.org/about-us.

10. "PACBI's Position on the Other Israel Film Festival (New York)," November 12, 2010, http://www.pacbi.org/etemplate.php?id=1411.

11. Nathaniel Popper, "Israel Aims to Improve Its Public Image," *Forward*, October 14, 2005, http://www.forward.com/articles/2070/.

12. Yuval Ben Ami, "About Face," *Haaretz*, September 20, 2005, http://www.haaretz.com/misc/article-print-page/about-face-1.170267?trailingPath=2.169%2C2.225%2C2.239%2C.

13. Ethan Bronner, "After Gaza, Israel Grapples with Crisis of Isolation," *New York Times*, March 18, 2009, http://www.nytimes.com/2009/03/19/world/middleeast/19israel.html.

14. Yitzhak Laor, "Putting Out a Contract on Art," Haaretz, July 25, 2008, http://

www.pacbi.org/etemplate.php?id=790.

15. Claudia La Rocco, "Gestures From an Explosive Movement Palette," *New York Times*, September 26, 2010, http://www.nytimes.com/2010/09/27/arts/dance/27batsheva.html?_r=3.

16. New York Campaign for the Boycott of Israel and Artists against Apartheid, New York City Chapter, "Why We Are Boycotting the Batsheva Dance Company," open letter, September 17, 2010, http://www.pacbi.org/etemplate.php?id=1362.

17. PACBI Newsletter, "NYT Reports Adalah-NY Boycott of Batsheva," PACBI, September 2010, http://www.pacbi.org/newsletter/september2010.php.

18. Jonathan Demme, quoted in Bob Thomas, "Entertainment Industry Fights Racism in South Africa," Associated Press, December 20, 1987.

19. Desmond Tutu, "Israeli Ties: A Chance to Do the Right Thing," *Times Live*, September 26, 2010, http://www.timeslive.co.za/world/article675369.ece/Israeli-ties—a-chance-to-do-the-right-thing.

20. This section is based on an article published under this title in *Dance Insider*, February 22, 2008, in reaction to the announcement of several theaters in New York of Israeli dance shows to coincide with Israel's celebration of its "60th Anniversary" (http://www.danceinsider.com/f2008/f0221_1.html).

21. Palestinian Non-governmental Organizations' Network (PNGO), "60 Years of Palestinian Dispossession," n.d., http://www.pngo.net/data/files/english_statements/08/PNGO-THT-HP5208(2).pdf.

22. See Omar Barghouti, "Putting Palestine Back on the Map: Boycott as Civil Resistance," *Journal of Palestine Studies* 35, no. 3 (Spring 2006): 51, http://www.palestine-studies.org/journals.aspx?id=6804&jid=1&href=fulltext, and Omar Barghouti, "The Light at the End of the Gaza-Ramallah Tunnel," *Electronic Intifada*, June 20, 2007, http://electronicintifada.net/v2/article7043.shtml.

23. Paulo Freire, *Pedagogy of the Oppressed* (New York: Continuum, 2006), 55.

24. In 2009 PACBI issued detailed "Guidelines for the International Cultural Boycott of Israel," http://www.pacbi.org/etemplate.php?id=1047.

25. Wall of Silence, "Faithless Join Boycott," n.d., http://www.wallofsilence.org/news.html.

CHAPTER 8: FIGHTING APARTHEID IN SOUTH AFRICA, CELEBRATING APARTHEID IN ISRAEL: OPEN LETTER TO NADINE GORDIMER

1. One of those letters was written by Haidar Eid, http://electronicintifada.net/v2/article9488.shtml.

2. The PACBI Call for Boycott is endorsed by dozens of the leading academic,

cultural, professional, and other Palestinian civil society unions and organizations: http://pacbi.org/campaign_statement/htm.

3. PACBI organized a petition signed by dozens of internationally renowned cultural figures opposing the "Israel at 60" celebration. The petition was prominently published as a paid advertisement in the *International Herald Tribune*: http://www.pngo.net/data/files/english_statements/08/PNGO-THT-HP5208 (2).pdf.

CHAPTER 9: BETWEEN SOUTH AFRICA AND ISRAEL: UNESCO'S DOUBLE STANDARDS

1. In a more recent statement, published July 11, 2010, PACBI explicitly exposed UNESCO's role in "covering up" the complicity of Israel's academic institutions in occupation, apartheid, and violations of international law. See PACBI, http://www.pacbi.org/etemplate.php?id=1307.

2. The full text of the Palestinian Call for Boycott—issued by the Palestinian Campaign for the Academic and Cultural Boycott of Israel (PACBI) and supported by tens of the most important Palestinian unions, associations and organizations in the occupied West Bank and Gaza—can be found at http://www.pacbi.org/etemplate.php?id=869. For recent articles arguing for academic and cultural boycott of Israel, refer to http://www.pacbi.org.

3. For a listing of the eight UNESCO-sponsored seminars and conferences against apartheid South Africa, organized between 1975 and 1991, see http://www.anc.org.za/6849?t=United%20Nations.

4. Desmond Tutu, "Apartheid in the Holy Land," *Guardian*, April 29, 2002, http://www.guardian.co.uk/israel/comment/0,10551,706911,00.html.

5. World Council of Churches, "WCC Central Committee Encourages Consideration of Economic Measures for Peace in Israel/Palestine," press release, February 21, 2005, http://www.oikoumene.org/gr/news/news-management/eng/a/browse/130/article/1634/wcc-central-committee-enc.html.

6. See, for example, the call for sanctions against Israel issued by War on Want and supported by British MPs and leading artists at http://wow.webbler.org/Echoes%20of%20South%20Africa%3F+8612.twl.

CHAPTER 10: WHAT WE REALLY NEED! A RESPONSE TO ANTI-BOYCOTT ARGUMENTS

1. A. B. Yeshoshua and Amos Oz, "Support Barak Conditionally," *Haaretz*, De-

cember 19, 2000.

2. Barbara Demick, "A Squandered Chance for Mideast Peace," *Philadelphia Inquirer*, January 16, 2001.

3. Danny Rabinowitz, "Not the Right of Return but Right of Return" (Hebrew), *Haaretz*, January 4, 2001.

4. Danny Rabinowitz, "Return of the Native," *Haaretz*, August 8, 2003, http://www.haaretz.com/print-edition/opinion/return-of-the-native-1.96622.

5. Uri Avnery, "The Right of Return," Media Monitors Network, 2000, http://www.mediamonitors.net/uri3.html.

6. Moshe Machover, "Why I Am Not an Israeli Peace Activist," *Weekly Worker*, October 7, 2010, http://www.cpgb.org.uk/article.php?article_id=1004122.

7. For more on this critique of what Palestinians call the "peace industry," see Faris Giacaman, "*Can We Talk? The Middle East 'Peace Industry,'*" *Electronic Intifada*, August 20, 2009, http://electronicintifada.net/v2/article10722.shtml.

CHAPTER 11: DERAILING INJUSTICE: PALESTINIAN CIVIL RESISTANCE TO THE "JERUSALEM LIGHT RAIL"

1. "Jerusalem Light Rail—Mass Transit System," Jerusalem Transportation Master Plan Team—Light Rail, http://www.stopthewall.org/downloads/pdf/Jerusalem_Light_Rail_Mass_Transit_System_Brochure_ENG.pdf.

2. In August 2007 John Dugard, then UN special rapporteur for human rights in the occupied Palestinian territory, described the wall to the UN General Assembly thus: "The 75-km wall being built in East Jerusalem is now almost complete. . . . This wall, which is built through Palestinian neighbourhoods and separates Palestinians from Palestinians, is an exercise in social engineering, designed to achieve the Judaization of Jerusalem by reducing the number of Palestinians in the city. It cannot conceivably be justified on security grounds." Dugard, "Report of the Special Rapporteur on the Situation of Human Rights in the Palestinian Territories Occupied Since 1967," August 17, 2007, http://unispal.un.org/UNISPAL.NSF/0/07FC0614021668418525736B005C8A82.

3. While East Jerusalem is recognized by the United Nations as part of the Palestinian territory occupied by Israel in 1967, the rest of the city, now called West Jerusalem, was also occupied militarily by Zionist forces in 1948 in violation of the partition plan, which envisioned placing the entire city under international jurisdiction.

4. Article 49 of the Fourth Geneva Convention specifically prohibits an occupying power from transferring members of its own civilian population into the territory it occupies. When extensive appropriation of property is involved

without military necessity, the infringement may amount to a war crime. Fourth Geneva Convention, 1949, available at http://www.icrc.org/ihl.nsf/ 385ec082b509e76c41256739003e636d/6756482d86146898c125641e004aa3c5.

5. In his March 2009 report to the UN Human Rights Council, Richard Falk, the current UN special rapporteur for human rights in the OPT, stated that "there are a variety of concerns about the Palestinian future in East Jerusalem, and allegations that Israel is engaged in a subtle, but cumulatively very efficient, process of 'ethnic cleansing' to ensure Jewish demographic dominance of the whole of Jerusalem. A variety of practices have elicited Palestinian complaints, and seem validated by independent observers" (http://www.transnational.org/Area_MiddleEast/2009/Falk_OralStatement _Gaza.html).

6. For more on this, see Ilan Pappé, *The Ethnic Cleansing of Palestine* (Oxford: Oneworld, 2006).

7. Akiva Eldar, "Israel Has Secret Plan to Thwart Division of Jerusalem," *Haaretz*, May 10, 2009, http://www.haaretz.com/hasen/spages/1084402.html.

8. The Grassroots Palestinian Anti–Apartheid Wall Campaign and the Civic Coalition for Defending the Palestinians' Rights in Jerusalem, "A Call to the Kingdom of Saudi Arabia Not to Contract Alstom Ltd. Its New Power Plant in Shoaiba," n.d., http://www.stopthewall.org/downloads/pdf/briefing %20Alstom.pdf.

9. See the map in the brochure at http://www.stopthewall.org/downloads/ pdf/Jerusalem_Light_Rail_Mass_Transit_System_Brochure_ENG.pdf.

10. In its advisory opinion titled "Legal Consequences of the Construction of a Wall in the Occupied Palestinian Territory" (July 9, 2004), the ICJ stated, "The Court concludes that the Israeli settlements in the Occupied Palestinian Territory (including East Jerusalem) have been established in breach of international law" (http://www.icj-cij.org/docket/files/131/1677.pdf).

11. The Israeli Coalition of Women for Peace keeps an up-to-date list of Israeli and international companies implicated in violations of international law in the OPT: http://www.whoprofits.org/.

12. Negotiation Support Unit, "Jerusalem Light Rail" (fact sheet), March 2007.

13. Association France Palestine Solidarité, "Communiqué de l'AFPS sur l'état de la procédure engagée par l'AFPS et l'OLP relative à la construction et à l'exploitation d'un tramway en Cisjordanie," December 15, 2008, http:// www.france-palestine.org/article10614.html.

14. Association France Palestine Solidarité, "Action en justice de l'Afps (et de l'OLP) contre la construction et l'exploitation d'un tramway à Jérusalem-Est," May 3, 2009, http://www.france-palestine.org/imprimersans.php3?id _article=11680.

15. Directive 2004/18/EC of the European Parliament and of the Council of 31

March 2004 on the coordination of procedures for the award of public works contracts, public supply contracts, and public service contracts, http://eur-lex.europa.eu/LexUriServ/LexUriServ.do?uri=CELEX:32004L0018:EN:NOT.

16. For more on the BNC's make-up and activities, see its "about" statement: http://www.bdsmovement.net/?q=node/126.

17. "Final Declaration and Action Plan of The Bilbao Initiative," November 4, 2008, http://www.bdsmovement.net/?q=node/213.

18. "Public Launch of the Palestinian Civil Society Strategic Position Paper towards the UN Durban Review Conference," November 28, 2008, http://bdsmovement.net/?q=node/222.

19. The Civic Coalition for Defending the Palestinians' Rights in Jerusalem and the Grassroots Palestinian Anti-Apartheid Wall Coalition, "Call to the Kingdom of Saudi Arabia," http://www.stopthewall.org/downloads/pdf/briefing%20Alstom.pdf.

20. Abbas Al Lawati, "Palestine Urges Withdrawal of Rail Contract," Gulf News, May 30, 2009, http://www.gulfnews.com/Region/Middle_East/10318479.html.

21. Ibid.

22. Adri Nieuwhof, "Principled Dutch ASN Bank Ends Relations with Veolia," Electronic Intifada, November 26, 2006, http://electronicintifada.net/v2/article6076.shtml.

23. Aurine Crémieu, "Rubrique 'en mouvement' Israel et Territoires Occupes: Un tramway hors-la-loi," Amnesty International, March 1, 2006, http://www.amnesty.fr/index.php/amnesty/s_informer/la_chronique/mars_2006_sommaire/israel_et_territoires_occupes.

24. Joakim Wohlfeil, "Veolia Loses 3.5 Billion EUR Contract in Sweden," Diakonia, press release, January 20, 2009, http://www.diakonia.se/sa/node.asp?node=2807.

25. Adri Nieuwhof, "Divestment Campaign Gains Momentum in Europe," Electronic Intifada, March 24, 2009, http://electronicintifada.net/v2/article10418.shtml.

26. Ibid.

27. West Midlands Palestine Solidarity Campaign, "West Midlands PSC 'Bin Veolia' Campaign," press release, March 26, 2009. http://www.palestinecampaign.org/index7b.asp?m_id=1&l1_id=4&l2_id=25&Content_ID=546.

28. This comes from a rough English translation of the original statement in French at http://www.ism-france.org/news/article.php?id=11649&type=communique&lesujet=Boycott.

29. Adri Nieuwhof, "Installation Criticizing Occupation, Veolia Causes Stir," Electronic Intifada, March 12, 2009, http://electronicintifada.net/v2/article10388.shtml.

30. "Jerusalem Rail Operator Jumps Ship, Tel Aviv Group Isn't Even Responding,"

Haaretz, August 6, 2009, http://www.haaretz.com/hasen/spages/1091186.html.

31. Ibid.

32. Ibid.

33. Adri Nieuwhof, "Veolia Whitewashes Illegal Light Rail Project," *Electronic Intifada*, August 26, 2010, http://electronicintifada.net/v2/article11488.shtml.

34. http://www.connex.co.il/index.asp?num=5 (accessed on September 13, 2010, since removed); see Diakonia, "Veolia Publishes Discriminatory Ad for Jerusalem Light Rail," press release, Alternative Information Center, August 27, 2010, http://www.alternativenews.org/english/index.php/topics/jerusalem/2829-veolia-publishes-discriminatory-ad-for-jerusalem-light-rail.

35. Adri Nieuwhof, "Veolia Tries to Spin Its Involvement in the Occupation," *Electronic Intifada*, April 22, 2010, http://electronicintifada.net/v2/article11225.shtml.

36. Ibid.

37. Islamic Human Rights Commission, "IHRC Welcomes Veolia's Plan to Abandon Light Rail Project Connecting Illegal Israeli Settlements to Jerusalem," press release, June 11, 2009, http://www.ihrc.org/.

38. Ireland Palestine Solidarity Campaign, "Major Victory for Pro-Palestine Boycott Campaign: Dublin City Council Passes Anti-Veolia Motion," press release, May 10, 2010, http://cosmos.ucc.ie/cs1064/jabowen/IPSC/ipsc/displayRelease.php?releaseID=335.

39. Scottish Palestine Solidarity Campaign, "Swansea Follows Dublin and Votes to Boycott Veolia for Human Rights Violations," June 28, 2010, http://www.scottishpsc.org.uk/index.php?option=com_content&view=article&id=3456:swansea-follows-dublin-and-votes-to-boycott-veolia-for-human-rights-violations&catid=368:successes&Itemid=200263.

40. Who Profits from the Occupation?, "Veolia Environnement," http://www.whoprofits.org/Company%20Info.php?id=581.

CHAPTER 12: BOYCOTTS WORK: OMAR BARGHOUTI INTERVIEWED BY ALI MUSTAFA

1. The internationally adopted definition of apartheid can be found in the International Convention of the Suppression and Punishment of the Crime of Apartheid: http://www.icc-cpi.int/NR/rdonlyres/6C2AB560-3E9D-401D-ACD8-A6F7C3AA7F6E/248661/372818.PDF. It can also be found in the 2002 Rome Statute of the International Criminal Court: http://untreaty.un.org/cod/icc/statute/99_corr/cstatute.htm.

2. US State Department, Bureau of Democracy, Human Rights, and Labor,

"2009 Human Rights Report: Israel and the Occupied Territories," March 11, 2010, http://www.state.gov/g/drl/rls/hrrpt/2009/nea/136070.htm.

3. For more on Israel's regime of occupation, colonialism, and apartheid, see "United against Apartheid, Colonialism and Occupation: Dignity and Justice for the Palestinian People," October 2008, Civil Society Position Paper for the Durban Review Conference, Geneva, April 20–24, 2009, http://bdsmovement.net/files/English-BNC_Position_Paper-Durban_Review.pdf.

4. Chris McGreal, "Worlds Apart," *Guardian*, February 6, 2006, http://www.guardian.co.uk/world/2006/feb/06/southafrica.israel.

5. PACBI, "Boycott 'Ariel' and the Rest! All Israeli Academic Institutions Are Complicit in Occupation and Apartheid," February 10, 2010, http://www.pacbi.org/etemplate.php?id=1175.

6. For more on the normalization of the military in the Israeli academic establishment, see Lisa Taraki, "The Silence of the Israeli Intelligentsia," *Counterpunch*, September 10–12, 2010, http://www.counterpunch.org/taraki09102010.html.

7. For more on the modern history of Palestinian popular-civil resistance, see Roger Heacock and Jamal Nassar, eds., *Intifada: Palestine at the Crossroads* (New York: Praeger/Greenwood, 1990); Naseer Aruri, ed., *Occupation: Israel over Palestine* (1st ed., Washington, DC: Association of Arab-American University Graduates, 1983; 2nd ed., 1989)—includes several chapters on pre-intifada politics and society); Joost Hiltermann, *Behind the Intifada: Labor and Women's Movements in the Occupied Territories* (Princeton, NJ: Princeton University Press, 1991); Zachary Lockman and Joel Beinin, eds., *Intifada: The Palestinian Uprising against Israeli Occupation* (New York: South End Press, 1989).

8. This argument opposing academic boycott on principle has become moot with many of its staunch supporters suddenly joining a call for academic and cultural boycott of the Israeli colony of Ariel and all other colonies built on occupied Palestinian territory. Despite the narrow focus of this "settlements-only" boycott, it clearly vindicates the Palestinian BDS campaign's insistence that boycotts should not exempt any institution that is deeply implicated in a system of colonial subjugation, ethnic cleansing, and apartheid just because it is an academic or cultural entity.

9. Judith Butler, "Israel/Palestine and the Paradoxes of Academic Freedom," *Radical Philosophy* 135 (January–February 2006).

10. Oren Ben-Dor, "Academic Freedom in Israel Is Central to Resolving the Conflict," *CounterPunch*, May 21/22, 2005, http://www.counterpunch.org/bendor05212005.html.

11. For more on the apartheid reality of Israel, see Karine MacAllister, "Applicability of the Crime of Apartheid to Israel," *Al-Majdal*, Summer 2008, http://

badil.org/en/al-majdal/item/72-applicability-of-the-crime-of-apartheid-to
-israel.

12. For more on the one democratic state solution and the moral and logical
problems of the binational solution, see Omar Barghouti, "Re-imagining
Palestine: Self-Determination, Ethical Decolonization and Equality," *ZNet*,
July 29, 2009, http://www.zcommunications.org/re-imagining-palestine-by
-omar-barghouti.

CHAPTER 13: BOYCOTTING ISRAELI SETTLEMENT PRODUCTS: TACTIC VERSUS STRATEGY

1. Joakim Wohlfeil et al., *Illegal Ground: Assa Abloy's Business in Occupied
Palestinian Territory*, SwedWatch Report 22, Diakonia, Church of Sweden,
and SwedWatch, October 2008, http://www.diakonia.se/documents/public/
IN_FOCUS/Israel_Palestine/Report_Illegal_Ground/Report_Mul-T-lock_
081021.pdf.

2. Ma'an News Agency, "Israeli Winery Leaves Premises in Illegal West Bank Settlement," August 31, 2008, http://www.maannews.net/eng/ViewDetails.aspx
?ID=204774.

3. For example, Al-Haq, a leading Palestinian human rights organization
based in Ramallah, praised the Barkan Wineries move, saying: "As a Palestinian human rights organisation committed to the promotion and protection of human rights of the Palestinian people in the Occupied Palestinian
Territory (OPT), Al-Haq welcomes the decision by Barkan Wineries, an Israeli subsidiary of Tempo Beer Industry Ltd. Drinks, to remove its activities
from the industrial zone of the illegal settlement of Barkan, in the northern
West Bank, and transfer them into Israel." Open letter to Dutch diplomatic
representatives and Heineken Nederlands, October 4, 20008, http://www
.alhaq.org/etemplate.php?id=393.

4. Donald Macintyre, "Britain to Crack Down on Exports from Israeli Settlements," *Independent*, November 3, 2008, http://www.independent.co.uk/news/
world/middle-east/britain-to-crack-down-on-exports-from-israeli-settlements
-986854.html.

5. Barak Ravid and Anshel Pfeffer Agencies, "Britain to EU: Clamp Down on
Imports from Settlements," *Haaretz*, April 11, 2008, http://www.haaretz.com/
news/britain-to-eu-clamp-down-on-imports-from-settlements-1.256586.

6. Richard Falk, Note on Legal Status of BDS Campaign with respect to Israel,
by courtesy of the author [TEXT SENT TO THE BNC—NOT PUBLISHED]
September 19, 2010.

CHAPTER 14: OUR SOUTH AFRICA MOMENT HAS ARRIVED

1.   See, for example, UN Special Rapporteur John Dugard, *Human Rights Situation in Palestine and Other Occupied Arab Territories*, A/HRC/7/17, January 2008.

2.   Ali Abunimah, "Extremist West Bank Settlers Help Stir Acre Violence," *Electronic Intifada*, October 15, 2008 http://electronicintifada.net/v2/article9892.shtml.

3.   Omar Barghouti, "Is the UN Complicit in Israel's Massacre in Gaza?," *Electronic Intifada*, January 1, 2009, http://electronicintifada.net/v2/article10089.shtml.

4.   Robert Kagan, "Power and Weakness," *Policy Review*, no. 113, June 2002.

5.   The Palestinian BDS Campaign has consistently rejected all forms of racism, including Islamophobia, Zionism, and anti-Semitism (www.BDSmovement.net).

6.   "Israel, Palestine and the Hypocrisies of Power: An Interview with Noam Chomsky," August 22, 2007, http://www.kibush.co.il/show_file.asp?num=22676.

7.   Richard Falk, "Slouching toward a Palestinian Holocaust," June 29, 2007, http://www.transnational.org/Area_MiddleEast/2007/Falk_PalestineGenocide.html.

8.   Ibid.

9.   CIDSE Seminar Report, *The EU's Aid to the Occupied Palestinian Territory*, Brussels, November 7, 2008.

10. For more on this see, Ilan Pappé, *The Ethnic Cleansing of Palestine* (Oxford: Oneworld, 2006).

11. Daniel L. Byman, "How to Handle Hamas," http://www.brookings.edu/articles/2010/0825_hamas_byman.aspx (originally published in *Foreign Affairs*, September/October 2010).

12. B'Tselem, "Human Rights in the Occupied Territories: 1 January 2009 to 30 April 2010," June 2010, http://www.btselem.org/Download/2009_Annual_Report_Eng.pdf.

13. Gisha, "Due to Gaza Closure, 40,000 Students Refused from UNRWA Schools," September 15, 2010, http://www.gisha.org/index.php?intLanguage=2&intItemId=1871&intSiteSN=113.

14. Ida Audeh, "Israel's War Crimes in the Gaza Strip," *Countercurrents.org*, January 21, 2008, http://www.countercurrents.org/audeh210108.htm.

15. "Gaza's Stunted Growth Problem," *New York Times*, March 21, 2009, http://topics.blogs.nytimes.com/2009/03/21/gazas-stunted-growth-problem/, excerpted from "Health in the Occupied Palestinian Territory, *Lancet*, March 4, 2009.

16. Chris McGreal, "Palestinians Hit by Sonic Boom Air Raids," *Guardian*, November 3, 2005, http://www.guardian.co.uk/world/2005/nov/03/israel.

17. "Health in the Occupied Palestinian Territory," *The Lancet*, March 4, 2009, http://www.thelancet.com/series/health-in-the-occupied-palestinian-territory.

18. Karen Koning AbuZayd, "This Brutal Siege of Gaza Can Only Breed Violence," *Guardian*, January 23, 2008, http://www.guardian.co.uk/commentisfree/2008/

jan/23/israelandthepalestinians.world.

19. Shulamit Aloni, "There Is No Fixed Method for Genocide," *Counterpunch*, March 7, 2003, http://www.counterpunch.org/aloni03072003.html.

20. Palestinian Centre for Human Rights, "Weekly Report: On Israeli Human Rights Violations in the Occupied Palestinian Territory," January 15–21, 2009, http://www.pchrgaza.org/files/W_report/English/2008/22-01-2009.htm.

21. "Map: Gaza Offensive—Week One," *BBC News*, January 5, 2009, http://news.bbc.co.uk/2/hi/middle_east/7805808.stm.

22. R2E Campaign, Open Letter to International Academic Institutions, January 17, 2009, http://right2edu.birzeit.edu/news/article706.

23. Amnesty International, "Attacks on Ambulance Workers in Gaza," January 28, 2009, http://www.amnesty.org/en/news-and-updates/news/ambulance -20090128.

24. Peter Beaumont, "Israeli Soldiers Killed Unarmed Civilians Carrying White Flags in Gaza, Says Report," August 13, 2009, http://www.guardian.co.uk/ world/2009/aug/13/israeli-soldiers-gaza-deaths-allegations.

25. Alan Cowell, "Gaza Children Found with Mothers' Corpses," *New York Times*, January 8, 2009, http://www.nytimes.com/2009/01/09/world/middleeast/ 09redcross.html?_r=1&em.

26. UN Office for the Coordination of Humanitarian Affairs, "Field Update on Gaza from the Humanitarian Coordinator, 27–29 January 2009," http:// www.ochaopt.org/documents/ocha_opt_gaza_humanitarian_situation_report _2009_01_29_english.pdf.

27. "Israel's Bombardment of Gaza Is Not Self-Defence—It's a War Crime," open letter signed by thirty-one judges, law professors, and others, *Sunday Times*, January 11, 2009, http://www.timesonline.co.uk/tol/comment/letters/ article5488380.ece.

28. Amnesty International, "Time for Accountability in Gaza and Southern Israel," January 26, 2009, http://www.amnesty.org/en/appeals-for-action/time -accountability-gaza-and-southern-israel.

29. Human Rights Watch, "Israel/Gaza: International Investigation Essential: UN Should Ensure Impartial Inquiry Into Serious Violations by Both Sides," January 27, 2009, http://www.hrw.org/en/news/2009/01/27/israelgaza -international-investigation-essential.

30. B'Tselem lagged behind international human rights groups in exposing the full scope of Israel's atrocities during Cast Lead and later attacked the credibility of the Goldstone Report.

31. B'Tselem, "Israel Is Using Phosphorous Illegally in Gaza Strip Bombings," January 12, 2009, http://www.btselem.org/English/Gaza_Strip/20090112_Use_of _White_Phosphorus.asp.

32. Oxfam International, "Gaza: Aid Agencies Call for Suspension of Enhanced EU-Israel Agreements," press release, January 7, 2009, http://www.oxfam.org/

en/pressroom/pressrelease/2009-01-07/gaza-aid-agencies-call-suspension
-enhanced-eu-israel-agreements.

33. Rory McCarthy, "Gaza Truce Broken as Israeli Raid Kills Six Hamas Gunmen," *Guardian*, November 5, 2008, http://www.guardian.co.uk/world/2008/nov/05/israelandthepalestinians.

34. JTA News Service, "MP Kaufman Likens Israelis to Nazis," January 26, 2009, http://jta.org/news/article/2009/01/16/1002308/mp-kaufman-likens-israelis-to-nazis.

35. Noam Chomsky, "'Exterminate All the Brutes': Gaza 2009," *ZNet*, January 20, 2009, http://www.zmag.org/znet/viewArticle/20316.

36. Alan Hart, "The New Nazis," *AlanHart.net*, January 13, 2009, http://www.alanhart.net/the-new-nazis/.

37. Ben Birnbeg et al., letter to the editor, *Guardian*, January 10, 2009, http://www.guardian.co.uk/world/2009/jan/10/letters-gaza-uk.

38. International Jewish Anti-Zionist Network (IJAN), "International Holocaust Rememberance Day," January 26, 2009, http://www.ijsn.net/home/.

39. For more details on this, refer to Omar Barghouti, "On Refugees, Creativity and Ethics," *ZNet*, September 28, 2002, http://www.zcommunications.org/on-refugees-creativity-and-ethics-by-omar-barghouti.

40. Michael Ben-Yair, "The War's Seventh Day," *Haaretz*, March 3, 2002, http://www.haaretz.com/hasen/pages/ShArt.jhtml?itemNo=136433.

41. International Convention on the Suppression and Punishment of the Crime of Apartheid, http://www.icc-cpi.int/NR/rdonlyres/6C2AB560-3E9D-401D-ACD8-A6F7C3AA7F6E/248661/372818.PDF.

42. International Criminal Court, Rome Statute, 1998, http://untreaty.un.org/cod/icc/statute/99_corr/cstatute.htm.

43. "United against Apartheid, Colonialism and Occupation: Dignity and Justice for the Palestinian People," October 2008, Civil Society Position Paper for the Durban Review Conference, Geneva, April 20–24, 2009, http://bdsmovement.net/files/English-BNC_Position_Paper-Durban_Review.pdf.

44. Aron Shai, "The Fate of Abandoned Arab Villages in Israel, 1965–1969," *History and Memory* 18, no. 2 (Fall 2006). See also Meron Benvenisti, *Sacred Landscape: The Buried History of the Holy Land* (Berkeley: University of California Press, 2000); Walid Khalidi, "Why Did the Palestinians Leave, Revisited," *Journal of Palestine Studies* 134, no. 2 (1995); Slaman Abu Sitta, *Atlas of Palestine 1948* (London: Palestine Land Society, December 2004); Ilan Pappé, *The Ethnic Cleansing of Palestine* (Oxford: Oneworld, 2006).

45. In the official Israeli translation, this 1952 law is wrongly titled "Law of Nationality."

46. Roselle Tekiner, "Race and the Issue of National Identity in Israel," *International Journal of Middle East Studies* 23, no. 1 (February 1991): 39–55.

47. Committee on Economic, Social, and Cultural Rights, *Consideration of Re-*

ports Submitted by States Parties Under Articles 16 and 17 of the Covenant, December 4, 1998, http://www.cesr.org/downloads/CESCR%20Concluding %20Observations%2019th%20session.pdf.

48. Jonathan Cook, "Anthology of Bigotry," *Al-Ahram Weekly Online,* no. 855, July 25–August 1, 2007, http://weekly.ahram.org.eg/2007/855/re92.htm.

49. Jack Khoury, Eli Ashkenazi et al., "Poll: 68% of Jews Would Refuse to Live in Same Building as an Arab," *Haaretz,* March 22, 2006, http://www.haaretz.com/news/ poll-68-of-jews-would-refuse-to-live-in-same-building-as-an-arab-1.183429.

50. Ronnie Kasrils and Victoria Brittain, "Both Palestinians and Israelis Will Benefit from a Boycott," *Guardian,* May 25, 2005, http://www.guardian .co.uk/education/2005/may/25/highereducation.uk1.

51. David Hirsch, "The War Game," *Observer,* September 21, 2003, http://www .guardian.co.uk/world/2003/sep/21/israelandthepalestinians.bookextracts.

52. PACBI, "PACBI Salutes Canadian Academic Trade Unionists," February 25, 2009, http://www.pacbi.org/etemplate.php?id=954.

53. PACBI, "Quebec College Federation Joins the BDS Campaign," March 14, 2009, http://www.pacbi.org/etemplate.php?id=971.

54. PACBI, "The BNC Salutes South African Dock Workers Action!" February 3, 2009, http://www.pacbi.org/etemplate.php?id=916.

55. PACBI, "Hampshire College Becomes First College in U.S. to Divest from Israeli Occupation!" February 11, 2009, http://www.pacbi.org/etemplate.php?id=930.

56. PACBI, "Power of Student Action Forces University to Divest Its Holdings in Major Arms Companies," February 27, 2009, http://www.pacbi.org/etemplate .php?id=959.

57. PACBI, "Why Support the U.S. Campaign for the Academic and Cultural Boycott of Israel?" February 8, 2009, http://www.pacbi.org/boycott_news _more.php?id=926_0_1_0_C.

CHAPTER 15: AFTER THE FREEDOM FLOTILLA ATROCITY: BDS TAKES OFF

1. David Hirst, "The War Game" (excerpt), *Observer,* September 21, 2003. http://www.guardian.co.uk/world/2003/sep/21/israelandthepalestinians .bookextracts.

2. International Committee of the Red Cross, "Gaza Closure: Not Another Year!" June 14, 2010, http://icrc.org/web/eng/siteeng0.nsf/htmlall/palestine -update-140610.

3. "Report: Israel Seizes Oxygen Machines Donated to PA," *Haaretz,* June 26, 2010, http://www.haaretz.com/news/diplomacy-defense/report-israel-seizes

-oxygen-machines-donated-to-pa-1.298385.

4. For an analysis of the BDS campaign's origins and progress, see Omar Barghouti, "BDS: A Global Movement for Freedom and Justice," *Al-Shabaka*, May 5, 2010, http://al-shabaka.org/policy-brief/civil-society/bds-global-movement -freedom-justice.

5. Henry Seigman, "Israel's Greatest Loss: Its Moral Imagination," *Haaretz*, June 11, 2010, http://www.haaretz.com/jewish-world/israel-s-greatest-loss-its-moral -imagination-1.295600.

6. Jeff Halper, "An Open Letter to the Israeli Jewish Public: Support the Gaza Flotilla!" *Canadian Dimension*, May 31, 2010, http://canadiandimension.com/ articles/3053/.

7. Ben Saul, "Israel's Security Cannot Come at Any Price," Drum Unleashed, June 2, 2010, http://www.abc.net.au/unleashed/stories/s2915343.htm.

8. Daniel Machover and Roy Amlot, "In Law Israel Has a Case to Answer," *Times* (UK), June 3, 2010, http://www.timesonline.co.uk/tol/comment/ letters/article7142646.ece.

9. "Karin Arts Co-Authors Letter about Israel for Dutch Newspaper," International Institute of Social Studies of Erasmus University Rotterdam, June 3, 2010, http://www.iss.nl/News/Karin-Arts-co-authors-letter-about-Israel-for -Dutch-newspaper.

10. Office of the High Commissioner for Human Rights, "Human Rights Council Decides to Dispatch Independent Fact Finding Mission to Investigate Israeli Attack on Humanitarian Boat Convoy," June 2, 2010, http:// www.ohchr.org/EN/NewsEvents/Pages/DisplayNews.aspxNewsID=10095 &LangID=E.

11. "Secretary-General 'Shocked' by Deadly Raid on Gaza Aid Flotilla," UN News Centre, May 31, 2010, http://www.un.org/apps/news/story.asp?NewsID=34863 &Cr=gaza&Cr1=.

12. Agence France-Presse, "Israeli Leaders Should Be Brought to Justice: UN Rights Expert," *Gulf News*, May 31, 2010, http://gulfnews.com/news/world/ other-world/israeli-leaders-should-be-brought-to-justice-un-rights-expert-1 .635049.

13. Agence France-Presse, "Nicaragua Suspends Diplomatic Ties with Israel," *Ynetnews*, June 2, 2010, http://www.ynetnews.com/articles/0,7340,L-3897773 ,00.html.

14. Franz Wild, "South Africa to Recall Its Ambassador to Israel Over Raid on Aid Flotilla," *Bloomberg*, June 3, 2010, http://www.bloomberg.com/apps/news ?sid=a_vBbjBZJ6LM&pid=20601087.

15. "Ambassador Çelikkol Back in Ankara for 'Consultations,'" *Today's Zaman*, June 3, 2010, http://www.todayszaman.com/news-212110-100-ambassador -celikkol-back-in-ankara-for-consultations.html.

16. Associated Press, "Israel to Deport Remaining Gaza Flotilla Activists,"

Guardian, June 2, 2010, http://www.guardian.co.uk/world/2010/jun/02/israel-deport-gaza-flotilla-activists.

17. Agence France-Presse, "Norway Calls for Boycott on Arms to Israel," *Swedish Wire*, June 1, 2010, http://www.swedishwire.com/nordic/4809-norway-calls-for-boycott-on-arms-to-israel.

18. Global BDS Movement, "In Response to Israel's Assault on the Freedom Flotilla: BNC Calls for Action," June 1, 2010, http://bdsmovement.net/?q=node/710.

19. South African Transport and Allied Workers' Union, "Palestine–Zimbabwe–Swaziland Must Be Free!" n.d., http://www.satawu.org.za/international/10-international.

20. Global BDS Movement, "Palestinian Trade Union Movement Calls on International Dockworkers Unions to Block Loading/Offloading Israeli Ships," June 7, 2010, http://bdsmovement.net/?q=node/712.

21. Patrick Craven, "SATAWU Condemns the Israeli Act of International Piracy," Media Release List of the Congress of South African Trade Unions, June 3, 2010, http://groups.google.com/group/cosatu-press/msg/a2ff0baff48201c4?pli=1.

22. Ibn Kafka (pseud.), "The Swedish Dockers' Union Decides on a Blockade against Israeli Ships and Goods," *Ibn Kafka's obiter dicta—Divagations d'un juriste marocain en liberté surveillée*, June 3, 2009, http://ibnkafkasobiterdicta.wordpress.com/2010/06/03/the-swedish-dockers-union-decides-on-a-blockade-against-israeli-ships-and-goods/.

23. "Press Release from the Swedish Dockworkers Union, Section 4, Gothenburg," *Band Annie's Weblog*, June 23, 2010, http://bandannie.wordpress.com/2010/06/23/press-release-from-the-swedish-dockworkers-union-section-4-gothenburg/.

24. Greg Dropkin, "Dockworkers, Worldwide, Respond to Israel's Flotilla Massacre and Gaza Siege," *Counterpunch*, July 13, 2010, http://www.counterpunch.org/dropkin07132010.html.

25. Patrick Craven, "COSATU Condemns Israeli State Piracy," Congress of South African Trade Unions, May 31, 2010, http://www.cosatu.org.za/show.phpinclude=docs./pr/2010/pr0531d.html&ID=3395&cat=COSATU%20Today.

26. Tahir Sema, "SAMWU Declares, Every Muncipality an Apartheid Israel Free Zone!" South African Municipal Workers Union, June 4, 2010, http://www.samwu.org.za/index.php?option=com_content&task=view&id=621&Itemid=1.

27. Jonathan Kalmus, "Unite Votes to Boycott Israel," *Jewish Chronicle Online*, June 4, 2010, http://www.thejc.com/news/uk-news/32579/unite-votes-boycott-israel.

28. Jonny Paul, "British Trade Union Calls for Boycott," *Jerusalem Post*, June 24, 2010, http://www.jpost.com/International/Article.aspx?id=179475.

29. Jonny Paul, "Britain's Largest Academic Union Cuts Ties with Histadrut," *Jerusalem Post*, June 2, 2010, http://www.jpost.com/International/Article.aspx?id=177210.

30. Charlotte Haarvik Sanden, "Hent Hjem Ambassadøren I Israel," Norweigan Broadcasting Corporation, June 1, 2010, http://www.nrk.no/nyheter/norge/1.7148110.

31. Agence France-Presse, "40% of Norweigans: Ban Israeli Products," *Ynetnews*, June 2, 2010, http://www.ynetnews.com/articles/0,7340,L-3898052,00.html.

32. Victoria Colliver and David R. Baker, "Hundreds in Oakland Protest Gaza Blockade," *San Francisco Chronicle*, June 21, 2010, http://www.sfgate.com/cgi-bin/article.cgi?f=%2Fc%2Fa%2F2010%2F06%2F20%2FBA0G1E28CV.DTL.

33. "Northern Illinois Conference Votes to Divest from Companies That Benefit from the Occupation of Palestine," Peace with Justice Coordinators, June 17, 2010, http://pwjcoordinators.blogspot.com/2010/06/peace-with-justice-coordinators_17.html.

34. Cal Divest From Apartheid, "The Evergreen State College Passes Divestment Campaign," June 3, 2010, http://www.caldivestfromapartheid.com/2010/06/03/the-evergreen-state-college-passes-divestment-campaign/.

35. PACBI, "Hampshire College Becomes First College in U.S. to Divest from Israeli Occupation!" February 11, 2009, http://www.pacbi.org/etemplate.php?id=930.

36. Martin Rowson, "Martin Rowson on the Gaza Flotilla Attack," *Guardian*, June 5, 2010, http://www.guardian.co.uk/commentisfree/cartoon/2010/jun/05/martin-rowson-gaza-flotilla-attack.

37. PACBI, "Palestinian Filmmakers, Artists and Cultural Workers Call for a Cultural Boycott of Israel," August 6, 2006, http://pacbi.org/etemplate.php?id=315.

38. PACBI, "Call for Academic and Cultural Boycott of Israel," December 12, 2008, http://www.pacbi.org/etemplate.php?id=869.

39. Iain Banks, "Small Steps towards a Boycott of Israel," *Guardian*, June 3, 2010, http://www.guardian.co.uk/world/2010/jun/03/boycott-israel-iain-banks.

40. Stéphane Hessel, "Gaza Flotilla: Global Citizens Must Respond Where Governments Have Failed," *Huffington Post*, June 15, 2010, http://www.huffingtonpost.com/stephane-frederic-hessel/gaza-flotilla-global-citi_b_612865.html.

41. "Gaza Aid Flotilla: Henning Mankell Calls for Sanctions on Israel," *Telegraph*, June 2, 2010, http://www.telegraph.co.uk/news/worldnews/middleeast/palestinianauthority/7795692/Gaza-aid-flotilla-Henning-Mankell-calls-for-sanctions-on-Israel.html.

42. Alice Walker, "You Will Have No Protection," *Electronic Intifada*, June 4, 2010, http://electronicintifada.net/v2/article11319.shtml.

43. John Berger et al., "IoS Letters, Emails, & Online Postings," *Independent*, June 6, 2010, http://www.independent.co.uk/opinion/letters/iiosi-letters-emails

-amp-online-postings-6-june-2010–1992480.html.

44. Helle Klein, "Det är nog nu—bojkotta Israel!" *Aftonbladet*, January 12, 2009, http://www.aftonbladet.se/ledare/ledarkronika/helleklein/article4164419.ab, and "Bojkotta Israel," *Aftonbladet*, June 5, 2010, http://www.aftonbladet.se/ledare/article7248085.ab.

45. "A Boycott of Israeli Goods Is Now Necessary," *Sunday Tribune*, June 6, 2010, http://www.tribune.ie/news/editorial-opinion/article/2010/jun/06/a-boycott-of-israeli-goods-is-now-necessary/.

46. City Mouse Online, "Klaxons and Gorillaz Sound System Cancel Israel Shows, Apparently Due to Gaza Flotilla Raid," *Haaretz*, June 4, 2010, http://www.haaretz.com/news/national/klaxons-and-gorillaz-sound-system-cancel-israel-shows-apparently-due-to-gaza-flotilla-raid-1.294191.

47. Agence France-Presse, "The Pixies Pull Out of Israel Gig," *Australian Broadcasting Corporation News*, June 7, 2010, http://www.abc.net.au/news/stories/2010/06/06/2919568.htm?section=justin.

48. Devendra Banhart et al., untitled post, June 14, 2010, http://www.devendrabanhart.com/news/2010/06/14.

49. Janine Zacharia, "Israel's Feeling of Isolation Is Becoming More Pronounced," *Washington Post*, June 22, 2010, http://www.washingtonpost.com/wp-dyn/content/article/2010/06/21/AR2010062104706.html.

50. David J. Prince, "Israeli Raid on Gaza-Bound Flotilla Draws Mixed Artist Reaction," *Billboard.com*, June 11, 2010, http://www.billboard.com/news#/news/israeli-raid-on-gaza-bound-flotilla-draws-1004097608.story.

51. Palestinian Campaign for the Academic and Cultural Boycott of Israel, "A Victory for Ethical Responsibility of International Artists: PACBI's Reaction to Elvis Costello's Cancellation of Two Gigs in Israel," May 18, 2010, http://www.pacbi.org/etemplate.php?id=1236&key=santana.

52. Gary Rosenblatt, "Jewish Week: Marketing a New Image," *Israel21c*, January 20, 2005, http://www.israel21c.org/opinion/jewish-week-marketing-a-new-image.

53. Nathan Guttman, "Boycott Targets Stars from Elvis to Elton," *Forward*, May 19, 2010, http://www.forward.com/articles/128185/.

54. Aidan Girt et al., "500 Artists against Israeli Apartheid," *Tadamon!*, February 25, 2010, http://www.tadamon.ca/post/5824.

55. PACBI, "John Berger and 93 Other Authors, Film-Makers, Musicians, and Performers Call for a Cultural Boycott of Israel," December 15, 2006, http://www.pacbi.org/etemplate.php?id=415.

56. Palestinian Non-governmental Organizations' Network, "60 Years of Palestinian Dispossession," http://www.pngo.net/data/files/english_statements/08/PNGO-THT-HP5208(2).pdf.

57. Boycott from Within, http://boycottisrael.info/.

58. Jerusalem Media and Communications Centre, "Knesset Moves to Criminalize Boycott Supporters," June 10, 2010, http://www.jmcc.org/news.aspx?id=1066.

59. Omar Barghouti, "Our South Africa Moment Has Arrived," *Palestine Chronicle*, March 18, 2009, http://palestinechronicle.com/view_article_details.php?id=14921.

CHAPTER 16: LEADERSHIP, REFERENCE AND THE ROLE OF ISRAELI ANTICOLONIALISTS: OMAR BARGHOUTI INTERVIEWED BY MAXINE KAUFMAN-LACUSTA

1. Omar Barghouti, "The Boycott and Palestinian Groups: Countering the Critics," *Counterpunch*, October 21, 2008, http://www.counterpunch.org/barghouti10212008.html.

CONCLUSION: IF NOT NOW, WHEN?

1. Paulo Freire, *Pedagogy of the Oppressed* (New York: Herder and Herder, 1972).
2. The fact that all the main political parties have endorsed BDS cannot substitute for their still lacking actual involvement in the campaign inside historic Palestine and around the world.
3. See, for example, Boycott from Within (BfW), http://boycottisrael.info/, Alternative Information Center (AIC), http://www.alternativenews.org/, and Who Profits from the Occupation?, http://www.whoprofits.org/.
4. The Cairo Declaration, produced and endorsed by representatives of solidarity groups from more than forty countries who protested in Egypt as part of the Gaza Freedom March, provides a distinguished example of such principled solidarity: http://cairodeclaration.org/.
5. Several of these recommendations were adopted at a civil society peace and justice forum held in Bilbao, the Basque Country (Spain), in November 2008, with the participation of dozens of Palestinian, European, and Israeli progressive organizations endorsing BDS: "Final Declaration and Action Plan of the Bilbao Initiative," November 4, 2008, http://www.bdsmovement.net/?q=node/213.
6. For more on the academic boycott, see www.pacbi.org.
7. See, for instance, the Guidelines for the International Academic Boycott of Israel, http://www.pacbi.org/etemplate.php?id=1108, and the Guidelines for the International Cultural Boycott of Israel, http://www.pacbi.org/etemplate.php?id=1047.
8. Major Christian Palestinian figures issued the Palestine Kairos Document calling on churches around the world "to say a word of truth and to take a position of truth with regard to Israel's occupation of Palestinian land" and explicitly endorsing "boycott and disinvestment as tools of justice, peace and security": December 15, 2009, http://www.kairospalestine.ps/sites/default/

Documents/English.pdf.

9. Alternative Tourism Group, n.d., http://www.atg.ps/.

10. BDS Movement, "Stop the Jewish National Fund," n.d., http://stopthejnf .bdsmovement.net/node/4.

11. Norway, for example, banned testing submarines destined to Israel in its territorial waters and facilities. "Norway Bans Testing of Israel-bound Submarines," Homeland Security Newswire, October 1, 2010, http://homeland securitynewswire.com/norway-bans-testing-israel-bound-submarines.

12. The EU-Israel Association Agreement and the MERCOSUR-Israel FTA are high-priority targets in this context.

13. See, for instance, Naomi Klein's statements in this regard at a lecture last year in Ramallah covered by *Haaretz*—Yotam Feldman, "Naomi Klein: Oppose the State Not the People," *Haaretz*, July 2, 2009: http://www.haaretz .com/hasen/spages/1097058.html.

14. Desmond Tutu, "Israeli Ties: A Chance to Do the Right Thing," *Times Live*, September 26, 2010, http://www.timeslive.co.za/world/article675369.ece/ Israeli-ties—a-chance-to-do-the-right-thing.

15. T. Skouteris and A. Vermeer-Kunzli, eds., "The Protection of the Individual in International Law: Essays in Honour of John Dugard," special issue, *Leiden Journal of International Law*, 2007, 6.

ACKNOWLEDGMENTS/SOURCES

Several chapters in this book are based on articles and essays published over a period of six years in the following sources. Some arguments and facts may therefore appear in more than one chapter for the sake of maintaining the internal coherence of each chapter. In some cases, the text was slightly updated or otherwise modified to reflect recent developments; in other cases, substantial rewriting or additions were required.

Chapter 3 is based on a lecture given at the first international conference on the academic boycott of Israel, sponsored by the British Committee for the Universities of Palestine (http://www.bricup.org.uk/) and endorsed by PACBI, held at SOAS in the University of London, in December 2004.

Chapter 4 is based on the critique of the "On Academic Boycotts" statement by the American Association of University Professors (AAUP), published in the AAUP publication *Academe* in the September–October 2006 issue, as part of a series of articles debating the Palestinian call for an academic boycott against Israel. It is available at http://www.aaup.org/AAUP/pubsres/academe/2006/SO/Boycott/Critics.htm#omar.

Chapter 5 was published in *DevISSues* in April 2008 and available at this address: http://www.iss.nl/DevISSues/Articles/Just-Intellectuals-Oppression-Resistance-and-the-Public-Role-of-Intellectuals.

Chapter 6 was originally published in *CounterPunch*, June 2005, http://www.counterpunch.org/barghouti06012005.html.

Chapter 7 is based on an article that first appeared in *Dance Insider*, September 12, 2008, http://www.danceinsider.com/f2008/f0912_1.html/.

Chapter 8 can be found online at http://www.pacbi.org/etemplate.php?id=725.

Chapter 9 was first published in *Electronic Intifada*, March 3, 2005, http://electronicintifada.net/v2/article3654.shtml.

Chapter 10 is based on an article first published in *Electronic Intifada*, October 23, 2008, http://electronicintifada.net/v2/article9906.shtml.

Chapter 11 is based on an article first published in the *Jerusalem Quarterly*, Summer 2009, http://www.jerusalemquarterly.org/PDF/issues-pdf/38issue.pdf.

Chapter 12 first appeared in *Electronic Intifada*, June 1, 2009, http://electronicintifada.net/v2/article10562.shtml.

Chapter 13 comes from *Electronic Intifada*, Novermber 11, 2008, http://electronicintifada.net/v2/article9948.shtml/.

Chapter 14 is based on an article first published in *Palestine Chronicle*, March 18, 2009, http://www.palestinechronicle.com/view_article_details.php?id=14921.

Chapter 16: Portions of this interview appear in the afterword to the trade paperback edition of Maxine Kaufman-Lacusta, *Refusing to Be Enemies: Palestinian and Israeli Nonviolent Resistance to the Israeli Occupation* (Ithaca Press, 2011).

INDEX

ABOUT HAYMARKET BOOKS

Haymarket Books is a nonprofit, progressive book distributor and publisher, a project of the Center for Economic Research and Social Change. We believe that activists need to take ideas, history, and politics into the many struggles for social justice today. Learning the lessons of past victories, as well as defeats, can arm a new generation of fighters for a better world. As Karl Marx said, "The philosophers have merely interpreted the world; the point, however, is to change it."

We take inspiration and courage from our namesakes, the Haymarket Martyrs, who gave their lives fighting for a better world. Their 1886 struggle for the eight-hour day reminds workers around the world that ordinary people can organize and struggle for their own liberation.

For more information and to shop our complete catalog of titles, visit us online at www.haymarketbooks.org.

ALSO FROM HAYMARKET BOOKS

Gaza in Crisis: Reflections on Israel's War Against the Palestinians
Noam Chomsky and Ilan Pappé

The Pen and the Sword: Conversations with Edward Said
David Barsamian, introductions by Eqbal Ahmad and Nubar Hovsepian

*Between the Lines: Readings on Israel,
the Palestinians, and the U.S. "War on Terror"*
Tikva Honig-Parnass and Toufic Haddad

Hopes and Prospects
Noam Chomsky

*The Palestine Communist Party 1919–1948:
Arab and Jew in the Struggle for Internationalism*
Musa Budeiri

Diary of Bergen Belsen: 1944–1945
Hanna Lévy-Hass, foreword by Amira Hass

ABOUT THE AUTHOR

Jenna Barghouti

Omar Barghouti is an independent Palestinian commentator and human rights activist. He is a founding member of the Palestinian Campaign for the Academic and Cultural Boycott of Israel (PACBI) and the Palestinian Civil Society Boycott, Divestment and Sanctions (BDS) campaign against Israel. He holds bachelor's and master's degrees in electrical engineering from Columbia University and a master's degree in philosophy (ethics) from Tel Aviv University.